THE PARIS SPY

ALSO IN THIS SERIES

THE NEW LONDON SPY
THE NEW YORK SPY

THE PARIS SPY

A DISCREET GUIDE TO THE CITY'S PLEASURES
EDITED BY RAYMOND RUDORFF

ILLUSTRATED BY KAFFE FASSETT

ANTHONY BLOND

© *Copyright* 1969

Printed in Great Britain by R. & R. Clark, Limited, Edinburgh

954926

914·436.　28/4/70

Introduction

To publish yet another guide book on Paris needs no apology. First, the *Paris Spy* is not a guide-book like the others. Secondly, the majority of such books seem to have been written and produced on the assumption that the average visitor to Paris is a sober-minded art and architecture lover whose time-table will consist mostly of visits to museums and monuments and lengthy walks through streets of 'historical interest'. Food, drink and more worldly entertainment are relegated to the introduction or a short, 'handy' section. In other words, the emphasis is on erudite pleasures. To know that Alfred de Musset lived for so many years in such and such a house or to see the Etruscan room in the Louvre is all very well but as a pleasure that only Paris can give it is strictly limited.

This is all the less appropriate as Paris' main appeal undoubtedly lies in its reputation as *the* city of Pleasure. Our grandfathers went to Paris for a spree, to eat, drink and make merry and, whether they admitted it or not, for headier and more private pleasures. Most of those who can afford to do so (exchange controls allowing) continue to go to Paris for largely the same reasons. It is for such people that the *Paris Spy* has been written.

But have the pleasure-giving capacities of Paris declined in recent years? Many think so. The Algerian War, plastic bombs and political strife in the early sixties, the riots and strikes of 1968 have hardly been an encouragement to tourism. Prices have risen sharply and continue to do so. That legendary Parisian rudeness is even less legendary. The social and political outlook is as unsettled as ever in this volatile, unpredictable country. With the Gaullist government there came somewhat of a clamp-down on the more uninhibited pleasures of Paris. People who want to go to a 'swinging, wide-open' city go to London, Copenhagen or Amsterdam.

In some respects, Paris appears strangely old-fashioned. For gambling, music and cheap but good clothes, foreigners visit London rather than Paris. For both the puritanical and the dissolute, Paris is hardly the Babylon that it was held to be in the eighteen-nineties, the late nineteen-forties and early fifties. The city is less popular now than it used to be with American would-be expatriates enamoured of old Europe and 'civilised living'.

But you cannot kill a city in a few years. Paris is people and people demand pleasures whatever the regime or the state of their economy

Older generations may moan the passing of *their* golden age but each new generation will create its own pleasures, its own night-clubs, cafés, bars, restaurants, discothèques and cabarets, dances and songs, styles and fashions. Our contributors have all borne this in mind and in asking them to tell you of Paris' pleasures today, we encouraged them to pay as much attention to the ephemeral as the traditional. A gourmet friend of ours, an expert in matters of gastronomy, has written about the great restaurants of Paris that existed a generation ago and which are likely to exist at least another generation. Another colleague will tell you about some bars that are now fashionable and which may well be semi-deserted two years hence. Some of the best shops we list may have moved by the time you read this 'Spy'. We make no apology for changes that may occur, for addresses and suggestions that may become out-of-date: a city is not a fossil.

What we have tried to do is present Paris to you as it is *now*. We have some articles on churches, museums and art—but only as suggestions, not as detailed descriptions. Other guides do that. We treat night clubs and drinking in as much detail and with the same seriousness as clothes and topography. Food buying and antiques, art galleries and gambling, useful addresses and unusual shops—all are equally important. We have selected a few quarters of Paris and tried to give their *feel*, and overall impression rather than a long geographical-historical description which would be as wearisome as it would be out-of-place in a book such as the *Paris Spy*. And we have done all this with the firm conviction that the pleasures of this beautiful city are still among the best that the world has to offer—even if they cost more than they used to.

The reader will find nothing about sport, music, theatre, in the *Paris Spy*. The Paris newspapers and the Paris edition of the *New York Herald Tribune* will do that for you. We have not tried to be comprehensive or encyclopaedic with the impersonal tonelessness that this all too often implies. Our team have been encouraged to be personal, prejudiced, and selective. Many of the articles were originally written in French. We have not tried to 'anglicize' them too much since they are written by Parisians with attitudes and style that are part of their city and even in English we want to keep this flavour, this essential French-ness of Paris.

Paris is people, we said. We have written about some of the people who live in Paris: *clochards* and homosexuals, Catholics and Arabs. To write a comprehensive book on all the different societies and people who make up Paris would be a fascinating undertaking which would fill volumes. Again we have merely selected. 'Arab Paris' hardly comes under the heading of 'pleasures', we agree, and the pleasures afforded by prostitutes or mingling with the 'underworld' may be dubious, risky and expensive but they are a part of Paris—part of the context in which people inhabit and enjoy the city. And how can you enjoy a city completely without knowing at least something of its more private, human side?

Finally, we have tried to encourage your curiosity, to wake interest and a desire to become your own Paris spy. We have opened some doors for you: it's up to you to go through them. The more doors you go through and the more you discover for yourselves after we've sent you on your journey of discovery, the better pleased we'll be. And the more pleasure Paris gives you as a consequence, the more Paris will always be Paris to us all.

Contents

List of Illustrations

Contributors

DANIEL AUDEMARE

JEAN-MARIE BENOIST

NICOLE BLACK

PETER BUCKMAN

MIGUEL DEL CASTILLO

MICHEL DESGRANGES

GOFFREDO FOFI

CLAUDE FREGNAC

ROBERT GIRAUD

IGOR GOURINE

JOAN HARRISON

MICHAEL HENNESSEY

GEORGES HUGO

HENRY KAHN

CHRISTIAN LEDOUX

GIANCARLO MARMORI

MARCEL MONTARRON

EDOUARD RODITI

JEAN-LUC DE RUDDER

RAYMOND RUDORFF

GILLIAN TINDALL

SAM WHITE

BERNARD DE ZOGHEB

Christmas and January

The French are far from sharing the Anglo-Saxon longing for Christmas family reunions. Even more, the secret wish of every sophisticated Parisian is to avoid them completely. The result is that hundreds of thousands flee from the capital to skiing resorts. Those unfortunates who have to stay celebrate with their family in the traditional manner, complete with turkey. Dinner over, they go to Midnight Mass—quite irrespective of whether they pray or attend church during the year (they may even be Communist), thus recovering their spirits and rediscovering the pleasant feeling of being both French and Christian. The old Catholic rite has lost none of its magic. The choirboys belonging to the famous group of the Petits Chanteurs à la Croix de Bois are a great attraction in services in the main churches. The best midnight services are at Notre-Dame and at a few of the wealthier parish churches such as the Madeleine and Saint-Roch. They are rather pompous although the liturgy has been modernised recently.

New Year's Eve in Paris is the real celebration: a group of friends will go to a gaily decorated restaurant for a huge meal, then dance and whoop it up with friends of their friends, and eventually go out and paint the town red. This is called *Le Réveillon* (a word that always excites the Parisian's imagination). Lack of inhibition is the general rule—even in the streets. People hug and kiss each other, shout 'Bonne année!', play practical jokes and use their car hooters without restraint.

The 'Fête des Rois' on January 6th is a cosier, more discreet, social ceremony, still coloured by a vestigial religious feeling. This is the time for nice little boys and girls to visit their aunts and uncles and share a cake known as a *galette* in which a model of the infant Jesus is hidden. The finder becomes King or Queen for the occasion and chooses his or her future spouse from among the company.

February

Cold and dry, according to legend. Starts on its second day with Candlemas (purification day) and continues with periods of fast until the Mardi gras pancake day which celebrates the official ending of the fast. Huge carnival in Nice. Paris much the same as in

January. The Christmas skiers come back while the fashionable and wealthy tan themselves in Megève (world's greatest density of beautiful girls per square foot) or slither down the steep slopes of the Val d'Isère. Well-known figures in the arts, cinema, television, politics and sober businessmen enjoy their first pure air of the year before late evening whiskies in crowded night-clubs. As in August, Paris is deserted by the 'smart set'. Occasional frost in the Ile de France. St Valentine's day on the 14th, but flowers are very expensive. Fruits, confits and marrons glacés are at their best.

March

Paris wakes from its winter torpor. More cars; people start going out at week-ends to do up their cottages (*maison de campagne*). Schoolboys and students begin to think about their Easter holidays. Three picturesque festivities: first, a carnival with a procession in Arpajon (the renowned homeland of the asparagus, 10 miles south of Paris). The second comes at the end of the month: the animated Foire à la Ferraille et aux Jambons (Iron and Ham Fair) in boulevard Richard Lenoir, alongside and above Canal St-Martin. Lastly there is a fun fair, the Foire du Trône, from the 30th until late in April at Pelouse de Reuilly. Various University Balls such as that of the Ecole Normale Supérieure (where President Pompidou graduated; the students' posters mention that he can get in free), the scholarly Ecole des Chartes, etc. Exhibition of bulbous plants at Parc de Bagatelle. International cat exhibition the 2nd and 3rd March for the pleasure of middle-aged society ladies. The Salon des Indépendants, first artistic event of the year.

April

Very windy month, occasional sudden showers of hail; beautiful skies. A happy month, beginning with All Fools' Day heralding the beginning of Spring. Birds chirping, budding flowers in parks. The lively Foire du Trône goes on until the end of May. Fashion buyers throng into the Salon du Prêt-à-porter Féminin where the new Parisian Summer styles and trends are expertly shown by young unknown models (Porte de Versailles; for about a week). Camping and Caravanning Fair on the last ten days of the month. Two other specialised exhibitions, also at the Porte de Versailles, are the International Fur Industry Fair and the International Scientific

2

Technical Book and Magazine Fair. About the middle of the month, on a Sunday, is the Prix du Président de la République, first important race of the Paris season. On the last Sunday, an international swimming race on the Seine through Paris from the Pont de Bercy to the Bassin d'Iéna. All competitors wear flippers. First bullfights in Arles. National Deportation Remembrance Day on the 28th: flowers laid and solemn speeches delivered at the Monument des Déportés, Ile de la Cité.

May

Starts with the Fête du Travail Bank Holiday. Paris completely deserted. Anyone may sell lilies-of-the-valley without a licence on that day. People go to Bois de Chaville to pick the lilies. All very romantic with the air full of sweet scent. You are expected to offer a delicate 'bouquet de muguet' to the ones you love. This month is full of bank holidays (*fêtes légales*), both patriotic and familial. On the 8th, the anniversary of the German capitulation of 1945. On the second Sunday of the month, the Fête Jeanne d'Arc: a little ceremony takes place around the gilt statue of Joan of Arc in the Place des Pyramides. On the last Sunday, French children pay homage to their mothers by offering them poems and presents. Most festivals throughout France are held between May and September. The Mai de Versailles opens the season of artistic events with its concerts, recitals, plays and ballets. Saint-Germain-des-Prés has its own festival of the arts for a week in the middle of the month. At Versailles, the festival ends with a vast flower show (*Floralies*) on the 30th and 31st. Salon de Mai for three weeks at the Modern Art Museum. At the Foire de Paris (18th until the end of the month), inventors of all kinds exhibit their trivial or ingenious contrivances during the celebrated Concours Lépine. People less mechanically minded go to the Salon de la Nature. In the last week of the month, an exhibition of farm animals in the Place du Tertre in Montmartre. In the same week, Paris waiters take part in their annual race across the city, holding trays covered with full glasses.

June

Big flower shows to coincide with (expected) first hot weather. International flower show at Versailles (again) and at Bagatelle with

3

bouquet competitions. Display of roses at the Parc de l'Haye-les-Roses until July. The big Paris attraction is the Festival du Marais, with musical and dramatic events held in the buildings and court-yards of the noble 17th-century mansions in the ancient Marais district. Open air opera and theatre—weather permitting. More worldly events are the Prix des Drags at the Auteuil race-course and the Prix de Paris at Longchamp (end of the month). Two important horse races at Chantilly during the first half of the month: the Prix du Jockey-Club and the Prix de Diane. Garden party of the Nations in the gardens of the Cité Universitaire on the last Sunday of the month. The colourful, noisy fun fair on the boulevard Richard Lenoir continues until the 20th. At Nogent on the river Marne (celebrated by Zola and Maupassant), a Marché Commun des Chansons with charming old *guinguette* music and 1900 style music halls or *cafés-concerts* during a week in the middle of the month. Famous and time-honoured Foire du Lendit at Saint-Denis: cavalcades, illuminations, folklore, food from different regions. Prize-giving day in all *lycées* on or around the 15th. Le Mans 24-hour car race and Reims Grand Prix at end of the month. Greatest excitement of all: the three-week Tour de France cycling race.

July

Schoolchildren and students desert Paris. Hordes of tourists. Traffic as bad as ever with nearly everyone wishing he could be anywhere but Paris. The Festival du Marais lingers on, to be followed by the Festival Estival held in Paris' sober churches. Illuminations all over France, those in the gardens of Versailles (*Les Grandes Eaux*) being one of the most spectacular. Classical performances of plays by Racine, Corneille and Marivaux given every evening in the Tuileries Gardens until September 4th. From the 11th to the 21st, the 'free Commune of Montmartre' is gaily bedecked with flowers. *The* big day is of course the 14th, Bastille Day. Paris squares decorated with multicoloured lanterns, flags and bunting and platforms for the popular evening balls. Festivities begin at 10 am with a long military parade along the Champs-Elysées in the presence of the President of the Republic and his ministers. The fun begins after sundown. Dancing in the streets, on bridges, even on the tops of parked cars. Local orchestras and brass band of the School of Fine Arts provide music while non-dancers watch elaborate fireworks display in the Tuileries gardens. Non-stop pandemonium at the main line Paris railway stations. For the rest of the month Paris is socially, commercially and artistically dead.

August

For many, the best time to see Paris. Little traffic, few inhabitants about, beautiful weather and Prussian blue night skies. Most offices close for holidays as well as restaurants, literary cafés and hundreds of small shops. Librarians are on holiday but there is still a lot that can be visited quietly. Very few concerts or plays but there are the cinemas, the Festival Estival and the *soirées* in the Tuileries. For horse racing addicts there is the Prix d'Europe at Enghien. On August 15th Bonapartists (if any) may still celebrate Napoleon's birthday. Otherwise the social, cultural and sporting life of the nation has moved to the mountains, the seaside and fashionable watering places.

September

By the middle of the month Paris is back to normal again. Theatres reopen, business starts up and the major art exhibitions begin. Schools open on about the 15th and the season of commercial fairs and exhibitions begins with the International Leather Week at the Porte de Versailles. Illuminations and window display competitions are held along the rue de Rivoli and rue Saint-Honoré during the rue de Rivoli Grande Quinzaine for a fortnight. 'Bean Fair' at Arpajon followed by a 24-kilometre walk. Beginning of the athletic season. Paris gourmets impatiently wait for reports on the year's new vintage. A wine harvest festival is held in the Parisian suburb of Bagneux, although there are no longer any vineyards there. Snails begin to appear and are captured by chefs. For one week, towards the end of the month, the international Biennale of Antique Dealers, Jewellers and Decorators at the Grand Palais. Royal Oak at Longchamp in the middle of the month; Grand Prix d'Eté at Vincennes.

October

Starts with the long-awaited Motor Show and a well-attended second-hand car display for ten days at the Porte de Versailles.

B

The very popular Salon de l'Enfance (a kind of 'Home and Family' affair) opens towards the end of the month. Parliament opens and the Budget is presented. Rain frequent throughout October. Nature-lovers can go to the Dahlia Show at the Parc de Sceaux or the Chrysanthemum Show at the gardens of the Porte d'Auteuil. The 'most beautiful cat in the world' on display among admiring mink-coated ladies at the Hôtel Continental. Festival International de la Danse de Paris opens at the Théâtre des Champs-Elysées towards the end of the month and continues throughout November. Famous writers, playwrights and composers gather to pass judgement on both ultra-conservative and ultra-avant-garde performances. Every second year: the Semaines Internationales Musicales de Paris. Music-lovers might find an old harp or an Edison phonograph among the treasures of bric-a-brac and old junk at the Foire de la Ferraille held every year on the boulevard Richard Lenoir (5–12th). Near the foot of the Eiffel Tower you can watch a six-hour speed-boat race on the Seine, the Six heures de Paris, in the first week of the month and then go to Longchamp on the first Sunday to watch the Prix de l'Arc de Triomphe. For something slower, see the cycle race up the winding rue Lepic to the Place du Tertre in Montmartre. The slowest competitor wins (second Sunday).

November

All Saints Day. Solemn family lunches followed by even more solemn visits *en masse* to relatives' graves to lay chrysanthemums in honour of the departed. Rain. Seine threatens to rise to flood level. Fashion dealers come from all over the world for the Winter Collections presented at the Salon International du Prêt-à-porter Féminin. Do-it-yourself maniacs go to the Salon du Bricolage. Ambitious debs in search of future top executives go to the Bal de l'X at the Opera House. A very grand occasion with stiff *Polytechniciens* in uniform with epaulettes, cocked hats and swords. Interesting Jazz Festival on first day of the month with many visiting celebrities in the jazz world. November 11th: Fête de la Victoire, a bank holiday with particularly solemn official celebrations. November 22nd: General de Gaulle's birthday. The 25th is Saint Catherine's Day. As she is the patron saint of students, philosophers and young girls this can be an especially merry occasion. Employers give their young secretaries presents.

December

Christmas fever in the shops. Traffic jams worse than ever. Night clubs full every night. Season of literary prize giving (the Goncourt being the most prestige-worthy). The General of the Republic usually gives a speech to the nation before visiting yet another foreign state. Feverish scenes at the Gare de Lyon with dozens of extra trains running to the French Alps. School holidays start about four days before Christmas. Traffic jams even worse.

Hotels

Paris has a plethora of old hotels and hardly any modern ones—with the notable exception of the Hilton. You can stay in the Ritz or the Plaza-Athénée if you're rich, and exist for less than a pound a day in Montmartre or on the Left Bank. Paris really has hotels to suit every purse, from the elegant and old-world luxurious to the picturesque or sordid.

People live, study, die, make love, plot revolutions and starve in Paris hotels. Some people who came to Paris to live years ago are still in the hotel they first stayed in. Flats are expensive and scarce. Coco Chanel lives in the Ritz because she likes it.

We can only give you our own brief selection of a few hotels, ranging from the famous to the inexpensive and convenient, and remind you of one Golden Rule: unless you come to Paris in the dreariest winter months, do try to book in advance. You'd be surprised how even the smallest and dingiest hotel can be full up when there's a Motor Show or another big event. Paris is nearly always crowded—except in August.

Though the number of hotels in Paris has barely increased since the last World War, Parisian hôtellerie has made some effort to renew its premises and sanitary equipment. A few discreet hotels have even succeeded in attracting exacting clients who dare to expect comfort, courtesy and pleasant surroundings. Such habitués always go back to the same hotel, wisely booking in advance.

But when foreigners leave their homes and worries to visit Paris, the chances are that they will show greater interest in the city than in their hotel. Nevertheless, to choose a bad hotel in a holiday resort is a disaster. The more fortunate tourist in Paris needs no such home from home: he spends most of his time sightseeing and meandering through unknown streets.

Businessmen need comfort, a private telephone with sufficient extensions, the swift and efficient service of reliable staff and a resourceful barman. He considers the money he spends there an investment.

The international set have tried most 'palaces' (as Parisians call their larger and grandest hotels) and they have made their choice for all time. But the basic need of the ordinary visitor in search of a hotel is a few hints to avoid unpleasant mistakes, and information as to his rights, for hotel managers are subject to strict government regulations.

Official regulations you should know about

Hotels registered by the Office du Tourisme are divided into five main categories according to the number of rooms, general comfort, standard of equipment, extra facilities, number and type of staff. The unhurried visitor can compare the merits of the four-star de luxe hotel to those of the one-star hotel where the reality of his means will perhaps encompass him—for everyone knows that Paris is now the most expensive city in the world.

Only the prices charged by four-star de luxe hotels are free from any restrictions; the others are not. Members of the Syndicat général de l'industrie hôtelière de Paris include some 1,400 hotels with a total of about 60,000 rooms.

If you are on your own and the hotel cannot provide you with a single room and offers you a share in a room for two persons, the price must be reduced by at least 20%.

If you need an extra bed in your room, the price cannot be increased by more than 30%.

Do not be surprised if the hotel charges you 1·5 F or 2·0 F every time you use a common shower or bathroom; it is their right, but they don't always do it.

And if you stay over 60 days at a one- or two-star hotel, you are entitled to a minimum 30% reduction on the price of your room.

Booking your room

Certain seasons see Paris invaded by armies of visiting politicians, businessmen and provincials drawn by one of the great annual commercial exhibitions. These convergences of foreigners and provincials occur mainly in September, October and June. Your choice will then be considerably limited, sometimes to the point of your being sent to an obscure suburban hotel. It is therefore best to book in advance (from ten days to four weeks ahead for the better hotels).

A quick and proven method is to send a cheap and laconic telegram using the International Hotel Telegraph Code. This is how the Code works:

a room with one bed = Alba; with one large bed = Aldua; a room with two beds = Arab; with three beds = Abec; two rooms with one bed each = Belab; with two beds each = Board; a child's bed = Kind; Private bathroom = Bat; connected rooms = Conex.

Choosing an area

Ideally, your first encounter with Paris should be as total as possible. Pick a part of the city which corresponds most closely with your own ideal of Paris.

Avoid some areas like the plague: the well-to-do residential 16th arrondissement is dull, stodgy and empty of charm and life. The 17th is without beauty but more lively and cosmopolitan. The 11th, 12th, 19th and 20th arrondissements are noisy and predominantly working-class districts and too far from all places of interest for the tourist. But if you can afford it and want to savour the classical beauty of Paris in the very heart of the Right Bank, then you must contrive to stay in the neighbourhood of:

Concorde, Palais-Royal, Louvre (1st and 8th arrondissements)
For comfort and beauty combined, by far the best choice of an area in which to find your hotel. The 1st arrondissement is the smallest and least populated in Paris. It has the noblest surroundings and great monumental set-pieces: the Tuileries with its gardens, the Louvre Museum, the Place de la Concorde and the Opera House. You will be near the now-lamented Halles where the all-night restaurants are still pulling in the Paris-by-night crowds, the rue de Rivoli, rue Saint-Honoré, rue de la Paix and Place Vendôme —the homes of Parisian elegance at its most sumptuous.

Three celebrated 'palaces' are all within a minute's walk from the Place Vendôme. A fourth faces the Place de la Concorde. They are:

RITZ **** DE LUXE. 15 PLACE VENDOME. 073 28–30. RITZOTEL-PARIS
170 rooms and 60 private suites. Built in 1705, this historic and classically beautiful building is as famous a Paris institution as Maxim's. It has a staff of 500 constantly attending to the needs of some 200 worldly clients, including Coco Chanel who lives there permanently. The great halls are furnished with reproduction Louis XV furniture but the most beautiful private suites on the

first floor are all 'classified' by the Ministry of Fine Arts. All the bathrooms have been modernised but the rooms are delicately decorated in 1900 style with appropriately intimate lighting and pastel colours. There are 60 rooms for the personal staff of the clients, with appropriately connected bells. Three bars, a grill-room and a discreet entrance in the rue Cambon. Single room: from 115 F to 170 F. Double room from 150 F to 225 F. The suites overlooking Place Vendôme cost between 300 F and 750 F. 15% service. Breakfast 8 F.

MEURICE **** DE LUXE. 228 RUE DE RIVOLI
Another entrance in rue du Mont-Thabor.
073 32–40, 742 01–79. MEURISOTEL-PARIS
Undoubtedly one of the very best 'palaces' in Paris. As aristocratic as the Ritz, with a clientèle including members of the Spanish Royal family and other crowned heads of Europe; Salvador Dali, Noël Coward, Yul Brynner and Mme Florence Gould, who is known for her literary suppers at the hotel. Suites furnished with antique furniture. 184 rooms; single 110 F; double from 180 F to 200 F. 36 suites from 300 F. Service 15%.

LOTTI **** DE LUXE. 7–11 RUE DE CASTIGLIONE. 742 93–84
OTELOTTI-PARIS
World-famous and a favourite with international business tycoons. Advisable to book 4 to 6 weeks in advance. 135 rooms. Single room from 80 F to 100 F. Double room from 105 F to 185 F, breakfast included. 15% service.

CRILLON **** DE LUXE. 10 PLACE DE LA CONCORDE, (8e).
265 24–10. CRILONOTEL-PARIS
If you want to feel that you own the Place de la Concorde, stay at the Crillon. This is how the cream of Anglo-American society have achieved their air of tenure. You will be welcomed in English, treated with care and served with geniality. The 18th-century Place is very noisy but the impressive edifice with its Greek columns will envelop you in its dignified tranquillity. 220 rooms. Single room from 104 F to 115 F. Double room from 173 F to 190 F, breakfast not included.

VENDOME **** I PLACE VENDOME. 073 48–24.
VENDOMOTEL-PARIS
The favourite hotel of the English aristocracy before the Ritz was opened. With its 39 rooms and 9 suites, it is more intimate than

the 'palaces'. Single room 86 F; double room 123 F. Haute cuisine at the restaurant.

SAINT-JAMES ET D'ALBANY **** 211 RUE ST-HONORE; 202 RUE DE RIVOLI. 073 02-30. JAMALBANY-PARIS
Pleasant garden; façade on the Jardin des Tuileries. Frequented mostly by distinguished middle-aged foreigners. Excellent service and atmosphere. Book well in advance—particularly during exhibition times. 207 rooms and 15 private suites. Single room 80 F; double room 98 F, all included. Free parking.

CONTINENTAL **** 3 RUE DE CASTIGLIONE, (MAIN ENTRANCE, RUE DE RIVOLI). 073 18-00. CONTENTAL-PARIS
From the main entrance, you can see both the Jardin des Tuileries and the Place Vendôme. Huge, rococo and bombastic, the Continental belongs to a lost epoch. It was made into a Nazi headquarters during the occupation and, obviously, has had to recover from the experience. Much has been done to renew its installations and it is now regaining a prestige that one could have thought lost for ever. Quite a memorable experience to stay a few days in such solemn surroundings, designed by the architect of the Opera House. It also has an open-air restaurant, a garden, 350 rooms and 30 suites. Single room from 75 F to 115 F. Double room from 127 F to 173 F, breakfast included.

BRIGHTON *** 218 RUE DE RIVOLI. 073 27-80.
76 rooms. Beautifully situated, facing the Tuileries, the Louvre and Place Jeanne d'Arc. Single room 76 F; double room 90 F, all included. Restaurant.

HOTEL DE FRANCE ET CHOISEUL *** 239 RUE ST-HONORE. 073 41-92. FRANCHEUL-PARIS
125 rooms. Large very quiet interior garden, which is extremely rare for the area. A room with a bathroom is 50 F and a double 71 F, with breakfast extra at 7 F.

MONT-THABOR *** 42 RUE DU MONT-THABOR. 073 22-73.
104 rooms. Singles between 49 F and 54 F. Double room 58 F to 68 F, breakfast extra at 6 F. Restaurant.

OXFORD ET CAMBRIDGE *** 11 RUE D'ALGER. 073 28-45
Not so obviously touristy. Modest décor but very well situated in a quiet little street, facing the Continental. 82 rooms. Single from 35 F to 46 F. Double room from 54 F to 68 F, breakfast not included.

LOUIS LE GRAND ★★ 3 RUE ROUGET DE L'ISLE. 073 37-57.
OTELBLET, PARIS
55 rooms. Single room 45 F; double room 60 F. Lift.

*Champs-Elysées, Etoile, Faubourg St-Honoré, Madeleine (8th arrondisse-
ment)*
To the west of the 1st arrondissement. The 8th is where the French
President lives in the official luxury of the elegant 18th-century
Elysée Palace and where most of the international millionaire set
congregate. Not so classically 'Parisian' as the 1st arrondissement.
Several of the greatest 'palaces' as well as several smaller hotels of
the highest repute.

GEORGE V ★★★★ DE LUXE. 31 AVENUE GEORGE V. 359
89-71/9. GEORGEHOTEL-PARIS
Built in 1928 with about 300 rooms and 100 suites, this giant palace
has styleless modern furnished rooms with up-to-date bedding and
a private safe in the walls. The impressive hall with Louis XIV
tapestries and baroque sculptures leading to richly decorated lifts
walled with red leather panels looks far better than the sad-coloured
corridors of the upper floors. But the view over Paris on the top is
worth paying for. From Simenon to Paul Getty, every personality
is known by name to the concierge. Lonely clients are sometimes
discreetly solicited by some of the beautiful single ladies who
wander along the Avenue George V or, more rarely, in the hotel
halls themselves. .... No air conditioning or sound-proofing, but
the management will give you a 30% reduction for any stay over a
week. Single room 130 F; double room 220 F. Suites: 330 F for
one person, 550 F for two. $15\frac{1}{2}$% service; breakfast not included.

PLAZA-ATHENEE ★★★★ DE LUXE. 23-27 AVENUE MONTAIGNE.
225 14-90, 359 85-23. PLAZATENE-PARIS
The decoration is perhaps a bit pompous but likely to please a
North and South American clientèle craving for grand surroundings
and antique furniture. The rooms are very large and well-kept,
with Louis XV and XVI furniture. Graceful, flower-filled courtyard.
200 rooms and 50 suites. Single room from 130 F to 170 F; double
room from 220 F to 330 F; suites from 350 F to 780 F. (Breakfast
and 15% service not included.) Book in advance for September,
October, May and June.

BRISTOL **** DE LUXE. 112 FAUBOURG ST-HONORE.
359 23-15. BRISHOTEL-PARIS
Undoubtedly one of the few real 'palaces' in Paris. Bright and
elegant clientèle composed mainly of diplomats and distinguished
Americans; luxuriously decorated suites with air conditioning (also
in the restaurant); private parking for 40 cars; private dining-rooms;
impeccable service. 220 rooms and suites. Single room from 120 F
to 160 F; double room from 160 F to 240 F. Suites from 275 F to
1,000 F. 15% service and breakfast not included.

Other hotels 'de grande tenue', at about the same price include:
PRINCE DE GALLES **** DE LUXE. 33 AVENUE GEORGE V.
225 39-90. PRINCE-GALOTEL
Calm, almost intimate. For international businessmen. 230 rooms.
Single room from 104 F to 127 F. Double room 173 F to 207 F,
breakfast not included.

ROYAL MONCEAU **** DE LUXE. 35 AVENUE HOCHE.
227 78-00. ROYOTEL-PARIS
Within easy walking distance of the Arc de Triomphe. Elegant
international clientèle. Private garden. 260 rooms. Single room from
94 F to 138 F. Double from 125 F to 189 F, breakfast extra at 9 F.

BERKELEY **** I RUE DE PONTHIEU, 225 02-24. 7 AVENUE
DE MATIGNON
Very quiet, facing the Champs-Elysées. Well reputed restaurant
'Le Berkeley'. Bar. Residential hotel for people who want to stay
long—you will if you enjoy the finest French food. Large and
small suites. 14 rooms. Between 85 F and 145 F, breakfast not
included.

Three excellent hotels are situated around the quiet and pleasant
Place François Ier, five minute's walk from the Seine and the
Rond-Point des Champs-Elysées:
BELLMAN **** 37 RUE FRANÇOIS Ier. 359 62-51.
BELLMANOTEL-PARIS
Small hotel frequented by international show business people.
40 rooms, all with bath. About 90 F for one person, 100 F for two,
all included. Bar and restaurant.

SAN REGIS **** 12 RUE JEAN GOUJON. 259 41-90
55 rooms, all with bath. 8 private suites. Luxurious hotel patronised
by Americans. Single room 80 F; double room 110 F, all included.
Book well in advance. Restaurant.

ROYAL-ALMA **** 35 RUE JEAN GOUJON. 225 83-30/31/32.
HOTROYALMA-PARIS
84 rooms, all with bathroom or shower. Bar and restaurant. Charming hotel decorated with taste in contemporary styles. Single room: 60 F, double room: 90 F.

Overlooking the Champs-Elysées and Avenue de Matignon is the
ELYSEES-PARK **** 2 RUE JEAN MERMOZ. 359 31-96/99.
PARKOTEL-PARIS
Very central, attracts an international set. Stylish furniture. Restaurant. 60 rooms and 12 suites. The prices of the rooms vary between 90 F and 200 F.

If you want a quiet, cheaper hotel near the Champs-Elysées, then try the
BERRI *** 8 RUE FREDERIC-BASTIAT. 359 27-50. BERRIOTEL
Every modern facility. Round the corner from rue d'Artois. No bar. 38 rooms. 58 F for a room with a bath. Breakfast extra at 7 F.

AMINA *** 4 RUE D'ARTOIS. 225 80-93
31 rooms, all with bathrooms. 60 F for a single, 66 F for a double. Breakfast 6 F. If you need a much cheaper hotel in the same area, go to the

PARIS * 19 RUE DE PONTHIEU. 359 27-44
39 rooms, 15 of which have running water. None have a telephone. This is one of the hotels run on a classified scale of rates, the *Barême officiel*. As a hotel improves (or otherwise) its position in the scale changes, so in these cases it is not possible to give any reliable prices. At this hotel breakfast, however, is not included and at the moment stands at 3.50 F.

Elderly people might like the generally very quiet hotels in the 'Quartier de l'Europe' which is completely deserted at night. Walk around the northern part of Gare St-Lazare along any street named after a European capital. You will probably come across some exiled Russians with a smattering of English who will willingly guide you since they will themselves have stayed in some of these hotels.

Opéra, Grands Boulevards, Bourse (9th arrondissement)
Very busy commercial district for businessmen mainly.

COMMODORE **** 12 BOULEVARD HAUSSMANN. 770 93-00, 770 66-03

Near the Opera House. Attracts many French and foreign business-men. 200 rooms. Restaurant. American bar. From 60 F to 100 F. 25% service.

GRAND HOTEL DU PAVILLON **** 36-38 RUE DE L'ECHIQUIER, (10e) 770 17-15/16/17
Halfway between the Gare du Nord and the Stock-Exchange. Métro Bonne Nouvelle, on the Grands Boulevards. 200 rooms. Good food and large range of vintage wines. From 64 F to 86 F, all included.

VILLA TREVISE ** 12 CITE TREVISE. 824 89-56/57.
Situated in a private passage near the Stock-Exchange and Folies-Bergère. 29 rooms entirely renewed, with telephones. Parking. 'Bar select.' Lift. Interpreter. *Barême officiel.*

Montmartre, Pigalle (9th arrondissement)

PROUST *** 68 RUE DES MARTYRS. 378 43-31/32. OTELPROUST-PARIS
Rue des Martyrs is a market street going up to Pigalle with many attractive spots. 38 rooms entirely renewed in 1966. Restaurant renowned for its *cassoulet* and *foie gras*. American bar. Free television and radio-sets. From 65 F to 80 F, all included.

Bois de Boulogne (16th arrondissement)

RESIDENCE FOCH **** 10 RUE MARBEAU. 727 99-10
This hotel opened in 1964 and is situated in a very quiet and anony-mous street off Avenue Foch (the Paris equivalent of Park Lane). For the rich who want the best. Refined decoration, attentive and well-groomed staff. 26 rooms, 11 suites. From 120 F to 170 F for two. Easy parking. 2 minutes' walk from the Bois.

Auteuil: (South of the Bois)
LA RESIDENCE DU BOIS *** 16 RUE CHALGRIN. 727 50-59
A luxurious small 'hôtel particulier' with 23 old-style furnished rooms and access to lovely garden. Great comfort and 'cuisine bourgeoise' for those who want to keep the almost civilised Bois de Boulogne for themselves. Parking. About 90 F for two, all included.

LEFT BANK *(5th, 6th, 7th and 15th arrondissements)*
Saint-Germain, Odéon, Quartier Latin
These are certainly the most lively districts of Paris, as well as the

most cosmopolitan. You could stay there a fortnight without a moment's boredom. Numerous cafés, cinemas, and interesting crowds.

On the embankment:

RELAIS-BISSON **** 37 QUAI DES GRANDS-AUGUSTINS, (6ᵉ) 326 71-80
25 rooms and 3 suites. One of the loveliest hotels in Paris. Authentic antique furniture, paintings by established masters. Restaurant for gourmets. Bar. Rooms with view on the Seine: 75 F for one person, 100 F for two; rooms with view on inside courtyard: 60 F and 75 F. Suites: 130 F.

HOTEL DU QUAI VOLTAIRE *** 19 QUAI VOLTAIRE, (7ᵉ) 222 28-11, 548 42-91
Very pleasant hotel facing the Tuileries and Palais du Louvre (if you don't mind the persistent traffic). Intellectual clientèle. 34 rooms from 35 F. Bar and restaurant.

Within 5 minutes' walk of the Seine:

PONT-ROYAL **** 7 RUE MONTALEMBERT, (7ᵉ) 548 42-50. PONROYTEL-PARIS
Wealthy and brilliant clientèle including James Baldwin, Françoise Sagan, and other successful writers, top pop painters and film producers from the States. The quiet and cosy basement bar is the early evening headquarters of some of the most reputed French writers and poets such as Queneau, Aragon, etc. (Gallimard's head-office is just round the corner.) There is a good restaurant and grill-room, shops, theatre agency. The rooms are comfortable but not luxurious. All of them have a bathroom and a refrigerator. 90 rooms and 5 suites. From 80 F.

CAYRE *** 4 BOULEVARD RASPAIL, (7ᵉ) 222 10-82. CAYROTELAC-PARIS
Round the corner from boulevard St-Germain. 124 rooms, 85 with bathrooms. Another agreeable and central haven for visiting writers. Bernanos once lived there. Bar and restaurant. From about 40 F to 75 F. Near-by garage.

BOURGOGNE ET MONTANA *** 7 RUE DE BOURGOGNE, (7ᵉ) 468 20-22/23. BOURGONTEL-PARIS
View overlooking the French Parliament (Palais-Bourbon), the Seine and Place de la Concorde. A beautifully situated, quiet, and

comfortable hotel. Unpretentious atmosphere attracting many sophisticated foreigners. 'Cuisine soignée.' 42 rooms, half of them with bathrooms. From 30 F to 90 F.

HOTEL DE NICE ET DES BEAUX-ARTS ★★★ 4 BIS RUE DES BEAUX-ARTS, (6e) 326 54-05/06
One minute's walk from the Seine and the Institut (magnificent building where the solemn 'Académie Française' hold their obscure debates over the definition of words). Now famous in England and the United States as an ideal home from home. Free parking. You can rent a studio with kitchen and the services of the hotel. (100 F per month). 40 attractive rooms from 30 F to 60 F. Book at least a month in advance (a few months for a studio).

SOLFERINO ★★ 91 RUE DE LILLE, (7e) 705 85-54
Now a lovely and refined small hotel of 35 rooms near the Seine. Good service and prices. Lift. From 28 F to 40 F. Telephone in every room.

SCANDINAVIA ★★ 27 RUE DE TOURNON, (6e) 633 45-20
Near the Théâtre de l'Odéon (now Théâtre de France). Quaint and original decoration with ancient Spanish furniture. Young international clientèle. 22 rooms and 3 suites. 55 F for a single or double bedroom, service included. Breakfast 4 F. Telephone in every room.

MONT BLANC ★★ 28 RUE DE LA HUCHETTE, (5e) 033 49-44
With its noisy musical environs, the hotel is situated in what is perhaps the most lively and picturesque street in the whole Latin Quarter, just off the Place St-Michel. There are 41 rooms, and you are likely to have friendly encounters with your neighbours. From 20 F to 40 F. Telephone in each room. Lift. Restaurant and bar. Service and breakfast included.

LONDRES ET MALAQUAIS ★★ 3 RUE BONAPARTE, (6e) 033 67-41
Off the embankment. Recently renewed and very pleasant. Telephone in each of the 31 rooms. From 17 F to 35 F.

LOUISIANA ★ 60 RUE DE SEINE, (6e) 326 97-08
Full of young artists and writers and a bevy of eager Anglo-Saxon girls on an extended fling in Paris. 60 rooms with telephone. Lift.

5 minutes' walk from Café de Flore. Single room with bathroom: 30 F; without, 20 F. Double room: 40 F and 25 F.

LE LYS ★ 23 RUE SERPENTE, (6e) 326 97-57
Picturesque and well-kept 18th-century hotel off the Place St-Michel. Happy habitués. 22 rooms, from 18 F to 30 F all included.

MARRONNIERS ★ 21 RUE JACOB, (6e) 033 91-66
Very pleasant courtyard. Hotel has been entirely renewed. Welcoming atmosphere. Stronghold of artists and intellectuals. 18 rooms from 14 F to 35 F, with telephone.

If you have no particular hotel in mind, just walk around the Latin Quarter and Saint-Germain. It won't be long until you fall in love with some arresting little street with its newly-cleaned buildings. Try the Ile de la Cité, Ile Saint-Louis, the Panthéon, Place Monge and Maubert-Mutualité areas. There are plenty of cheap hotels in picturesque surroundings providing you don't mind the traffic.
A few very cheap hotels which we can recommend:

HOTEL DES GRANDS HOMMES, 17 PLACE DU PANTHEON, (5e) 033 38-93
The names of Balzac, Stendhal, André Breton (who wrote *Nadja* there) are connected for various reasons with this hotel facing the impressive and austere Panthéon mausoleum. Still a place of pilgrimage for many postgraduates. 41 rooms from 9 F to 13 F. Book in advance for the autumn and winter.

STELLA ★ RUE MONSIEUR LE PRINCE, 326 43-49
Round the corner from rue Racine, near Odéon. Gregory Corso and some other less known English speaking poets used to live there in the 60's. The owners make you feel one of the family. 22 rooms from 8 F to 11 F, for one or two persons.

GRAND BALCON ★ 5 RUE DAUPHINE, (6e) 326 43-28
Building looks like the sharp prow of a battle-ship. It has a balcony overlooking a very lively carrefour, opposite the café-restaurant *Procope*. It is run by friendly people. 26 rooms from 11 F to 14 F, service included. One room for 3 persons: 16 F. No advance booking necessary.

LE SELECT ** I PLACE DE LA SORBONNE, (5ᵉ) 033 29-01
Anonymous hotel strategically situated opposite the Sorbonne,
2 minutes from the Jardin du Luxembourg. 66 rooms with telephone. Lift. 22 F with a double bed.

Champ de Mars (Eiffel Tower), Invalides, (7th arrondissement)
Official area full of wide avenues with trees and gardens and refined
town mansions now occupied by various ministries. Always quiet
at night.

DERBY-HOTEL *** 5 AVENUE DUQUESNE, 468 12-05.
DERBY-HOTEL
Near the gentle avenue de Breteuil, behind the Hôtel des Invalides.
Parking. Bar. Lift. 13 suites with kitchens. 43 rooms with telephone.
Between 35 F and 55 F. Breakfast extra at 5.50 F.

HOTEL SPLENDIDE ** 29 AVENUE DE TOURVILLE, 468 24-77.
SPLENHOTEL-PARIS
Beautifully situated across avenue de Breteuil. Same amenities as
the Derby. 5 private suites. 47 rooms. Single with bath 43 F. Double
with bath 48 F. Breakfast not included.

And 200 yards west of the Eiffel Tower, the
HILTON **** DE LUXE, 18 AVENUE DE SUFFREN, (15ᵉ) 273
92-00. HILTELS-PARIS
The latest giant newcomer to the Paris hotel scene. A thoroughly
American-inspired, prestige-seeking caravanserai with 492 rooms—
all with radio and television (French television programmes only).
The eleven-storey building looks even heavier and more obtrusive
than the London Hilton. So much for architecture. The interior
was designed at huge expense by Raymond Loewry, a famous
expounder of industrial aestheticism, with one of the 3 restaurants
and gardens in 'authentic' Wild West style. Like all other Hiltons,
it's a miniature self-contained city. Numerous pretty girls in constant
attendance. Latest novelty: paper pyjamas at 15 F a pair: blue and
red-striped for men, white and spotted with pink flowers for women.
They are called 'pacojamas' and designed by Paco Rabanne. Should
the Hilton catch fire during the night, imagine the Marx-brothers-
style sight of its striped and flowered clientèle fleeing down the
corridors.... Single rooms 118 F, 147 F, 176 F; double rooms
147 F, 176 F, 205 F. Private suites from 410 F to 880 F. 15% service;
breakfast not included.

RESIDENCE PLAZA MIRABEAU **★★★** 10 AVENUE EMILE ZOLA, (15ᵉ) 250 72-00

A luxurious residential hotel with 25 apartments with kitchen and bathroom. Very popular during last ten years, especially with embassies who send their staff there until they can be found more permanent quarters and families waiting for a suitable flat. But you can stay even for one day and there is no need to give long notice when leaving. Special prices arranged for long stays. Quiet area near the Pont Mirabeau and the Métro Javel. Studios with kitchen and bathroom: 62 F to 67 F per day; 2-room apartments: from 72 F to 87 F for two persons (10 F extra for an additional bed). 15% service.

HOTELS (disreputable)

Paris is famous for its *maisons de passe* where rooms may be hired by the hour for obvious purposes but naturally we can't give you any precise addresses. As a general rule, Paris hôteliers are fairly tolerant of amorous encounters if conducted with suitable discretion, but don't like letting their rooms for less than 24 hours. Some hotel porters will be ready to supply addresses for a small consideration but of course you might find an obliging taxi-driver. If you and your companion can't afford about 30 F then try some of the more decrepit hotels on the east side of the boulevard Sébastopol. You might even be given new stimulus by the sight of some of the weirder inmates who stay there for several days at a time. The number of hours you want to stay may be negotiated with complete lack of embarrassment on either side.

Pleasure seekers with a better knowledge of the ways of the capital go to more salubrious and discreet 'hotels' which don't advertise themselves as such. The building, usually respectable and bourgois in appearance, will be situated in a quiet side street. There will always be a bar next door or on the premises itself to give a reassuring air of casualness to what is an illicit 'house of rendezvous'. If you spend about 70 F on drinks you will be accosted by a girl belonging to the establishment but strictly speaking it is not a brothel since you can bring your own partner. 'Amateurs' are also to be found in the bars. One such place operates in the rue Bayen (17th arrondissement) but you must bring your own companion. Another is in the rue Boursault (17th arrondissement).

If you go to a very proper looking six-storey building in the rue Sainte-Beuve (6th arrondissement; Métro Vavin) the pattern of approach is somewhat more devious. You make your way to the kitchen, wait there alone for a few minutes then order a coffee and await developments. You may find yourself in the company of similarly lustful members of both sexes. This sanctuary is opposite the 'Canne à sucre' and there is a nearby bar.

Two registered hotels offering a modest degree of comfort, a bedroom and a salon are in the rue Danielle Casanova and the rue de la Pompe (2nd and 16th arrondissements respectively). They will provide you with the necessary intimacy and discretion for about 20 F at any time of the day. The first has a sign in dedication to Stendhal who is said to have lived there.

Near the Métro Cluny another establishment offers the attraction of 'blue' films. A drawing pin in the wall inside signifies that performances will be held that night.

Outside Paris, in the neighbourhood of the Ville d'Avray, the Roi René has a bar where orgies are arranged, both by and for genuine connoisseurs of such activities. You must order a drink for yourself which will cost you 30 F but you are not obliged to buy one for any of the ladies you might be taking with you. A chauffeur will take you to a house not far away. He is, incidentally, the barman who has just served you your drink.

And if you can't afford a hotel at any price. . . .

If you are in the unhappy predicament of being unable to find even a few square feet of hotel space at a derisory price, don't despair. True, you can do as the *clochards* do and make shift with a railway station, embankment or bridge, but the most comfortable solution by far is to go to the international telephone exchange in the central post office in the rue du Louvre. Ask for a number abroad where you know there will be no answer (Madame Tussaud's in London, a cinema in Switzerland, a small shop you know somewhere . . .). Pretend dismay when told that no one is answering and announce your intention of trying again later. Then have a nap. It's not the best way of getting a full night's sleep but at least you're warm and there are a number of all-night cafés in the neighbourhood.

Tourists with camping equipment can use the camping ground in the Bois de Boulogne which has the usual amenities and charges the usual fees. You can sleep there in your own car but remember: you are not allowed to park anywhere else in the Bois (whether because it's against the law or because the police don't like it is a matter of conjecture). If you are caught you might be charged with soliciting others to join in organised orgies. Until quite recently, the Bois was notorious as a place where similarly inclined parties would signal to each other with their headlights before joining up to head for some flat or villa.

Buying Antiques

The French, it's well known, have a mania for antiques and old furniture. Their flats are often pretty ancient too. A wealthy Parisian will generally still prefer to pay the earth for a Louis XV chair than buy a Charles Eames chair or a comfortable sofa.

There has been a craze for buying art nouveau (called 'le modern style' by the French) antiques and bric-à-brac. Now it's 1920-style stuff. Tomorrow it'll be the Thirties.

Paris is full of every kind of antique shop. Buying antiques is a risky business everywhere but the shops we've listed are among the best of their kind.

Antique Dealers become more numerous every month and more and more often they hardly deserve the name. Any leisured society lady (or just any lady) with a comfortable amount of capital behind her can decide to open a 'boutique' to sell 'amusing' objects—usually only to friends and relatives. You go there to meet your friends, to have a cup of tea or a whisky, to chat—it's the kind of boutique which has taken the place of the Marquise de Sévigné, the Rumpel Mayer, and even the bar of the Ritz of the Twenties. It's also an excellent excuse for going to London two or three times a year to 'stock up' and treat yourself to some cashmere woollies. The ravaging effects of the vogue for the 'English style' on French taste are almost beyond belief in Paris. Most of these boutiques are decorated with chintz or rather doubtful tartans and cater for a well-off clientèle impressed more by 'class' than originality. They come to buy 'Regency' furniture, ships' chests, 'Adam' mirrors and copper lamps, all recently made in England and shipped over wholesale at prices unknown on the other side of the Channel.

Still, Paris does have some antique dealers worthy of the name. A large number of them are to be found on the Left Bank, in a quadrilateral area approximately bordered by the Luxembourg and the Seine on one side, the boulevard Saint-Michel and the rue du Bac on the other. A short walk in this district will give you an idea of what Paris has to offer you in the way of antiques. On the other side of the Seine, a few famous, luxurious and highly reputed antique dealers continue to reign over the antique market.

La Lanterne Magique Shop, rue Coctlogon

Furniture and objets d'art

Late 17th–18th centuries (the 'golden age' of French classical furniture)

Left Bank

BUVELOT, 9 quai Voltaire, Paris 7
Very beautiful furniture, all in perfect condition and beautifully displayed.

GROTNOT ET JOINEL, 23 quai Malaquais, Paris 6

MARCEL HEIM, 42 rue de Varenne, Paris 7
The pieces on display in the window only give a faint idea of the treasures kept in the three huge upper storeys. Only to be seen by *bona fide* appointment.

NOTGATCH, 194 boulevard Saint-Germain, Paris 7

MLLE. RÉMY, 200 boulevard Saint-Germain, Paris 7
The pieces of furniture here are all 'in their juice' (dans leur jus) as the antique dealers say. It simply means that they have only undergone a minimum of restoration. The chairs in particular have kept their original paint intact. Prices are high in consequence.

SOUFFRICE (galerie Voltaire), 33 quai Voltaire, Paris 7

E. TOUZAIN AINE, 27 quai Voltaire, Paris 7
In the former Hôtel de Villette where Voltaire died in 1778. On the first floor you can still see a *salon* decorated with woodwork dating from the great man's lifetime.

Right Bank

AVELINE ET CIE, 20 rue de Berri, Paris 8

BENSIMON, 20 rue Royale, Paris 1
Very beautiful 18th-century furniture and *objets d'art*. Also has silverware and jewellery.

BRANTOME, 50 rue de Berri, Paris 8

MAURICE CHALOM, 17 Place Vendôme, Paris 1

SAMY CHALOM, 38 faubourg Saint-Honoré, Paris 8

DOUCET, Place Beauvau (94 faubourg Saint-Honoré), Paris 8

FABIUS FRÈRES, 152 boulevard Haussman, Paris 8

FERSEN, 18 avenue Matignon, Paris 8
Beautiful chairs admirably covered with brocades made after original period designs.

JANSEN, 9 rue Royale, Paris 8
Jansen is the accredited decorator of royal houses, industrial magnates, Greek ship-owners, the Rothschilds, etc. Furniture of very high quality. The 'Boutique Jansen' is an extremely elegant gift shop run by young, pretty and charming society girls. One of the 'best addresses' in Paris.

KRAEMER ET CIE, 43 rue de Monceau, Paris 8
M. Kraemer's collection is on display in a superb private mansion in the Plaine Monceau. Advisable to telephone for an appointment.

ETIENNE LEVY, 178 faubourg Saint-Honoré, Paris 8

ANDRE MAVON, 238 faubourg Saint-Honoré, Paris 8
Beautiful 18th-century furniture and objects mounted in gilt bronze.

RAMSAY, 54 faubourg Saint-Honoré, Paris 8
Beautiful furniture and old woodwork. Ramsay also does interior decorations.

SELIGMANN ET CIE, 23 Place Vendôme, Paris 1
The shop is small and the few rare and beautiful pieces on display only give a slight idea of the treasures owned by the firm.

YVONNE DE BREMOND D'ARS, 20 faubourg Saint-Honoré, Paris 8

'Haute Epoque', Renaissance and 'Louis XIII'

A distinction must be made here between a few great antique dealers selling first-rate pieces at a price beyond the reach of the average collector, and the shops offering rather rustic-style, generally late-17th century pieces, all in the so-called 'Louis XIII style'. In the first category we suggest:

BACRI, 6 rue Copernic, Paris 16
In a private house.

BRIMO DE LAROUSSILHE, 58 rue Jouffroy, Paris 17
Also in a private house.

NICOLAS LANDAU, 3 rue de Duras, Paris 8
Each of the exquisite objects kept by M. Landau, in a charming maisonnette tucked away at the end of the shady courtyard, has a story attached to it. Its owner will tell it to you with consummate art.

TAILLEMAS, 17 quai Voltaire, Paris 7

You will also find good Renaissance and Louis XIII furniture at:

A LA VIEILLE REMISE, 16 rue des Saints-Pères, Paris 6
Don't expect pieces here to be rare or of exceptional quality.
What you will find, piled up in a kind of warehouse, are regional
furniture or wood furnishings of the 18th or 19th century. They
are plain, genuine, honest and good value, even if they do often
need repairs.

MICHEL COQUENPOT, 25 rue de Bourgogne, Paris 7

JAQUET, 40 rue des Saints-Pères, Paris 6 and 18 rue de Seine, Paris 6

LEONARDI, 8 avenue de Friedland, Paris 8

MICHEL MEYER, 56 rue du Four, Paris 6

PERPITCH, 240 boulevard Saint-Germain, Paris 7

Empire style and Charles X

ANDRE MANCEL, 42 rue du Bac, Paris 7

ROGER IMBERT, 157 faubourg Saint-Honoré, Paris 8

JEAN CHELO, 5 rue Lamennais, Paris 8
A specialist in light-coloured wood furniture of the Charles X period.

A NAPOLEON, 33 boulevard Raspail, Paris 7

'English' style

MADELEINE CASTAING, 21 rue Bonaparte, Paris 6
The English style, particularly that of the Regency period, was
'invented' in France by Madame Castaing immediately after the
war. The mode spread throughout France with surprising rapidity
and still survives strongly. Needless to say, most of her imitators
have neither her knowledge of the subject, nor her imagination and
decorative fantasy. Of her followers we may mention:

JOHN DEVOLUY, 3 rue Jacob and 1 rue de Furstenberg, Paris 6
Furniture of the period and also fittings, candélabre, etc., made
after his own designs.

FRED GUIRAUD, 9 rue de Belloy, Paris 16

RAOUL GUIRAUD, 90 rue de Grenelle, Paris 7
He is also a very fashionable interior decorator.

HAGNAUER, 10 rue de Seine, Paris 6

ANDREE HIGGINS, 54 and 66 rue de l'Université, Paris 7

'Art nouveau' and 'art déco' ('1925 period')

After having long been despised and relegated to the lumber room as the last word in 'bad taste', furniture and objects of the 1900 period have come back into favour in the last ten years. Prices have soared up tremendously although it must be admitted they were rock bottom to begin with. The fashion for objects of the twenties is more recent but now well established among collectors who won't be considered as *avant-garde* for very much longer.

CACTUS BAZAR, 35 Passage Choiseul, Paris 2
Shop belonging to the charming actress Sophie Desmarets. The stock is varied and very amusing. Although it has been spoilt by neon lights, the Passage Choiseul is still lively and full of charm. Facing the Cactus Bazar is Catherine Harlet's model agency. If you're lucky you may catch more than one glimpse of some of the most famous models of both sexes whom you see every day in the papers.

COMOGLIO, 22 rue Jacob, Paris 6
Incredible and varied bric-à-brac of every imaginable kind of furniture—many pieces are hired to film companies. 18th-century pieces to be found side by side with astonishing Second Empire and 1900 pieces in the most fantastic styles.

J. DE CUSSET, 19 rue Bonaparte, Paris 6
Furniture and glassware of the 1900 period and the mid-twenties.

JACQUES DAMIOT, 3 chaussée Pont-de-Grenelle, Paris 15
In a private house. After having made the Second Empire style fashionable again, M. Damiot was one of the first to take an interest in late 19th-century decorative art.

DENOEL, 21 rue Guénégaud, Paris 6
Mostly furniture and knick-knacks of the mid-twenties.

MME FILLON, 23 rue Bonaparte, Paris 6
Late 19th-century glassware and furniture.

GERARD LEVY, 17 rue de Beaune, Paris 7
Only a few pieces from M. Gérard Lévy's magnificent collection of 1900-period objects are on display in his shop, together with highly interesting objects from archaeological excavations.

GABRIELLE LORIE, 21 quai Voltaire, Paris 7
One of the oldest and finest collections of glassware by Gallé, assembled before the war when the works of the great Nancy

craftsmen were almost completely neglected. 19th-century English and French furniture.

Frames and gilt-wood furniture

MME BAC, 37 rue Bonaparte, Paris 6

LEBRUN, 155 faubourg Saint-Honoré, Paris 8

SERGE ROCHE ET ROTHIL, 279 rue Saint-Honoré, Paris 1
French and Italian picture frames, mirrors, painted and gilt furniture.

Antique textiles

FULGENCE, 75 rue La Boétie, Paris 8
Admirable collection of antique textiles and costumes.

Carpets and Hangings

BENADAVA, 6 rue Royale, Paris 1
Oriental carpets, 18th-century French carpets and tapestries.

DARIO BOCCARA, 184 faubourg Saint-Honoré, Paris 8
Oriental and European carpets, Gobelins, Beauvais and Aubusson tapestries (all of outstanding quality) are magnificently displayed on each of the three enormous floors of the shop.

ROBERT DE CALATCHI, 135 boulevard Haussmann, Paris 8
Ancient Oriental carpets.

CATAN, 129 avenue des Champs-Elysées, Paris 8
Oriental carpets, Aubusson, *savonnerie* and *petit-point* carpets.

GALERIE PERSANE, 132 boulevard Haussmann, Paris 8
Ancient Oriental carpets.

TARICA, 43 faubourg Saint-Honoré, Paris 8
Very beautiful ancient Oriental and Spanish carpets.

European and far-Eastern ceramics

BRICUS A BRACUM, 68 rue Bonaparte, Paris 6
A charming shop. Madame Latel, the owner, has a fine selection of 1900-period glassware (Gallé, etc.), crystal and tableware, mostly dating from the late 19th century and all of very high quality.

VAN DER MEERSCH, 23 quai Voltaire, Paris 7

NICOLIER, 7 quai Voltaire, Paris 7
Admirable choice of porcelain and faïence ware from almost

all countries, of the 16th, 17th, 18th and early 19th centuries.

PIERRE DE REGAINY, 6 rue de Beaune, Paris 7
Porcelain of the very highest quality, enamels, knick-knacks, and glassware, mainly of the 17th and 18th centuries.

LECOMTE ULLMANN, 75 faubourg Saint-Honoré, Paris 8
Ceramics, mostly of the 18th century; small collectors' pieces.

Antique gold and silver, jewellery

In Paris, don't expect to find the same splendid silver you may often have seen displayed in London shops. Hardly any French silverware of the 17th and 18th centuries has survived changes in fashion, and the melting-down ordered at the end of the reign of Louis XIV and during the Revolution. The few rare pieces that did survive are either in museums, large collections, or in the hands of a few dealers who, having managed to buy them at a sale, soon sell them to a selected list of clients. Prices are absolutely sky-high. Silver of the Empire period, and especially that of the late 19th century, is less rare and correspondingly cheaper.

If you are looking for *art nouveau* style jewellery made by the finest craftsmen of the period such as Vever and Lalique, then don't miss:

MARC GARLAND, 23 rue du Bac, Paris 7 and 346 rue Saint-Honoré, Paris 8

JOSEPHINE, 1 rue Bonaparte, Paris 6
Silver ware of the 18th and, above all, 19th century.

KUGEL, 7 rue de la Paix, Paris 2
M. Kugel is one of the great international dealers and only a very small part of his extraordinary collection is on display in his Paris shop. Apart from French silver ware, he has a selection of gems mounted in gold and silver and some German goldwork worthy of the greatest museums.

OXEDA, 334 rue Saint-Honoré, Paris 8
Antique silver ware and jewellery.

PIERRE ANDRIEUX, 66 faubourg Saint-Honoré, Paris 8
Beautiful antique and modern silver ware. Very classical in style and of the highest quality.

ALEXANDRE POPOFF, 86 faubourg Saint-Honoré, Paris 8

Silver, some fine porcelain (Meissen in particular) and charming mid-19th-century paintings.

AU VIEUX PARIS, 4 rue de la Paix, Paris 2
Specialises in French 18th-century silver.

A LA VIEILLE CITE, 350 rue Saint-Honoré, Paris 8
Antique gold and silver and jewellery. Many pieces of Russian origin.

MASALI, 73 rue des Dames, Paris 17
Don't go into this shop situated in the popular district around the Place Clichy expecting to find a soup-tureen by Germain decorated with the arms of France. But if you are looking for some honest silver ware, mostly of the late 19th century, or even a few downright 'cubic' pieces of the thirties, then you may find them at a reasonable price among an incredible collection of *bric à brac*. You can also haggle without risking the glacial, scornful 'no' of dealers in the 'high class districts'.

Antique clocks and watches

DIETTE, 4 avenue Matignon, Paris 8
Incomparable collection of clocks of every period. Everything of the highest quality.

AU VIEUX CADRAN, 59 *ter*, rue Bonaparte, Paris 6
Watches, clocks. Some antique jewellery.

Far-Eastern art—Primitive art

MICHEL BEURDELEY, 4 rue de l'Elysée, Paris 8
By appointment only. The greatest French expert in Eastern and far-Eastern art.

BEURDELEY ET CIE, 200 boulevard Saint-Germain, Paris 7
A delightful shop run by Michel Beurdeley's son. Beautiful Chinese and Indian objects on display in a very modern, very elegant, very simple setting.

COMPAGNIE DE LA CHINE ET DES INDES, 39 avenue de Friedland, Paris 8
Chinese ceramics, lacquer and sculptures from the earliest periods to the 18th century.

LE CORNEUR-ROUDILLON, 206 boulevard Saint-Germain, Paris 7
Primitive art.

LOO, 48 rue de Courcelles, Paris 8
The monotony of the highly conventional Plaine Monceau district

is charmingly broken by M. Loo's Chinese house, with its red
balustrades and pagoda-shaped roof. First-rate collections inside.

CHARLES RATTON, 14 rue de Marignan, Paris 8
Primitive, Egyptian and early Western art.

MAURICE RATTON, 17 rue de Grenelle, Paris 7
Primitive art.

Sarah Bernhardt's Chair, M. Guirche's '1900 Room'

Eating in Paris

Eating is what some people come to Paris for. Paris still has some restaurants which are the glory of the civilised world. We're happy to introduce you to them but expect them to be more expensive than anything you have yet come across at home. They're worth the price, though, if you really appreciate food at its finest. You can also eat cheaply and well in Paris— if you know where. We'll try to help you. And of course you can eat all kinds of exotic foreign food. Ever tried cous-cous? or Vietnamese cooking?

The Great Restaurants

Perhaps the first thing to be said about going to eat in one of Paris' great restaurants is that they are very, very expensive. On the other hand, they are among the best in the world, and quality is always expensive. Also, any owner will tell you how overheads and taxes have soared in the past few years and how salaries have risen as a consequence. If these restaurants were less expensive, it would simply mean that the chefs and personnel were of the second rank. It is precisely because the great restaurants insist on remaining faithful to their standards and traditions, that they can only have the best staff obtainable and must pay for them accordingly.

For you to enjoy and appreciate the very high quality of French *haute cuisine*, there are few fixed rules but you must, let us say, be in a certain frame of mind. A great meal is like a ritual and you should prepare yourself for it beforehand. Nonetheless, there are certain things you should know when you have arrived at the table of your choice: in the first place, don't talk too much or too loudly. The famous gastronome, statesman and consul under France's 1st Republic, Cambacérès, used to tell his noisier guests at table: 'Be quiet, how do you expect us to know what we're eating!' He was quite right. Secondly, don't be impressed by the sonorous titles of some of the dishes on the menu. If you see something described as 'à la Grand Duc de . . .' it may well have been invented for the occasion, because 'it sounds nice'.

Don't be afraid to ask the *Maître d'hôtel* (head waiter) for explanations: that's what he's there for. If, as happens rarely, he either refuses to tell you exactly what you want to know in complete detail, or else assumes a stupid air of superiority because you are a foreigner (and therefore an absolute ignoramus who can be told and given anything), then leave at once.

Many Americans, especially, tend to forget or to be unaware that apart from the salad and ice-cream, all the main dishes in French high cuisine demand to be accompanied by wine. If, for reasons of health perhaps, you can't drink wine, then ask for water. Beer may be drunk in certain very rare cases, but tea, coffee or milk will always destroy the taste of a sauce. So will any apéritif or spirit.

When choosing a wine, tell the *sommelier* (wine waiter) exactly what you are going to eat. You needn't be ashamed of telling him that you have no intention of ordering any of the great vintages, if your means are limited. In a good restaurant, even the cheapest wines available will be of excellent quality for their price. But do beware of the occasional waiter who will advise you to try the 'little rosé' of the house. There are practically *no* great rosé wines and the often-heard remark that rosé wines go with any dish is pure superstition. They may not clash with anything—admittedly—but they certainly do not harmonise with anything particular and enhance nothing. They can ruin even the most delicious meal: a fact which all too many Frenchmen would do well to remember.

Some people who wish to pass as 'connoisseurs' find it amusing to send back a bottle of wine after tasting it, saying that it's 'corked'. This may sometimes be true, but unfortunately so many pretentious snobs and pseudo-gastronomes have done this to show off, that you must be absolutely and utterly certain of your judgement before raising any objection in a great restaurant where every possible care has been taken of the wine and where any obvious defect will immediately be noticed by the waiter.

You should be sure to book your table well in advance, by telephone, spelling your name out with great care. If you're not an expert in great French cooking, then ask for the specialities, or for the chef to compose a meal for you which he will do with pleasure.

When you pay your bill, it is advisable to leave about 5 per cent extra, in addition to the service if you feel you have been particularly well looked after and at least another 5 francs to the *sommelier*.

Finally, if you wish to enjoy a really pleasurable meal in any of the great restaurants we have listed and described, you should know that some are rather too quiet and even a little depressing at lunch times. From experience, the best places to go for lunch are the Grand Véfour, Ledoyen or Prunier rather than Maxim's or the Tour d'Argent where the clientèle tends to be composed mainly of businessmen, talking business most of the time. Moreover, the most elegant and beautiful *Parisiennes* who grace these establishments tend to rise later and later and the sight, if not the company, of a lovely woman always goes well with a superb meal.

CHEZ DENIS, 10 rue Gustave-Flaubert, Paris 17. Tel: WAG 40-77. Closed Mondays and from 22nd July–15th September. Until 11 pm.

According to an old French adage, you should roll your tongue seven times in your mouth before speaking. Even more circumspection is needed before mentioning this particular restaurant.

Its chef—its very great chef—Denis is arrogant, self-satisfied and subject to daily fits of increasing intensity of megalomania. The staff, which he seems to have recruited haphazardly during his bouts of evil humour, rival him in his rudeness when they are not simply looking absent-minded. As for the décor, it is comfortable and reminiscent of the time when all things British and whisky were the rage, but that's all. In other words, neither the décor nor the welcome, and even less, the service can justify a visit to *Chez Denis*.

All that remains is the cooking and this, it must be admitted, places the restaurant at the very summit of Paris gastronomy. Its inspiration is mainly Aquitaine and its specialities are those the like of which you will find nowhere else in Paris. Their quality is incomparable. It is worth bearing everything to taste such delights as Monsieur Denis' *ris de veau en gelée, confit d'oie à l'oseille, selle d'agneau aux légumes, foie gras de canard*. A special mention must be made of the truly fabulous *homard à la bordelaise*—a dish whose perfection is proof enough that behind his roguish and insolent demeanour, the chef is one of the most sensitive and inspired cooks in the world.

Criticise Denis as much as you like then, but not for his food or his high prices. And if you are one of those 'phlegmatic' Englishmen the French so love to imagine, try not to lose your temper or your famous *sang-froid*. . . .

CLOSERIE DES LILAS, 171 boulevard du Montparnasse, Paris 6. Tel: DAN 70-50. Every day until 2 am.

Despite the advice of traditionally ill-informed gastronomic experts, we have decided to include this most luxurious of all Parisian intellectual centres in our list of the very greatest Paris restaurants. All you have to do to be convinced of the truth of our judgement is to savour such specialities as the *poularde en vessie*, specially prepared by an accomplished young chef who gets better every day, and, among the fish dishes, the *loup grillé à la farigoulette*— so infinitely superior to that served at the nearby *Méditerrané* in the Place de l'Odéon, one of the most crazily overestimated restaurants on the Left Bank.

Other good reasons for going to the 'Closerie': its *carré d'agneau aux aromates, œufs bénédictine* and *filet sauté Stroganoff*.

The 'Closerie' was also a great literary cafe: Hemingway, Picasso, Giacometti, Beckett, Gide and Sartre have all been there. Why not you?

DROUANT, Place Gaillon, Paris 2. Tel: OPE 53-72. Open every day until 10.30 pm. Closed in August.

The restaurant and the famous literary event known as the Prix Goncourt are inseparable. In 1896, the two members of the young Académie Goncourt decided to meet every first Wednesday of every month in this already famous restaurant where Clemenceau could sometimes be seen treating his friend Claude Monet to a meal. Seven years later, in 1903, the little dining room known as the 'Table Ronde' was set aside on a certain Monday every December for the election of the Goncourt winner. But if you are a gastronome, don't go on that day. The first floor rooms, stairs and entrance will be crammed with journalists, photographers and lookers-on. Better go on the other days when Drouant welcomes some of the best-fed businessmen in Paris from noon until ten thirty.

The writer Huysmans used to sneer at Drouant but he was wrong and has remained wrong ever since. This great restaurant in the little Place Gaillon has never lost its quality and the service is consistently satisfactory in every respect.

The cuisine: specialities of the house include the *paupiette de poulet de Bresse Lucullus*, the *terrine de caneton rouennaise* and its exquisite woodcock *pâté*. As for the fish and shellfish: they deserve a chapter of their own. They are beyond the shadow of a doubt among the most delicious in Paris: sole fillets, *homard Drouant*, *saumon sauce verte*, *suprême de barbue* and a classic *bouillabaisse*. They are served with the famous *blanc de blanc* of the *maison*. But don't let the great reputation of this wine prevent you from discovering some of the less-publicised treasures of the cellar. . . .

GRAND VEFOUR, 17 rue de Beaujolais, Paris 1. Tel: RIC 58-97. Closed Sundays and in August.

Even the fact that the Golden Book of the Grand Véfour contains all the names of the Tout-Paris and the show world cannot diminish our very favourable opinion of the (generally *Bordelais*-orientated) cuisine prepared by Raymond Oliver and his élite chef. The fact is that it's smart in Paris to deny that a restaurant can be both fashionable and 'serious'.

Let it be said straight away that if the Grand Véfour is so fashionable it is due far more to the television success of its bearded and genial owner than to any reputation gained by the constant presence of film starlets whose culinary culture is restricted to salads and 'rare' steaks.

This preamble is necessary if you are to understand our judgement that follows: television personality or not, the fact remains that Raymond Oliver is a very great cook indeed. His preparations are often original (sometimes downright audacious), always skilled and they never disappoint. But it happens all too often that his many extra-culinary activities keep this debonair and outrageously 'ham' master of cuisine from his saucepans. His buying of rare books on culinary theory and history and his many television appearances have tended to lower the extremely high quality of his cuisine, justly dominated as it is by his famous *poulet au homard, toasts au crevettes Rothschild*, the *pigeon Rainier, œufs Louis Olivier*, the *coulibiac*—dedicated to his late neighbour Colette—the *crêpes Mélusine aux pommes soufflées, ballotine de volaille duc de Chartres*, some remarkable specialities that were created as homage to his departed friend Jean Cocteau, and his boned thrushes, the *grives Georges Sand désossées*, stuffed with *foie gras* and cooked in pastry. This last speciality owes its name to the fact that Georges Sand was a habituée of the Café de Chartres (the first name of the Grand Véfour) and it is for the same reason that all the ashtrays reproduce one of the writer's hands.

Cellar: not up to the level of the cuisine. Mostly consists of the few thousand bottles brought from his birthplace at Langon by Raymond Oliver who has refused to lay down the really great vintages. This is his main and very great defect. Nothing can excuse it—certainly there is no justification whatsoever for his fear of putting wines costing more than 30 francs on the list destined for a clientèle largely composed of international millionaires.

One last word: As with all restaurants in the same category, you should telephone Raymond Oliver the day before you wish to come to lunch or dinner. For the rest—leave it to him. He knows better than anyone else how to compose a meal. If you're English, make your nationality known to him since he tends to take anyone without his own brand of Bordeaux accent for an American and he may decide he can't possibly reserve a table that day for anyone from the States. Admittedly, this bias is gradually disappearing but, you never know. . . . An uncertain rolling of your R's, or an over-nasal final consonant might be enough to revive it. . . .

LAPEROUSE, 51 Quai des Grands-Augustins, Paris 6. Tel: DAN 68-04. Every day except Sundays in the summer. Until 10 pm.

The extreme variety in the sizes of the many dining rooms and fourteen *salons* on the ground floor and two upper floors of this most discussed of Paris restaurants reflects the inequality of the cuisine. Alas, it must be admitted that this inequality is a constant and major characteristic of the cuisine directed by Monsieur Topolinski. But despite the vagaries of the cooking, the service remains impeccable.

The specialities of the house all belong to the category of the so-called 'brilliant cuisine': *crème de faisan* (in season), *turbot soufflé aux deux sauces, foies de volailles à la crème, rognons* and various *gratins: œufs, artichauts, langoustines, coquilles Saint-Jacques,* etc. Such rustic dishes as *bœuf bourguignon* also make their regular appearance on the reasonably priced menu which concludes with an impressive list of desserts.

Nowadays, the great prestige of Lapérouse is due largely to its charming décor and situation, as an ancient private mansion flanking the Seine. With its low ceilings, its little salons with their delicate lighting and Louis Seize fittings, wall paintings with cherubs or parrots, hunting scenes and occasional portraits and landscapes, Lapérouse is a perfect lovers' rendezvous. Each salon even has a sofa where after-dinner conversations can be continued and if the cooking is not likely to inspire great memories, at least memories of amorous encounters and intrigues have survived, as in the room where Raymond Poincaré once established his headquarters, with its mirrors bearing such diamond-incised inscriptions as 'Nana 1880' or 'To Dédé for life'. . . . Say what you like about the meal, but admit that Lapérouse *is* pretty.

LASSERRE, 17 avenue Franklin-Roosevelt, Paris 8. Tel: ELY 53-43 and 67-45. Closed on Sundays and in August. Until 11 pm.

Décor: extraordinarily luxurious and even somewhat heavy. Hinged roof on the first floor so that you can eat under the stars on a fine summer's evening. Hanging garden, Louis Quinze panelling, decorative ceramics, paintings, etc.

Service: couldn't be more perfect.

Cuisine: unvaryingly, supremely refined. The great specialities of the house include the *poularde Grand Palais*, the *gratin de ris de veau*, *poussin Viroflay*, the *bar à l'oseille* (remarkable), *pannequets* (pancakes) Grand Marnier and sumptuous oysters (as soon as you have finished each one it is whipped off your plate with a fork and a spoon by the waiter). Beautifully laid tables: flowers, silver tableware, crystal glasses.

Cellar: said to contain nearly three hundred thousand bottles collected since 1927 when the restaurant was founded by a genial native of the Béarn. He was as successful in *cuisine* as in business and gathered his faithful clientèle by founding a *club de la casserole*, with each member being given a key-ring with a little silver casserole containing an aspirin.

Many amateurs of great cuisine find such gimmickry—not to speak of the décor—rather irritating. But don't be put off. The *cuisine* is what matters most and is one of the greatest in Paris.

LAURENT, 41 avenue Gabriel, Paris 8. Tel: ELY 14-49. Closed on Sundays and in August. Until 11 pm.

When Laurent was founded in 1842, the spacious avenue Montaigne which it now overlooks was called *l'Allée des Veuves* ('Widows' walk') no doubt in honour of the continual presence of lonely ladies seeking for a kindred soul, who more often than not, might have begun the task of consoling them by dining them in one of the intimate private rooms on the first floor of the restaurant which earned the charming title of 'Chalet des Amoureux'.

Nowadays, the lovers have gone and been replaced by sober-visaged international economists and dedicated gastronomes but the waiters remain as discreet as ever. One rule still observed insists that 'the *maître d'hôtel* should knock before entering and not remain more than two or three seconds in front of a door behind which state secrets are being disclosed'. The bill is less mysterious: it is always very high indeed.

Specialities include: *foie de canard au muscat, gratin de homard au whisky, sole à l'estragon, poussin farci.* Several dishes are of Italian inspiration such as the excellent grilled scampi.

Cellar: interesting. We strongly advise you to listen to the highly informed and often imperious wine waiter. His advice is to be treasured.

LEDOYEN, Carré des Champs-Elysées, Paris 8. Tel: ANJ 47-82. Closed on Sundays. Until 10 pm.

Once one of the top restaurants in Paris, Ledoyen sadly declined after the last war. Now, under the direction of Gilbert Lejeune, this famous old restaurant in its lovely gardens just off the Champs-Elysées is rapidly recovering its former prestige. By the time you have read this it is more than probable that certain typical Ledoyen specialities such as its *poussin aux œufs d'or* and *sole souffleé* will be again esteemed for what they are: some of the most remarkable, unique gastronomic delights to be found in Paris today!

LUCAS CARTON, 9 Place de la Madeleine, Paris 8. Tel: ANJ 22-90. Open every day. Until 11 pm.

No restaurant would be better qualified to begin this brief survey of Paris' top eating places, if we had not decided on an alphabetical order.

Don't listen to anybody who denigrates this restaurant in the Place de la Madeleine. We firmly believe it to be the greatest in all Paris, which is to say, in the world. Cynics may sneer and say that the only thing that is great about it is its prices. They are wrong. Of course it *is* tremendously expensive and the price you pay at the end may destroy your memories of an incomparable meal—if you are a small-minded, 'occasional' gastronome. The fact is that everything—absolutely everything prepared by the present chef of the Lucas Carton, a pupil and the successor of the illustrious chef Soustelle' is admirably planned, prepared and served, from the simple dish of whiting known as *merlan en colère* to the less simple *gigot d'agneau* with its exquisite *pommes sarladaises* (truffled potatoes), to the most elaborate specialities including that peak of all French cuisine, the *lièvre à la royale*, and the *poularde étuvée au porto*, etc.

And then there is the wonderful and strangely little-known décor of the ground-floor dining room which was designed by the great

French artist Majorelle and made in sycamore and elm in his own studios at Nancy. This masterpiece of sculpted, *fin de siècle* panelling —at the time it cost 400,000 gold francs—is still one of the most accomplished examples of the best of French *art nouveau*. The private dining rooms are extraordinarily charming. One of them was used on November 10th by Marshals Foch, Haig, Joffre and General Pershing when they arranged the armistice for the following day.

The *carte* only gives a faint idea of the treasures to be found in the cellars. More than 120,000 bottles including some extraordinary vintages are kept in the disused corridors of the Madeleine *métro* station. The Grand-Echézeaux and the Romanée Conti are particularly superb.

Service: as quick and discreet as you could possibly wish for.

We can have nothing but praise for the atmosphere, the quality of the linen, couverts, table ware, lighting and carpets. They all contribute to the charm and dignity of the most incomparable of all Paris' great restaurants.

MAXIM'S, 3 rue Royale, Paris 8. Tel: ANJ 27-94. Closed on Sundays. Suppers served after midnight.

Was *Maxim's* all it was made out to be? No doubt it was. Plenty of enthusiastic and authoritative accounts show that what was once the uncontested headquarters of Paris pleasure in the palmy days before the First World War counted an admirable *cuisine* and cellar among its other attractions.

And today . . ? Under the management of Monsieur and Madame Vaudable the great restaurant of the rue Royale has two *cuisines*. One produces a run of indifferent dishes not worth even a line or two in this guide, the other sometimes produces miracles. They're called *selle de veau Orlov*, *potage Milly-by*, *homard New-Bourg*, *sole Albert* and *omelette du curé* and when one of them comes on your table it's a sign that Alex Humbert—one of the greatest living cooks —is busy in his kitchen. This happens quite frequently. All you have to do is to order your meal in advance and let the management compose your meal with him. If you want to see the chef make the most of his skill and experience and all the resources of his kitchen, then order a *chartreuse de perdreaux*.

Wines: only the greatest champagnes, and an important selection of Bordeaux and Burgundies, as well as almost every other wine from almost everywhere.

Décor: Famous and rightly so. Charmingly *art-nouveau* mahogany panelling and *fin de siècle* paintings.

Service: seventy years of perfection.

Yes. It is still worth going to *Maxim's*. . . .

PRUNIER, 9 rue Duphot, Paris 1. Tel: OPE 11-40. Closed on Mondays and from mid-June to September. Until 11 pm.

Surprisingly enough, this sister of the famous London establishment of the same name is undeservedly little-known in Paris these days. But though neglected by gastronomes who should know better, it is still one of the great sea-food restaurants of Paris and a place of glorious traditions.

It was born with the 20th century and the rather charming solemnity of the service is a survival of a time when the art of eating well was accompanied by certain rituals which were all so many expressions of 19th-century *savoir-vivre* at its most refined. But Prunier is far from being a relic from the mythical 'good old days' and the finest traditions are still faithfully perpetuated there in an astonishingly pure *art nouveau* background with a 1920 entrance that would have made a perfect setting, with its black marble and gold-sprinkled walls, for a Jean Harlow film.

As far as the *cuisine* goes, connoisseurs say that the high quality is much the same as that to be found in the London branch, but even so, no praise is too high for its 'house' oysters—the finest and freshest in all of Paris and its wonderful fresh caviar, specially treated every April by the master of the London and Paris Pruniers: the incomparable Jean Barnagaud.

TAILLEVENT, 15 rue Lamennais, Paris 8. Tel: BAL 05-08 and ELY 39-94. Closed on Sundays and in August. Until 10 pm.

One of the adjectives that has most frequently been applied to this excellent restaurant is that of 'classic'. But about ten years ago, the chef Lucien Leleu decided to render permanent homage to his great predecessors in the provinces, whether they were famous or, in his opinion, unjustly neglected, and day by day each region was honoured by its own *plat du jour*. If you had the means and the inclination, it was possible for you to go to Taillevent's to eat *à la Bourgogne* one day, a speciality of Provence the next, a Norman or a Breton dish the next and so on. But recently, André Vrinat, has tempered his son's audacities by reimposing on the *cuisine* the great, simple, 'classic' lines of *cordon bleu* cooking, illustrated at its most outstanding by such specialities as *ris de veau taillevent, escargots Talleyrand, truffes en pâte, gratin de langouste*, etc.

Décor: restrained. Taillevent is set in a former private mansion with an imposing staircase, and sober wood-panelling. The general lack of affectation and pomposity is in perfect keeping with the spirit that reigns in the kitchen. There are certainly other restaurants in Paris where the principles of French cooking are more spectacularly —if not showily—illustrated and some where these same principles are cheerfully and brilliantly turned topsy-turvy but none where the highest and most demanding traditions of French *haute cuisine* are more rigorously maintained. There is no better place for an initiation into the mysteries of French gastronomy at its most— again, only the word 'classic' will do. . . . The name of the restaurant itself is revealing of its attachment to traditions since *Taillevent* was the nick-name of Guillaume Tirel, author of the 'Viandier', the first known treatise on French cooking, written in the 14th century.

Cellar: famous for its great Yquem, Château Lafite and Romanée Conti. Other less expensive and memorable wines of outstanding quality for their price. We particularly recommend the Château Les Combes.

TOUR D'ARGENT, 15 Quai de la Tournelle, Paris 5. Tel: ODE 23-31. Closed on Mondays. Until 10 pm.

The 'hostellerie de la Tour d'Argent' was founded in 1582. It became an immediate success after Henry III of France had dined there with his *mignons*. The largely affected 'preciosity' of his guests inspired the owner Routreau to create forks for them. The first, made by a goldsmith, had only two brass prongs. Later, King Henry IV came often to dine, eating with his fingers. He enjoyed the heron *pâté* so much that he granted Routreau various privileges and a coat of arms. In the 17th century, the duke of Richelieu (the nephew of the famous cardinal) first offered his forty guests an extraordinary new beverage: coffee. As you see, the Tour d'Argent is rich in history. It even managed to keep going in 1870 during the Siege of Paris, although the raw materials used were a little unusual —to put it mildly. You may see a menu of that time if you wish.

The *cuisine*: very, very elaborate. Gastronomes tend to be divided over it. Some hold that the *filets de sole cardinal* (with shrimps), the *croustade de barbue Lagrené, filet Marco-Polo au poivre vert, noisettes de Tournelles* and other specialities of the chef Ducreux are all so many glories of contemporary *haute cuisine* while others regard the preparation of these dishes as being part of an outmoded culinary aesthetic of the 19th century. These serious questions are debated by the experts in the glassed-in sixth floor of the restaurant. In any case, nothing could be further removed from the so-called *cuisine rustique* or *bourgeoise* than the repertory of dishes that Claude Terrail dispenses to his international clientèle.

Most famous of all the dishes served in the Tour d'Argent is the *canard au sang* which is almost a symbol for the restaurant. Contrary to what some chroniclers have written (and still write), the *canard au sang* was not created here but at Rouen or in the immediate neighbourhood. Experts still quarrel over exactly where it was first created in its final form. In any case it seems to have been introduced into Paris by a Monsieur Lecoq—the great patron of the 'Tour' in the early days of Napoleon's Empire. However, we don't really think it is one of the greatest glories of French *cuisine*.

Be that as it may: the tradition of serving each duck with a numbered card only goes back to 1890 when the future Edward VII ate the 328th official victim. Fifty-eight years later, Princess Elizabeth and the Duke of Edinburgh were served nos. 185,397 and 185,398.

Part of the cellar has been made into a museum (a 'wine pantheon' complete with *son* and *lumière*). It's one of the most famous in the world. A short time ago, it contained about two hundred thousand bottles laid carefully down near the personal store of the La Rochefoucauld family.

Eating Cheaply

Now that you have eaten at the Grand Véfour or Taillevent, you'll probably have to eat cheaply for the rest of your stay. This doesn't necessarily mean eating badly.

Paris still has many little eating places that have kept their local 'sympathetic' flavour and where you can get good, if simple, French cooking into the bargain. Some you'll discover for yourself—others we're happy to suggest to you.

First, can you eat cheaply in Paris? Prices have been rising steadily and there is every sign that they will continue to do so. The great restaurants are some of the most expensive in the world and there is no lack of bad expensive. Many Parisians will sadly tell you that good cooking in Paris is a fast disappearing tradition (if indeed it ever was a tradition—the question is open to debate). But what about the little *bistrot*, 'just round the corner', where the *real* Parisian goes for his lunch or dinner, where the *cuisine* is done by the *patron* and his family, where the menu is small but lovingly composed *and* inexpensive? Is it a myth? Can one really eat well for as little as, say, 10 francs?

If cheapness, irrespective of quality, is what you are after then you might as well settle at once for the 'self-service' cafeterias that have been increasing in number in the last few years. It's sad, it's a *faute de mieux* solution, but at least you know exactly what you are going to spend. But, 'self-service' restaurants are the same the world over and the mere fact of being able to place a quarter litre bottle of indifferent *vin ordinaire* on your tray is unlikely to radiate French gastronomic lustre over your formica-topped table. A tiny portion of egg mayonnaise, a diminutive and rather resistant steak with a few rapidly cooling 'French-frieds', a piece of bread, a banana— was it for this you came to Paris?

Of course, if you don't care about food none of this matters and you might as well bring your own sandwiches and sit on a park bench in the Luxembourg or on the quays if the weather is fine. But if you want a hot meal that is not prefabricated and that pleasant feeling that you are eating in a manner both civilised and cheap, like a true Parisian 'who knows where to go', then you must be adventurous. You must search out the little restaurant of your choice where you will spend not more than ten or fifteen francs. But before you go on your quest, a few words of warning:

Paradoxically, if you are hypnotised by the sum of ten francs (roughly the average at present for a cheap meal of three courses) you may well do better to go to a little restaurant of the utmost simplicity where your meal will only cost you seven or eight francs all included. Ten francs, or just under, is a dangerous target when searching for a restaurant. You are a tourist of limited means, you look in your wallet and decide that one ten-franc note is all that you are going to spend on your meal. Under no circumstances are you going to break into a second note. It's your ideal price. Unfortunately many restaurant proprietors who rely on a passing trade (either tourist or provincial) know only too well the attractions of the menu at ten francs or under. They will hang out a sign like this:

MENU 10 FRANCS

Pain, service, couvert.
Tout compris.

or: MENU TOURISTIQUE

9·50 Francs
etc.

As an added inducement, you may be offered a quarter litre of wine or a glass of beer for the same price. The trap is sprung.

What you are most likely to get is something like this: a plate of undistinguished soup or a microscopic *hors-d'œuvre* (grated carrot or a pathetic herring fillet), a brown, evil-looking *bifteck* and a few potatoes, a little *crème caramel* or apple sauce/wedge of cheese/small and wrinkled apple, all served in quick succession with a small carafe of sour wine. You will finish this banquet feeling hungry, ill-tempered, disillusioned, and wondering whether it's worth finishing your wine and ordering coffee. An hour or two later, you will probably be chewing a ham sandwich and remembering the gloomy atmosphere of the restaurant with a shudder. Paris can be *so* depressing!

You will often see 'cheap' restaurants advertising their *Steak-frites* or ¼ *poulet-frites* at six or seven francs. Avoid them. All over Paris such 'steaks', chicken quarters and fried potatoes have the same dry metallic taste as though they had been mass-produced the week before and kept in cold storage. Paris is the capital of 'chips with everything' and the quality is usually deplorable. If you want a really good steak you must go to a reputable *grille* and pay at least twelve francs for the meat alone.

Beware of all restaurants which advertise in their windows anything other than the menu. If the place is good, then the menu is enough—and the number of people eating there is also a good recommendation. Anywhere that is half empty before two o'clock in the afternoon is usually bad.

For some mysterious reason, restaurants where the menus are handwritten are better than those where they are typed.

Try not to go in a café or *brasserie* where they advertise set meals, especially on main thoroughfares, unless they are very tiny. The best *brasseries* (like the *Flo* or the *Bofinger*) don't need to offer set-price meals. And do keep away from places where the word *frites* is given any special prominence: they are probably the only filling thing you will get apart from bread. And never, never go into an empty restaurant. There is no more horrible experience than to be served a cheap and nasty meal in a deserted restaurant where the waiter is obviously trying to be rid of you.

Food is very expensive in Paris and you simply can't expect to eat anything palatable or copious except in a restaurant with small overheads and a faithful local clientèle. The smaller the place, the simpler the décor, the better. Go to the ones where everything is *à la carte: poulet chasseur, three francs; rable de lapin, four francs; cassoulet toulousain, 3.75 francs*, etc. If there is a small zinc bar inside that's even better. The meal will be cheap but not *too* cheap. The cooking may be simple but at least it *is* cooking and will be done with care and affection. The *hors-d'œuvre* will be small, but the main course generous and piping hot. You will hardly ever be cheated when the bill is added up. No need to tip unless your lack of French has made the process of ordering unduly long and complicated, for ten or twelve per cent will be added to your bill for service. As prices are at present, your meal will cost you just under ten francs.

Some Parisian restaurants put the accent on generosity rather than *fine cuisine* and you may be surprised to find that many Parisians attach quite as much importance (if not even more) to the former rather than the latter. If you simply want to stuff yourself then we recommend a restaurant like the tiny *Chez Marcel* in the rue Saint-Lazare (a few yards on the left going down the road from the back of Notre-Dame de Lorette station.) A menu at eleven francs offers a choice of twenty-one *hors-d'œuvre* followed by steak

or chicken with mountains of 'French fried' and a half carafe of
vin ordinaire. On the left bank, *La Boucherie* in the rue des Ciseaux
(opposite Saint-Germain-des-Prés) is open until two in the morning
and offers substantial *pâté* or a mixed salad followed by steak for
the same price, with as much wine as you care to drink. Here again
quantity is King. You will find others like it throughout Paris, all
full of people who don't seem to have eaten for a week.

If you want to eat at rock bottom prices, then seek out (if you
have the patience to do so) a little worker's *bistrot* (always in a
narrow side street), or go to the counter of the *Pied du Cochon*
(excellent *plat du jour* at 3.50 francs, very good *vin ordinaire* at
ninety *centimes* a large glass and divine Camembert; open day and
night). You have to stand at the counter to eat. If you are studious,
go to the 1900 style *Colbert* in the rue Vivienne, just behind the
Bibliothèque Nationale (menu at 4.50 francs; lots of intellectual
atmosphere). All these places have atmosphere into the bargain.

If you are a student, artist or poet on the Left Bank, go to *Chez
Wajda* in the rue de la Grande Chaumière (next to the famous
studios of the same name) where you will eat simply but well for
about seven francs or at *Rosalie's* on the other side of the boulevard
Montparnasse in the rue Campagne Première (full of memories
of the thirties).

But above all, if you want *ambiance*—that almost indefinable
French word that means more than 'atmosphere' and not quite
'environment'—as well as a cheap meal, you could do no better
than to keep to the heart of Left Bank Paris, either around St-
Germain, on the Seine side of the boulevard, or the Latin Quarter
proper. This is where young Paris comes to eat, and cheap as the
restaurants often are, they *do* make an effort and are designed to
feed the young and hungry. Here, you need not be afraid of décor
or set-price menus. Often, the restaurant has been designed by
some needy student from the Beaux-Arts for fun as well as money.
The little restaurants in and around the rue de la Huchette and rue
Saint-Séverin, or the delightful Place de la Contrescarpe, rely on a
young clientèle and they are always jolly and noisy. Food is honest,
even if there is a tendency to rely too heavily on *steack* and *frites*,
and they are nearly always crowded. The pseudo-cheap restaurants
here haven't a hope of surviving. The atmosphere of youth is
friendly and refreshing and you will often find yourself striking up
a friendly conversation with the people at your table or next to
you. Yes, eating cheaply can be fun in Paris. . . . And even if you

do have to break into your second ten franc note, you won't have any regrets afterwards. If you absolutely must spend less, then you will just have to make do with that sandwich (which is half a French loaf) and glass of *vin ordinaire*. After all, that, too, is Paris.

Guide to cheap but honest restaurants :

Workers *bistrots*: they aren't in the least bit interested in being advertised. Anyway, half the fun is finding them.

ROCK BOTTOM PRICES

Le Colbert, rue Vivienne, Paris 2. Menu 4.50 francs.

Le Pied de Cochon, 6 rue Coquillière, Paris 1.
At the counter only. *Plat du jour*, 3.50 francs. Open day and night.

Chez Wajda, 11 rue de la Grande Chaumière, Paris 6.
About 8 francs. Not after 9 pm. Shut on Mondays.

Rosalie, 5 rue Campagne Première, Paris 14. About 10 francs.
Until 10 pm. Shut Sundays.

La Chinoise, rue Mouffetard, Paris 5.
Chinese *and* French cooking! Very jolly and picturesque. A few outside tables. Until 12 pm. About 10 francs.

Madeleine, rue de la Sourdière, Paris 1.
Adorable. Family-run. Classic French, simple cooking. Very local atmosphere. Closed Mondays. Until 9 pm. only. About 9-10 francs.

Self-service Cluny, 98 boulevard Saint-Germain, Paris 5.
Yes, a 'self-service'. This one is not bad at all. Open till 12 pm. Anything between 5 and 10 francs.

ABOUT 10-15 FRANCS

Brasserie Flo, Cour des Petites Ecuries, Paris 10.
Very 19th-century atmosphere. Copious Alsatian *choucroutes*. Until 10 pm. Closed Sundays.

Chez Pierre, 9 rue Saint-Lazare, Paris 9.
Closed Mondays. 11-franc menu with enormous variety of *hors-d'œuvres*. Tiny but jolly. Go there if starving.

La Petite Chaise, 35 rue de Grenelle, Paris 6.
Open every day. One of the oldest restaurants in Paris. Until 10 pm. Honest but unexciting 11-franc menu. Eat *à la carte* if possible.

Le Fénelon, rue Hautefeuille, Paris 6.
Real French *bistrot* atmosphere and food. Full of teachers from the Lycée Fénelon. Closed Sundays.

Le Tison d'Or, 34 rue Duret, Paris 16.
A new restaurant just off the avenue Foch. A good place to go if stranded in millionaire's Paris. Excellent *hors-d'œuvre*, meat and fish. 9 francs. Dessert and wine extra.

Vagenende, 142 boulevard Saint-Germain, Paris 6.
A riot of French *art nouveau* décor. Very pretty indeed, but food wildly varying in quality. Best if you go in a party. Until 2 am.

Julien et Petit, 48 rue de l'Université, Paris 7.
Delightful Basque-Breton *bistrot*. Very genteel atmosphere. Until 10.30 pm. Closed Mondays.

Orientale, 10 rue Grégoire de Tours, Paris 6.
Franco-Greek cuisine. Very crowded, very amiable service. Closed Thursdays. Until 10 pm.

Au Vieux Casque, rue Cardinale, Paris 6.
Specialises in *kebabs*. Closed Sundays. Open until 11 pm.

Aux Beaux-Arts (chez Poussinot), rue des Beaux-Arts, Paris 6.
Closed Sundays. Until 11.30 pm. Excellent *bourgeoise* cooking, especially *ragoûts* and beef. Snails are cheap and good (7 francs the dozen).

Etchegorry, 41 rue Croulebarbe, Paris 13.
Hard to find, but it's worth it. Basque cooking and very copious. Closed on Tuesdays. Until 11 pm.

La Vieille Trousse, boulevard Saint-Germain, Paris 6.
Turkish and French cooking. Drink *raki* there. Between 8 and 11 francs.

The Bistrots of Paris

The real bistrot is the working man's café. It's small, cosy and old-fashioned. You go in to drink at the bar with the patron *and your neighbourhood friends. They're not for tourists, but that needn't stop you going in one. If you speak French you'll find they're much better than the cafés for feeling the life of a district: the popular everyday life of working Paris.*

Some bistrots (and cafés also), specialise in wines. They're for connoisseurs. Often the owner knows the vineyard proprietors personally. Some of the best wine bistrots have prizes awarded to them once a year. Here, drinking wine is a serious matter. . . .

The name is derived from the Russian 'bistro' meaning 'quickly' which was introduced into Paris at the time of the Napoleonic Wars by hungry soldiers. The expression became a name, and the name stuck—to a special, very French type of eating place. The typical Paris *bistrot*: a few tables and chairs, a zinc-topped bar, a *patron* behind the counter, the hiss of an old-fashioned coffee machine, the same advertisements on the walls (MIDI, SEPT HEURES—L'HEURE DU BERGER), the same Martini or Ricard trademarks on the water carafes and ash-trays, the same smoke-stained poster on the wall with the full text of the law relating to 'public drunkenness' . . .

The atmosphere, of course . . . the little prostitute endlessly making up and mysteriously disappearing between two drinks of *crème de menthe*, a gaunt old man ruminating on his sandwich, a couple sitting on the *banquette* in the back, holding hands and pondering on the eternal mystery of their love, a man counting his coins for lack of anything else to do, a few card-players using matchsticks for tokens, three local business tycoons doing their accounts around a celebratory bottle of champagne, an ordinary passer-by who wanders in and out, unnoticed by the dice-players at the bar, a glass of *blanc sec* . . . the haze of Gauloise smoke. The world in a nutshell—the world of the *bistrot*. . . .

Paris has 40,000 *bistrots* and cafés of various sizes, shapes, colours and categories. In some you can buy tobacco, stamps and lottery tickets (the *café-tabac*), in most you can telephone and in all you can go to the lavatory. Sometimes you can bring your own food to the *bistrot*, you can play cards, you can read and write, or you can just sit and think. No one is likely to bother you. You have a sitting room, a study or a club for the price of a coffee.

The real Paris *bistrot* is more than a café. It is essentially a local, popular institution dependent on a faithful clientèle. The most typical *bistrot* of all is the working-class *bistrot*—the proletarian equivalent of the *Deux Magots* or *Café de la Paix*. If you want to see the authentic Paris *bistrot* you must go to a working-class district—the north-east of Paris perhaps. Take the Métro to the *Jaurès* station, for instance, and walk along the Canal Saint-Martin, along the Quai de la Loire. You are back in the world of Marcel Carné, Jacques Prévert and all those old films of the thirties, the Paris of Inspector Maigret and Jean Gabin. There, each *bistrot* has become half-camouflaged by the grime of years and the smoke of countless passing tugs and barges. This is the area of the Paris coal-depots and every *bistrot* is packed with men in clothes as coal-black as their faces, drinking beer out of pint glass mugs, the froth on their lips making them look like giant golliwogs. In many little *bistrots* throughout Paris you will see the sign VINS ET CHARBONS. These are the *bougnats*—hundred per cent working class—where the counter is *le zinc* and housewives come to buy firewood and paper sacks of coal—a strange but hallowed juxtaposition.

Bistrots are rarely called *bistrots*. Their names are as time-honoured and as unoriginal as their interiors: *Café du Port*, *Café de La Marine*, *Au Rendez-vous des Pêcheurs*, *Au Soleil du Levant*. Some names proclaim their speciality such as the *Galoche d'Aurillac* off the Place de la Bastille where you can still buy wooden clogs (*galoches*) as well as cooked meats, sausages and country hams. In the district of Les Halles, such names as *Aux Mandataires*, *Aux Mareyeurs* proclaim the occupations of the regular clientèle. In the rue Croissant, near the great newspaper offices, the *Roule-Toujours* is the *bistrot* of the newspaper porters, and near the Hôtel de Ville, *Le Bâtiment* is always packed with stonemasons.

Don't be afraid of going into even the humblest Paris *bistrot*. You will be neither welcomed nor rejected and a glass of wine is still only 30 centimes. The *bistrot* is open to all but it reserves its favours for the happy few to whom it has become a private club. You will remain an outsider but if you didn't, the *bistrot* would have lost its meaning.

Each Parisian has his own *bistrot* which has become part of his everyday familiar landscape, part of the daily round of life. Even if it isn't in his own quarter, it is always the one 'at the end of the street', or 'two steps' from his place of work, or the one by his bus terminus. A Parisian may well have two *bistrots*—one near his home and the other near his work which he has found after long exploration and a judicious process of selection. The *bistrot* of his choice becomes *his bistrot* and becomes an extension, both in the concrete and in the abstract, of his public and private life.

Every regular customer there lives part of the life of his neighbour before the knowing eyes of the *patron* who knows everybody and everything. Every pretext—the 14th of July, a birth or a death—is good enough for a ritual *tournée* when round succeeds round of drinks. Certain words and expressions become obligatory for the members of the club. Almost every *bistrot* has its own myths, folk-lore and language and every now and again a new word will be invented almost casually at the bar, giving fresh spice to monotonous existence. In certain East End *bistrots* some years ago, a glass of red wine was known as a 'Stalin', a *rosé* as a 'Socialist', a glass of mineral water as a *chômeur* ('unemployed person'), and a glass of milk as a *Mendès* (after Mendès-France, notorious for his propaganda in favour of milk rather than wine-drinking). The terms have dated, and illustrate an epoch, but they are still used by the old habitués. The *bistrot* is essentially conservative.

Nowadays, with change, much is lost of that which gave the *bistrot* its independence from all other cafés, its *raison d'être*, its special atmosphere and its originality. With the coming of plastic and formica, many *bistrots* have become anonymous and purely functional. Neon lights, a medley of bright but garish colours, glass and mirrors, new tables and chairs, square and squat, designed with almost surgical precision, and white coated waiters have all robbed the old *bistrots* of their soul and turned them into vulgar *cafés*. There has been a mania for 'renovation' and an invasion of a new clientèle for whom the *bistrot* is a Coca Cola and a pinball machine.

Even so, you can still find the old-style *bistrot* or *zinc*. You will recognise them at once, from their wood or zinc-topped bar, their marble-topped tables, their sparse decorations and their colours—as faded as a workman's blue dungarees. Revealingly, few of their clients are young people. But they offer a haven of peace and fellowship, of community-feeling and recollection of times past, far away from the machine-gun stutter of tills and one-armed bandits. The wine they offer does not necessarily come out of the giant tanks and warehouses of Bercy-sur-Seine or Charenton, but you can still taste the grape. They are part of the old Paris of a thousand villages and have kept their rustic, provincial air. The *bistrot* is essentially *rustic*, and why not? Wine doesn't grow in Paris and in the *bistrot* wine is king.

Statue of Bacchus in the Luxembourg Gardens

Drinking Wine in Paris

Paris is by no means the ideal place to drink French wines, any more than London is the Mecca of the beer drinker. All too often you will be given the same rather acid Muscadet, the same insipid Côtes du Rhône, a below average Beaujolais or Alsace wine, and the same metallic red or white *ordinaire*. There are, of course, some honourable and even outstanding exceptions—cafés where you may be sure that what you drink will be genuine and where you may enjoy some of France's greatest wines, specially chosen by the owner who is a connoisseur catering for connoisseurs. We offer you gladly a short selection of *bistrots* specialising in fine wines, but first a few words of advice:

Wine is served in two different sized glasses: the *verre* and the *ballon*. The *ballon* holds about half as much again as the *verre* but will cost twice as much.

Don't be surprised if you pay as much as 2.50 francs for a *ballon* of fine wine: it *is* expensive but it *is* a fine wine.

If you simply want an ordinary glass of ordinary red or white wine, ask for a *rouge* or *blanc ordinaire*.

If the patron suggests you eat something (a piece of bread and cheese, a slice of *saucisson*) with one of the better wines, take his advice. The wine will taste even better.

Never switch from red to white or vice versa: the *patron* will lose all interest in you as a wine customer.

Drink at the counter: you won't learn anything from the *patron* or waiter if you sit down at a table. Besides, it'll cost you more.

And now, the places to go:

RIGHT BANK

L'ami Pierre, 7 rue des Déchargeurs, Paris 1, closed Sundays.
Typical Les Halles *bistrot*. A favourite with porters before the market was moved to Rungis. Excellent Beaujolais wines of the last vintage.

Bar des Bof, 7 rue des Innocents, Paris 1, closed Sundays.
Another former Les Halles bar. Closes at 7 pm. Again, specialises in genuine Beaujolais wines.

Au Beaujolais, 4 rue des Petits-Champs, Paris 1.
Excellent selection of Loire and Alsace wines. The Sancerre is

outstanding. Magnificent cheese and ham sandwiches.

Au Sancerre, rue des Petits-Pères, Paris 2.
Near the Banque de France. As the name implies, a place to drink Sancerre. Also fine Alsace wines and Beaujolais, Morgon, etc.

Grand Comptoir, 4 rue Pierre-Lescot, Paris 1.
Restaurant with *zinc* bar where you can drink excellent Beaujolais.

Ma Bourgogne, 19 Place des Vosges, Paris 4.
A *café tabac* in the loveliest old square in Paris. Excellent Loire, Alsace and Beaujolais wines. Ham sandwiches made with country bread.

Le Pied du Cochon, 3 rue Coquillière, Paris 1.
Restaurant with *zinc* counter. The speciality here are the large glasses of excellent (and very strong) red and white wine of the establishment: the *Réserve*. Probably the best *vin ordinaire* in Paris.

Pétrissans, 30 bis avenue Niel, Paris 17.
One of the great wine-shops of Paris, with a counter for tasting—happily!

Simon, rue Lepic, Paris 18.
Wine shop with bar on way up the winding rue Lepic towards the Butte Montmartre. Wonderful selection of just about every French wine.

Tabac Henri IV, 13 Place du Pont-Neuf, Paris 1.
On the Ile de la Cité facing the equestrian statue of Henry IV. A tastefully modernised *café tabac*. Wonderful Loire wines, good Rosé and Beaujolais wines. Try the ham and brown country bread—they make a wonderful light lunch with a couple of glasses of Morgon.

La Tartine, 46 rue de Rivoli, Paris 4.
Now one of the best wine *bistrots* in Paris but, curiously enough, has a mostly local clientèle. Especially fine burgundies and Beaujolais. Ask for a *tartine* with Beaujolais cheese.

LEFT BANK

Chaudet, 20 rue Geoffroy-Saint-Hilaire, Paris 5.
Undoubtedly, one of the very best wine shops anywhere. Every great French wine is on sale there and there is an enormous number of rare and little known wines (from the Savoy, the Pyrenees and Provence for instance). When drinking wines at the bar, ask Monsieur or Madame Chaudet for their advice—and take it ('first

you will drink a Saint-Emilion—and then, after a Juliénas, our Mercurey . . .'). Closed on Sundays and shuts at 9 pm which, perhaps, is just as well or you'd spend all evening there getting mellower and mellower. Buy a bottle to take away afterwards. You can get a first rate 'little' wine for 2 or 3 francs.

Fraysse, 21 rue de Seine, Paris 6.
Closed on Sundays. Famous for its Pouilly-Fuisse and Quincy.

Pacquez, 8 rue de l'Industrie, Paris 13.
Closed on Sundays, open till 9 pm only. A wineshop and *bistrot*. Go there for Beaujolais and burgundies.

Le Sauvignon, 80 rue des Saints-Pères, Paris 6.
A nice small *bistrot* with wines from the Loire and the Beaujolais regions.

Le Sancerre, 22 avenue Rapp, Paris 7.
Some of the best Sancerre and ham in Paris.

Finally, if you see a sign in the window of any little Paris *bistrot* proclaiming: ENFIN, LE BEAUJOLAIS NOUVEAU EST ARRIVÉ! you know what to do. This happy event takes place in the winter around New Year.

Foreign Restaurants

*You may not wish to eat French food. You may not even like it. Cous-
cous, Chinese and Vietnamese cooking are not for you. Never mind, you
can still survive in Paris on Greek, Italian, Persian or Russian food.
Here's a baker's dozen of good foreign restaurants to choose from, listed
by nationality.*

African: LE BAOBAB, 7 rue de l'Université, Paris 7. Lit. 08-80.

American: LA TRINQUETTE, 1 rue Gustave-Courbet, Paris 16. 704
59-53.

Belgian: BEULEMANS DE PARIS, 204 boulevard Saint-Germain,
Paris 7. LIT 73-30.

Greek: LA TAVERNA, 44 rue Sainte-Anne, Paris 2. 742 53-60.

Hungarian: LE TOKAY, 43 rue Montpensier, Paris 1. RIC 32-32.

Indian: TAJ MAHAL, 56 bis rue de la Fédération, Paris 15. FON 85-90.

Italian: GILDO, 153 rue de Grenelle, Paris 7. INV 54-12.

Japanese: LE TOKIO, 22 rue Delambre, Paris 14. DAN 45-00.

Mexican: MEXICO LINDO, 19 rue des Canettes, Paris 6. DAN 43-55.

Persian: LA ROSE D'ISPAHAN, 87 rue de Miromesnil, Paris 8 *and*
44 rue de Naples, Paris 8. 522 67-51.

Russian: DOMINIQUE, 19 rue Bréa, Paris 6. DAN 63-92.

Spanish: LA VENTA, 33 rue Guénégaud, Paris 6. DAN 69-83.

West Indian (French): LE REQUIN CHAGRIN, Place de la Contrescarpe,
Paris 5. ODE 18-87.

One of the more interesting side-effects of the break up of an
empire can be observed in the *cuisine* of the former mother-country.
For all sorts of reasons, economic and otherwise, many of the best
cooks in the colonies follow their late overlords home and establish
restaurants that cater to the gastronomic nostalgia of retired
expatriates or to the exotic tastes of a younger generation. London's
Oriental restaurants have thus, in recent years, attracted some of
the best Indian, Pakistani or Goanese cooks from the Indian sub-
continent and East Africa; Holland has attracted many of the best
cooks from Indonesia. French *cuisine*, famous for two centuries for

its passionate resistance to any foreign influence, may likewise, within the next few decades, become thoroughly transformed by the invasion of foreign cooks who have now endowed Paris with some of the world's best Russian, Greek, Armenian, Turkish, Vietnamese and Arab restaurants.

The highest concentration of Arab restaurants is to be found in the narrow streets between the boulevard Saint-Germain and the Left Bank embankments of the Seine, especially between the rue Dauphine and the Place Maubert. At 24 rue Maître-Albert, *Le Djurdjura* offers an excellent *couscous* at a very moderate price. In the rue Saint-Séverin, the rue de la Huchette and the rue de La Harpe, a good dozen Arab restaurants compete with Vietnamese, Greek and Italian rivals. At 21 rue de la Huchette, the *Dar-el-Beida* can almost be said to be a luxury restaurant; at 27 rue de la Huchette, the *El-Djezair* even offers an Oriental-style floorshow. At number 22 on the same street, the *Pâtisserie Tunisienne* is very popular for its Arab pastries; at number 20, the *Pâtisserie de Delphes* offers excellent Greek pastries and Turkish-style coffee.

At 9 rue Saint-Séverin, *Le Vieux Paris*, a modest-priced but good Arab restaurant, competes with *La Grèce*, a Greek restaurant in the next building, as well as with a surprising number of rivals in the near-by rue Xavier Privas, where *Le Latin*, at number 22, offers Arab specialties; *Le Mitsuko*, at number 17, represents Japanese gastronomy, *La Belle Etoile*, at number 15, *Chez Saighi*, at number 16, and *Le Privas*, at number 9, advertise Arab menus, whereas the *India Restaurant*, at number 11, offers Indian food and the *Long-Van*, at number 20, and the *Long-Phuong*, at number 12, both cater to lovers of Indo-Chinese food.

In the rue de la Harpe, *Les Balkans*, at number 3, and the *Restaurant Franco-Hellénique*, at number 5, both specialise in Greek or Turkish food. At number 13, *Les Brochettes* is slightly more luxurious and caters to customers who might not be content with the more modest Latin Quarter atmosphere of most of the other Oriental restaurants in this neighbourhood. At 13 rue Serpente, on the other side of the boulevard Saint-Michel, the *Restaurant d'Athènes* has long been haunted by lovers of *döner Kebab* and other such Greek or Turkish delights.

At 4 rue Grégoire de Tours, *L'Orestias* has for many years been the most popular Greek restaurant among the less wealthy intellectuals of Saint-Germain-des-Prés. *Chez Zorba*, in the same street, is a tiny and modest-priced Greek snack-bar. At 6 rue Grégoire de

Tours, *La Baie d'Along* has an established reputation among lovers of Indo-Chinese food. While at number 10, *Le Typique* is Spanish-Algerian, offering most of the Arab and Spanish specialties of Oran.

The orthodox Jewish gourmet who is not afflicted with a *Yiddishist* nostalgia for *gefillter Fisch* or *Kreplach à la Sholem Aleichem* can have a field-day in Paris, where some of the best Sefardic-Jewish cooks from Algeria and Tunisia now compete for the privilege of titillating his palate. Oriental-style Jewish restaurants are concentrated mainly in three areas of Paris: around the rue du Faubourg Montmartre and its side-streets, in the old Jewish quarter between the Right Bank embankment of the Seine and the Saint-Paul mètro-station, and in the Tunisian-Jewish quarter in Belleville. Many of these restaurants are very small; the best policy is to browse around and to allow one's sense of smell to dictate the final choice. *Cachere* (Kosher) *Merghez* sausages, highly-spiced, are one of their specialities, as well as *boukha*, a strong liqueur made of figs.

A great number of modest but very pleasant Arab restaurants are scattered throughout other neighbourhoods of Paris, especially on the Left Bank in the 15th arrondissement. Generally speaking, one can safely patronise any restaurant that is run by a Berber from Kabylia. Actually, most of the best Arab restaurants in Paris are owned and run by Kabyle Berbers, by Moroccans or by North-African Jews who hail from Algeria or Tunisia. Moroccan restaurants are often more luxurious: their menu may thus include such delicacies as *pastilla*, a pigeon-pie that is a specialty of Fez, *mechoui* roast lamb or *tagine* (meat or chicken stewed with vegetables). Algerian and Tunisian restaurants tend to limit themselves to *couscous*, *tchouktchouka* and simpler Arab fare. At 112 boulevard de Grenelle, *Le Djurdjivia* and, at 164 boulevard de Grenelle, *Le Tahar* both deserve to be listed as better-known Arab-style restaurants of the 15th arrondissement.

Some of the more expensive Moroccan restaurants in the Champs-Elysées neighbourhood cater to gourmets who also require an elaborate Oriental setting and a floor-show of belly-dancers and Arab music.

The *Restaurant Téhéran*, 12 rue Brey, is famous for its Iranian food. Its menu includes a number of Armenian specialities as well as Iranian caviar.

Cafés and Bars

There's nothing like a French café. Paris has thousands of them. Unfortunately a lot have been modernised with disastrous results. Others are noisy and garish. But they're still the meeting place par excellence. In most of them you can drink until late at night if you want to; or you can sit for hours over a cup of coffee and watch all of life go by. No one will disturb you: it's one of the advantages of the French café. You can even write a book in one: it's often been done. You can telephone in nearly all of them, buy cigarettes if they're a café-tabac, and bet on horses if they have the sign up of P.M.U.

Here is a list of some of the most typical Paris cafés.

Right Bank

ALEXANDRE, 53 avenue George-v, Paris 8.

Big, expensive café typical of the Champs-Elysées district. A good place for observing the well-heeled fauna of the 8th arrondissement in their natural surroundings—particularly near the bar.

LA BELLE FERRONNIERE, 53 rue Pierre-Charron, Paris 8.

Smart in a flashy sort of way and a favourite with *Paris-Match* reporters, photographers and aspiring models as well as estate agents and businessmen. Much more a 'local' during the day than any of the Champs-Elysées cafés.

CAFE DE LA PAIX, 12 boulevard des Capucines, Paris 9.

To most tourists—particularly Americans—the Café de la Paix is one of the 'musts' of Paris, like the Louvre or the Eiffel Tower. It's almost as big and very luxurious. There is a good if expensive snack-bar, a sumptuously appointed restaurant and a wide, almost always crowded *terrasse*. Some of the older generations of boulevardiers still haunt it and can be seen admiring the pretty Scandinavians and Anglo-Saxons who never fail to turn up there. In 1944, during the Liberation, it was De Gaulle's first stop in Paris.

CAFE DU TROCADERO, 8 Place du Trocadéro, Paris 16.

A favourite with the gilded youth of the district. Expensive, neon-lit, and devoid of any really definable character—like too many other cafés in this part of Paris.

CHEZ FRANCIS, 7 Place de l'Alma, Paris 8.

Not as fashionable as it once was but a typically sumptuous right-bank café with a good and expensive restaurant and a well-situated *terrasse*. A good place to recover after visting the two near-by museums of modern art.

FOUQUET'S, 99 avenue des Champs-Elysées, Paris 8.

One of the 'greats' of the Right Bank cafés and certainly by far the most fashionable of those on the Champs-Elysées. Huge *terrasse*, cosy bar, good and not-too-expensive restaurant with one of the longest and most astonishing wine-lists in the city. Fouquet's is particularly famous for having long been a favourite rendez-vous for show-business people (particularly in the cinema) and the girls there tend to be prettier than in any of the neighbouring cafés.

LE MARIGNAN, 33 avenue des Champs-Elysées, Paris 8.

Another huge Champs-Elysées café—brash, brassy and expensive but still a magnet for those tourists who fondly imagine that sipping an overpriced coffee on this unattractive boulevard is really living it up in Paris.

NAPOLITAIN, 1 boulevard des Capucines, Paris 9.

A survivor from the 'Belle Epoque', that golden age of Paris during the 1890's and pre-1914 era. All that now remains of its former glory is its name. Once a favourite meeting place for writers and journalists, it is now just another tourist-haunted café from which to watch endless traffic jams.

ROND-POINT DES CHAMPS-ELYSEES, 1 avenue Matignon, Paris 8.

A large and once fashionable café-restaurant with one of the most pleasant *terrasses* in the neighbourhood, which makes up for a lot.

Left Bank

LE BONAPARTE, 42 rue Bonaparte, Paris 6.

An interesting example of how one of the old, glorious Left Bank haunts (memories of Sartre, Greco, etc.) can be modernised almost out of existence. Mostly patronised by students and deserted by the older generation of intellectuals who once congregated there.

63

CLUNY, 20 boulevard Saint-Michel, Paris 6.

Alas, yet another old-established Left Bank café to have undergone 'modernisation' or 'redecoration', losing a great deal of its sober, solid old-fashioned charm in the process! Still, the result could have been far worse and the glasses of dry Muscadet are probably the biggest and cheapest you can get at any café of comparable size.

LA COUPOLE, 102, boulevard du Montparnasse, Paris 14.

The 'Coupole' is still one of the main attractions of modern Montparnasse and a surviving monument of the swinging 1920's and 30's. It is also the most amusing and lively of all the Left Bank café-restaurants and a Mecca for practically every artist and tourist in the district. Occasional rumours have it that the 'Coupole' is going to be pulled down, transformed, turned into a 'Drugstore', 'bowling alley', etc., but so far it has survived, paintings, décor, atmosphere and all. . . .

DEUX MAGOTS, 170 boulevard Saint-Germain, Paris 6.

For about half a century the 'Deux Magots' was one of the great rendez-vous of intellectuals and writers in Paris and one of the temples of 'existentialist' thought in the heady post-war years when Sartre and Simone de Beauvoir held court there. The décor hasn't changed much since then, but in general the clientèle has, although the bill proudly states that the place is still the 'rendez-vous of the intellectual élite'.

LE DOME, 108 boulevard du Montparnasse, Paris 14.

The 'Dôme' is another famous relic of the glorious early years of the century when Modigliani, Picasso and others met there. It has a certain scruffy charm and the clientèle who gather round the horseshoe-shaped counter late at night are what an old-fashioned guide book would call 'mixed'. They have a tendency to speak Spanish with a Latin-American accent.

FLORE, 172 boulevard Saint-Germain, Paris 6.

Only a few steps away from the 'Deux Magots' and rather more authentically Parisian in a camp sort of way. Usual Saint-Germain associations: Sartre, Beauvoir and Camus, etc., all drank there. Still popular with writers, critics and publishers and the more Bohemian of the smart set. But upstairs, it is almost entirely homosexual in ambience.

LIPP, 151 boulevard Saint-Germain, Paris 6.

The most fashionable café-brasserie on the boulevard. 'Lipp' was famous for being the haunt of 4th Republic politicians. Since De Gaulle came to power it has become somewhat less political and a little more worldly. It's much smarter to sit inside than outside on the small *terrasse*. The beer and white wines are excellent and not too expensive and the *choucroute* is abundant.

LE QUARTIER LATIN, 6 place Edmond-Rostand, Paris 6.

One of the quieter, more comfortable of the Latin Quarter cafés and a splendid place for observing the *Boul' Mich'* student crowd.

LA RHUMERIE MARTINIQUAISE, 166 boulevard Saint-Germain, Paris 6.

Crowded, lively and the best place to drink rum-punches in Paris.

LA ROTONDE, 105 boulevard du Montparnasse, Paris 6.

Only the name remains of the original Montparnasse café where Modigliani, Picasso and other celebrities used to carouse in the mythical early 1900's when they weren't at the Dôme or elsewhere. The coffee tends to be better than across the road, and that's about all we can find to say about the place.

LE SELECT, 99 boulevard du Montparnasse, Paris 6.

Much nicer than the 'Rotonde' with its pleasantly ageing décor and sober interior. It has its habitués who refuse to go anywhere else in Montparnasse except for the Coupole every now and again. Popular with elderly Spanish exiles and determinedly intellectual young *Montparnos*.

And some Bars . . .

Right Bank

BAR BELGE, 75 avenue de Saint-Ouen, Paris 17.

For beer-lovers. Some of the finest Belgian beer in the world is served with love and devotion by Julien Forêt, the Belgian-expatriate owner. Try his cold meats from the Ardennes and his Dutch cheeses.

BAR ROMAIN, 6 rue Caumartin, Paris 9.

One of Paris's oldest bars, dating from 1905, with thirteen

Brasserie Lipp, boulevard Saint-Germain

academic paintings of Roman scenes, left by some forgotten artist, supplying most of the décor. A favourite with surviving boulevardiers, showbiz people from the Olympia, and key-ring collectors (the patron is 'President of the Club of Key-ring collectors' and has a magnificent collection of his own on display).

LA CALVADOS, 40 avenue Pierre-Ier-de-Serbie, Paris 8.
Fashionable bar-restaurant for playboys, rich socialites and high-powered businessmen. Food, music and some of the prettiest women in Paris.

CINTRA, 6 Square de l'Opéra, Paris 9.
Famous, old-fashioned and eminently respectable bar. Quiet, comfortable atmosphere. Good port and some sherries.

CLUB DU CHAMPAGNE, 5 Chaussée d'Antin, Paris 9.
The bar for champagne. They have an astonishing selection.

CRILLON BAR, Hôtel Crillon, 10 place de la Concorde, Paris 8.
American-type bar, mostly tenanted by Americans and Sam White of the London Evening Standard. Quiet, rather conspiratorial.

FORUM, 4 boulevard Malesherbes, Paris 9.
Quiet, comfortable bar for wealthy businessmen and racehorse owners.

GEORGE V, Hôtel George-V, 31 avenue George-V, Paris 8.
One of Paris's most famous hotel bars. Huge and sumptuous. Rudolph Slavik the barman is an institution and one of the best cocktail-mixers in the world besides being a mine of information for his friends. Largely north- and south-American clientèle.

HARRY'S BAR, 5 rue Daunou, Paris 2.
Over fifty years' old and now a venerable institution. No longer as fashionable as it once was and rather a tourist haunt but still worth visiting, if only for its excellent beers and whiskies. American-Scandinavian-type clientèle, mostly young and enthusiastic. Andy, the owner, is a Scotsman.

RELAIS-PLAZA, 21 avenue Montaigne, Paris 8.
Elegant bar for the international set. Splendid variety of cocktails at splendid prices.

BAR DU RITZ, 38 rue Cambon, Paris 1.

Now the most elegant of all Paris hotel bars. Smooth, discreet service, décor in the best possible taste and a jewel of a barman, Bertin, who will invite you to try his 'Ritz special'. Try it.

LE TROU DANS LE MUR, 23 boulevard des Capucines, Paris 2.

The first 'English bar' to come to Paris early in the century. Old-fashioned décor, good Scotch, Irish, Canadian whiskies and Bourbons and several distinguished French showbiz habitués.

Left Bank

CLOSERIE DES LILAS, 171 boulevard du Montparnasse, Paris 6.

Old-established 'American bar' in a luxury restaurant on the site of what used to be one of the most revered of all Left Bank 'literary' cafés. The place has certainly changed since Hemingway went there, but there is still no more civilised place to drink on the Left Bank.

FALSTAFF, 42 rue du Montparnasse, Paris 14.

Strange mock-Tudor interior, reminiscent of a Younger's Scotch pub in London. Sartre, Beckett and a sprinkling of foreign journalists are occasionally to be seen there as well as a number of ladies of interesting reputation.

LE FIACRE, 4 rue du Cherche-Midi, Paris 6.

Bursting at the seams almost every night and a Mecca for the more exotic representatives of 'gay' Paree as well as for hordes of curious tourists in search of 'sophisticated Paris'. Far too crowded to drink in comfort, but who goes just to drink?

JACKY'S FAR WEST SALOON, 11 rue Jules-Chaplain, Paris 6.

The famous old 'Jacky's bar' has become a small, undistinguished bar above a discothèque with 'Wild West' décor. More for moneyed teenagers than for serious drinkers.

MONTALEMBERT, Hôtel du Montalembert, 3 rue de Montalembert, Paris 7.

Almost exclusively for literary drinkers: publishers, authors and agents. At its liveliest around apéritif time.

LE NUAGE, 5 rue Bernard-Palissy, Paris 6.

One of the most popular bars in Saint-Germain-des-Prés for

writers, journalists, painters and smart young would-be 'intellectuals of the left'.

PETITS PAVES, 4 rue Bernard-Palissy, Paris 6.
Beneath the restaurant of the same name. Another 'literary-intellectual' hang-out. Popular with card-players.

PONT-ROYAL, Hôtel du Pont-Royal, 7 rue de Montalembert, Paris 7.
Soberly appointed bar for publishers and writers and their agents. A good place to spot French literary celebrities during the winter season.

ROSEBUD, 11 bis rue Delambre, Paris 14.
A favourite with the literary-artistic-bohemian élite of Montparnasse. Reputed for its *chile con carne* and large glasses of excellent red wine. Gilles is an extraordinary barman—one of the best in Paris.

LE VILLAGE, 7 rue Gozlin, Paris 6.
One of the great bars of the immediate post-war period in Saint-Germain-des-Prés. Now rather faded but still charming. Clientèle largely made up of nostalgic habitués. The two owners are brothers, Greek, and were born at Colombey-les-deux-Eglises—General de Gaulle's home.

Paris Bars

by Sam White

Sam White, doyen of the Corps Journalistique in Paris, authority on Right Wing, Right Bank bars and principal propper-up of the Crillon, was finally nailed, when on a visit to London, in the bar of the Hyde Park Hotel, Knightsbridge, by the publisher and spoke as follows:

AB: You were saying, Sam?

SW: I was saying that it's almost literally true of bars in Paris that they are almost entirely for foreigners.

AB: That's not all bars, is it? I mean, you're talking about the Right Bank bars.

SW: Certainly I'm talking mainly of Right Bank bars, but in general Parisians, even so-called Bohemian Parisians, don't make a practice of going to bars.

AB: Well, who would be propping up the Crillon?

SW: In my absence the Crillon totters.

AB: What do you mean by that?

SW: It's in danger of falling down. The Crillon is, in the evening, one of the dreariest bars in the world. At lunchtime it's fairly lively, mainly because it's used by the two embassies. One adjoins it: the American embassy. And the other, the British embassy, is quite near.

AB: What about the Press?

SW: It's used also by a limited number of journalists, very few English and quite a few Americans. But the practice of journalists using the Crillon has fallen off very much in recent years because journalists, like everyone else, are affected by the cost of living.

AB: Where do they go?

SW: They go home.

AB: What about the bar of the George V?

SW: Well, that, I find—oh no, let's get back to the Crillon.

AB: Right.

SW: Because the Crillon has this reputation of being used by journalists and diplomats, it's also fairly regularly patronised by the French Secret Service police—which gives it such touch of romance as it might have. The Crillon bar was used very heavily by the CIA, but then that became so widely known that the CIA now retreat to a bar in the basement of the Crillon.

AB: Called?

SW: It has no name—it's simply the basement bar.

AB: What do these people drink?

SW: The Americans?

AB: Yes.

SW: Oh, Scotch—Scotch and—er—

AB: O.K., that's the Crillon. But supposing you were wanting— you felt quite expansive and expensive, and you wanted to have a fling, where would you go for an amusing Right Bank bar?

SW: I would say that for purely social purposes the Lotti bar is one of the pleasantest.

AB: Do you know the names of the barmen at these places—it helps a lot?

SW: Well, Louis at the Crillon. I don't know the name of the bar- man at the Lotti, but that I could find out quite easily. What other bars are there?

AB Well, what about the Georges Cinq, for heaven's sake?

SW: No, the George V, frankly, depresses me. It's so overwhelm- ingly and oppressively foreign, especially American, that one has the feeling simply of being in another capital.

AB: Where would a pretentious Frenchman go to be seen?

SW: One of the really amusing bars in Paris, strictly for lunchtime use, is the Plaza Athénée bar—the Relais, the Relais Plaza. Now that—especially during the fashion collection time—is an absolute joy. That's because it's full of models, and even at ordi- nary times it's full of people from the fashion industry—er— the fashion business, and it's also used by society women as a rendez-vous place with their women friends—as distinct from their men friends. And so it provides an atmosphere of chic and animation and pretty women which is quite unique in Paris.

AB: Would you say that Scotch is the sort of standard drink throughout?

SW: I would definitely say so.

AB: Supposing you wanted to show off, if you had a beautiful girl friend, where would you go?

SW: Oh, I would take her to the Plaza—the Relais Plaza.

AB: What about night-time? What about the Village, for instance?

SW: Oh well, that's on the Left Bank.

AB: Yes, sorry. O.K.

sw: Well, at night-time, there again I use the Village a lot because one can run into friends there quite easily—and the kind of friends one would never meet.

AB: I'm not thinking, Sam, of you. I'm thinking of the people who will be reading this book. They want to know what places to go to—just for fun, for expense, for showing off, or whatever you like. For instance, what would you say about the Ritz—I mean, it's got that lovely corridor, and then there's a bar at the end.

sw: Well, yes, the Ritz. I'm very fond of the Ritz. But now they've opened a new bar, which is extremely attractive: the one on the Place Vendôme. That is very pleasant because it overlooks the Place Vendôme and it overlooks the gardens of the Ritz. But the old Ritz bar is still—I think, from the point of view of people I might run into—the best.

AB: Is there any particular protocol you should observe when operating in French bars? I mean, what do you tip, for instance? And how do you get the eye of the waiter? Are there any little tricks?

sw: The most obvious thing not to do is to call the barman 'garçon'.

AB: What do you call him?

sw: Barman.

AB: What about tips?

sw: About tips? It's a very simple procedure: if you drink at the bar, then in most bars in Paris now the tip is included—there's no need to add anything extra.

AB: People get neurotic about this—shouldn't you in fact put a few of those copper coins down?

sw: It depends: if it's your first time ever, yes. But if you've in any way become a regular and the tip that's included is 15%, then certainly not. But if you sit down at a table, then obviously you must tip over and above the 15%.

AB: There's a difference between the standing up and sitting down?

sw: Quite. But even sitting down, I would make the tip, you know, quite small and in no relation to the price. I would always bear in mind that 15% has already been added for service.

AB: Sure. Now you talked about the Plaza Athénée, the Ritz, and the Lotte—there must be somewhere else in the swanky—

sw: There is a very small, very intimate bar—which again is noted for the very pretty women who use it—the Belmont.

AB: Where's that?

sw: In the rue François Probien.

AB: What goes there?

72

sw: A lot of models. And it's very small, with a very friendly Spanish barman.

ab: Called?

sw: Carlo? Pedro? No, I can't remember.

ab: Talking about Harry's Bar—

sw: Now Harry's Bar still has considerable atmosphere and charm—

ab: Although it's American-owned—

sw: Yes, although it's American-owned, technically. And it caters for American taste. But what happened is that it's very, very popular with the French, especially with the French young.

ab: What sort of young French would you mean? What would they be, in the Bourse?

sw: In the Bourse, in advertising, in the theatre and journalism. But one of its great qualities is the drinks—they're really excellent. And there's a splendid professionalism about it—the service is good, and the barmen know what you want—if it's a good dry Martini, a whisky sour or a gin fizz.

ab: What about the traditional cafés, like the Café Fouquet or the Café de la Paix? Any smart place on the Right Bank—what do you have to say about them? Would you advise people to go there?

sw: The Fouquet is very pleasant. There's a terrace. It's patronised mostly by sporting people.

ab: What does that mean, sporting people?

sw: Oh, jockeys, racing people generally, trainers, sports writers— you know, the more posh, prosperous pugilists and cyclists. But it's mainly a 'turf' crowd.

ab: If you had a hot story and you wanted to find out if it was true, where would you go to check up?

sw: Well, it would depend on the story.

ab: A political story.

sw: If it were a political story, say, my rendez-vous would be made at the Crillon. And in any case I'd go to the Crillon in the hope of meeting someone who would throw some light on it. If it were a fashion story, I'd go to the Plaza Athénée.

ab: Supposing you were a bored tourist, and you saw somebody you'd like to talk to, how would you approach them in any of these bars? Or wouldn't you?

sw: If you were thinking of picking up a girl, the most civilised approach is to say to the barman, 'Est-ce que vous pensez que mademoiselle est seule?'

ab: Thank you.

Food Buying in Paris

Expensive but a joy to the eye. No city has prettier bread and pastry shops. The markets are a 'must', the fish is glorious, the meat is nearly always well cut and the cooked meats and speciality shops are outrageously tempting. Even the supermarkets know how to entice.

The open street markets of Paris are fun even if you don't want to buy anything. They hold their own in spite of the supermarkets because the freshest fruit and vegetables in Paris are still to be found there. They are the only places where one is certain to find fresh-cut herbs of all sorts—basil, marjoram and fennel from the South of France as well as great bunches of fresh thyme and rosemary, sorrel and the small grey échalotes, so necessary for many sauces.

The best open market is the Neuilly street market which runs from the Place du Marché in the avenue de Neuilly right up to the Pont de Neuilly. It moves up and down the Avenue according to the day of the week. Most of the stall-holders have been running the same stands for years and the quality of their produce is high. Many of them specialise in one thing only such as asparagus when it is in season, melons from the Charantais, the finest, smallest haricot verts or the early sweet white peaches from the Perpignan district.

Other big street markets are to be found in the Marché St-Honoré in the rue St-Honoré, the rue du Seine, the rue St-Charles in the 15th arrondissement and the rue Poincelet in the 17th. There is also the Marché des Ternes in the rue Bayen, a covered street market which attracts shoppers from all over Paris.

While the freshest things obviously go to the early shoppers the cheapest are sold off around mid-day when the stall-holders are packing up to go home. Then one can get two or three small lettuces for 6d, or two pounds of peaches for 1/6d. or two pounds of fresh herring or mackerel for 2s. It is the time when the thrifty middle-aged housewives with large shopping baskets scoop up their bargains, and when over and above the yells and back-chat of the stall-holders the shrill harsh voices of the Spanish and Portuguese 'bonnes' can be heard bargaining over the priced down soft fruit or fresh sardines.

MEAT AND POULTRY

There was once an elegant fashion writer who so loved the French rolled joints of tender beef that she would wrap three or four pounds up in towels and stuff them into her typewriter for the journey home to London. Until the day a bloody chunk rolled out under the interested gaze of a customs officer and the acid-tongued artist who accompanied her said 'Anne, I always suspected you of murder'.

If you long for French Charolais beef, or the tender Pré Salé lamb, tender entrecôtes or Normandy veal here are the addresses of three of the best butchers in Paris:

Bernard, 82 rue Réaumur. The owner, M. Dubois, sells his meat at the same price as the Halles or central markets and has such an enormous clientèle that he still makes a profit. He sells meat, poultry, game and charcuterie, all of first-class quality.

The Grande Boucherie, 96 rue de Courcelles, and Letève, 36 rue Paul Barruel are rather more expensive but their meat is beautifully prepared and presented. The Grande Boucherie specialises in young lamb and M. Letève in Côte de Bœuf and entrecôte.

Tripe. One of the best shops is Paturel, 7 rue Gombouse and 38 Place du Marché St-Honoré. M. Paturel supplies all the main hotels as well as several famous restaurants with liver, sweetbreads, calves heads, brains and tongue, as well as prepared tripe.

Poultry and Game. Delaunay-Leveille, 16 rue de Sèze and 13 rue Marbeuf. One of the oldest established and best game shops in Paris.

Sausages. Mme Françoise Steels, 71 bis rue de la Tombe-Issoire. Mme. Steels comes from the Auvergne but her sausages come from every region in France. She has cervelas and rosette from Lyon, fresh sausages from the Lot, dried sausage from the Haute-Loire and Savoie as well as wonderful fresh boudin from the Mayenne. She also sells fresh pâtés and terrines and smoked hams of all sorts.

FISH

Prunier, the best fish restaurant in Paris, is also the best fish shop with an enormous choice of all fresh and smoked fish. At both addresses, 9 rue Duphot and 16 avenue Victor-Hugo, the ground floor is a shop. The prices are the same as any other good quality retailer. One of the few places where you can buy the elusive French caviar from the Gironde when it is in season.

75

Other good addresses: Sevenet, 57 rue de Passy and 95 rue Lecourbe, Queyroy et Fils, 112 rue Rambuteau.

Oyster Stalls. The oyster stalls outside the following restaurants sell to the public as well as supplying the restaurant:

Dessirier, 9 Place Pereire.

Rech, 62 avenue des Ternes.

Ocean Paris Bar, 20 avenue de Neuilly.

Louis xiv, 8 boulevard St-Denis.

CHEESE

Androuet, 41 rue d'Amsterdam is still the biggest and best cheese shop in Paris. M. Androuet is a 'maître fromager'. He owns the hôtel particulier where he has a shop on the ground floor, a cheese restaurant on the first floor and his own large apartment above that. He is in the great tradition of master artisans. A jolly square man who loves wine as well as cheese, his apartment is full of glorious antique furniture and his cellars of glorious cheeses.

Rech, at 62 avenue des Ternes, is a restaurant famous not only for its magnificent oysters and shellfish but also for its camembert. You can buy from the oyster stall outside the restaurant or from the maître d'hôtel. A camembert from Rech cost 4 francs, about 1/6d, more than you would pay at a cheese shop, but it is worth it. Rech have cheese cellars on the premises as well as in Normandy. Each one sold or eaten in the restaurant is matured to just the right degree.

Another famous cheese merchant is M. Hubert who has a restaurant called A la Ferme St-Hubert, 70 rue de Tocqueville, and who also sells his cheeses in the Neuilly open market. Tuesday, Thursday and Saturday in front of 151 avenue de Neuilly; Wednesday, Friday and Sunday in front of 34 avenue de Neuilly.

Two other good addresses: M. Cantin, 2 rue de Lourmel and Carmes, 24 rue de Levis.

WINES

Brossault, 22 rue des Capucines has a traditional and deserved reputation for its Bordeaux wines. Here you can buy all the great years as well as the more ordinary 'petit Bordeaux de table' selling at 3 francs and 4.75 francs a bottle (that is between 6s. and 7s. 6d.). Many connoisseurs know of the Brossault reputation for good claret and think of it as rather a snob shop. But its cheaper and more everyday wines have a great following amongst their regular clientèle. They also have wonderful *eau de vie* liqueurs. Their Framboise is out of this world. It costs 45 francs (about £4) a bottle and is worth every centime.

Jean Baptiste Besse, 48 rue de la Montagne-Sainte-Geneviève, is a wine merchant who loves his trade. He has a large following in Paris not only because his cellars are good but because he always seems to have time to advise even the one-bottle buyer.

Petrissans, 30 bis avenue Nie, have been installed there since 1895. There is a wine bar by the side of the shop where you can taste your wine before buying it.

HAND-MADE CHOCOLATES

The Chocolatiers and Confiseurs of France still make hand-made chocolates and sweets in traditional style. The chocolates are rich and expensive and so are the sweets. They make gifts and thank-you presents to hostesses—more than just something for the kids.

Le Lotus d'Or, 5 rue de Suresnes specialise in hand-made chocolates made by a maître chocolatier in Compiègne.

Joubin, 7 Place Tristan Bernard. M. Joubin is a Pâtissier who also makes all his own chocolates and sweets. The chocolates are delectable but cost 9s. for a quarter of a pound. Around Easter time he really lets himself go and produces monumental set pieces in chocolate as well as eggs. He has a famous chocolate cake of incredible smoothness which, alas, costs £2 10s. for a two-pound cake.

Spécialités de France, 44 avenue Montaigne. Sweets and chocolates from all the different regions of France as well as crystallised fruits. Here you will find the chocolates known as 'Puits d'amour', calixons, the marzipan sweets from Aix-en-Provence, barley sugar from the Vosges, pâtes de fruits from Nice and the famous soft nougat from Senequier in St-Tropez.

HONEY

La Maison de Miel, 24 rue Vignon, is an old-fashioned shop which sells eighteen different sorts of honey. They specialise in honey from the Alps and from the Vosges mountains as well as acacia, broom and pine honey.

Les Abeilles d'Or, 12 rue Royer-Collard specialise in honey from Southern France, thyme, lavender and rosemary honey.

THE EXOTIC AND THE RARE

Hédiard, 21 Place de la Madeleine, famous for the variety of their home-made jams and sirops, fruit juices, fresh and preserved fruits. They also sell their own special mixture of peppercorns in a small glass jar which is like no other freshly-ground pepper.

Fauchon, 26 Place de la Madeleine, is just like Fortnums, selling the same kind of luxury goods. If you want to take prepared snails back home, Fauchon's are the best in Paris. Their large Burgundian snails are purged with thyme and herbs which give them a very special flavour.

'Pubs'

Pubs have come to Paris in the last few years. They're as English as the French imagine an English pub to be and you can drink bitter in them. You can also have afternoon tea, various snacks and a 'real English breakfast' at any time. They're not quite pubs as we know them but they're certainly not cafés as the Parisians know them. But they're all the rage now.

Anglomania being what it is in Paris, it was inevitable that the English pub should eventually cross the Channel. But one thing you can't export to Paris is the atmosphere of the real, old-fashioned, institutional British boozer and the Paris 'pubs' haven't even tried. For one thing they're open all day and they close late. There's no pleasure in trying to beat the clock with just that one last round and no one will bellow 'Time gentlemen, PLEASE!'. They're also much more expensive than their English models. A half pint of Watney's Red Barrel (the beer most frequently available) will cost you about 4 shillings and it won't have quite the same taste as English bitter: they haven't learned how to keep it yet.

The Paris pubs started, as was to be expected, as a gimmick and they haven't quite managed to shake off their air of 'an amusing and oh, so very English novelty!' which is a pity as some are much more comfortable (and better decorated) than the now average Paris café which is a noisy nightmare of harsh lighting and coloured plastic. If you're a nostalgic English expatriate, it's no good trying to compare them with the genuine London article. Still, they're fun to meet people in and you can always save paying for an expensive lunch by taking a French business colleague there instead of the Tour d'Argent or Lapérouse.

Not all 'pubs' in Paris are English in their inspiration. The name has stuck and been applied to several other establishments which are more like the 'Drugstores' at Saint-Germain-des-Prés or on the Champs-Elysées. The thirsty journalists of 'Le Monde' drink across the road at the 'Pub Haussmann' which is anything but a pub (rue des Italiens, Paris 9) and the term has been applied indiscriminately to other brasseries and cafés. The 'Pub Renault', for instance, is nothing but a flashily decorated 'drugstore-type' snack joint on the Champs-Elysées. The four 'pubs' that follow are all of the English type which means that their décor has been copied from English pubs with varying degrees of accuracy, they make a point of serving English beers and you can enjoy the 'typically English breakfast' there in the middle of the afternoon like one Paris society lady of our acquaintance who imagines that serving tea and breakfast is one of the main *raisons d'être* of the English pub. The French still have a lot to learn about our institutions. . . .

TAVERNE DE LONDRES, rue du Sabot, Paris 6.
Set in a quaint little street off the rue de Rennes. The exterior of this recently opened Paris 'pub' is a more convincing pastiche of a London pub than the interior which is frankly 'drugstore' in style. They serve Watney's beer and the 'real English breakfast' as follows:
> Fresh orange juice.
> Cereals (cornflakes—rice crispies)
>   or Porridge.
> Eggs, bacon, tomato, toast.
> Toast, butter, marmelade [*sic*],
> Breakfast tea, coffee or chocolate.

Price: 12 francs. Prices of drinks are exorbitant: a half of Red Barrel is 2.70 francs; a cuppa (with milk or lemon) from a pot is 3.30 francs; current brands of whisky (Bell's, Black and White, Teacher's): 7.40 francs; other whiskies from 8 to 35 francs (Chivas Regal Royal Salute) and if you want a sherry it'll cost you about 8.50 francs. At these prices you might as well go to the 'Flore' or any nice little bar in the neighbourhood.

SIR WINSTON CHURCHILL, 5 rue de Presbourg, Paris 16.
Decorated by Paris's, most fashionable café/drugstore decorator, Slavik. Lots of wood and discreet lighting. Watney's beer again (they also serve brown ale) and food served. Expensive drinks. Frankly, all a bit camp and not very English.

BEDFORD ARMS, rue Princesse, Paris 6.
Next to 'Castel's' and part of the same establishment (see page 260). Pretty cut glass and mirrors, expensive prices, beer, and a very, very cliquey atmosphere and clientèle. The Duke of Bedford agreed to lend his name to the place.

PUB SAINT-GERMAIN, rue de l'Ancienne-Comédie, Paris 6.
Open day and night. Dark lighting, comfortable seats and cubicles and a nice long bar. Somewhat (but not much) less expensive than the others and very 'Latin Quarter' in atmosphere.

'Drugstores'

They've opened one in Chelsea now—it was inspired by the Paris Drugstores which have been booming ever since they opened. They all have jazzy decorations, sensationally good loos and are quite useful for buying cold foods, papers, etc., at most hours of the day and night. They're a strange hybrid, not quite American, not quite French and rather too gimmicky to be natural. But they're spreading. . . .

DRUGSTORE-CHAMPS-ELYSEES, 133 avenue des Champs-Elysées (near the Arc de Triomphe).
Open until 2 am. The first of the Paris 'drugstores'. Quite good cold snacks, comfortable eats at the bar, lots of tourists and Paris teenagers with money to spend. You can buy 'souvenirs', papers, perfumes, etc.

DRUGSTORE SAINT-GERMAIN, 149 boulevard Saint-Germain, Paris 6.
Open until 2 am.
The most famous or notorious of the Paris drugstores. Opened about three years ago with a bang, on the site of a nice old café with excellent oysters, the 'Royal Saint-Germain'. You can eat upstairs in a rather Daliesque décor in dubious taste, there is a hot-dog and snack bar, shops, a paper shop, a book-shop (in the basement), a tobacco counter and quite a good cold foods and wine and spirits shop. It's usually packed and popular with a certain kind of young fauna hanging around the entrance for various and fairly obvious reasons.

DRUGSTORE OPERA, 6 boulevard des Capucines, Paris 9.
Until 2 am. Restaurant-snack bar with emphasis on sandwiches and hamburgers and a décor largely composed of huge stills from famous films.
And if you walk along the boulevard Poissonnière towards the Porte Saint-Denis you will find the

MADRID-MINI-DUGSTORE
on the site of the old and glorious literary café of 50 years ago, the 'Madrid'. No further description is really necessary at this point: it's too depressing.

WIMPEY BARS

A few years ago, an enterprising French businessman, Jacques Borel, decided there was a fortune to be made by introducing the 'Wimpey-burger' to his fellow countrymen, advertising them as 'a complete meal in a roll'. There are now about a dozen Wimpey Bars in Paris. They look very much like the English ones and serve the usual range of 'burgers' which don't need any further description since nothing tastes more like one Wimpey than another Wimpey, wherever it is.

A Guide to Paris Art Galleries

In the last few years dealers have been lamenting the parlous state of modern art in Paris. Even so, there is no shortage of galleries. Some are world famous and have a glorious history; others are amusing, avant-garde and even ephemeral. Here's what every would-be collector should know about the art scene in Paris today.

Only towards the middle of the nineteenth century did Paris gradually gain recognition as the Western world's main centre and market for contemporary art. Ever since the Renaissance, Florence, Rome and Venice had attracted young artists from far and wide. Later, for a while, Amsterdam had been an important centre for trading in the works of old masters and living artists. During the first half of the nineteenth century, Rome had been the meeting place of Romantic painters and sculptors who flocked there mainly from Germany, France and England, but also from Scandinavia, Russia and America.

Around 1850, Paris had to compete, as an art centre and art market, with Munich and Düsseldorf as well as with Rome. But Paris soon obtained an important lead over these rivals, thanks to the world-wide success of two groups of French painters: the landscape painters of the Barbizon School and, after 1870, the Impressionists. Gradually Barbizon, Paris, Pont-Aven and other rural colonies of French painters attracted more and more artists from abroad; at the same time, the Paris dealers and galleries slowly won for French art and for the art of foreign-born artists of the School of Paris a world-wide market that has only in recent years begun to be challenged by artists and dealers of the School of New York and of the English School.

Today, Paris can still boast of more commercial art galleries than any other city in the world except New York. In April, May and June of each year, at the peak of the Paris art season, a professional critic may find himself invited to as many as a hundred different exhibition-openings each week. A systematic tour of the most outstanding Paris art galleries can turn out to be almost an introductory course in the history of French art and of the art of the Western world since the middle of the eighteenth century.

For French eighteenth-century painting, two Paris dealers of world-wide repute can always be relied upon to provide a varied choice of works of acknowledged masters: Wildenstein's, at 57 rue La Boétie, and Cailleux, at 136 rue du Faubourg Saint-Honoré. Whereas Cailleux also specializes in paintings by the somewhat off-beat French Impressionist master Monticelli, Wildenstein's Paris gallery, like his galleries in London and New York, can also boast of being able to show at all times, to an interested collector, as varied a choice of works of almost any school of Western art as one would be likely to see anywhere else in the world, except in a major museum. The Paris branch of another important New York firm of art dealers, M. Knoedler et Cie, at 85 bis rue du Faubourg Saint-Honoré, can also produce, on request, some very remarkable paintings by a wide range of artists of the past and of the present. Knoedler's also handle the work of Emmanuel Pereire, one of the more subtle younger French painters of recent years.

For nineteenth-century French art, especially of the Romantic School, one should visit the gallery of Daber, at 103 boulevard Haussmann; also, at 2 rue des Beaux-Arts, Aubry and, around the corner at 12 rue de Seine, Jonas or, at 6 rue de Seine, Le Pavillon des Arts. These four dealers have specialised in recent years in salvaging the reputations of such neglected nineteenth-century French masters as the sculptor Barye and, among painters of the Barbizon School, Narcisse Diaz, Harpignies and Trouillebert. Hector Brame, at 68 boulevard Malesherbes, is one of the older firms of Paris dealers, famous in the nineteenth century as the gallery that stocked the works of Corot; though no longer very active or felicitous in its choice of contemporary artists, Hector Brame's gallery still has a valuable stock of masterpieces of nineteenth-century French art.

Several galleries which handled and launched the work of French Impressionist masters are still in business; they can show to the interested collector, works of outstanding quality and merit by painters of fifty or more years ago, but have all too often neglected to keep up with any more recent trends of French art. At 137 boulevard Haussmann, the Galerie Serret-Fauveau has some fine paintings by Guillaumin and Lebourg and, among living artists, by Volovick, who was at one time a close friend and associate of Soutine and other older masters of the so-called 'Ecole juive de Paris'.

Durand-Ruel's gallery, at 37 avenue Friedland, remains a Mecca for collectors of French Impressionists. The founder of this firm, close on a hundred years ago, was the first to market their works on a large scale and to sell them to those far-sighted American collectors who have since left their collections to Museums such as New York's Metropolitan and Chicago's Art Institute. Durand-Ruel's stocks still include a great number of paintings and drawings of the French masters of the period between 1870 and 1900 and especially of Camille Pissaro. Bernheim-Jeune et Cie, at 83 Faubourg Saint-Honoré, followed Durand-Ruel's example a couple of decades later and, in addition to valuable stocks of Monet and other Impressionist masters, still has the world's most important stock of works by Bonnard.

An art-lover who is interested in off-beat Post-Impressionist masters should not fail to visit the tiny Galerie 'Les Deux Iles', 1 Quai aux Fleurs, on the Ile de la Cité, behind Notre-Dame. There he will always find an exciting choice of works, often minor but always delightful, by painters of the Gauguin circle, such as Schufflenecker and Emile Bernard. At the Galerie Katia Granoff, on the Place Beauvau in the rue du Faubourg Saint-Honoré, one finds an interesting choice of Impressionist and Fauvist works; Katia Granoff's passion for impasto effects and for greens and earth-colours tends, however, to impose a surprising unity on her selections of works of otherwise very varied painters. Her gallery is nevertheless the only one to handle the work of Amédée Ozenfant, a much neglected major Cubist and Post-Cubist or Purist master whose colour-harmonies and rational composition often contrast surprisingly with Katia Granoff's other choices.

The works of French Fauvist and Cubist masters remained for two or three decades very 'speculative' investments, so that many of the dealers who first tried to launch them are no longer in business. Daniel-Henri Kahnweiler's Galerie Louise Leiris, at 47 rue Monceau, has long handled Picasso's work and also the work, among others, of the Surrealist master, André Masson. For works by Léger, Kupka and Jacques Villon, one should visit the gallery of Louis Carré, at 10 avenue de Messine. For Chagall, Kandinsky and Miro, the Galerie Maeght, at 13 rue de Téhéran. For Vlaminck and Van Dongen and other Fauvists, in addition to the Galerie Katia Granoff, Paul Petrides, at 53 rue La Boétie, is always worth a visit. H. Bénézit, at 20 rue Miromesnil, often shows a few surprising works by masters of the period from 1910 to 1930; recently, I saw there Tal-Coat's remarkable but little-known portrait of Gertrude Stein. Berggruen et Cie at 70 rue de l'Université, specialises in established reputations, ranging from Klee and Picasso to such younger masters of colour-lithography as Paul Wunderlich; Berggruen's stock of modern prints and drawings always includes some very exciting items.

The Galerie Jeanne Bucher, at 53 rue de Seine, is one of the very few major galleries of the twenties that has survived the Depression of the thirties. After handling for many years the works of second-generation Cubists and Surrealists, it has become very eclectic and now exhibits such painters as Vieira du Silva and such sculptors as Hajdu. Works by Cubist and Surrealist masters of the period from 1920 to 1939 can moreover be found scattered in a great number of other galleries. The Galerie Zerbib, in the rue des Beaux-Arts, thus handles work of the late Alfred Reth, one of the first Cubists and, unfortunately, of the most neglected. The Galerie Suillerot, 8 rue d'Argenson, likewise handles the work of the Cubist painter Henri Hayden. Edouard Loeb, at 53 rue de Rennes, has long specialized in the work of masters who were at one time considered too extremist by other dealers.

André François Petit, at 122 boulevard Haussmann, has in recent years collected and exhibited works of Surrealist Masters, ranging from the more famous, such as Dali, Max Ernst, Victor Brauner and Tanguy, to the more way-out, such as Bellmer, Savinio, Dorothea Tanning, Toyen and Richard Oelze. Nowhere else in Paris can one find, at any time, such a varied and carefully selected choice of Surrealist art. Jacques Tronche, at 122 boulevard Haussmann, is less exclusively devoted to the Surrealist cause and also has some good examples of the work of Dubuffet and a few other more esoteric modern artists in addition to Surrealists and, among these, especially Matta.

Surrealist art is also well represented in the following Left Bank Galleries: Le Point Cardinal, which exhibits Max Ernst, Dorothea Tanning, Matta and Josef Sima at 3 rue Jacob; the Galerie du Dragon, 19 rue du Dragon; the Galerie Iolas, 196 boulevard Saint-Germain, which exhibits Matta, Magritte, Brauner, Léonor Fini and Niki de Saint-Phalle's fabulous *Nana* figures; the Galerie Jacques Desbrières, 27 rue Guénégaud, which exhibits Léonor Fini, Yüksel Arslan, Michel Henricot, Barlach Hoyer and a whole group of younger and somewhat more manneristic Post-Surrealists; and, at 5 and 6 rue Visconti, the Galerie 3 + 2 and the Galerie 3 + 3, which both specialise in the more erotic and way-out Surrealist and Post-Surrealist painters, ranging from Bellmer, Roldàn and Yüksel Arslan to the legendary Berlin artist Friedrich Schroeder-Sonnenstern. The Galerie 'La Roue', 16 rue Grégoire de Tours, shows mainly drawings and smaller works by artists who have only recently achieved success.

The Galerie Claude Bernard, in the rue des Beaux-Arts, has long been a major centre for contemporary European Sculpture. Wotruba, Cesar, Penalba, Hiquily, Ipousteguy and many others exhibit there. This gallery also exhibits painters and has distinguished itself, among younger Paris galleries, by its open-mindedness in showing outstanding foreign artists, such as Richard Lindner, from America, and the great German Expressionist, Georg Grosz.

Lovers of abstract art will find its various trends well represented in many Paris galleries. The Galerie de France, at 3 rue du Faubourg Saint-Honoré, has long been the headquarters of French Abstract or 'lyrical' Expressionnism, as represented by such painters as Manessier, Soulages and Hartung. For the more austere trends of Op Art and Kinetic Art, the Galerie Denise René, at 124 rue La Boétie, remains almost unrivalled, whether in Europe or America: its range extends from the pioneers and masters of this movement, such as Herbin, Josef Albers and Vasarély, to such younger representatives as Le Parc and Karl Gerstner. Denise René also maintains a Left Bank branch at 196 boulevard Saint-Germain.

Pop Art is best represented in Paris by the Galerie Ileana Sonnabend, at 12 rue Mararine; it handles in Europe most of the New York stars of this movement as well as some of their more outstanding European colleagues. The Galerie Darthea Speyer, in the nearby rue Jacques Callot, opened in 1968, specialises in the work of a few American painters, such as Peter Saul, and European sculptors, such as Stahly. On the Right Bank, Iris Clert, at 28 rue du Faubourg Saint-Honoré, has acquired a world-wide reputation for the spectacular openings of her shows of way-out European and American painters and sculptors, among whom the American sculptor Zev distinguishes himself by creating some of the most complex bronzes that have ever been achieved. The Galerie Mathias Fels, at 138 boulevard Haussmann, handles a few younger Post-Surrealist painters, such as Camacho and Bertholo, as well as some way-out younger artists who belong more strictly to the school of Pop Art. The near-by Galerie Ariel, at 140 boulevard Haussmann, has a preference for Expressionist painters whose work hovers on the border-line between figurative and non-figurative art and distinguishes itself by its very painterly quality: Bitran, Gillet and Tabuchi are among its more interesting younger painters.

Far from exhausting the list of Paris galleries that deserve the attention of a sophisticated art-lover whose curiosity is not limited to the style of a single school, these suggestions can claim only to illustrate the wide range of styles and schools that are represented on the Paris art-market. In general, Paris art galleries are grouped, on the Right Bank, between the rue du Faubourg Saint-Honoré, with its many side-streets, and the boulevard Haussmann. In this area, the Galerie André Schoeller, at 31 rue Miromesnil, should also be included among the more interesting younger galleries. At 8 rue du Cirque, the Galerie Henriette Gomès proves to be one of the more esoteric Paris galleries, handling almost exclusively the work of the painter Balthus. Beno d'Incelli, at 43 rue Miromesnil, runs his gallery on broadly eclectic principles, but with a flair for quality; Cargaleiro, a Portuguese painter, is one of his more promising younger artists.

The other major concentration of Paris art galleries is to be found between the boulevard Saint-Germain and the embankments of the Seine, especially on and off the rue de Seine. In an afternoon devoted to gallery-cruising in either of these areas, a good dozen galleries can easily be visited.

Collectors of modern prints, in particular, will enjoy visiting the Left Bank Galleries. In the rue des Beaux-Arts, the Galerie Claude Bernard always has, in its print department, a broad choice of prints by modern artists; in the rue de l'Université, Berggruen is also to be recommended. The Librairie de la Hune, on the Boulevard Saint-Germain between the Café de Flore and Les Deux Magots, offers perhaps the best choice of art books as well as of modern prints and, in its gallery, regularly exhibits the works of such well-known graphic artists as Hayter, Johnny Friedlander and Gregory Mazwrovsky.

The Paris market offers such a vast choice of art of every kind and style it can cater to almost every taste and, if one has patience, knowledge and luck, can even yield surprising bargains. Nearly every week, some lucky connoisseur manages to salvage, from the confused array of odds and ends of the *Marché aux Puces* in the Northern suburb of Clignancourt, some work of real value that was sold to him for a song. Georges Romane, a well-known figure among Left Bank Bohemians, has been convinced every week for the past twenty years that he has just found in Clignancourt a lost masterpiece by a famous painter of the past. Though he is very often mistaken, you cannot be wrong fifty thousand times, and some of the thousands of drawings and paintings that he has salvaged from the Paris Flea-markets have proven to be works of real value.

Nearly every year, a few wise collectors manage likewise to purchase from a Paris art gallery, at a modest price, some works of an unknown contemporary which, within a couple of years, will be worth ten times what they originally cost. Many foreign art lovers therefore come to Paris almost exclusively to discover new talents in whose works they can invest. A number of smaller Paris galleries exhibit only such artists, whose works may well turn out to be shining examples of this kind of capital-growth.

But the art world remains, even in a boom, a gambler's market. Of the thirty thousand artists of all kinds who now live or exhibit in Paris, less than five hundred, at best, can be expected to achieve any fame or success, and no prophet can guide you completely unerringly in your choice of those who are least likely to fail. Your best guide is at all times your own knowledge and taste, which you can improve and refine as the years go by. If you consistently pick duds, you might be wiser to collect postage-stamps.

Some Paris galleries have nevertheless proved to be, in recent years, particularly felicitous in their choices of younger artists. The former Galerie Flinker, now renamed Galerie Daniel Gervis, at 34 rue du Bac, has exhibited a surprising number of painters who very soon achieved fame on both sides of the Atlantic: Hundertwasser, Jenkins and Maeda, among others. The Galerie Seder, at 25 rue des Saints-Pères, has specialised in modern prints and lithographs and has also been wise, or lucky, in many of its patronage of new artists.

Among those smaller Paris galleries that exhibit mainly young artists whose works are still relatively inexpensive, the Galerie Jacques Casanova, in the arcade of the Galerie Montpensier of the Palais-Royal, distinguishes itself by being particularly eclectic: its range of interests extends from abstract to figurative, from fantastic to realist art. Other such smaller galleries generally remain faithful to a single trend: the Galerie Solstices, 44 rue des Tournelles, between the Place de la Bastille and the Place des Vosges, handles the work, among others, of a group of very promising young Moroccan painters, ranging from the late Ahmed Cherkaoui, a truly remarkable colourist, to Benkemoun, a newcomer to Paris whose prices are still very reasonable. On the nearby Place des Vosges, the Galerie

Jeannette Ostier handles only Japanese art of the classical periods: its stock can at any time compete with the collections of all but the best Japanese museums.

If only because its immigration policies are more liberal, France continues to attract from the Americas, from all over Europe and now from Asia, Africa and Australia too, more young artists of talent than its two major rivals in the art world, London and New York. Though France itself may no longer produce as many outstanding artists as it did in the heyday of Impressionism and Post-Impressionism, the School of Paris can still boast that among its many foreign-born painters and sculptors it harbours, encourages and markets more artists of real talent and originality than any other city in the world.

Museums

Not just the Louvre. Paris has a wealth of small, intimate museums to delight the curious as well as the culture vulture, some magnificent private collections on view to the public, two museums of modern art, and one of the eeriest collections of wax-works anywhere. . . .

There are nearly a hundred museums in Paris and its neighbourhood. As a general rule you pay for admission except on Sundays. There are reductions for students and if you have taken the trouble beforehand to get a cultural *laisser-passer* from the Council of Europe at Strasbourg you may even get in free (although in some of the smaller museums a baffled attendant may never have heard of the Council of Europe and treat your card with great suspicion).

Our selection of museums follows in alphabetical order—except for the Louvre. It's the biggest museum in the world. There's no missing it and it is the one that most visitors go to—which is not always a good thing since if you are unwisely determined to do it all at once you're not very likely to be interested in the rest of our list. Some people have to spend the whole of the following day recovering from the Louvre—so be warned!

MUSEE DU LOUVRE
Open from 10 am to 7 pm except Tuesdays. Lecture tours in French and English starting from the Pavillon Denon at 10.30 am and 3 pm and on Friday evenings only at 9 pm (starting from whichever gallery is being visited at the time). Entrance 2 francs.
Not only the world's biggest museum, but also the world's largest palace. It was begun in 1204 and only finished in 1870. It was first a fortress (you can see the moat that M. Malraux has uncovered), then a royal palace, and only comparatively recently did it become a museum. The first great collections were made by François I and later by Louis XIV. In 1746, some of the vast royal collections were transferred from Versailles, but most of them ended up in the Luxembourg Palace. It was not until the Revolution, in 1793, that the present museum was born as the Central Museum of the Arts, and not until the following year that it was declared open to all citizens.

Another great collector was Napoleon (who also gave his name to the museum for a while), aided and abetted by Baron Denon, who 'acquired' a magnificent collection in the course of the Italian campaigns. A lot of the works had to be given back after the downfall of the Empire but even so, paintings by Giotto, Fra Angelico and Veronese were part of the booty that remained. The Louvre has gone on gobbling up collections and precious masterpieces ever since, by more legal means. They are now divided into six huge departments: 1. Greek and Roman Antiquities. 2. Oriental Antiquities. 3. Egyptian Antiquities. 4. Medieval, Renaissance and Modern sculpture. 5. Paintings and drawings (including the very important engraving and drawings department: the *Cabinet des Dessins*), and 6. General works of art.

The Louvre is particularly famous for its magnificent Egyptian collection, much of which came from Napoleon's ill-fated Nile Expedition. But the most famous single work in the whole museum is undoubtedly Leonardo's *Mona Lisa*. It has now been 'demoted' for some reason. No longer in the great painting gallery, it has been relegated to a dimmer, smaller room near by. After you've found it you might like to know that there's a restaurant in the Louvre, in the Pavillon Mollien.

The Louvre is more than just one museum. Apart from housing the Ministry of Finance, the great building includes:

The Musée des Arts Décoratifs
Entrance at 107 rue de Rivoli. From 10 am to 12 noon and 2 pm to 5 pm. Closed on Tuesdays.
Vast permanent collections of furniture and furnishings, art objects, tapestries and other examples of the applied arts. There is a reference library and many important exhibitions are held in the museum throughout the year.

For late 19th-century French painting and especially the Impressionists, you must go to the

Musée du Jeu de Paume in the Tuileries Gardens, near the Place de la Concorde. From 10 am to 12.45 pm and from 2 pm to 5 pm. Closed on Tuesdays.
The museum dates from the time of the very important Caillebotte bequest. Caillebotte, himself a painter, was a great friend and admirer of the Impressionists. He gave his collection to the state and when it was accepted by the Louvre there was a great contro-

versy as the works were not thought 'respectable'. They went to the Jeu de Paume in 1920 and it is now the best and the most representative collection of Impressionist and immediately pre-Impressionist paintings in the world. Later paintings by Gauguin, Douanier Rousseau, etc., are also displayed.

The **Orangerie** in the same gardens is the sister museum to the Jeu de Paume. It is mostly used for temporary exhibitions and permanently displays Monet's famous *Water Lilies*.

MUSEE DE L'AIR, 2 rue du Vertugadin, Meudon. From 9 am to 5 pm except on Saturdays and Sundays when it is open from 10 am to 12 noon, and 2 pm to 6 pm.
Worth going out of Paris to see. A delightful collection of flying machines from the earliest days (many of them never got off the ground). Still in process of arrangement and a little chaotic.

MUSEE DE L'ARMEE, Hôtel des Invalides, Paris 7. From 10 am to 12.15 pm and from 1.30 pm to 5 pm (5.30 pm in summer).
Arms and armour and every kind of military relic with a heavy bias towards Napoleonic exhibits. Rather disorganised since you never know in advance quite which rooms will be open.

BALZAC'S HOUSE, 47 rue Raynouard, Paris 16. Every day from 1.30 pm to 5 pm except Tuesdays.
A pretty 18th-century country house and garden in the midst of dreary Passy. Every kind of Balzac relic for the enthusiast. The great man wrote the last part of his *Human Comedy* there.

MUSEE CARNAVALET, 23 rue de Sévigné, Paris 3. 10 am to 12 noon and 2 pm to 5 pm. Closed on Tuesdays.
One of the most delightful, prettiest museums in Paris inside a superbly elegant late-Renaissance and 17th-century mansion. Everything relating to the history of Paris: objects, paintings, relics, maps and curiosities. Wonderful little ivory model of the guillotine, faience model of the Bastille, Napoleonic relics, etc. The models of old Paris streets and squares are not to be missed.

CENTRE DE DOCUMENTATION DU COSTUME, 79 avenue de

la République, Paris 11. From 2 pm to 6 pm except on Saturdays and Sundays.

More than 1,500 costumes of the last two hundred and fifty years as well as innumerable drawings and photographs.

MUSEE CERNUSCHI, 7 avenue Vélasquez, Paris 8. From 10 am to 12 noon and from 2 pm to 5 pm (or until 6 pm in winter). Closed on Tuesdays.

A beautiful collection of Chinese and Japanese art. A smallish but very elegant display for the connoisseur.

MUSEE DE CLUNY, 6 rue Paul-Painlevé, Paris 5. From 1 am to 5 pm. Closed on Tuesdays.

A set of 27 rooms inside ancient monastic buildings and devoted mainly to medieval arts and crafts. There is a wonderful Gothic chapel and a famous series of tapestries: 'The Lady and the Unicorn'. One of the best laid-out small museums in Paris and only a few steps away from the cafés on the boulevard Saint-Michel.

MUSEE COGNACQ-JAY, 25 boulevard des Capucines, Paris 2. From 10 am to 12 noon and 2 pm to 5 pm. Closed on Tuesdays and public holidays.

A very elegant, very 'Parisian' collection of 17th- and 18th-century art. Well worth visiting, if you happen to be passing by, for its works by Rembrandt, Tiepolo and Watteau.

CONCIERGERIE, 1 Quai de l'Horloge, Paris 1. From 10 am to 12 noon and 1.30 pm to 5 pm.

A grim reminder of the Terror during the French Revolution. You can still see Marie-Antoinette's cell and the prisons where aristocrats (and others) waited before being carted off to the guillotine. Very gloomy, very impressive. Also various relics of the Revolution.

MUSEE DU CONSERVATOIRE DES ARTS ET METIERS, 292 rue Saint-Martin, Paris 3. From 1.30 pm to 5.30 pm (10 am to 5 pm on Sundays). Closed on Mondays.

Despite its rather off-putting title, the museum is housed in a delightful old priory. Devoted to science and industrial techniques but we guarantee that even the most inveterate museum-hater will be fascinated by its wonderful collection of automats and robot-dolls, many made in the 18th century by Vaucanson, a mechanical wizard. The automats are only made to perform one Sunday every three months, unfortunately.

MUSEE DE LA CONTREFAÇON, 16 rue de la Faisanderie, Paris 16. From 9 am to 12 noon and from 2 pm to 5 pm except on Saturdays and Sundays.
Even the apparently 18th-century building is a fake, being built in 1900. A museum devoted to the art of the counterfeiter. Fascinating and very discouraging for would-be forgers. Every kind of fake from banknotes to patent medicines.

MUSEE DELACROIX, 6 rue de Furstenberg, Paris 6. From 10 am to 12 noon and 2 pm to 6 pm between May 1st and November 1st. The great painter Delacroix's studio as he left it, overlooking one of Paris' smallest and prettiest squares, near the church of Saint-Germain-des-Prés. Paintings, sketches, relics, etc.

MUSEE D'ENNERY, 59 avenue Foch, Paris 16. Sundays only, from 1 pm to 5 pm.
A strange place that belonged to a once-popular playwright. Lots of Chinese and Japanese knick-knacks and an 'Armenian' room. Very suitable for lovers' meetings, plotting or simply for sitting and thinking if you've been caught by the rain on Sunday afternoon while strolling down Paris' smartest residential avenue.

MUSEE DES GOBELINS, 42 avenue des Gobelins, Paris 13. Open Wednesdays, Thursdays and Fridays only, from 2 pm to 5 pm. Beautiful tapestries from the world-famous workshops.

MUSEE GREVIN, 10 boulevard Montmartre, Paris 9. Every day from 2 pm to 7 pm.
Wax works, tableaux, a Palace of Mirages, distorting mirrors. A strange place that would make a wonderful set for a fantastic or horror film. Much, much more impressive than Madame Tussaud's in London.

MUSEE GUIMET, 6 Place d'Iéna, Paris 16. From 10 am to 5 pm. Closed on Tuesdays.
The Musée Guimet houses the Asiatic Art department of the Louvre. Wonderful collections of Oriental art. World-famous

Japanese and Chinese masterpieces and unrivalled display of sculptures from Cambodia and Greco-Buddhist sculptures from northern India and Pakistan. One of the world's best displays of Far Eastern art.

MUSEUM D'HISTOIRE NATURELLE, Jardin des Plantes, 57 rue Cuvier, Paris 5. Gardens open from 8 am until sunset. Zoological, mineralogical, etc., collections open from 1.30 pm to 5 pm except on Tuesdays. A small zoo and vivarium open from 9 am to 5 pm. A strangely old-fashioned place with a rather mysterious air. Can it be the old 19th-century buildings with their astonishing frescoes and reliefs by official, government-sponsored artists? Or the display of prehistoric animals? Great fun for children anyway.

MUSEE DE L'HOMME, Palais de Chaillot, Paris 16. From 10 am to 5 pm. Closed on Tuesdays.
One of the finest anthropological and archaeological museums in the world, specialising in African, Asian and early pre-Columbian American arts and crafts. Beautifully laid out. There is a cinema, a photo collection, a record collection, library and restaurant with a bar. The collection of primitive art is incomparable.

MUSEE VICTOR HUGO, 6 Place des Vosges, Paris 4. From 10 am to 12.30 pm and 2 pm to 5 pm. Closed on Tuesdays and public holidays.
Souvenirs, relics, portraits and paintings all connected with Hugo's life and works and, above all, a wonderful collection of over 300 of the writer's strange, almost Surrealist drawings.

MUSEE JACQUEMART-ANDRE, 178 boulevard Haussmann, Paris 8. From 12 noon to 5 pm (until 6 pm in winter). Closed on Tuesdays. Once the private residence of M. and Mme Jacquemart-André with fine collections of 18th-century French art and Italian art and furniture left as a bequest to the Institut de France. Contains frescoes by Tiepolo, three paintings by Rembrandt, paintings by Carpaccio and Ucello, etc.

MUSEE DE LA MARINE, Palais de Chaillot, Paris 16. 10 am to 5 pm. Closed on Tuesdays.
Next to the Musée de l'Homme in the right wing of the Palais de Chaillot. Everything for enthusiasts of naval history: paintings,

models of ships, relics, etc. On Wednesdays, the rooms are illuminated until 11 pm.

MUSEE GUSTAVE MOREAU, 14 rue La Rochefoucault, Paris 9.
One of the most intimate of all Paris' little museums. Moreau was one of the most imaginative and unusual 19th-century French artists with a distinct penchant for Surrealist-type, dream-like compositions. His house is as he left it when he died, crammed with paintings, sketches and drawings and various curious knick-knacks.

Musée Gustave Moreau

MUSEE MUNICIPAL D'ART MODERNE, 11 avenue du Président-Wilson, Paris 16. From 10 am to 5 pm. Closed Tuesdays. In the east wing of the building.
A recent museum, inaugurated in 1961. Like its twin museum in the other wing, it specialises in modern painting. A famous work there is Raoul Dufy's delightful fresco painting made for the Electricity Pavilion of the 1937 Paris Exhibition. Unfortunately, like the Musée National d'Art Moderne, it is rather a cold and uninspiring place and certainly not as comprehensive and as well

laid-out as the New York Museum of Modern Art, for example. In fact, neither of the two Paris 'modern art' museums is *really* modern enough.

MUSEE NATIONAL D'ART MODERNE, 11 avenue du Président-Wilson, Paris 16. From 10 am to 5 pm. Closed on Tuesdays.
Not to be confused with the Musée Municipal d'Art Moderne. One is a state museum, the other, the museum of modern art of the *town* of Paris. This one is in the west wing of the building—the Palais de Tokyo. It was founded in 1937 for the Paris Exhibition and, as the name says, is devoted to modern painting of the 20th century, mostly French: Bonnard, Matisse, Braque, Picasso, etc.

MUSEE NISSIM DE CAMONDO, 63 rue de Monceau, Paris 8. From 2 pm to 5 pm except Sundays when visiting hours are 10 am to 12 noon and 2 pm to 5 pm. Closed on Tuesdays.
A step into the age of Louis XVI in a private mansion. Nissim de Camondo was an aviator killed in the First World War. His father was a great art lover and collector and beautifully reconstructed the interior of an 18th-century art patron's mansion. Contains the very best of French 18th-century furniture as well as paintings and art objects.

PALAIS DE LA DECOUVERTE, Grand Palais, avenue Franklin-Roosevelt, Paris 8. From 10 am to 12 noon and 2 pm to 6 pm. Closed on Fridays.
Wonderful place for schoolboys. A 'Palace' of science with a Planetarium, cinema and masses of working models of everything scientific.

MUSEE DU PETIT PALAIS, avenue Alexandre III, Paris 8. 10 am to 5 pm. Closed Tuesdays.
Many exhibitions are held here. The permanent collection is rich in 19th-century French painting and art objects. The building itself and its frothy, painted ceiling are very 1900-style and many people prefer them to the actual exhibits.

MUSEE DE LA PREFECTURE DE POLICE, 36 Quai des Ofrèvres, Paris 1. Every Thursday from 2 pm to 5 pm except on public holidays.
Grim and fascinating. A kind of 'black museum' full of murderer's tools and weapons and other relics with a sinister history.

MUSEE RODIN, Hôtel Biron, 77 rue de Varenne, Paris 7. From 1 pm to 5 pm. Closed on Tuesdays.
Many of Rodin's greatest works on view in the mansion, the courtyard and the gardens which are among the most beautiful in Paris. The great sculptor's erotic works are also kept somewhere in the house but it's up to you to get to see them.

MUSEE DU VIEUX-MONTMARTRE, 17 rue Saint-Vincent, Paris 18. Every day from 10 am to 12 noon and 2 pm to 5 pm. Closed on Tuesdays.
A wonderful reminder of the days when Montmartre *was* Montmartre in an old 18th-century house. Drawings and relics of Montmartre's most famous inhabitants, and posters by Toulouse-Lautrec.

Churches

Paris has all kinds of churches, from the sublime to the sinister—churches for Baptists, Greeks, Armenians, Seventh Day Adventists, Mormons, Americans, Russians, Rumanians and Welsh as well as a Mosque and a Great Synagogue—and only a few of them are beautiful.

Here is a selection of Paris' Catholic churches. Some are depressing, many are badly lit, even more have never quite recovered from being pillaged and vandalised during the French Revolution, but each has its own kind of fascination. . . .

Unlike Rome, Paris is not a city of glorious churches. Her claim to architectural distinction and beauty lies elsewhere, in her lovely riverside, her theatrical vistas, grand set-pieces, tree-lined avenues and tangle of picturesque little streets. Take away all the Paris churches with the exceptions of Notre-Dame and the Sacré-Cœur, and the overall aspect of the city will be practically the same.

Most of the *real* Paris churches, Catholic of course, are rather sober affairs, looking as if they had known better days. Many were pillaged during the Revolution and consequently have little of the sumptuousness of their Italian or Spanish cousins. What few art treasures they still contain are badly lit and even worse publicised. Some churches don't even look like churches: witness that curious essay in Greek classicism, the Madeleine. Others that are built as churches, like the Panthéon, are secular edifices. As for what is probably the prettiest church in the city (its dome is certainly the loveliest), the Val-de-Grâce, it is about as Parisian as a Neapolitan pizza. The 6th arrondissement may contain the heart of Catholic/ intellectual Paris but its largest church, the Saint-Sulpice, is more like a huge grey tomb than a monument to a living faith and has a frankly puritanical air—a quality shared by many other Paris churches. It is one of the most prominent of the great churches (thereby qualifying as a 'monument') but it is still far from beautiful.

Even more prominent is the vast white basilica, the Sacré-Cœur, towering over the northern Paris skyline. Seen from a distance it has a certain fairy-tale charm but on close inspection it is just another huge monument built in a rather pedantic Romanesque-cum-Byzantine style. But of course, the most (deservedly) famous and prominent Paris church of all is Notre-Dame and it is with this great cathedral that we advise you to begin your tour of the city's churches. None will be as beautiful but they are all different and have their own curiosity, if not artistic, value. Moreover, the very fact that so many of them are so little explored should be a challenge to the lover of Paris ancient. And don't forget to take a torch. . . .

NOTRE-DAME, Paris 4.
One of the greatest and earliest Gothic cathedrals of Europe. So much has been written about it that all we shall say here is that it is now being scrubbed clean for the first time in its eight-hundred year life and that the best way to make a thorough visit is to join a group tour. To see Midnight Mass celebrated here at Christmas is an unforgettable experience. Medieval miracle plays were performed on the parvis outside during the Christmas season until a few years ago and may be resumed soon. The building was restored in the first half of the 19th century by the great French architect Viollet-le-Duc. Not many people know that the famous gargoyles are also his own work.

A brass compass inscribed *Kilomètre Zéro* is set in the parvis and all road distances in France are calculated from it.

SAINTE-CHAPELLE, off the boulevard du Palais, Ile de la Cité, Paris 1.
Generations of French schoolmasters have told their charges that this is a 'gem of Gothic art'. They are quite right. It was built, as a shrine, in less than 3 years by France's saint-king, Louis IX, after he had acquired the Crown of Thorns and a fragment of the True Cross from the commercially-minded Venetians. Although somewhat restored in the 19th century the stained glass is the oldest in Paris with over 1,000 Biblical scenes. There are two chapels: a lower with forty columns, and an upper, approached by a spiral staircase on the left. The whole structure is astonishingly delicate and is like a casket with jewelled, glowing windows—one of the most perfect reliquaries ever made. The actual relics are now in Notre-Dame.

SACRE-CŒUR, 37 rue du Cheval-de-la-Barre, Paris 18.
Stupefyingly huge and conspicuously ugly. 328 feet long, 164 feet wide; the dome is 197 feet high. Interior covered with lavish

mosaics and frescoes, all in uninspired late 19th-century–early 20th-century styles. You can visit the spacious crypt for 50 centimes and the dome for 1 franc. Magnificent view—which is what you have really come for anyway. The whole thing was built as an act of penitence and to symbolise national reconciliation after the 1870 war and the tragic Commune uprising of the following year, with more than 3 million subscribing to the building fund.

SAINT-PIERRE-DE-MONTMARTRE, 2 rue du Mont-Cenis, Paris 18.
Quite dwarfed by its horrid neighbour, the Sacré-Cœur, but one of the most historic Romanesque churches in Paris with a wonderful vaulted roof and beautifully carved Romanesque pillars and capitals.

CHAPELLE EXPIATOIRE DE LOUIS XVI, Square Louis-XVI, Paris 8.
Not really a church but built by order of Louis XVIII by Percier and Fontaine to commemorate the memory of Louis XVI and Marie-Antoinette who had been buried on this site (once the cemetery of the Madeleine) until they were removed to the basilica of Saint-Denis in 1815. Open every day in the afternoon (entrance is in the rue Pasquier) and well worth visiting for the statues of the unhappy royal pair. More than 3,000 victims of the Revolution and nearly 1,000 of the Swiss guards who died defending the Tuileries in 1792 are buried outside.

SAINT-AUGUSTIN, 46 boulevard Malesherbes, Paris 8.
Paris has no shortage of ugly churches. This one was built in the 1860's and is one of the more grandiose monstrosities.

SAINT-NICOLAS-DU-CHARDONNET, 30 rue Saint-Victoire, Paris 5.
One of the most interesting churches in the Latin Quarter. The exterior is unfinished and uninteresting but inside there are some magnificent paintings (a Crucifixion by Pieter Breughel II in the presbytery; works by 17th-century French artists) and a family chapel with beautiful statues by Charles Le Brun.

SAINT-NICOLAS-DES-CHAMPS, 254 rue Saint-Martin, Paris 3.
A Gothic church much altered in the late 16th century. The great attractions here are the south portal, the fine 14th-century altar-

piece with paintings of the Life of Christ and some superb French paintings of the 17th century.

SAINTE-MARGUERITE, 36 rue Saint-Bernard, Paris 11.
Worth going out of the way to this church in the east end of Paris for its curious wall paintings in the Chapelle des Ames du Purgatoire by the Italian 18th-century artist Brunetti and the presumed tomb of Louis XVII, the Dauphin, who may or may not have died in the Temple. Bones of a child and those of a young man were found in the tomb when it was dug up in the last century but like all good mysteries it is still unsolved.

SAINT-MERRI, 78 rue Saint-Martin, Paris 4.
Very pretty but badly restored façade in a late Gothic style and remains of fine carvings and 16th-century stained glass inside. The church bell is the oldest in Paris.

SAINT-DENIS-DU-SAINT-SACREMENT, 68 bis rue de Turenne, Paris 3.
An early 19th-century neo-Grecian style church with a fine front and probably the gloomiest interior of any church in Paris. Atmosphere of stifling melancholy guaranteed to produce instant depressions.

SAINTE-ELISABETH, 195 rue du Temple, Paris 3.
A 17th century church. Foundation stone laid by Marie de Medicis and many fine bas-reliefs and paintings which could be better lit and which were last cleaned in 1926.

SAINT-ROCH, 296 rue Saint-Honoré, Paris 1.
Another handsome baroque church. The foundation stone was laid by Louis XIV in 1653 and several other stones on the façade are still marked by cannon balls and bullets of the time young Bonaparte quelled an anti-government Royalist revolt there in October 1795 by mowing down the opposition with grapeshot. Numerous 17th- and 18th-century works of art inside but, glacial atmosphere.

SAINT-PAUL-SAINT-LOUIS, 99 rue Saint-Antoine, Paris 4.
Another fine example of the Italian 'Jesuit' style of church architecture in Paris. Lovely portal; painting by Delacroix (Christ on the Mount of Olives) in the left transept.

SAINTE-MADELEINE, Place de la Madeleine, Paris 8.

One of the biggest churches in Paris and, of course, a more or less exact copy of a classical Greek temple. It was begun in 1764; work was interrupted by the Revolution and then enthusiastically resumed under Napoleon who wanted to dedicate it as a 'Temple of Glory' to the soldiers of the Grand Army. It was only finished in 1842 and became one of Paris' smartest society churches (very chic for weddings). Gloomy inside and artistically quite undistinguished but good religious music can sometimes be heard there.

SAINT-LOUIS-DES-INVALIDES (Hôtel des Invalides), 2 avenue de Tourville, Paris 7.

Not to be confused with the Dôme des Invalides which contains Napoleon's Tomb. It was built at the same time as the Hôtel des Invalides and is as full of Napoleonic and military relics and tombs as you might expect. Flags, standards, banners everywhere inside, from Africa, Morocco, Crimea, etc., monuments to marshals and generals, and tombs in profusion. As you go in, on the right you can see the funeral carriage used for Napoleon at Saint Helena. In the Chapelle Napoléon: 3 flagstones from Napoleon's tomb at Saint Helena, his former copper sarcophagus and a death-mask.

SAINT-LOUIS-EN-L'ILE, 21 rue Saint-Louis-en-l'Ile, Paris 4.

A dark but very beautiful 17th-century church full of fine paintings and statues. It really is worth making the effort to see them. Take a torch.

SAINT-EUSTACHE (métro station: Halles).

What Notre-Dame is to Paris, Saint-Eustache is to the Halles district. Huge, imposing and still grimy on the outside, the church is a characteristically Parisian mixture of the French 'classical style', the Gothic and the Renaissance. Begun in 1532, completed in 1654 and then more or less rebuilt in the mid-18th century. During the Revolution a 'feast of Reason' was held there in 1793 and two years later it became a 'Temple of Agriculture'. A magnificent organ, sculptures galore and some fine stained glass windows. Fine concerts are held there. Louis XIV's great minister Colbert is buried in the first chapel to the left facing the apse behind the altar.

SAINT-GERMAIN-DE-CHARONNE, 4 place Saint-Blaise, Paris 20.
One of the prettiest and oldest churches in Paris. It was begun in
the 11th century in full Romanesque style, is the only church in
Paris to have kept its graveyard around it and still looks what it was
for so many centuries: a country church.

SAINT-GERMAIN-DES-PRES, 3 Place Saint-Germain-des-Prés,
Paris 6.
The oldest church in Paris with its Romanesque tower of the 11th–
12th centuries. Full of ancient carvings but largely restored inside
in the 19th century. The little patch of greenery to the north of the
church is full of fragments of sculptures from a former Lady Chapel
of the 13th century built in the grounds of the old abbey of Saint-
Germain-des-Prés.

SAINT-SULPICE, Place Saint-Sulpice, Paris 6.
A gigantic monster of a church dwarfing the square in front of it
in the heart of 'pious Paris'. It is rather funereal and the unfinished
tower looks even sinister, particularly at night, but it is famous for
two great fresco-paintings by Delacroix—Jacob fighting with the
Angel and Heliodorus expelled from the Temple—in the first
chapel on the right as you go in. If you can get hold of the sacristan,
ask to see the huge crypts underneath, with remnants of an earlier
church.

VAL DE GRACE, 277 rue Saint-Jacques, Paris 5.
The prettiest, most Italianate dome in Paris. It was originally
designed after Saint Peter's at Rome by the great architect François
Mansart and the massive altar with its six twisting columns was
inspired by Bernini's altar in Saint Peter's. Great fresco by Pierre
Mignard in the dome. The church is often illuminated at night, and
if you stand at the end of the rue Val de Grâce on the Boulevard
Saint-Michel at night and look down at the face, the view is
breathtakingly beautiful.

SAINT-GERMAIN-L'AUXERROIS, 2 Place du Louvre, Paris 1.
One of the most famous churches in Paris. Its bells gave the signal
for the start of the massacre of Protestants on Saint Bartholomew's
Eve, August 24th, 1572. Marvellous medieval Gothic sculptures, a
gilt-wood altar-piece and some stained glass. The two portals of
the transept are particularly fine.

SAINT-LEU-ET-SAINT-GILLES, 92 rue Saint-Denis, Paris 1.
One of Paris's really dark and gloomy churches, but full of fine sculptures if you can see in the dark.

SAINT-SEVERIN, 1 rue des Prêtres-Saint-Séverin, Paris 5.
One of the most beautiful and curious Gothic churches in Paris. Besides being a centre for good works, with a soup kitchen in its cloister well-known to *clochards* and visiting beatniks, it was a great favourite with writers like Huysmans and the late 19th-century 'Satanists'. Revealingly, most of the old second-hand bookshops nearby specialise in alchemy and black magic. Concerts and occasional exhibitions of sculpture in the cloister and grounds.

SAINT-ETIENNE-DU-MONT, 1 place Sainte-Geneviève, Paris 5.
A curious exterior: great medley of different styles of the Gothic and Renaissance periods. Inside, the wonderful rood-screen is famous and unique, concerts are held; an archbishop of Paris was murdered here in 1857 by a defrocked priest and more little old ladies in black seem to come here than to any other church in Paris.

SAINT-GERVAIS-ET-SAINT-PROTAIS, 2 rue François Miron, Paris 4.
Now thoroughly cleaned up and beautiful. A fine 17th-century façade and Gothic interior. A splendid organ and many important concerts. The choir of Saint-Gervais is particularly worth hearing. The church was hit by a German shell in March 1918 when 75 worshippers were killed and a large part of the roof had to be restored.

SAINT-JULIEN-LE-PAUVRE, 1 rue Saint-Julien-le-Pauvre, Paris 5.
Originally a 12th-century Gothic church which lost its portal and tower in 1675. It was used as a chapel for the old Hôtel-Dieu, but since 1889 it has been used for the Byzantine Catholic rites.

SAINT-MEDARD, 141 rue Mouffetard, Paris 5.
A lovely old church built between the 15th and 17th centuries, with a somewhat curious history. It was taken over by Protestants for a while in December 1561 and in the 18th century the 'Convulsionists' of the Jansenist sect danced wildly over the deacon's tomb to the great scandal of the faithful. It is all very sedate now and concerts are held from time to time.

NOTRE-DAME-DES-VICTOIRES, Place des Petits-Pères, Paris 2.
Commissioned by King Louis XIII to celebrate the capture of La
Rochelle from the Protestants, and built in an Italian Baroque
Jesuit style but only finished in the early 18th century. It was used
as a Stock Exchange during the Revolution, but now its gloomy
interior is particularly famous for its wealth of ex-votos—more than
30,000 of them.

SAINTE-CLOTILDE, 23 bis rue Las-Cases, Paris 7.
A curious example of 19th-century French neo-Gothic architecture
facing a rather English looking square. The organ is probably the
finest feature of the church. César Franck and Gabriel Fauré used
to play there.

Passy Cemetery

The Flea Market (Le Marché aux Puces)

Every great capital has its 'flea market': the Portobello Road in London, the Porta Portese in Rome, the Rastro in Madrid . . . Paris' 'marché aux puces' isn't what it once was, but what Flea Market ever is? Of course most of the dealers are experts; of course they're not likely to let a masterpiece go for a song. But you never know. . . . It might happen—and that's why you go there, hopefully hunting for that dust-covered rare first edition or that pair of 17th-century candlesticks. Or else, you go for the sheer fun of it all, because it is picturesque, because you can always find something amusing, because there's always some sort of bargain. . . .

A haphazard conglomeration of stalls, tables, stands and sheds—this will probably be your first impression of the Paris Flea Market. Yet if you look a little closer you will detect an order underlying the disorder that is one of the attractions of any junk market. Paris's Flea Market has its history, its tradition and its own rules.

About a century ago, the rag-and-bone men who sold old rags, scrap iron and various worthless odds and ends were expelled by the city authorities from their habitual sites in the city. They settled outside the city limits near the Porte de Clignancourt, in the north of Paris on a waste land, by permission of the military governor of Paris who was the proprietor. The picturesque medley of objects for sale, mostly rescued from dustbins and scrap heaps, soon attracted the attention of visitors avid for 'slumming' and professional junk men. After the amateurs came the professionals. Sensing that the site was becoming something of a fashionable attraction—dance halls and fairground attractions were set up—they decided to make it their permanent home. The rumour soon went around Paris that you could find outstanding bargains at the 'Puces', that if you were lucky you might pick up an old master for a song, discover antique furniture that simply needed a little cleaning and restoration to regain its original splendour, etc. It became 'the thing' to make a visit to the Puces. In about 1920, Romain Vernaison, the owner of a piece of land near the Porte de Clignancourt, had the bright idea of building wooden booths and shanties which he rented out to the junk men. The first of the many 'markets' of the Puces' was born.

Others soon followed: the *Marché Biron*, the *Marché Malik*, the *Marché Paul-Bert* and the *Marché Jules Vallès*. Together with the *Vernaison* there were five markets in all with a total of 2000 stands, not counting the pavement displays which continue to give the Puces its agreeably confused appearance.

Today, the Saint-Ouen flea market covers an area of about 125 acres between the avenue Michelet, the new peripheral boulevard, and the rue Lécuyer. The market is open on Saturdays, Sundays and Mondays—when the calm of the humble working-class suburb is shattered by the arrival of a crowd of sightseers and collectors. The atmosphere of the market varies according to which day it is: on Saturday dawn brings the professional antique dealers—mostly Parisian—on the look-out for a 'find', and then collectors of knick-knacks who spend the whole day quietly hunting through the stalls in search of some single object; Sunday brings the crowds *en famille*—children, grandchildren and grandparents in the best Paris Sunday outing tradition. On Monday the market is relatively calm again and you'll find that the junk men are likely to lower their prices rather than have to carry away their bulkier wares, but by then, of course, the choice is smaller.

When is the best time to go to the Puces?

If you are looking for anything special you couldn't do better than to get up early and join the dealers on Saturday morning. If you simply want to stroll through the market to savour the atmosphere, with the hope of finding something unusual or a rare bargain—then you couldn't do better than to go on a Monday. But, as a general rule, *never* go on Sundays unless you like crowds.

You can find just about everything at the Puces. Whether you're looking for a Venetian chandelier, an Aztec piece of statuary, a Montenegrin medal, a Paris postal almanack for 1889, you may be sure of finding it somewhere. Everything is there. Prices are correspondingly varied. In the space of a few yards you can buy an unpainted wardrobe for thirty or forty francs or a Louis XV signed *commode* for several thousands—and this is the tragedy of the Puces today. What began as an authentic junk market is now tending to become a vast open-air antique fair.

The sad truth is that several of the shrewder Paris antique dealers with shops in the smartest Paris districts have realised that many Parisians who might hesitate to buy a really valuable piece on the rue du Faubourg Saint-Honoré are more likely to buy exactly the same thing if it is displayed amid the picturesque disorder of a 'flea market'. The price may be the same but the distinction is important. Snobbery makes people buy and the Puces is *chic*. The result is that a large part of the Puces—particularly the *Marché Biron*—is no longer a junk market. This does not mean that it has lost its interest—on the contrary a real collector will find a remarkable variety of rare and fine *objets d'art* in a restricted area and be sure that their authenticity is beyond doubt. Some of the more expensive stands even make a point of displaying the odd and amusing trifle at a reasonable price. So don't be too discouraged: even if you aren't going to furnish your country house from top to bottom with wares from the market you may still pick up something intriguing and have the agreeable sensation of discovery.

For the *real* Puces, go to the rue Lécuyer, the rue Jules Vallès or the *Marché Malik*. They are not exclusively junk markets but they are the heart of the old Puces. There a dealer specialising in Ming porcelain may one day buy the contents of a whole attic and offer you a rocking-horse or a broken accordion. Junk has a way of drifting everywhere throughout the market.

Go to the Puces in a spirit of adventure. First make a quick tour of the big, permanent markets, the *Biron* and the *Vernaison*, leaving yourself time to go back later. Then hunt through the stalls at your leisure but remember that not everything you see is for sale. The bookseller in the rue Lécuyer who specialises in out-of-print paperback thrillers also displays a magnificent collection of copper wares. Don't ask him their price—they are his personal collection and they help to bring people to his stand.

Never forget that a dealer at the Puces has his whims: he may readily sell you the chair he's sitting on but refuse to let go his magnificent grandfather clock simply because he wants to be able to tell the time that day.

The Flea Market is more than a commercial gathering: it is a fiercely individualistic world of its own. Don't worry about being a foreign tourist: xenophobia is unknown to the dealers. If the dealer likes your face or is having one of his good days he may well bring out some hitherto hidden treasure or lower his prices appreciably. On the other hand, he may sulk and do everything to discourage you from buying something that you've set your heart upon.

Can you haggle at the Puces? Certainly. With very few exceptions, there are no fixed prices. As a general rule, you can knock at least 10 per cent off the price asked. If the dealer likes you, then you'll pay even less. But never forget he's doing a job: don't ever try to make an obviously, ridiculously low offer after he's given you a price: you will only irritate him and he will refuse to lower his first price by one *centime*. To be a good buyer, you must be a good psychologist. And don't forget that on Mondays many dealers will be only too happy to do business at the very last minute and will let things go for prices they would have pronounced absurd on the previous Saturday.

Many newcomers to the Puces still succumb to the myth that if you're lucky enough, you may pick up a masterpiece for a song. That's one hope you would do well to abandon at once, all ye who enter here! You might just as well expect to find the Crown Jewels in the gutter. But *do* take a good look at some of the dust-covered objects you may see laid out on the pavements of the rue Lécuyer by one of those semi-down-and-out dealers who seem to specialise in old boots and spectacle frames. One friend of ours was lucky enough to pick up a splendid 18th-century silver tureen for a few francs, so don't be put off by dirt or dust. There is still the chance that it's hiding something worth while.

Although most people come to the Puces to buy, you can also sell there. If, at the end of your stay in Paris, you find yourself down and out, you can at least try to buy yourself your last meal or night in a hotel by selling your clothes. There's only one snag: to prevent stolen goods being sold, the law obliges the buyer to go to the seller's home. Nonetheless, if you go through the *Marché Malik* carefully you will eventually find someone who'll take your *suède* jacket or shoes and no questions asked.

You may now have spent the entire day at the Puces; you have acquired a French Romantic painting, a mahogany-mounted cigarette lighter, a set of false teeth, a fake *Art Nouveau* vase and a Florentine statuette, but have you *really* discovered the soul of the Puces? You will not have discovered its secrets and you may not have understood what it is that still makes it a world apart, a charming but anachronistic survival from the Paris of last century. If you want the true atmosphere of the Puces, then go into one of the many little *bistrots* frequented by the junk dealers who go in for a quick drink between sales. Go and drink a glass of red wine— ordinary *vin rouge*, for the Puces are anything but gastronomically distinguished—and you may understand why so many people come to the Puces not to buy but just for the love of it. At lunch-time, go to *Chez Louisette* in the *Marché Vernaison*, and try her *Bœuf gros*

Flea Market at Clignacourt

sel or *Moules marinières.* You can listen to an accordion being played in the company of working girls out with their boyfriends, sharp businessmen and well-known painters. It is there that you will savour an old-fashioned, traditional France—the France of the thirties, of the films of Carné and René Clair, a France that still manages to survive between the towering housing estates and the outer motorway.

A last warning: the Puces is the one place in Paris where you can still fall victim to the three-card-trick player—a swindle as old as it is skilful.

Although the Saint-Ouen Flea Market is, by definition, *the* Puces, it is by no means the only one in Paris. You will find similar 'flea markets' at the Porte de Montreuil (20th arrondissement), Bicêtre (Porte d'Italie) and the Porte Didot (14th). They are all miniature Puces, consisting only of a few pavement stalls along the boulevards. Even so, a miraculously good bargain is still possible. Unfortunately, these Puces are living out their last days as they are condemned by yet another motorway. The rag-and-bone merchants and junk-men there will be driven away but no doubt you'll meet them all again at Saint-Ouen.

Lastly, *do* visit the *Foire à la Ferraille* on the Boulevard Richard Lenoir, near the Bastille, if you are in Paris when it is held (twice a year: for nine days following the first Saturday in October and the nine days preceding Palm Sunday). Besides various sellers of cooked meats—whose presence remains something of a mystery— you will find rather more than 500 junk dealers who still uphold the authentic traditions of the Flea Market. It is there, perhaps, that you will find the *real* Puces.

Snob's Paris

Even if you aren't born one, you can acquire the outward signs and attributes of the real Paris snob by a judicious choice of where you hold your bank account, buy your ties, shoes, food, luxuries, necessities and trivia. Should your ambitions lie in this direction, here are a few tips and good addresses.

The status-requirements of the upper crust of any well-established society generally represent significant national characteristics. Englishmen of some social standing have long been reputed to prefer to wear clothes that are obviously not new; in recent years, however, a few such Englishmen have begun to follow more studiously the trends of sartorial fashion, if only to distinguish themselves from the mass of way-out younger people who masquerade in old clothes. In Madrid, too, it had been considered at all times *cursi* or 'in bad taste' to be too well-dressed; a diplomatic incident was only narrowly avoided a few years ago, when drab Señora Franco, on the occasion of an official visit, turned her nose up at elegant Evita Perón and muttered under her breath the damning word: '*Cursi!*'

The French upper class has long expressed, in many of its traditions and tastes, a preference for everything that smacks of the *Ancien Régime*, that is to say of the long-defunct French monarchy. The most elegant Parisian homes are thus to be found in some of the most ancient and dilapidated sections of the city: in the Ile Saint-Louis, in the Right Bank Marais, in the Left Bank faubourg Saint-Germain or in the area around the faubourg Saint-Honoré. However, with the growing shortage of available eighteenth-century homes, it has become acceptable, in recent years, to live in an apartment-house built even in the Art Nouveau style of *La Belle Epoque* around 1900. Only an ignorant foreigner or a social pariah would dream, in Paris, of living in one of the luxurious new suburban developments that flaunt all modern conveniences.

Ever since the French Revolution, the more snobbish representatives of the middle classes that it emancipated have preferred to live in the old *hôtels* or palaces that the great aristocratic families had built under the monarchy. This preference extends to adopting quite a number of other habits and customs of the way of life of the

Ancien Régime or at least of a good fifty years ago. Thus, in spite of the many political revolutions of the past two hundred and fifty years and of the recurring financial and economic crises, Paris remains one of the world's most conservative capitals. In order to be considered acceptable in good French society, a foreigner, whether a tourist or a resident, must adapt his own tastes and way of life to those of the French *élite* with which he seeks to associate.

One should be careful, for instance, to avoid choosing to live in any hotel that is less than fifty years old. In the luxury class, the Ritz, still haunted by the ghost of Marcel Proust; the Meurice, once patronized by royal families that nearly all live in exile today; the Crillon, which still has eighteenth-century *boiseries* on the walls of some of its rooms; the Saint-James et Albany, with its charming small garden; the Continental, with its flamboyant turn-of-the-century Oriental lounge; and the Lancaster, frequented by Anita Loos and the survivors of the Gin Age, all these socially recommendable; on the Left Bank, the Lutetia also has a certain turn-of-the-century charm, though it appears to have gradually succumbed to invasion from Madison Avenue which had already made the Hôtel du Pont-Royal an outpost of New York's expense-account society. Among the more modest hotels, the Pas-de-Calais and the Saints-Pères, both on the rue des Saints-Pères, the Hôtel d'Angleterre, in the rue Jacob, and the Hôtel de Suède, 15 Quai Saint-Michel, have a quiet distinction that can only add to your prestige.

If you intend to stay longer in Paris and decide to rent a furnished apartment, you must insist on its having precarious plumbing; if it happens to be in a building that has an elevator, the latter should be an ancient hydraulic collector's item that functions only intermittently, and then very slowly; when it descends, it should always release a heart-rending groan or a sigh such as one might well hear at midnight in a haunted castle. Modern garbage-chutes are absolutely taboo.

Though the best people in Paris generally pay cash for everything, or have charge-accounts, some have at long last adopted the deplorable Anglo-Saxon habit of paying by cheque. But many French tradesmen still expect all cheques to bounce. Should a foreigner be rash enough to flaunt a cheque-book, it should be one from a long-established private bank. Unless you happen to be Swiss, you would scarcely be expected to bank with any of the older Protestant banks, such as Mallet Frères et Compagnie, Neuflize, Schlumberger et

Théâtre Palais-Royal

Compagnie, Odier, Bungener, Courvoisier et Compagnie, or Hottinguer et Compagnie, some of which have been in business in Paris and Geneva since before 1789, nor indeed with any of France's ancient provincial banks, such as Varin Bernier et Compagnie. But you will always impress favourably by drawing your cheques on Rothschild Frères, or Heine et Compagnie, a firm that was founded by a first-cousin of the poet Heinrich Heine, or on Morgan et Compagnie, should any of these agree to handle your account.

Nothing can be more damning than to offer your guests, in your home, such new-fangled beverages as Scotch or canned fruit-juice. For close on a hundred years it has been fashionable in the best French homes to offer—and to refuse—a none-too-appetizing

mixture of sweetened fresh orange-juice and tepid water, or of water with a thick and very sweet fruit-syrup bottled either by Tanrade, who have a shop in the rue Vignon, or by Hédiard, Place de la Madeleine. The only socially acceptable canned foods are sardines, tuna-fish and, oddly enough, green peas; goose-liver should always be purchased in a sealed stoneware jar, as should some kinds of mustard.

Modern art, displayed at home, is highly suspect. The best people in France purchase contemporary art, only, if at all, as an investment which they exhibit as unwillingly as they would their holdings in income-bearing and taxable securities. Exceptions are, however, such paintings and sculptures as happen to be gifts made to you by

I

artists who are personal friends. Should you own a Picasso, you should have purchased it before 1930, at a time when only lunatics dared invest even small sums in such controversial work. Society surgeons or dentists may on the other hand display in their homes examples of the most up-to-date abstract art, provided that these have been received from the artist in payment for some dentures or a prostate operation.

A good bookstore to patronize is Galignani's, at 224 rue de Rivoli. It was founded around 1800 and Lord Byron is reputed to have been one of its customers. In spite of this, Galignani's department of pornography offers a less varied choice of *erotica* than most other bookstores in its immediate vicinity. When Bulwer Lytton wrote *Pelham*, describing the life of an ideal and fictional dandy of over a hundred years ago, he made his hero buy his newspapers and books from Galignani's, which also published, in those days, the European continent's only English-language gazette, *Galignani's Messenger*, of which the novelist Thackeray was a sub-editor, in the more impecunious and inglorious years of his expatriate youth. The Galignani family, before moving from Italy via London to Paris, had also published books, in Latin or Italian, as early as 1520, mainly in Padua.

For your visiting-cards, for the engraved livery-buttons of your footmen (if you can still find any to employ), and for your personal note-paper, the firm of Agry, heraldic engravers at 14 rue de Castiglione, can offer you a fund of professional experience acquired since 1825 in handling this kind of order for sixteen thousand of the world's leading families, including most of the French nobility and even an occasional Indian Nawab or Rajah. The installation of Agry's diminutive but exquisite store is moreover a perfect example of interior decoration of the style which, between 1820 and 1830, characterized the reign of King Charles x of France.

Lovers of antique commercial interior decoration will likewise purchase their tea, coffee, chocolate and vanilla from the firm of Debauve et Gallais which, at 30 rue des Saints-Pères, still displays one of Europe's most perfect eighteenth-century shop-fronts and interiors.

At 233 rue Saint-Honoré, you can still order your trunks, suitcases and other travel-goods from Goyard Aîné, a firm that was founded in 1792 and presumably profited at the very start from a boom when half the aristocracy of France had to buy trunks and pack its valuables in a hurry to seek refuge from the Revolution in

London, in the many princely courts of Germany or in distant St. Petersburg.

Any gentleman of refinement and culture who needs a shave or a hair-cut must feel bound to patronize, at 18 rue Saint-Roch, the *coiffeur* whose tiny shop, founded in 1630, protrudes like a wart from the outside wall of the church of Saint-Roch. With the present trend towards less sober male fashions, this heir to the traditions of a true contemporary of the immortal Figaro can be expected to know how to powder a periwig, should our Flower-children decide to revive such a long-extinct mode.

Time passes, but your alarm-clock can be purchased only from Bréguet, 28 Place Vendôme, *Horlogers de la Marine et de l'Aéronautique*. Long before the hand-painted rococo balloons of the eighteenth century allowed the first aeronauts to rise triumphantly above breathless crowds of spectators, Bréguet was already manufacturing clocks and watches. Before the word *diversification* had been coined by management consultants, Bréguet had begun to manufacture precision-instruments, much as the firm of Peugeot, which began work as makers of grinders for pepper and coffee, later diversified its production and manufactured bicycles, and then automobiles. The best families in France thus own clocks that have ticked in their homes for over two centuries, except when, every few years, they have been returned briefly to Bréguet's workshop to be cleaned or otherwise serviced.

One can indeed still live in Paris, in many respects, as if time had stood still since 1788, or at least since *La Belle Epoque*, when Russian bonds were considered a safe investment. If you can afford it in terms of time and money, you can make a sport of patronizing only those Parisian hotels, restaurants and other places that are at least fifty years old, if not a hundred or more. After partaking of a perfect gourmet's lunch in the magnificent *Art Nouveau* setting of Maxim's, you may saunter from the rue Royale to the rue de la Paix to buy a diamond necklace from Mellerio dit Meller, at 9 rue de la Paix. Probably the oldest firm of jewellers in the world, Mellerio, which was in business four hundred years ago in the rue des Lombards, has supplied to the archbishopric of Paris, in the last few centuries, many of the masterpieces of the goldsmith's and silversmith's art that are now displayed to tourists in the *Trésor* of Notre-Dame Cathedral. And should you happen to own one of the late James Dean's wisdom-teeth, only Mellerio can be trusted to design an appropriate reliquary for it.

Bookshops

Book-shops and browsing in them are two of the many joys of Paris. Several of the best Left Bank shops are open until ten or even midnight and the variety is amazing. There are book-shops for would-be magicians, for science-fiction addicts, for revolutionaries, for Poles, Italians, Americans and English, Spaniards, surrealists, artists, cooks and collectors of old comics, pulp magazines and everything else. Here are a few of them.

Paris still has just about everything the confirmed bibliophile could wish for. The tradition of the 'book beautiful' is strong, and luxurious volumes illustrated with signed lithographs and etchings by well-known (and world-famous) modern artists are regularly produced. For the serious book-collector, there are antiquarian booksellers specialising in everything from fine early Voltaire editions to a complete set of illustrated Jules Verne editions and for the science-fiction addict in search of rare numbers of *Weird Tales* or *Astounding Science Fiction*, there are one or two highly specialised shops for a clientèle that reads English just as much as French. And then, there is always the pleasure of just browsing and where better to browse on a fine day than in the stalls alongside the Seine?

Unfortunately, the *bouquinistes* of the quay-sides are no longer what they used to be. This most famous aspect of biliophiles' Paris has become complacent and irremediably commercial. Ten years ago, so book-hunters say, you could hope to find some rare edition of an illustrated 18th-century novel, a valuable old print, or a 'curiosity', all for a few francs. Now, the best you can hope for is some 19th-century ephemera, or a set of 18th-century colour plates— probably more expensive than in a shop. Most *bouquinistes* seem content to stock cellophane-wrapped remainder copies, evilly printed editions of the French classics, and thousands of books so unreadable that the publishers could seem only to have been running a charity for hopeful authors. And, of course, there are the 'dirty books', mostly at prices rather more outrageous than the contents. The centre of the pornographic book trade is no longer Paris and customers now go to London, Amsterdam and, best of all, Copenhagen.

All the Seine *bouquinistes* can offer by way of 'dirty books' are old copies of Henry Miller, French translations of the *Kama Sutra* and a selection of anodyne works with alluring titles like *The Pleasures of Voluptuousness* or *Sisters of Sappho*—about as 'naughty' as the Folies-Bergère. One bookseller near the Senate is still supposed to keep a stock of 'licentious literature' for octogenarian senators to read during debates, but you will be ill-received if you ask a bookseller to show you anything 'spicy'. The best you can hope for are some of Maurice Girodias' *Olympia Press* titles, on sale in all the main bookshops. Really pornographic and erotic French books are jealously kept by a few antiquarian booksellers for French collectors only. They are for home consumption. *L'amour* is no longer a prime French export. Book-hunting in Paris now certainly is an 'innocent pleasure' but none the less worthwhile for that.

If you simply want something to read in English during your stay in Paris, W. H. SMITH in the rue de Rivoli and BRENTANO'S in the avenue de l'Opéra have the best stocks. For paper-backs, the best places are the basement of BRENTANO'S and the NOUVEAU QUARTIER LATIN, 78 boulevard Saint-Michel. They get everything – or almost everything from England and the States. For French paperbacks, *the* place is LA POCHADE (157 boulevard Saint-Germain) and for French books generally, the centre of the trade is around Saint-Germain-des-Prés and the Latin Quarter. LA HUNE (170 boulevard Saint-Germain) and LE DIVAN (Place Bonaparte) specialise in fine modern editions and art books in French and English. On the Boulevard Saint-Michel, the LIBRAIRIE 73 (at the same number) has everything for the student and a good selection of 'serious' non-fiction in both French and English. The JOIE DE LIRE (rue Saint-Séverin) is open till midnight every day except Sunday, and has everything for the budding revolutionary: it also has the largest selection of political books in Paris and the owner, Monsieur François Maspero, was the victim of several right-wing plastic bomb attempts during the dark days of the Algerian war. Near by, facing the Seine and Notre-Dame, Mr. Whitehead's SHAKESPEARE & COMPANY bookshop (English and American books) continues the traditions of the twenties and thirties. Young poets and writers are still welcomed and a limited number of homeless expatriates can even be put up for a night or two (the shop sleeps seven). Unfortunately the atmosphere is a little self-conscious.

For really rare and valuable old books, go to DURTAL (open in the afternoons only) in rue Jacob (number 6), LARDANCHET (100 faubourg Saint-Honoré), PIERRE CHRETIEN (178 faubourg Saint-Honoré), LES ARCADES (8 rue de Castiglione) and E. LOEWY (184 boulevard Haussmann). If you want old religious works in French (you might), the centre is in and around the rue Saint-Sulpice. The shops in and near the rue Saint-Séverin specialise in magic and alchemy. ALAIN BRIEUX (48 rue Jacob) has a wonderful collection of old scientific and medical books and Madame Simone Barbier at the LIBRAIRIE SIMONE BARBIER (14 rue de l'Université) has everything you could wish for on Paris.

For works in English and French on the cinema, the 'odd', the bizarre and the erotic (works of the Marquis de Sade) and American comics (*Mad* magazine, *Batman*, etc.) go to the delightful MINOTAURE in the rue des Beaux-Arts or the TERRAIN VAGUE in the rue de Verneuil. They specialise in everything 'way-out'. The MANDRAGORE in the rue des Grands-Augustins specialises in thrillers and old detective stories—mostly in French—and CLAUDE LABARRE has old children's books as well as a charming collection of antique toys and games (22 rue Dauphine). For 'horror film' and comic addicts, JEAN BOULLET has a very odd shop indeed in the rue du Château. He would like to know if you have any old children's books you want to dispose of—parcutilarly with illustrations (Kate Greenaway, Beatrix Potter, Arthur Rackham). For browsing and just 'books'— you'll find every sort of bookshop from the dingy to the luxurious near the boulevard Montparnasse, the Latin Quarter near the Bibliothèque Nationale, and between the boulevard Saint-Germain and the river. Good hunting!

Woman's Paris

Paris is a 'woman's city', made to flatter feminine vanity and to cater to every woman's whim—so they say.

A woman in Paris may not only come for clothes. She may have her problems. Where to have their hair done? Where to go if she's about to have a baby? How to cope with just living in Paris?

The author has lived as a foreigner in Paris for many years. She had to find out almost everything for herself. Now she's going to help you.

Paris has always been, and is still, a woman's city, providing you set out on the right foot—or with the right person. Some women hate it. These are usually professional or businesswomen who find Paris a battleground of erratic telephones and closed obstinate faces determined to resist any fast modern method. But for a woman with time on her hands, even if it is only a snatched week-end, Paris can produce the kind of feminine pleasure that is a combination of smells, sounds, looking one's best (or the illusion of doing so) and an almost nineteenth-century conformism that shatters many a forward-looking English mind.

To start out on the right foot, one should have a Parisian look. And this can be acquired easily, if expensively, at a really Parisian Beauty Salon, such as Carita, Guerlain or Orlane, the three best. This is not to decry E. Arden or H. Rubenstein, but their salons are pretty much the same all the world over and their finished product is international, not Parisian.

The Parisian look is understated and casual with the right scent being far more important than heavy blue eyeshadow. An elegant Frenchwoman would rather wear a sweater to a dinner party than a too décolletée overdressed cocktail outfit.

Of the three salons mentioned, Carita's, 11 faubourg Saint-Honoré, is the most fun. Their beauty care is excellent. Presided over by Mme Dulac, they have a variety of special herb and plant lotions that Madame has spent years in perfecting. One of the few salons who will send you out with a really natural as opposed to a made-up look.

Guerlain, 68 Champs-Elysées, has the best scent smells. All their beauty products are scented with the various Guerlain perfumes and great attention is paid to allergic or delicate skins. Their shops in the Champs-Elysées and at 2 Place Vendôme and 29 rue de Sèvres on the Left Bank are unique. The assistants will spray their scents on to special pads for you, advise and cosset. An hour spent in choosing just the right scent will not be considered by anybody as a waste of their valuable time.

Orlane, 163 avenue Victor Hugo, is the most modern of the three. They go in for the very French idea that you shock your face and body with high powered jets of icy water or vapour. Their make-up is very light with a speciality of very good sun creams and ski make-up.

HAIRDRESSERS

If you feel shy and the reverse of glamorous pluck up your courage and go to the Carita Hair salon, 11 faubourg Saint-Honoré or their branch at the Hôtel Hilton, avenue de Suffren. The two Carita sisters, Maria and Rosie are a voluble pair who work in their own salon and all their assistants take trouble to make a woman look her best.

Maria Carita, with a voice like a whip-lash, believes that any woman has the right to look her best and the harder the case the more trouble is taken.

It all costs money, at least three times what you would pay in London.

Gin, 47 rue Bonaparte, specialises in eccentrics. Her salon is full of a wonderful collection of bric-à-brac. She enjoys creating the kind of style that will cause a stir at a party and will then happily brush it all out for you the following day into a more wearable look at no extra cost.

Jacques Dessange, 37 avenue Franklin Roosevelt, is the specialist in wigs of all kinds. You can borrow one for the evening for just over £2.

Madeleine Plaz, 1 avenue du Président Wilson, has a deserved reputation for dyeing and tinting, particularly for what the French call 'mèches', streaked hair giving a sunburst effect.

Desfosse, 19 avenue Matignon, has a team of expert cutters. As might be expected, specialises in short styles. The salon also has a male beauty specialist who has created his own eyelash dye claimed to be resistant to sea water.

A WOMAN ON HER OWN

A woman on her own can go happily into almost any café or restaurant, even the most luxurious, but should avoid hotel bars. These are considered the preserve of ladies prepared and even eager to find a companion for the evening.

The top luxury restaurants do not freeze out the single woman, but treat her with courtesy and attention.

René Lasserre of Lasserre, 17 avenue Franklin Roosevelt, perhaps the most chic and expensive of the three-star group, makes a special point of seeing that a solitary woman diner is well looked after.

He says 'The sort of woman who comes here on her own is someone who would automatically choose this class of restaurant or who comes because she longs for a gourmet meal—in either case we see that she feels happy.'

On the other end of the scale it is better to choose a fairly large brasserie type restaurant than the 'little *bistrots*'. Principally because the *bistrot* type restaurant tends to have a regular clientèle and if it is good they like to cram as many people to a table as possible.

You can sit on a café terrace and be unmolested but not in a public garden or the Bois de Boulogne.

You would not get into the two ultra-chic night clubs Régine or Castel on your own unless you personally knew either Régine or Castel. You could go to a Chansonnier like La Tête de l'Art, 5 avenue de l'Opéra, or the famous bar Echelle de Jacob, 10 rue Jacob, which used to be the kind of place where new singers were discovered. It is still worth a visit and an evening can be spent sitting quietly watching a procession of singers, mimes and comedians, some good, some bad. Of course, there is always The Lido if all else fails. The show is slick. You must book a table and a woman on her own would tend to get badly placed.

IF YOU GET INTO ANY TROUBLE OR ARE STRANDED

Do not automatically assume that the Embassy will bail you out. The consular section get very tetchy with tourists who run out of money. What they do is give you a voucher for a ticket (usually the most uncomfortable route) and then give you quite explicit instructions on how to pay them back.

IF YOU GET SICK

or are about to have a baby. Ring the British Hospital, 48 rue de Villiers, Levallois, tel: 737 52-58.

The switchboard girls speak English and they have a large and well-run maternity ward. They have a special hospital service at the disposal of all tourists as well as a service of private doctors speaking English. They will accept payment in Sterling or any arrangement you can make to pay in England. This is a voluntary hospital run by private contribution.

Most Paris hotels have a doctor whom they will call in for you if you need one. You will have to pay him in Francs, though, and on the spot.

If you are sick, but transportable, Air France will always get you a seat on the next plane and organise a car-ambulance to take you to the airport. You just call the main Air France office: 535 66-00.

WHERE TO STAY

If your idea of Paris is book stalls, art students, night clubs and cheap restaurants, choose:

Hôtel Angleterre, 44 rue Jacob.

In a street packed with antique shops and atmosphere. Quiet well-kept hotel. Prices start at £2 10s. for a single room without bath.

Mont Blanc, 28 rue de la Huchette.

Noisy but cheap. The street is full of jazz clubs and wandering beatniks. Prices start at £2 for a single room.

Hôtel de Suède, 15 Quai St-Michel.

View of the Seine but this adds to the price of the room. Single room without bath, around £3.

If you have slightly more money:

Hôtel Port-Royal or *Montalembert*, next door to each other in the rue du Bac.

Prices start at just over £4 for a single room. Nearly all the rooms have baths or showers.

If you want peace and quiet in costly beautiful surroundings tucked away so that no-one would think of finding you there try:

La Résidence du Bois, 16 rue Chalgrin, 16th arrondissement.

This is a small private mansion with antique furniture and there is a private garden. The smallest room would cost between £5 and £6 a night, the most luxurious, £15.

Résidence Foch, 10 rue Marbeau, also 16th arrondissement.
Small hotel of great elegance. A single room would cost between £6 and £8 a night. Guests are made to feel that they are staying in a luxurious private house.

Boutique/Gallery, boulevard Saint-Germain

Women's Clothes

Where to buy. Where and how to see the latest fashions. Where to acquire Parisian chic. Boutiques and haute couture.

Some fashion journalists have complained in recent years that Paris is no longer what it was in the world of high fashion. French housewives come to England for Marks and Spencer's. Clothes are expensive in Paris— very often more than twice what you would pay in London. But still, Paris always manages to turn up with something surprising—out of the ordinary, amusing, or outrageous—and at their best, French clothes still have that 'something' you won't find elsewhere.

And even if you can't afford the clothes, you can always enjoy the window-shopping.

The *Haute Couture* is still far and away the best thing that Paris has to offer any woman interested in clothes. Obviously very few women can afford to buy a made-to-measure dress from a big House, but it is not all that difficult to get an invitation to see a show if you avoid the main collection times. All you need is a passport to prove that you are not connected with the dress trade, an assured manner and an outfit that doesn't look too poverty-stricken.

Mlle Dominique at Yves St-Laurent, the girl who decides whether to give you an invitation or not, says with a not-so-light laugh: 'Obviously, we don't hand out invitations to package tours.' And that acid little sentence rather sums it up.

You don't need money. Only professional buyers need that. And they have to pay between £400 and £800 a seat, preferably in dollars.

Until you have actually seen the clothes of a first-rate designer you cannot expect to realize why such a fuss is made about Haute Couture. Pictures and headlines picking out the more eccentric designs and published by newspapers and magazines twice yearly never really convey the blend of texture, colour, cut and design that distinguishes the work of a really great dressmaker.

Seeing the effect of a perfectly-made dress at close hand is like eating a meal cooked by a master chef. It teaches you what to avoid.

And to acquire that knowledge to help you buy cheaper clothes it is worth braving the dragons disguised as charming young women who guard the doors of the famous dress houses.

Remember never to try at the start of collection times for professional buyers and the press, which run from the last week in January to the middle of February and from the last week in July to the middle of August. March and September, when the majority of private clients buy their wardrobes, are the best months. The Haute Couture show then is just the starting point to get your eye in. Luckily nearly all the big houses have boutiques either on the same premises or special boutique shops. The prices, which range from £25 to £150, are more or less the same at the nameless boutiques with which Paris is strewn. So why not, while you are about it, have the name for the same price?

It is best to choose one where the chief designer supervises the boutique clothes.

This is true of Cardin, Givenchy, Pipard of Nina Ricci, Philippe Venet. Courrèges and Yves St-Laurent give as much time and attention to their cheaper-priced collections as they do to their main ones. At Christian Dior the boutique and Miss Dior collections are done by Philippe Guibourgé, a first-rate designer who has established himself strongly during the past few years.

Here, House by House, is what you do to get into a dress show, plus a few other tips that might be useful.

CHRISTIAN DIOR, 30 avenue Montaigne, tel. ELY 93-64.
They prefer you to call in person if you want an invitation. This is so that the charming dragon can give you a quick professional once-over. Not for snob value but just to make sure you have no connection with the trade. Like customs officials winkling out professional smugglers the dragons have a sixth sense. You ask for the Service de Représentation and if you pass the test an invitation will be sent to your hotel or Paris address.

The Dior Boutique is next door on the corner of the rue François Premier and the avenue Montaigne, and the Miss Dior shop is next to it in the rue François Premier itself.

Dior is for women who like to dress up a bit and the Miss Dior Shop has a splendid collection of short dinner dresses and cocktail dresses. (Average price £40.)

YVES ST-LAURENT, 30 bis rue Spontini, tel. PAS 43-79.
As we have mentioned they don't receive tourists. You should go

in person and ask for Mlle Dominique who will ask to see your passport and then turn you over to a vendeuse or high-class sales-lady who will give or send you an invitation. This is a bit of a bore if you have no intention of buying anything, but can be braved out if you are determined.

If your courage fails, not to worry. Yves St-Laurent gives more time and attention to his Boutique and ready-to-wear clothes than almost any other designer. The clothes sold at Yves St-Laurent Rive Gauche, 21 rue de Tournon, tel. DAN 07-05, are very similar to the Haute Couture collection and his prices give the best value in Paris for clothes with a name to them. They range from £15 for a skirt, £25 to £30 for a two-piece to £60 or £70 for an evening trouser suit outfit.

PIERRE CARDIN, 118 faubourg Saint-Honoré, tel. BAL 06-23. Telephone for an invitation. Ask for the Public Relations office then give your name and Paris hotel. When you go to the show you will have to take your passport with you.

His Boutique is at the same address and is full of delicious bits and pieces as well as made-to-measure clothes. The basement has been converted into a special children's wear department with Cardin-designed clothes for babies, toddlers and children up to twelve years of age.

Across the river on the Left Bank in boulevard Saint-Germain is Cardin Junior which takes care of teenagers.

Cardin is probably the easiest of all the Houses to get into to see a show. If you are in the VIP category your visit will be smoothed for you by Mme Hervé Alphand, wife of the former French Ambassador to Washington.

COURREGES, 40 rue François Premier, tel. ELY 72-17. Second Floor. Call round and ask to see Mme Baudoin, taking your passport with you. Go several days in advance as the collection is not presented every day and the salon is small. The Couture Future, the boutique collection, is at the same address.

CHANEL, 31 rue Cambon,
This is classic couture and an historic monument combined. Tele-phone first. You will be assigned a vendeuse who will send you an invitation and take charge of you. Again, you are likely to be asked for your passport. The enormous mirrored salon is unique. So are

the clothes. Mlle Chanel doesn't make boutique clothes, she just lets the copyists buy a model for £800 and reproduce it if they can.

It is acknowledged, even in Paris, that the best Chanel copyist was and still is Geoffrey Wallis of Wallis Shops, London.

You stand a much better chance of getting an invitation if you are thin. Mlle Chanel, whose word is law to her staff, doesn't like fat girls. She thinks they are un-chic.

LANVIN, 22 faubourg St-Honoré.
PHILIPPE VENET, 62 rue François 1er.
NINA RICCI, 20 rue des Capucines.
For these three, follow the same formula; call or telephone first and show your passport.

Nina Ricci has a special boutique collection show in the mornings. Philippe Venet is worth a visit just to look at his coats which are superbly cut.

GIVENCHY, 3 avenue George V.
Givenchy has just recently opened a Boutique at 66 avenue Victor Hugo. He has always specialised in amusing and unusual accessories and the Boutique is fun.

Cheap clothes of eccentric design are cheaper and more eccentric in England. In Paris it is better to go for quality.

DOROTHY BIS
This is far and away the best fun shop. Mr. Dorothy Bis, Elie Jacobson, practically invented the Paris cheap Boutique trade and was the first man to give a chance in Paris to new young stylists who have since made a name for themselves—Emmanuelle Khanh, Paco Rabanne, Michèle Rozier and Christiane Bailly. The first metal dress that Paco Rabanne ever made was done for Dorothy Bis in 1960.

Small, round and ebullient he goes to about two hundred collections a year to choose clothes, as well as the styles which he commissions specially. He has a nose like a ferret for a cheap best seller. And when one hears him murmur, 'Beefsteak, pommes frites', at a collection it always means that this is a model he is going to buy and sell by the hundred and is going to provide him with his daily bread or, as he prefers to call it, his steak and chips.

He has three boutiques: Dorothy and Dorothy Bis on the Left

Bank, 37 rue de Sèvres, and Dorothy Ter on the Right Bank in the rue Marbeuf, just off the Champs-Elysées.

A Dorothy Bis dress starting price is around £8. Very cheap for Paris.

If you are a small girl with a large bust and slender hips it is worth a trip out to the 14th arrondissement to—

LAURA, 104 avenue du Général Leclerc.
Laura is Sonia Rykiel who not only owns the Boutique but designs the clothes she sells as well as some special designs that she does for *Elle* magazine.

Sonia Rykiel, Hélène Vacher and Arlette Nastat of Réal all started up about the same time. They are friends and all design for their own particular shape. They felt their type of small feminine woman, typically Parisian, was overlooked.

The Réal shop in the Faubourg St-Honoré is the couture version of the same idea.

Laura is a very good shop for sweaters and knit dresses. Mme Rykiel has them specially woven for her in Italy. She goes to Milan twice a year to choose colours and supervise patterns and knit.

Her prices go from about £17 to £25 for student or young style dresses and average about £25 for 'La femme de trente ans'. Each season she designs about forty different exclusive models.

Paco Rabanne's own studio-cum-boutique is at 33 rue Bergère.

It is a mixture of workroom, showroom and photographer's studio with painted black walls and masses of steel tubes and projectors. When the paper rolls on the walls are pulled down it is transformed into a photographic studio.

Paco himself is usually to be found there amongst examples of all his different models. Rhodoid dresses, knitted fur coats, paper dresses, bathing suits in plastic, raincoats in moulded plastic, pyjamas, shirts, and bathing suits for men made up in tough washable paper, plastic handbags, shoes and jewellery. His prices range from about £2 for a pair of moulded plastic boots to several hundred pounds for a knitted fur coat. You can order from his shop.

Emmanuelle Khanh works from her home, 20 rue Le Verrier, and is gradually moving away from straight designing to concentrate more on accessories, leather goods, umbrellas, underwear, swim suits. Her accessories and umbrellas can all be bought in the big stores, Printemps, Galeries Lafayette, etc., as well as Dorothy Bis, 37 rue de Sèvres and Vog, 34 rue Tronchet.

Vog also specialised in the exclusive V de V ski wear and rainwear designed by Michèle Rozier. Is a good place for unusual sunglasses designed by Paco Rabanne and Michèle Rozier as well as a collection of plastic costume jewellery.

Two other smaller Boutiques worth a visit are VICTOIRE, 12 Place des Victoires, and KNACK, 104 avenue Victor Hugo.

Victoire is the shop window for designer Catherine Chaillet, who produces not only women's clothes and accessories but tableware, luggage and watches.

The ELLE BOUTIQUE at 127 Champs-Elysées is the place where you can buy clothes and accessories promoted by *Elle* magazine. One of the best go-ahead women's magazines with a world-wide reputation, *Elle* caters for the smart Parisian but their sizes rarely go above 14.

Most visitors to Paris know the ins and outs of the big stores Printemps and Galeries Lafayette, but it is perhaps worth mentioning that each of them now have a special floor devoted to the stylists' Boutiques.

At PRINTEMPS 'Choses' from St-Tropez, V de V and film star Michèle Morgan's designs all have their own stands.

At GALERIES LAFAYETTE you can find Pierre Cardin's ready-to-wear, sportswear by Mic-Mac (owned by Gunther Sachs, present husband of Brigitte Bardot) and a selection of Sonia Rykiel's designs.

PRISUNIC, the multiple store is good for cheap scarves, sun hats, all beach wear and cheap summer bits. Colours are good. Co-ordinated for years by Denise Fayolle who has built up Prisunic style and taste. Good and cheap children's clothes.

The three pilot stores where they try out all Denise Fayolle's new ideas are: Prisunic Caumartin, in the rue de Provence, just behind Printemps, Prisunic Elysées, in the Champs-Elysées, and Prisunic Ternes, in the avenue des Ternes.

Shoes

Shoes are half the price in England and made from better leather. Nothing beats the Italian stylists *but* some of the most beautiful hand-made shoes in the world are made by—

ROGER VIVIER, 24 rue François Ier.

Roger Vivier's shoes are worth looking at for their ideas and beauty. They are wildly expensive and he makes only small sizes, but each shoe is an exquisite object. He designs for most of the big couture houses. Model girls' feet are an object of great sorrow to him for most of the top model girls, though slim of waist are large of foot.

RENAST, 33 rue Tronchet.

Renast have adapted many of Vivier's ideas for the commercial market. They make very good boots. Not cheap. Shoes average £10 to £12 a pair and boots from £15 to £20.

A younger rival to Roger Vivier has just opened up:

ANDREA PFISTER, 4 rue Cambon.

A Swiss, born in Italy where his father is also a shoe maker, Andrea Pfister became known in Paris about three years ago when Michel Goma of Patou had him design shoes for the Patou collection. He makes accessories to match his shoes in a wonderful range of colours.

Very expensive but exclusive designs.

If you really can't afford to buy . . .

Getting one's clothes altered, remodelled, taken in or taken out is comparatively easy in Paris. Not only do dressmakers and sewing women exist but for people in a hurry there are a number of 'Clothing clinics' who specialise in this sort of work.

I can recommend from personal experience two who work well and quickly.

SILHOUETTE, 49 rue de la Victoire, tel. 874.14.82.

They will do any kind of job from taking up a hemline to completely remodelling a suit. Obviously they charge according to the amount of time needed. As an example, a skirt taken out at the waist, in at the hips and shortened will cost about £2.

RENOVIT, 25 rue Pierre Demours.

This is run by three tailors. As well as women's alterations they are specially good with men's suits. They will take an old-fashioned English style suit, shorten the jacket, slim down the trousers and transform a dismal looking object for a few pounds by giving it a completely new line.

Dressmakers

While on the subject of dressmakers here are the addresses of three specialists in their own line. They all work privately but have become known by having the word passed around by satisfied clients.

First on the list, the woman who makes made-to-measure swim suits. It is her speciality and she does nothing else. Her name is MME DENYSE ROUSSEAU and her address 127 rue Blomet way out in Paris' 15th arrondissement. Mme Rousseau charges about £7 to make a swimsuit and you can bring your own material and a picture of a suit you want copied. Or she will design one for you herself. She used to be a corset maker. She is swamped with orders during the summer months and you have to be prepared to wait at least two weeks for your swimsuit.

MME JOSEE, 12 rue de la Paix, is a dressmaker who works for the fashion magazines. She makes up patterns that are afterwards photographed. Many model girls who posed in her clothes are now her clients. She can copy any Haute Couture model from a photograph or drawing. She charges between £20 and £40 to make a dress, not counting the cost of the material.

ALICE LAROCHE, 48 rue de Richelieu, is an embroidress and button and belt maker. She works in every sort of material as well as in semi-precious stones and beading. She does a good deal of work for the big couture Houses and is always busy.

Men's Clothes

---

*Men's clothes have improved enormously in Paris in the last few years.
A lot of people think that they're better than women's clothes.*

*Carnaby Street styles came and went. Cardin and several other Paris
designers have elaborated new styles which owe little to Anglo-Saxon
inspiration. You can now dress as a dandy 'Left Bank style'. Or you can
be as traditional as you like in the Paris equivalent of the 'Jermyn Street
style'. There are plenty of clothes shops for Anglomaniacs. There's even
a Burton's at Paris. But leave 'English style' clothes to the French: you
didn't come to Paris to buy a tweed jacket did you?*

A few years ago, all Paris had to offer men in search of fashion were
a few rather sad and discreet shop windows with neat rows of pale
shirts soberly displayed. 'Respectable' men were not supposed to
take too much interest in sartorial problems, for fear of being thought
jokers or gigolos. To be really elegantly dressed meant not to be
noticed and if you were very rich the thing was to have a suit of
English cloth cut by an Italian disciplined by Parisian sobriety. As
for the others . . . well, you can still see a whole generation of
anciens combattants (ex-servicemen) with moustaches, berets and
straw hats, who believe that to change one's clothes too often is
morally unhealthy, to say nothing of being a ridiculous waste since
one suit for weekdays and another for Sundays are quite enough. . . .

This same parisimonious generation sent its children to school in
short trousers which were always too big (to 'allow for growth')
and then in equally oversize and practically indestructible long
trousers. The main thing was for clothes to be warm enough and to
last—apparently for ever. There was, in fact, a craze for long-lasting
clothes: people patched up their old suits, turned coats inside out,
worshipped cheapness and wear-proof cloth and the result can be
seen in any old school photograph of the time.

Then, all of a sudden, things changed. Pierre Cardin became
interested in men's fashion which he found too monotonous and
depressing, and his interest combined with the enthusiasm of the
modern generation precipitated the Paris scene into a timely metamorphosis: no more gigolos, or if there were any, they had become
lost in the crowd. Young people now wore very tight-fitting over-

coats and suits in the winter, and in summer went barefoot with skin-tight shirts. They took the greatest pains in choosing the right coloured shirt to go with their jackets or pullovers which they wore casually over their shoulders and as for their trousers—painstaking wasn't the word!

Some people have talked of 'de-virilisation' and claimed that even the most normal men were affected by the new contagion; they declared that this new taste in apparel was part of a syndrome—a renewal of the peacock instinct which tended to get the upper hand. It was only a matter of time, it was said, before the women would be asking the men to dance.

One thing is certain: like the males in the animal world, young men are now wearing the finest feathers and are out to seduce the female. Instead of being mere consumers of eroticism, in the 'Gaulish' tradition of their parents, they have become suddenly aware of their own face value. Masculine beauty has triumphed again and is demanding recognition.

Is it surprising then that so many boutiques should have suddenly sprung up? They are everywhere in the city now and you won't find one boutique for women that hasn't its masculine counterpart. The great couturiers have nearly all become interested in the husbands of their clients and Pierre Cardin reigns over them. He shows his collections throughout the world and has opened his main Paris boutique in the Place Beauveau overlooking the gardens of the Elysée Palace where you may perhaps see the President of France taking his walk. Elsewhere the countless new boutiques have a distinct flavour of Carnaby Street which seems to have offshoots on ever street corner of the capital. A recent television programme compared the Carnaby Street boutiques with their Paris cousins and even the names are the same: *Bus Stop, Punch, New Man, Dean*, etc.

It's quite impossible to give you all the details and addresses of the new boutiques, which even the oldest-established Parisian can no longer keep up with. What we can do is to give you the names of a few of the great ruling houses in the world of Paris fashion where you may go and indulge in the latest trends, and suggest a few itineraries to make your visit easier. First of all, let's begin at the top:

PIERRE CARDIN

The innovator; the first who had the nerve to recommend tight-fitting jackets and bright colours. He displays whole collections of

Workroom at Cardin's

male fashions, complete with models. Cardin has a number of luxury boutiques; alternatively, suits and shoes bearing his label can be found in quality shops and even in department stores.

TED LAPIDUS
Also a *couturier*. Specialises in a teenager style which can now be worn even by well-preserved forty-year-olds. Apart from his work-shops, he has three boutiques in Paris (including TEDD in the Place Victor Hugo) and a range in the Belle Jardinière department store.

RENOMA
After starting in the tailors' district, i.e. near the main boulevards on the Right Bank, the brothers Renoma have conquered the rue de la Pompe district and compelled other tailors to try to steal either their cutters or their clients.

CACHAREL
Not a boutique but the name of a stylist who has designed some very *à la mode* shirts in very beautiful colours.

CARVIL
For shoes, like BALLY.

PRISUNIC and INNO
Like Woolworth's, in every part of Paris. The *chic* thing to do is

to hunt around in them, as you would in your favourite junk or antique shop and come up with some amusing little item of clothing for next to nothing which, you will modestly say to those who compliment you on it, is from Prisunic or Inno. The fact is that the designers here are often original and their prices are unbeatable. But as their creations usually only reach these shops in small quantities, it's best to be there on the day they first appear. Worth looking out for: very beautiful silk ties for only 10 francs, and the sales at Inno.

Now, a few itineraries:
From the Place Vendôme to the 8th arrondissement:
The kind of people who stay at the Ritz or the Crillon, top antique dealers of the traditional kind, international financiers and society people go to some of the following places:

GELOT, 12 Place Vendôme, tel. OPE 78-49.
The most elegant hatter. Sheer perfection.

CHARVET, 8 Place Vendôme, tel. OPE 41-31.
A very refined shirtmaker. Also very handy as he's opposite the Ritz.

PIERRE FAIVRET, 165 rue Saint-Honoré, tel. 073 26-29.
The shirtmaker of the Place du Théâtre Français. Also has a range of ready-to-wear suits and dresses a few of the French actors who come for fittings. Rather hammy styles as you may see from the windows. . . .

WASHINGTON TREMLETT, 244 rue de Rivoli, Paris 1, tel. 073 24-60.
Very classic shirtmaker. Scarves and ties.

HILDITCH AND KEY, 202 rue de Rivoli, tel. 073 51-60.
Like the above, although very English in style. Perhaps not for tourists who want to forget Jermyn Street.

CERRUTI, 3 Place de la Madeleine, tel. 265 65-33.
Shirts, accessories and suits as well. The boutique has just been opened in Paris by masters of the Italian cut. They have a design shop in Italy but the models are made in Paris by a former Cardin

man. Prices begin at 550 francs for a ready-to-wear suit and at 1,700 francs for a tailored suit. One of the newest boutiques in Paris.

LANVIN, 15 rue du Faubourg Saint Honoré, tel. 265 14-40.
The very image of the provincial style at its most refined—that of the important industrialists and habitués of Deauville. Facing Hermès, another fine quality shop: extraordinary choice of shirt materials; extraordinary prices too.

PIERRE CARDIN, Place Beauveau.
A temple of masculine fashion and Paris male fashions in particular: walls lined in its creator's favourite green, with metal furniture (all the rage in Paris. After Oscar Gustin made a red copper décor for Molière's *Don Juan* at the Comédie-Française, the boutique went in for brass and Ungaro even had Oscar Gustin make metal brassieres). Even if you can't afford to re-stock your wardrobe completely, it's well worth seeing the window displays and, if possible, the shop itself. You can always go to the *Printemps* or the *Saint-Germain-des-Prés* afterwards to buy a suit with the Cardin label.

If you are a traditionalist, if you don't mind what you spend on quality, this itinerary will also lead you to some of the 'great' Paris tailors, i.e. those who dress Presidents of the Republic and Boulevard actors. They are generally tucked away on the first floor of some discreet block of flats and it's the done thing to have been going there for years or else to simply send them your instructions. Here are a few addresses:
PORTES, 194 rue de Rivoli, Paris 1, tel: 742 87-07.
FERUCH, 75 faubourg Saint-Honoré, Paris 8, tel: 359 40-00.
LARSEN, 7 rue de La Boétie, Paris 8, tel: 225 07-80.
BARDOT, 13 rue de la Boétie, Paris 8, tel: 265 39-90.
CIFONELLI, 31 rue Marbeuf, Paris 8, tel: 225 38-84.

The Champs-Elysées:
The district of businessmen in a hurry, provincials and tourists, a kind of great corridor with international playboys from Claridges and workmen rubbing shoulders on Saturday afternoons. The boutiques are very varied in quality and usually rather expensive (the rents are high), but a few are still popular with the true Parisian.

PRISUNIC ELYSEES, 60 avenue des Champs-Elysées, Paris 8, tel. 359 65-03.
Good for treasure-hunting if you haven't got anything special in mind.

O'KENNEDY, 50 avenue des Champs-Elysées, Paris 8, tel. 256 09-13.
One of the sanctuaries of the 'young' style adapted to the taste of the *grands boulevards* (see below).

EDDY, Passage du Lido, Paris 8, tel. 225 59-19.
A very good boutique with a range of ready-to-wear suits. It allowed itself to be overtaken somewhat by the 'youngsters' but soon made up for its temporary slackness. The crowds who patiently queue up for the sales are good proof of the quality of Monsieur's Eddy's wares.

ELYSEES SOIERIES, 65 avenue des Champs-Elysées, Paris 8, tel. 359 37-64.
A very good choice of shirts, in particular.

From the avenue Victor Hugo to the rue de la Pompe:
If you follow this itinerary you can see how male fashions have changed, the inter-generation conflict and the progress made recently in the design of clothes for men.
The avenue Victor Hugo is considered to be one of the best addresses in Paris and reflects the image of a still rather stuffy *haute bourgeoisie*. Furnishings, furs and fashions all have an air of comfortable distinction.

BARCLAY, 66 avenue Victor Hugo, Paris 16, tel. 553 95-65.

ROMOLI, 38–40 avenue Victor Hugo, Paris 16, tel. 704 36-72.

The Place Victor Hugo has already begun to change: a good seat on the terrace of a café will allow you to admire the gilded youth of the district (while their mothers and grandmothers take tea opposite at the 'Marquise de Sévigné') window-shopping at:

TEDD, 6 Place Victor Hugo, Paris 16, tel. 704 41-20 and 704 40-19.
One of Ted Lapidus's boutiques with a range of ready-to-wear suits.

The real centre of fashion for the youth of the 16th arrondissement is to be found somewhat further along, in the neighbourhood of the Lycée Janson de Sailly. There, around one boutique, a whole new shopping district is being born.

RENOMA, 129 bis rue de la Pompe, Paris 16, tel. 553 57-04.
We've already mentioned the Renoma phenomenon. His windows here are an object lesson.

MAYFAIR, 'boucherie anglaise', 128 rue de la Pompe, tel. 272 43-88.
The ironwork and hooks of the old butcher's shop that once stood here have been kept. The clothes which now hang instead of sides of beef are very, very youthful. And often very well cut.

The rue de Passy:
Neither the avenue Victor Hugo nor the rue de la Pompe, but an area half-way between the two for relatively modest purses. We aren't going to give you any particular address, but you might like to know that you can buy Rodier knitwear, Bally shoes, browse in an excellent Inno (where the men's range is very important), a '100,000 chemises' for shirts of course, a Burton's (yes, an English Burton's, with a truly remarkable 'young' section) and several very worth-while boutiques like *Vormese*, *Blaise* and *Dominique*, all at the end of the street, on the Chaussée de la Muette.

From the rue Saint-Guillaume to the Odéon, via Sèvres-Babylone:
You can, in fact, confine yourself to one or the other part of this important itinerary which is particularly rich in every kind of boutique. The centre is around Saint-Germain-des-Prés, with a political-science-student tendency facing the rue Saint Guillaume, a young-bourgeois tendency around the rue de Sèvres, a young-cinema tendency at Saint-Germain and a with-it student tendency by the side of the rue Mazarine. You can almost confine yourself to this district and its shop windows to have a fairly exact idea of what's happening at Paris.

FERUCH, 202 boulevard Saint-Germain, Paris 8, tel. 548 01-87.
A new boutique. A somewhat more light-hearted branch of the great tailor Feruch who launched the 'Mao-style' collar and the Hindu tunic. Prices aren't exactly low but the style is genuine and a visit is highly recommended.

ROMOLI, 187 boulevard Saint-Germain, Paris 8, tel. 222 24-44.
As on the avenue Victor Hugo, discreet hint of eccentricity is the
thing here. The recent suicide of Jack Romoli may not prevent the
survival of his boutiques which have already acquired their own
tradition. This one is suited to the public of the Political Science
Faculty.

DEAN, 18 rue de Grenelle, Paris 8, tel. 222 69-99.
A very successful imitation of a King's Road boutique. Made-to-
measure suits can be had there.

ARNYS, 14 rue de Sèvres, Paris 8, tel. 548 76-99.
Undoubtedly one of the best boutiques for ready-to-wear and
semi-made-to-measure. The interior decoration is a blend of what
Paris calls the English style and the Louis XVI—1910 style so dear
to Christian Dior. The window displays are nearly always a success
with real sophistication of colour. This season (1968) the ties were
particularly noteworthy.

100,000 CHEMISES, 55 rue de Rennes, Paris 6, tel. 548 52-71.
We've already mentioned the branch in the rue de Passy. A
leading firm for popular and cheap shirts. Only a short time ago a
rather apathetic effort was made to inject some new life into this
chain of shops. Hints of Cacharel and Carnaby Street have given it
some tone and you can find a few interesting models among a
rather poor offering that still leans towards traditionalism.

SAINT-GERMAIN-DES-PRES, 37–39 rue du Four, Paris 6, tel. 326
43-66.
A good medium boutique with samples of French or foreign tailors'
suits (including Burberry's) and a 'pop' range of Cardin's clothes.

TED LAPIDUS SAINT-GERMAIN, 52 rue Bonaparte, Paris 6, tel.
326 87-84.
Everything is new. Brass everywhere.

LORENZO, 43 rue de Rennes, Paris 6, tel. 548 84-20.
Has already been at Saint-Germain for ten years and is now doubled
by a boutique for women. Lorenzo is now called 'Zaza et Lorenzo'.

NEW MAN, 16 rue de l'Ancienne Comédie, Paris 6, tel. 033 77-54.

Tiny but very amusing with little Chinese-style posters giving slang indications of the latest in *liquettes* (shirts) and *falzars* (trousers).

The boulevard Saint-Michel:
Along the entire length of this boulevard you will find shirts, hats, and shoes. Students buy a lot of clothes now but they often come from the provinces, hence a certain provincial air along the boulevard: a certain soberness, a whiff of the bourgeoisie. . . .

And, of course, there are a Bally and a 100,000 Chemises. Blaise near the Luxembourg has astonishingly reasonable prices. Hundreds of other shops. You might care to idle there if you like the student-who's-not-taking-any-risks style. Worth knowing that there's a King's road-type-boutique half-way between the Luxembourg and the river. Its painted window and coloured suits brighten up the general surroundings.

The Grands boulevards:
If you start from the Madeleine, you will see some extremely sober window displays: MADELIOS in particular is a large shop still selling what passes for the traditional English style. The quality is genuine at least. A little further, LE CARNAVAL DE VENISE is a good, traditional shirt shop. Also, shoe shops, including the inevitable Bally. All rather serious.

But if you cross the avenue de l'Opéra, you will come to another district which seems quite picturesque after Richelieu-Druot. A number of shops on the way to the Place de la République were frankly awful before the advent of the *yé-yés* (some still are), but now they have acquired a new boldness and youthfulness, if not the best of taste. Anyway, they're all very colourful, with the tightest-fitting jackets in Paris, the squarest-tipped shoes and the most highly coloured underwear. Take a walk along the *grands boulevards*: you won't regret it. Besides the windows, there are posters for erotic films and the public to watch. You may also make some discoveries.

Finally, if you're tempted, here are three addresses:

BURTON, 14–18 boulevard Poissonnière, Paris 9, tel. 770 72-70.
But only the department for *jeunes gens.*

PUNCH, 24 boulevard Saint-Denis, Paris 10, tel. 770 44-34.
Male fashions no longer have much place in this very Carnaby-

Street style setting where you wander around to the sound of music among dresses and two-piece suits, but a young, slightly adventurous style is well represented.

RENOMA, 22 rue de Nazareth, Paris 3, tel. 272 43-88.
As always.

Such then are the places where you can try to transform yourself into a thoroughly up-to-date Continental. There are, of course, a great number of other boutiques we haven't mentioned and, especially, the big department stores, led by Les Galeries Lafayette and Le Printemps (which has a 'Brummel' boutique in which Pierre Cardin is well represented). Go there, look out for something new and if you see it, jump on it. But if you care neither for elegance nor fashion you can always try the Flea Market.

Paris Pompous

'L'art pompier' they call it in Paris. It's the equivalent of our own Victoriana in architecture and decoration: Paris at its most florid, the Paris of the Second Empire and Third Republic, of fin-de-siècle academic and official art at its most sumptuous, brazen and overpowering. And it is by no means always 'bad taste': after all, it is part of the life and style of a fairly recent past, the belle époque *as Parisians know it. . . .*

London has its Victorian relics, Rome its Baroque, New York its skyscrapers and Paris its Second Empire and Third Republic monuments and remains. The pompous, academic, 'official' art and architecture of the late 19th century gave Paris much of its 'style'. You may hate them, love them or simply be bored by them but almost no matter where you go in Paris, you cannot escape them. They are part of that new Paris that Baron Haussmann built for Napoleon III in his attempt to make this capital the most beautiful in the world. They range from the grotesque to the imposing. At their best they are breath-taking, at their worst, they are as florid and gradiloquent as a French politician's speech in the provinces at election time. They are part of what the French call *l'art pompier* and as such, undeniably fascinating for the confirmed Betjemanite. Anyway, they make a nice contrast to the new skyscraper blocks rising in the south of the city. . . .

Here is a list of some of the most notable examples of 'Paris pompier':

THE ALEXANDRE III BRIDGE

The most spectacular introduction to the pompous, high-flown Paris built and frescoed by the favourite artists of Napoleon III and late 19th-century Presidents of the Republic is this bridge, built by Resal and Alby and bristling with candelabra, a variety of Glories, hippogriffs and divinities from the ocean depths. Stand on the bridge on a fine evening when the sun is going down and admire the Grand Palais and the Petit Palais, two highly flamboyant buildings on the Right Bank, one surmounted with colossal chariots loaded with heroes and languid Victories, the other by a huge dome over a breathtakingly florid iron doorway. They were both built for the great Paris Exhibition of 1900.

THE GRAND PALAIS

Often used for exhibitions and fairs. Enormous portico decorated with such opulent and granitic works as Verlet's *Art*, Lombard's *Peace*, Labatut's *Music* with its violinist flanked by a Doric colonnade and, behind it, Martin's *Grandes Epoques de l'Art* in the purest 'Viennese–Pompeian' style. On the other side of the façade, a voluptuous polychrome fresco of *Défilé des Arts à travers les âges* and a pair of equestrian statues by Falguière. You may also go into the *Palais* by the monumental entry in the Champs-Elysées, encrusted with bas-reliefs with such themes as 'The arts and sciences rendering homage to the new century'. Inside, a sinuous staircase in a kind of *art-nouveau*-cum-Louis XV style: a mass of wrought iron and arabesques writhing upwards to a landing supported by porphyry columns covered with lianas and steel scrollwork.

THE PETIT PALAIS

Tympanum over the portico with the allegorical figure of Paris surrounded by the Muses, the Seine, the Ocean and the Mediterranean. Inside, admire the interior of the cupola with frescoes by Albert Besnard, one of the most prolific masters of the rhetoric-impressionistic school. On the ceiling, Idea lying back on a watery globe, Matter being raped by Pan, Paris offering an apple to a Greco-Roman Aphrodite, and a Christian Ideal in the shape of a sulky, shame-faced virgin.

THE HOTEL DE VILLE

Rebuilt in a kind of mock-Flemish-pseudo-Renaissance style by Ballu and Deperthes after it had been burnt down in the Paris Commune insurrection of 1871. Interior more interesting than exterior despite its 136 statues of famous people or allegories on the façade. Rooms covered with a multitude of late 19th-century frescoes in gilt medallions. Some 'tasteful' wall paintings by Puvis de Chavannes (see also *Panthéon*). Another grandiose ceiling painting by Besnard who probably painted some two or three hundred square yards of wall and ceiling in public buildings in Paris and the provinces: this time, he took as his theme 'Truth leading the Sciences and throwing its light upon mankind'—a bare-bosomed, high-spirited and obviously tipsy courtesan followed by a throng of imprecise but agitated allegorical figures wearing a medley of Spanish or Greek costumes. Go up the main staircase to see 'Victor Hugo offering his lyre to the city of Paris': Hugo is immediately recognisable. The great writer and poet is depicted preceding a procession of the figures of Tragedy, Drama and Idyll, all draped in Roman togas, and offering his lyre to a Paris sitting on a marble platform amid ballerinas, ungirt athletes and 'civic Virtues'.

THE ECOLE DE PHARMACIE

More wall paintings by the irrepressible Besnard in the great hall: 'Geological walk', 'Chemistry Lesson', 'Prehistoric Man', 'Mammoths', etc. A curious painting of a lady bathing, apparently in blissful ignorance of two Pleisosauri and an astonished Stone-age man who are looking on from the banks of the stream.

THE SORBONNE

A treasure-house of 'pompous art'. Impossible to list all its treasures. Our own favourites include Besnard's 'Life being reborn out of Death' in the chemistry amphitheatre, with its new-born infant greedily suckling the breast of its dead mother and the Puvis de Chavannes' decorations in the great amphitheatre. The artist, who was acknowledged by Gauguin as his greatest master, celebrated the fame and glory of the university with the lugubrious figure of the Sorbonne as a Virgin standing in the midst of a nude, Bacchic throng of 'cultural allegories' in the centre of a sacred wood. Go through the *Bureau des Renseignements Scientifiques*, decorated only by Gustave Surant's 'Massacre of the Barbarians by Hamilcar'; stop in the Guizot amphitheatre for Comerre's 'Ancient Greece unveiling herself to Archaeology' and then go into the *Salle Louis Liard* with its decorated ceiling by François Schommer, featuring an academic candidate with rather obscene allegorical figures of the Human Sciences and two cupids fluttering above his head. To conclude this summary tour of 'Sorbonne art', go into the library and look at Rochegrosse's frescoe 'The Song of the Muses awakening the Human Soul' with the figure of kneeling humanity, its nudity only just covered by flowing hair, about to listen to the voice of the Muses. Since the rector of the Sorbonne at the time of the painting found Humanity (who might well be a prostrated Mary Magdalen in a Biblical picture) indecent, the painter was obliged to cover her flesh by lengthening her tresses with a few vigorous brush-strokes at the very last minute on the day of inauguration.

THE PANTHEON

Where the 'great men of France' are buried and it looks like it. This vast, funereal edifice, originally designed by the architect

Soufflot as a church is now mainly interesting for its huge frescoes of scenes from the history of Paris by Puvis de Chavannes. They are often produced in children's schoolbooks.

THE PARIS OPERA

One of the finest permanent showpieces of Second Empire, official art. Built by Garnier, the opera house is a striking example of architectural eclecticism and imperial sumptuosity in the Hollywood *Ben Hur* manner. The design was approved in 1861 and the theatre inaugurated in 1875. Seen from the front it has the effect of a giant baroque chocolate box or a pastry cook's triumph at an Oriental banquet. Garnier's method of working was to accumulate details and materials. The front has a loggia with projecting gilt-bronze busts of famous musicians and librettists, seven Renaissance-style arches garlanded with statues and wreaths, a spacious attic bordered with antique-style masks and allegorical groups (Poetry and Harmony), and it is all topped by a flattened cupola and a triangular pediment with the figures of Pegasus and Orpheus in perilous flight. The sides of the theatre are rich in architectural nooks and crannies, tiny courtyards, flights of steps, statues of Hindu dancing girls or slaves holding lanterns on their heads and some astonishing candelabra.

As a landmark, the Opéra is the largest theatre in the world although its capacity is less than that of La Scala at Milan because of the space that Garnier preferred to use for staircases, corridors, vestibules, niches, etc. The monumental staircase is the pride of the Opéra, with its Carrara marble steps, Algerian onyx balustrades, bronze nymphs holding candelsticks and its great sweep. The most famous piece of sculpture in the whole place is Carpeaux's *La Danse* on the ground floor to the right of the façade: a group of drunken Bacchantes dance the *tarantella* around a Satyr who is playing a Neapolitan tambourine. The sculptor had first made his models for this piece drunk on hock in order to get them into the spirit of the thing.

THE BOURSE DE COMMERCE

The Bourse de Commerce, in the heart of Les Halles, is one of many public buildings which were intended to demonstrate the incontestable superiority of French architecture over that of the rest of the world. A circular building with four immense Corinthian columns and a Greek pediment over the main entrance, decorated with three Graces at the top. Interesting frescoed ceiling inside,

Buffet, Gare de Lyon

painted by Clairin: a pictorial hymn to commercial exchanges between the five continents with figures that might have come out of old illustrations to Jules Verne's novels: European merchants in furs or topees at the Pole or Equator, cowboys and Indians, etc.

THE GARE D'ORSAY
Built by Laloux (1898–1900) and once much used by visiting heads of state. It is a facsimile of a wing of the Louvre in reduced but far more massive form and is by far and away the most pompous of all Paris railway stations. A façade of nine huge rounded arches, each

crowned by a lion's head and topped by cornucopias and festoons and various figures representing provincial cities. The station now only serves a few suburban stations from underground platforms but the upper, disused part of the station is hugely impressive. It has a ghostly, cathedral like air which fascinated Orson Welles who shot part of Kafka's *The Trial* there. Try to see it if you can, although the public are not supposed to be admitted.

THE JARDIN DES PLANTES
A fine example of scientific Third-Republican-pompous art. An

ex-royal garden now known officially as the *Museum National d'Histoire Naturelle*. Visit Durtet's building with its galleries of Anatomy and Palaeontology: on the façade, a spectacular 'Man's fight against Wild Beasts' painted by a whole team of artists, and eight marble bas-reliefs with animal scenes. On the ground floor, frescoes depicting the progress of the human race and Stone Age anecdotes by Cormon who once taught Toulouse-Lautrec and who became famous for such works as 'Funeral of an Iron Age Chieftain' and 'Orang-Outang strangling an Indian'.

THE RESTAURANT IN THE GARE DE LYON
One of the most spectacularly decorated restaurants in Paris with its vaulted arches, its *putti*, Venuses, half-nude stucco athletes, frescoes on the theme of travel by Flameng, its heavy opaline candelabra, and solid seats. It overlooks the platforms and is a perfect place to have dinner before embarking on the Orient Express. The station itself was rebuilt and embellished in 1889 with a façade adorned by four water sprites in rather relaxed poses and a belfry that might have come straight from Renaissance Florence.

Art Nouveau and '1900' Style
Not really fair to include it in this section since it is neither official, academic or pompous. But despite destructions, the style has left its mark on the city—particularly in the entrances to Métro stations —and was considered the last word in modernity at the time.

MAXIM'S
Décor as pretty as a butterfly's wing with its curvilinear mahogany wainscoting, cedar-wood marquetry and copper fittings. Pretty mural paintings by Sonnier.

BRASSERIE LIPP
Even the waiters look '1900'. Majolica tiles by Fargue (jets of palm leaves and lilies) and a ceiling painted with African bowmen releasing arrows at terrified butterflies.

19 AVENUE RAPP
Illustrated in almost every history of architecture. A block of flats built by Jules Lavirotte with a façade covered with a frenzy of floral motifs, a wild-eyed bust of a long-haired Ophelia on the portico

with peacock-butterfly decorations on enamelled terracotta. Immense loggia, columns and sculptures of Adam and Eve.

34 AVENUE WAGRAM
The 'Ceramic Hotel'. By the same architect, decorated in the same sensuous-botanical style with writing plants and tendril motifs.

33 RUE DU CHAMP DE MARS
Another *art-nouveau* building with various kinds of lilies crawling and wriggling all over the façade.

Other buildings where architects and decorators indulged their passion for botanical and oceanographic decoration include 6 rue de Hanovre, Paris 2, 9 rue Claude-Chahu, Paris 16, and a house in rue de l'Abbé de l'Epée, Paris 5.

Excursions outside Paris

You may want to spend Sunday or the week-end outside Paris—particularly if you have a car.

Here are a few suggestions. Only a few, for otherwise you might be tempted to desert Paris for France. And France isn't Paris. And Paris, to so many people, is France. . . .

Impossible to give you any ideal itinerary for your trips around Paris. The countryside round about is rich in unexpected, unusual, charming and even mysterious attractions, but why not let you discover them yourself? The list is endless. Nonetheless, if you really want some suggestions, why not start your tour with:

VINCENNES

(Neighbourhood of Paris, Métro station: Vincennes.) The castle of Vincennes, an enormous building begun in the 12th century, has been unjustly neglected which is a pity since it is both impressive and historically fascinating. According to legend, the keep was built on the site of the oak tree under which the good king, Saint Louis XI, rendered justice—something every French schoolboy is supposed to know. Five French kings died in the castle and it was transformed into a state prison during the reign of a later, not-so-amiable, Louis. Famous prisoners who were locked up there for various reasons include the King of Navarre, the Great Condé, the Cardinal de Retz, Fouquet, Mirabeau and Diderot. A guide will take you to the moat to show you the exact spot where the last Duke of Enghien was shot by order of Napoleon I.

THE PETS' CEMETERY

Asnières (north-west Paris, near Clichy, on the Ile de la Recette—also known as Ile des Ravageurs). A visit here is a must for all pet lovers. This somewhat melancholy spot is especially famous for its tombs of dogs. See the monument to Barry, the famous Saint Bernard dog with its bas-relief and touching inscription: *Il sauva la vie à quarante personnes, il fut tué par la quarante et unième.* (He saved forty people's lives; the forty-first killed him.) Various tombstones bear the inscriptions of great French writers such as

Lamartine and Chamfort—particularly that of Pascal: *Plus je vois les hommes, plus j'aime mon chien* (The more I see of men, the more I love my dog). From Asnières, you can go on to:

ARGENTEUIL

(By way of Colombes.) Visit the Gothic crypt in the rue Notre-Dame. It is the sole surviving relic of the convent where Héloïse took the veil after being separated from her lover Abelard. Interesting municipal museum in the rue Pierre-Guienne in the former hospital built by Saint-Vincent-de-Paul. Beside an important collection of documents belonging to the Jansenist sect, a giant asparagus —the speciality of the region. In the season, the local restaurant will serve you asparagus that are truly 'out of this world'.

BASILICA OF SAINT-DENIS

Situated a few miles to the north of the city, this is the most fascinating and least visited of the great churches of the Paris region.

The basilica was first built in about AD 275 over the tomb of Saint Denis, the patron saint of France (to some scholars the Christianised version of the pagan Dionysius). The building was transformed and rebuilt several times until the Abbot Suger made it one of the glories of early Gothic architecture. Unfortunately, all that now remains of his particular creation are the central crypt and a few columns. After being altered and enlarged on several occasions between the 12th and the 14th centuries, the church and its tombs were severely damaged during the Revolution. Later restorations made by Napoleon I, Louis XVII and Louis-Philippe were all rather disastrous. Happily the great French architect Viollet-le-Duc gave it back its true character, starting work in 1859.

With its wonderful tombs and monuments, restored after 1816, it is a magnificent museum of French sculpture of the Middle Ages and Renaissance. The tomb of Louis XII and his wife Anne of Brittany, is a masterpiece of French Renaissance art. The royal couple has been twice represented: first lying naked on the sarcophagus, in a style of extreme realism, and then kneeling above, in front of a *prie-dieu*. The tomb of Henry II and Catherine de Medicis was the masterpiece of the architect Pierre Lescot and the sculptor Germain Pilon and is somewhat similar in spirit to that of Louis XII. Some distance away, a second monument to Henry II and Catherine de Medicis shows the two sovereigns lying down, in marble, on a bed of bronze.

Other highly impressive tombs include those of that doughty French warrior of the Hundred Years' War, Bertrand du Guesclin, the Constable Louis de Sancerre, the king Philip the Handsome, and the very sumptuous tomb of François I. You may well be the only visitor at the time in the great church, and the calm and darkness give it an air of unforgettable mystery and solemnity as you discover such astonishing works as Pierre Bontemp's marble urn which contains the heart of François I. In the crypt, built by the Abbot Suger to contain the relics of Saint Denis and his companions, is the resting place of the Bourbon monarchs of France, the tombs of Louis XVI and Marie-Antoinette, of Louis XVII, the Duke of Berry, his two children and the last of the great Condé family. The only reminder of the tragic victims of the Revolution is an absurd statue by Petitot of Marie-Antoinette in *decolletée* and on her knees. Go back into the church again: it is full of ghosts and sadness for those who appreciate them, and then back into the light of day.

Why not take a day's leave of Paris and go to:

SAINT-GERMAIN-EN-LAYE

With its noble château and forest this is a place not to be missed. The somewhat austere looking castle was twice destroyed, twice rebuilt, often embellished and restored in the last century. It contains one of the finest museums in France, outside Paris: the Musée des Antiquités Nationales, famous for its unique collection of Gaulish, Gallo-Roman and Frankish monuments and works of art, its Carolingian masterpieces and prehistoric relics. The museum has been recently reorganised and each object is beautifully displayed. Its treasures include an oculist's case of implements dating from the Roman conquest, a 5th-century Christian altar, gold cloisonné glasswork, and a magnificent collection of Gaulish and Gallo-Roman coins.

Near the station, in the Town Hall: some very beautiful tapestries and a painting by Hieronymous Bosch: *the Boatman*. After all this, why not go for a walk in the forest and dine in the charming *Restaurant Cazaudore*, near the forest (a mile and a half from the town)? If the weather is fine you can eat outside in the garden. There are also two charming hotels (the *Pavillon Henri IV*, and the *Pavillon Louis XIV*) if you don't feel like going back to Paris that night.

To the west of Paris, a few miles past the Bois de Boulogne, go for a walk along the banks of the ponds that the painter Corot immortalised in his paintings at:

VILLE D'AVRAY

Beautiful and rather nostalgic—especially in winter. Perfect for lovers. Near by, the magnificent forest of Saint-Cloud and the old château with its terrace from which you have a beautiful view of Paris in the distance. At Ville d'Avray, you may visit the *Villa des Jardies*. Balzac lived there. So did Léon Gambetta, the French President who died there in 1882 after being shot by his former mistress.

VERSAILLES

This is, of course, a 'must', but do take our advice and only go on a week-day, and even better, on a rainy day when you can escape the usual hordes of fellow-tourists. Although the greatest architects and artists of the 17th and 18th centuries had a hand in its building, the Palace has been nothing more than a majestic carcass ever since its original proprietor, Louis XIV, stopped living in it in 1715. Without the presence of the Sun King, without his ten thousand courtiers, the royal furniture and the court life so lovingly described by Saint-Simon, the vast edifice has lost the power to move the visitor. It is huge, tiring, cold and eminently unlovable. Some rooms, encumbered as they are by Napoleonic souvenirs and bits and pieces belonging to the generals and marshals of the Empire are in downright bad taste. Other rooms are crammed with bad paintings, mostly celebrating battles and colonial expeditions of the time of Napoleons I and III. What you should see are the delightful Opera house and the Royal Chapel.

In the grounds, it is worth visiting the Orangerie with its two great staircases (102 steps each): a solid building by the architect Mansart, without the slightest ornamentation and particularly splendid in summer when the orange trees have been taken out into the gardens.

Marie-Antoinette's famous *hameau* (hamlet) was built by Mique and Hubert Robert in the 18th century for court ladies who wished to enjoy the idyllic country life that was made so fashionable (in theory anyway) by Jean-Jacques Rousseau and his followers. With its 'dairy', its 'farm' and cottages (all restored in 1899) it is strangely moving and after visiting the vast Palace, you won't be surprised why poor Marie-Antoinette loved it so much.

TRAPPES

A few miles from Versailles, you can see the remains of the famous abbey of Port-Royal-des-Champs at Trappes, famous for being the headquarters of the Jansenists in the 17th century. Racine and Pascal were frequent visitors there. Pretty countryside nearby.

CHEVREUSE VALLEY

This valley to the south of Paris is a favourite with Parisians and has the advantage of being accessible by an extension of the Paris Métro (from the Luxembourg station). Best not to go on a Sunday, if you can help it.

Begin by stopping at Arceuil (2 miles from Sceaux) where tradition has it that the dead were buried in their wedding clothes until very recently. From a certain point you can see the ruins of a 2nd-century Roman aqueduct, a 17th century aqueduct, a 19th-century aqueduct built above it, *and* a modern aqueduct.

If you go through the VALLEY OF THE YVETTE you will come to the heart of the delightful valley of the Chevreuse and the ruins of the Château de la Madeleine can be seen rising some 250 feet above the little town. The walk to the top of its ivy-covered keep and two towers is steep, but the view is worth it. From Chevreuse, it is only a few miles to:

DAMPIERRE

with its great château belonging to the ducal family of the Luynes. From Dampierre, walk to Vaux-de-Cernay where an abbey dating from 1128 has been beautifully restored by Baroness Nathaniel de Rothschild. On your way back to Paris, if you have time, then stop at Longpont-sur-Orge. The church has a wonderful treasury of relics which were gathered together in the Middle Ages by Crusaders. They include a supposed robe of Christ, fragments of swaddling clothes of the Infant Jesus, a hair from the head of the Virgin Mary, a belt belonging to Saint Peter, etc.

SENLIS

One of the most interesting medieval towns within easy reach of Paris. It is well worth staying at least half a day there and exploring its many delightfully curious narrow streets with their old houses and noblemen's mansions. The cathedral was built in the 12th century and the façade dates from the 13th. There is a very elegant steeple and the interior, which was altered in the 15th century, is interesting. Facing the church, the remains of a Gallo-Roman wall and the royal Château which was built over the ruins of the Roman governor's palace. Several fine Gothic churches, the 12th-century chapel of the bishop's palace, and several fine old houses (the Town Hall and the *Hôtel des Trois Pots*) add to the charm of this delightful town. To the south-west of the town, on the left of the road to Chantilly, you may see the Roman arenas which were discovered by one of the mayors of Senlis. Excavations have revealed a vast complex of arenas which were built in the 3rd and 4th centuries. The tracks and the main entrances are clearly visible.

The former Eglise de la Charité has been transformed into a museum of glass-work which is quite unique in Europe. The keeper was once a great huntsman and will be only too ready to tell you of his boar-hunting experiences. If you decide to stay the night at Senlis, then go to the *Hôtel du Nord* which is deservedly famed for its *gratin de langoustes*.

And now, one of the most curious spots, not only in the Paris region but in the whole of France:

LE DESERT DE RETZ

(1½ miles south-west of Chambourcy, on the edge of the Forest of Marly.) This was formerly the domain of Roys or Rays, a fortified stronghold which fell into ruin during the Hundred Years' War. In 1712, the site was transformed by a certain Monseigneur de Mondille into what was called a 'jardin d'illusions' and what is now known as the 'Désert de Retz' ('désert' was the name given to the least cultivated parts of English-style gardens which were widely imitated in 18th-century France). What remains of Monseigneur Mondille's garden is one of the oddest man-made 'wildernesses' in the world, a kind of folly, half man-made, half nature-made.

The 'désert' is by no means easy to visit, but if you do manage to get in (persistance will do the trick) you will find yourself in a magnificently unkempt, wildly overgrown park containing, among other things, the ruins of a chapel, a little temple dedicated to the god Pan, a Chinese pavilion, an obelisk-shaped ice-cave, a pagoda and a tower built according to the instructions of the architect and painter Hubert Robert, a kind of huge truncated column surrounded by a ditch, with a central staircase, rooms on different levels and windows piercing the fluted sides of the column. It is all in a state of abandon, very romantic and hugely satisfying for lovers of the unusual.

MORTEFONTAINE

(On the road from Paris to Chantilly.) Mortefontaine has a château and a beautiful estate that once belonged to the Prince Bonaparte, and, above all, one of the most beautiful 'English' gardens in Europe. With fine trees, groves and ponds, it is all wildly romantic. The poet Gérard de Nerval loved to walk there while composing his visionary fancies.

Near the Forest of Chantilly, the beautiful artificial lake known as 'l'étang de la Reine Blanche' and, at the lower end of the lake, the Château de la Reine Blanche, a Gothic-style hunting lodge built in 1826 and owing its name to the fact that it stands on the site of a château once lived in by the mother of Saint Louis of France, Blanche of Castille. Her ghost still appears there, we are told.

If you are an amateur archaeologist, and if you are anywhere near Coulommiers, then you *must* make a 12-mile detour and go to:

JOUARRE

One of the most famous relics of Merovingian France. You will visit the crypt of a monastery founded in the 7th century during the reign of King Dagobert. The crypt is ninety feet long and contains a wonderful series of tombs of the founders of the monastery (one of the finest is that of Sainte Telchide) and Gallo-Roman columns in alabaster, porphyry and cipolin marble, surmounted with carved capitals of white marble from the Pyrenees. The columns almost certainly came from the former pagan temples of the neighbourhood.

Paris Underground

Underground Paris is honeycombed with tunnels, many dating from the Middle Ages. Secret passages are said to abound in certain districts but unfortunately about all you will be able to see of underground Paris apart from the Métro and cellar night clubs are the catacombs and the sewers. Here's how to do it. . . .

It is only slightly easier to see Paris underground than to see the inside of one's own body. Apart from official visits to the Catacombs and the sewers, no other mysterious, breath-taking or in any way spooky excursions are allowed. The Métro of course is a trifle compared to the thousand hidden caves, gaps and corridors which haunt underground Paris. 130 miles of Métro lines; 2,500 miles of sewers; 230 miles of quarry galleries make impressive statistics, but this means little to the seeker of underground excitement.

Paris is built on a soil pitted by holes like Gruyère cheese. A great number of its buildings are still resting on abandoned quarries concentrated around Montmartre and Pigalle (the Métro station 'Blanche' reminds us of the white plaster-stones that were dug up by the ton there), in the Trocadéro area, all around Montparnasse, in the South and around Père-La-Chaise, in the East. These quarries have been used by secret societies—political, occult and religious. Ignatius de Loyala founded the Order of the Jesuits in a quarry near Abbesses; the Free Masons held conferences and meetings underneath rue Mouffetard; witch-doctors gave performances of their magic craft there; all sorts of revels and orgies took place in these secret sanctuaries in the dark times of the Middle Ages as well as in the brighter days of the Renaissance. Now most of the entrances are blocked to prevent people from getting lost and to dissuade political agitators from finding suitable dens for their movements . . . like the Hood Men (*Cagoulards*) of 1937.

The sewers played an important role in the Liberation of Paris in 1944. The father of the ex-Premier, Michel Debré, set up the headquarters of his Health Department in just such a disreputable, dark and dank place to be free from Nazi intrusion. Twelve resourceful English soldiers made their escape through a secret corridor they found off a sewer and which led them to Saint-Denis, 8 miles North of Paris. Now, condescending guides will paddle you through the concrete entrails of Paris, commenting on the philosophy of detritus while holding their breath as long as they can.

Archeologists have made important discoveries while digging up vestiges of the Roman and Merovingian civilisations in Paris. Various objects including central-heating tiles were found underneath the Jardin du Luxembourg in 1957. In 1963, two skeletons dating from 200 B.C. were exhumed: a man and a woman buried side by side. The existence of a Merovingian cemetery was revealed ten years ago, under rue Pierre Nicolle, near the Observatoire. The dead hands were still holding a silver coin to pay Charon for their crossing of the Styx; and yet another ancient necropolis has been found at Saint-Marcel.

But the principal underground attraction is still the Catacombs, which hold the remains of some six million Parisians who had to be exhumed first from the Halles Churchyard and then from many more parish churchyards. The transportation of the corpses from Les Halles started in 1786 and went on in its macabre and unerring way for fifteen months. It is well worth paying a visit to the millions of huddled bones, few of which still belong to their original skeleton. There they are, heaped together in a land of insane order along the 800 yards of winding galleries, 60 feet underground.

Eminent visitors to the Catacombs have included Bismarck, Napoleon III, once his paternalist friend, Prince Oscar of Sweden, and Francis I of Austria. They, too, scribbled on the walls like so many ordinary mortals. Above the entrance a sign proclaims: 'Stop! Here lies the Empire of Death!' Once inside the maze of skeletons you can't help being impressed by what is, perhaps, the world's largest *memento mori*.

The elegant dandies of the 1890's had the wit to perceive the musical possibilities of this macabre necropolis with its excellent acoustics. They accordingly invited some prominent 'Academicians', scientists and other notables and held, in secret, a nocturnal concert of *danses macabres* by Chopin, Saint-Saëns and Liszt, played in all seriousness by some fifty musicians.

A more recent underground memorial worth visiting is situated at the Western end of Ile de la Citê. Raised by a national appeal and built in 1962 by G. H. Pingusson, it is dedicated to the two-hundred-thousand deported prisoners who had fought for the Resistance. Its smallness and simple design give the intimacy necessary for the appropriate meditation and a feeling of brotherhood with the courageous victims. In that sense it is in itself a real work of art, a movingly poetic conception as you see the sky and the gentle flow of the Seine from the pit of the sanctuary decked with 200,000 small twinkling crystals.

Another well-known underground place you cannot visit is Canal Saint-Martin, which runs for over a mile beneath the Boulevard Richard Lenoir in the 11th arrondissement. The canal reappears at the Quai de Valmy, near République, and it is always pleasant to watch the barges come out or sneak into the tunnel and the Ménilmontant 'Titis' (Cockneys) playing their tricks on the urban mariners.

But you can still enjoy wine-tasting at the Caves de la Tour Eiffel, 5 Square Charles Dickens, tel. 647 99-27, Métro Passy. It is a large cellar used by the owner, the Compagnie des Vedettes, as a wine museum. If you take a trip on the Bateaux-Mouches on the Seine, they will take you to the Caves as well. Spirits and wine are best kept in deep cellars as was proved at the outbreak of the last war, when thousands of rum bottles were deposited in the strong-rooms of the Banque de France in place of France's wealth—gold bars which were hastily shipped to America.

An interesting underground aquarium lies at the bottom of Palais de Chaillot. You can relax there on a hot summer day in the company of strange-looking fish from Mexico and China.

CATACOMBES
2 place Denfert-Rochereau, Cour du Pavillon. One hour visit. From 1st July to 15th, October every Saturday at 2 pm.

From 16th October to 30th June, 1st and 3rd Saturday of the month.

SEWERS
(visite des égouts): Place de la Concorde, at the foot of the Statue de Lille, the nearest large statue to Métro Concorde. A boat will take you from Concorde to Madeleine. No visits during 6 months of the year.
From 1st July to 15th October, 2nd and 4th Tuesday of the month. From 1st May to 30th June, every Tuesday.
In May, June, July, August and September, every last Saturday of the month as well.
Visits start at 2 pm, 3 pm, 4 pm and 5 pm on these days.

ARENES DE LUTECE
49 rue Mongc, Métro Monge. 1st-century Roman open theatre.

No visit organised yet, but you can have a look from the outside.

THERMES DE CLUNY
24 rue du Sommerard, Métro St-Michel, tel. 033 24-21. 2nd-century Roman baths. Unearthed after Napoleon I was taken to St-Helena.

Jazz

Where to hear the best jazz in Paris.

Not as easy as it was some years ago. Good jazzmen are now a rarity in Paris. But there are still a few places where the great traditions are maintained. We offer you a short guide.

One of the first things you learn when you take up residence in Paris is that you should have done it sooner. 'Paris', people never tire of telling you, 'isn't what it was.' Then, gaining stimulus and encouragement from the rueful, silent question mark on your face, they will add with retrospective relish, 'Now fifteen years ago you just couldn't beat Paris for night life (choucroute/girls/bread/ income-tax evasion/oysters/studying Arabic/apache dancing/sleeping under the bridges—you name it).'

And the disconcerting thing is that these long-term residents, their faces gaunt and haggard from a thousand wild bohemian nights of orgiastic indulgence during the golden days of St-Germain-des-Prés, are only too right. They can recall the days when she-ing on the nursery slopes of Pigalle was an excursion into the realm of erotic enlightenment and not a squalid exercise in nightlight robbery.

Paris has changed dramatically, and the transformation, sadly, has robbed it of the quintessence of its old appeal. The very Frenchness of Paris has leaked away. (Not a bit like London which has become more like London than even Brighton.) If Henri de Toulouse-Lautrec were to return to his beloved Paris today he would gaze in horror upon what had happened to the city under de Gaulle and surely punch *mon général* hard on the nose.

Drugstores, frozen food, canned wine, workable plumbing, credit accounts, supermarkets, self service restaurants—*plus ça change, plus c'est Américain*. They've even perfumed the Métro and are carting away, one by one, those incomparably pungent street urinals, the *vespasiennes*.

The blinding irony in all this is that the one area where Americanisation would have been most acceptable—the Paris jazz scene—has not only remained immune from this invasion but has actively repelled it. At this moment there is not a single front-rank American musician playing in any of the Paris jazz clubs.

M

Kenny Clarke, founder of the modern school of jazz drumming, who has been a Paris resident for twelve years, recalling the jazz scene of ten years ago, says: 'They were great days. I worked at the Club St-Germain for two years and at various times I was playing with or opposite Stan Getz, Miles Davis, J. J. Johnson, Art Blakey's Jazz Messengers and the Modern Jazz Quartet. People packed the club to see their idols in the flesh. I can't understand why this sort of thing doesn't happen now.'

The Club St-Germain is now a discothèque; and Kenny Clarke hasn't played in a Paris club since November 1966 when he completed seven years as resident drummer at the Blue Note.

There are three reasons why 'this sort of thing doesn't happen now.' One is called the Beatles. The second is a staggering rise in prices which has seen the cost of a beer shoot up to thirty shillings in some clubs and which in itself accounts for the fact that the audience in these clubs usually consist of a few tone-deaf millionaires.

The third reason is that in December 1965 the Paris Musicians' Union decided to enforce restrictions—already statutory but hitherto largely ignored—on the employment of foreign musicians in clubs, cabarets, radio, television and recording studios. The law, since 1933, has been that employment of foreign musicians in any musical group should not exceed ten per cent. This meant that, in theory, the all-American trio of drummer Kenny Clarke, guitarist Jimmy Gourley and organist Lou Bennett, would have immediately to be augmented by twenty-seven French musicians.

The campaign created a lot of misunderstanding and ill-feeling and the pros and cons of it are too complicated to go into here. Suffice it to say that the result was more employment for cons, less for pros.

Of course, there are some fine French musicians working in Paris, but most of them prefer the security of studio work to the gamble of playing in a club. And those few French jazz musicians who do make club appearances are sadly discovering the truth of the saying that no man is a prophet in his own country. French jazzmen like pianists Martial Solal and George Arvanitas, violinist Jean-Luc Ponty, tenor saxophonists Dominique Chanson and Michel Roques, have won considerable esteem outside France. But it has to be admitted that their appearances in Paris are not exactly sold out.

When tenor saxophonist Johnny Griffin opened the Jazzland club in the rue Saint-Séverin in the summer of 1965, he consistently packed the place night after night. Dexter Gordon, Sonny Rollins, Lee Konitz and other top American jazzmen all played in the club with conspicuous success; but as soon as the management tried to economise by employing less expensive French groups, the attendances declined and business slumped. In December 1966 Jazzland closed its doors for good.

Restrictions on the employment of American musicians and the indifferent drawing power of even the best French musicians have thus made the Paris jazz club scene more impoverished now than at any time since the war.

But, in Paris, as elsewhere, though jazz may get sick, it never dies, because it enjoys the devoted attentions of a handful of enthusiasts who revel almost as much in the challenge of making a living from jazz as in the music itself.

One such enthusiast is Madame Thérèse Ricard, former *patronne* of Le Chat Qui Pêche in the rue de la Huchette, who is undoubtedly the capital's first lady of jazz. This tiny, sprightly, sparkling woman has, in the face of all kinds of difficulties, maintained an uncompromising jazz policy at her club which has endeared her not only to fans but to a long list of American musicians.

Madame Ricard has a mischievous sense of humour, almost no English, and a rare brand of courage which has sustained her through all the hazards—financial and physical—involved in running a jazz cellar in the narrow streets of the Latin Quarter. She was once attacked by a maniac and wounded by his knife, but she carried on dauntless and resolute until last year.

Despite the language problem, she could reduce the most refractory jazz musician to a blushing schoolboy caught stealing the jam.

But then she regards jazz musicians as her children, is keenly aware of their problems and though she has been, necessarily, tough in business, she has never exploited the musicians she employed. On the contrary, she fed them, lent them money—frequently with no reasonable hope of its being repaid—and often accommodated them in her flat over the club.

Le Chat Qui Pêche is not the most comfortable club you ever saw. It is a pretty airless cave with low wooden benches and tables, approached by a rickety stairway which leads down from the dimly-lit bar on street level. The bar's walls are papered with photographs of musicians who have appeared at the club—Bud Powell, Donald

Byrd, Don Cherry, Eric Dolphy, Nathan Davis, Art Farmer, Jackie McLean, Ted Curson, Tony Scott, Don Byas, Dexter Gordon, Johnny Griffin, Chet Baker, and many more.

Across the street from Le Chat Qui Pêche—a distance of about three yards—is the Caveau de la Huchette, another jazz cellar which enjoyed its biggest boom in the late fifties when dixieland music was the religion of university students and 'Les Oignons' by Sidney Bechet sold a million copies. A more spacious *cave* than Le Chat Qui Pêche, the Caveau de la Huchette still attracts a hard core of student trad jazz enthusiasts who have rejected the canned music of the discothèque.

The Caveau de la Huchette employs only French bands and pursues a solidly dixieland policy. In fact, French groups playing modern jazz are almost non-existent—with the exception of two or three trios. Regularly appearing at the Caveau are groups like Maxim Saury's, Les Strapontins, Irakli's jazzmen and the Jazz O'Maniacs.

On the other side of the rue Saint-Jacques in the rue Galande is one of the most picturesque jazz caves in Paris—Aux Trois Mailletz—which has the mainstream/modern Dominique Chanson Quintet as house band and frequently features blues singer Memphis Slim.

This is a charming, stone-flagged cellar club reached by a narrow stairway whose ceiling is so low that you can bark your shins on it. Centuries ago the club was an inn which quenched the thirsts of the stonemasons who were building the Notre-Dame cathedral. It was from the mallet (*maillet*) of the stone masons that the club took its name.

Beneath the cellar is yet another cellar which dates back to the fourth century and which includes a tiny cell where the rebel poet François Villon is supposed to have been kept in solitary confinement after being brought from the Châtelet prison through a tunnel running beneath the Seine. This area of Paris is honeycombed with cellars and passages and economy-minded jazz fans have often toyed with the possibility of tunnelling through from the Trois Mailletz to the Caveau de la Huchette and then the Chat Qui Pêche in order to save some entrance fees.

The second cellar of the Trois Mailletz houses a genuine torture chamber and some of the instruments are still preserved. It is therefore probably prudent not to try to leave without paying your bill.

The Caméléon in the rue Saint-André-des Arts is yet another small cave with the musicians housed in an alcove of such modest dimensions as to limit the size of the band to a quartet. The chief merit of this club is that on most evenings it offers the opportunity of hearing George Arvanitas—one of the most versatile and hard-swinging pianists in France—fighting a winning battle with an upright and slightly out-of-tune piano. He is usually accompanied by Jacky Samson, bass, and Charles Saudrais, drums, and, from time to time the management provide the bonus of a star American soloist.

On these occasions it is advisable to arrive before 10 pm because of limited seating accommodation which, combined with the apparently mandatory dim lighting, can easily result in your sitting on a poorly upholstered Frenchman.

Completing the Left Bank's roster of jazz clubs are the Riverboat, also in the rue Saint-André-des-Arts, Gill's Club in the rue Sainte-Croix-de-la-Bretonnerie, both of which feature predominantly traditional music, and the Lady Bird in the rue de la Huchette which usually boasts a trio—and usually not one that is worth boasting about.

The principal stronghold of the French dixieland movement is the Slow Club in the rue de Rivoli—yet another *cave* where the bands of Claude Luter and Marc Lafférière alternate and where students come to tap their feet and dance a curiously archaic combination of jiving, jitterbugging and twisting.

The most internationally celebrated of all Paris jazz clubs is the Blue Note in the rue d'Artois on the Right Bank.

The Blue Note has a proud history. From January 1st, 1959 to November 1966, drummer Kenny Clarke was in almost continuous residence at the club and, during that period the long, narrow room rang to the superb sounds of such jazz celebrities as Bud Powell, Stan Getz, Ben Webster, Victor Feldman, Dexter Gordon, Johnny Griffin, J. J. Johnson, Zoot Sims, Pony Poindexter, Brew Moore, Kenny Drew, Lee Konitz, Jimmy Guiffre, Booker Ervin, Charlie Byrd, Elvin Jones, Mal Waldron, Sonny Stitt, Sonny Criss, Sahib Shihab, Martial Solal and many more.

In its heyday the club was run by the majestically built, chain-smoking American, Ben Benjamin, and was a focal point both for jazzmen and jazz lovers. Even though it was the most expensive jazz club in Paris, you didn't begrudge your twenty-five bob for a scotch because you could be certain to hear jazz music of a very high standard played by top musicians.

Today, however, with a change in management and policy and

Ben Benjamin only playing a minor role in the running of the club, it is suffering from a sad case of the *sic transit gloria mundis*. Live music, usually played by a French group, is featured only two days of the week. For the rest of the time the Blue Note functions as a discothèque.

If the jazz spirit is dying in the Blue Note, it is vibrantly alive in La Cigale, a unique establishment in the boulevard Rochechouart about seven prostitutes east of the Place Pigalle.

La Cigale is a classic French-type café, with copper-topped bar, ceiling-to-floor mirrors, a five-second shoe-wash type lavatory, the usual plastic and chrome décor and a ceiling discoloured from the smoke of a million and a half Gaulloises. But what makes it unique among Paris cafés is that it has a live jazz group every night of the week except Thursday, with matinées on Saturdays and Sundays.

The resident quintet is led by a remarkable 64-year-old multi-instrumentalist, Benny Waters, who was a sideman in the bands of King Oliver and Jimmy Lunceford. Waters is an immensely genial character who calls everybody Poppa Sam or Mamma Sam according to sex (although there is at least one regular Cigale customer who confuses him).

La Cigale is completely ordinary in every respect—except in the matter of atmosphere. Tourists weary of the Pigalle clip joints and rapidly discovering that Paris *la Nuit* can be Paris *l'ennui*, frequently wander into La Cigale and emerge hours later refreshed and invigorated by the lively, intensely swinging music provided by Benny and his musicians.

Benny plays tenor saxophone, soprano saxophone, alto saxophone and clarinet, sings some blues and specialises in what he calls 'tailgate endings', which are four-bar codas repeated almost ad infinitum until the whole place, right down to the normally inscrutable barman, is swinging like a demented pendulum. It is not sophisticated music, but it gets to the people and keeps bringing them back for more. That's why the Cigale continues to flourish long after many other jazz establishments have closed their doors.

Another reason for its continued popularity, of course, is the fact that it is the cheapest place to hear live jazz in Paris—a beer will only set you back 3 francs 50.

Although I have left the Living Room until last, it is really the club which anyone in search of jazz in Paris should visit first.

To be found in the rue du Colisée just off the avenue des Champs-

Elysées, the Living Room is the youngest jazz club in Paris—it was opened in 1963—but has taken over the Blue Note's role as the Mecca of visiting jazzmen and jazz fans. It also attracts a rich variety of writers, poets, film dubbers, eccentrics, actors and actresses, airline pilots, embassy officials, painters, English au pair girls and American businessmen anxious to explain about Vietnam.

The Living Room has the best grand piano of any Paris club—it almost bisects the oblong room—and its favours are shared by solo pianist Aaron Bridgers, a protégé of Art Tatum, and Art Simmons, who plays with bass and drum accompaniment.

The club gets its name from the intimate, homely atmosphere which is suggested by the open fireplace (which glows with a log fire in winter time) and confirmed by the welcome of Jocelyn Bingham, the ever-smiling West Indian manager, and the briskly but unostentatiously attentive barman, Gil.

Art Simmons, from West Virginia, has been a Paris resident since leaving the us Army in October 1949. His neat and tasteful playing fits in perfectly with the musical policy of the club. You won't find any wild, raving jazz at the Living Room, but neither will your sensitive ears be clogged with that musical molasses known as 'cocktail music'.

Simmons, a talented arranger, has drilled his trio into a tightly-knit unit using inventive treatments to liven up the most hackneyed of standard tunes and to bring to wider attention many great but neglected songs. His chord work is faultless and his right hand delicate and crisp; but, above all, he knows how to swing.

Aaron Bridgers uses a wider canvas, as is the privilege of the solo pianist, and while the influence of his master, Art Tatum, is manifest in his playing, he has also absorbed the message of more modern practitioners such as Bud Powell and Bill Evans.

The visitors' book at the Living Room is a pretty comprehensive Jazz Who's Who, and a list of the top line jazzmen who have visited the club and sat in with the resident musicians would fill several pages of this book.

With the Paris jazz scene in a continual state of flux—jazzmen come and go so rapidly that very often only a handful of people know of their presence in Paris—the safest way to check on the club scene at any given time is to call at the Living Room. This is because this club is the jazz forum of Paris—often late at night, musicians form the majority of the clientèle—and is an automatic port of call for visiting jazzmen.

And if you happen to be a musician yourself, there's a very good chance that you'll be able to sit in at the Living Room, provided you know a crotchet from a crowbar and that you don't rattle the bones behind the bar with triple fortissimo trombone choruses.

If, on the other hand, you are a celebrity spotter or inveterate name-dropper, the Living Room can often be relied upon to yield richly. Visitors to the club have included Ava Gardner, Sidney Poitier, Dame Margot Fonteyn, Harry Belafonte, Deborah Kerr, Jacques Tati, Orson Welles, Fernandel, Peter Ustinov, Omar Sharif, Nana Mouskouri, Françoise Sagan, Joe Louis, Shirley McLaine, Peter O'Toole, George C. Scott, and Christine Keeler.

The Jazz Clubs of Paris

BLUE NOTE, 27 rue d'Artois, Paris 8. Tel. BAL 18.92.
Nearest Métro: Saint-Philippe-du-Roule.
Open: Fridays and Saturdays only for live music, 10 pm to 4 am.
Music: Modern.
Prices: 17 francs 50 centimes for a drink at live music sessions; no entrance fee.

CAMELEON, 57 rue Saint-André-des-Arts, Paris 6. Tel. DAN 64.40.
Nearest Métro: Odéon.
Open: Every evening except Sunday, 10 pm to 2 am.
Music: Modern, usually the Georges Arvanitas Trio.
Prices: 15 francs for a drink; no entrance fee.

CAVEAU DE LA HUCHETTE, 5 rue de la Huchette, Paris 5. Tel. DAN 65.05.
Nearest Métro: Saint-Michel.
Open: Normally every evening from 9.30 pm to 1 am.
Music: Traditional French groups.
Prices: 7 francs for admission and first drink.

LE CHAT QUI PECHE, 4 rue de la Huchette, Paris 5. Tel. DAN 23.06.
Nearest Métro: Saint-Michel.
Open: Normally every evening from 10 pm to 2 am.
Music: Modern, often American soloists.
Prices: Admission normally 2 francs and drinks at 15 francs.

LA CIGALE, 124 boulevard Rochechouart, Paris 18. Tel. MON 59.29.
Nearest Métro: Pigalle.
Open: Every evening except Thursday, from 9.30 pm to 1.30 am.
Matinées Saturday and Sunday at 3 pm.
Music: Mainstream; Benny Waters Quintet.
Prices: About 5 francs for a drink; no entrance fee.

GILL'S CLUB, 7 rue Sainte-Croix-de-la-Bretonnerie, Paris 4.
Nearest Métro: Hôtel de Ville.
Open: Every evening except Monday from 9.30 pm till dawn.
Dancing matinée Sunday at 3 pm.
Music: Various.
Prices: 6 to 8 francs for a drink; no entrance fee.

LADY BIRD, 10 rue de la Huchette, Paris 5. Tel. DAN 50.60.
Nearest Métro: Saint-Michel.
Open: Every evening except Sunday from 10 pm to 2 am (to 3 am
on Friday and Saturday).
Music: Various.
Prices: 10 to 14 francs for a drink; no entrance fee.

LIVING ROOM, 25 rue du Colisée, Paris 8. Tel. ELY 25.29.
Nearest Métro: Saint-Philippe-du-Roule.
Open: Every evening except Sunday from 10 pm to 4 am.
Music: Modern; the Art Simmons Trio and solo pianist Aaron
Bridgers.
Prices: 15 francs for a drink; no entrance fee.

RIVERBOAT, 67 rue Saint-André-des-Arts, Paris 6.
Nearest Métro: Odéon.
Open: Friday, Saturday and Sunday from 9.30 pm to 2 am.
Music: Traditional French groups.
Prices: 5 francs for a drink; no entrance fee.

SLOW CLUB, 130 rue de Rivoli, Paris 1. Tel. CUT 84.30.
Nearest Métro: Louvre.
Open: Every evening except Monday from 9.30 pm to 2 am.
Music: Traditional French groups.
Prices: 7 francs for a drink weekdays, 9 francs at weekends; no
entrance fee.

AUX TROIS MAILLETZ, 56 rue Galande, Paris 5. Tel. ODE 00.79.
Nearest Métro: Saint-Michel.
Open: Every evening except Monday from 10 pm to 2 am.
Matinée on Sunday at 4 pm.
Music: Modern; Dominique Chanson Quintet.
Prices: Admission 3 francs; drinks at 13 francs.

NOTE: Prices subject to fluctuation—so be warned!

Film-goer's Paris

Paris is a wonderful city in which to go to the cinema. The variety is magnificent, the audiences are some of the most discerning and critical in the world, and for the English or Amerian film-goer who can't understand a word of French, there are some thirty cinemas showing his homeland's films undubbed. There's no doubt about it: in Paris the cinema is very much one of the fine arts. . . .

Film addicts are a special breed, almost a race apart from the rest of humanity. You will find them in their colonies and outposts in San Francisco and London, New York and Madrid, Berlin and Rome but their real capital is Paris. Paris is heaven for the cinephile. Paris is where all good film addicts go before they die.

Where should the film addict make for once he has arrived in Paris? If he is already fortunate enough to be an expert in his own country with Paris as the ultimate Mecca, he will know where to go in advance and he may even have some introduction into one of the main clans revolving around the reviews *Cahiers du Cinéma*, *Positif* and *Présence du Cinéma*. But only a few foreigners will be so lucky and it is well-known that the cinema clans in Paris tend to be closed rather than open groups and not particularly well-disposed towards newcomers. They have their own ritual and mythical reunions with the *Cahiers* crowd gathering (as you would expect) on the Champs-Elysées (for some reason they nearly all seem to be Corsicans) after having taken lessons from their arch-priest, the Pope Godard, and the *Positif* crowd meeting for Sunday drinks in the house of Robert Benayound, their leader and chief critic. The least important of the three clans, the *Présence du Cinéma* crowd, has its headquarters in the *Macmahon* cinema on the avenue of the same name. The films there are usually of solid American workmanship, by Lang, Mankiewicz, Walsh and Losey, in his American period (his English films being too problematical and not 'classical' enough), as well as run-of-the-mill musicals (Koster) and less 'serious' types of Western (Hathaway). Above all, the classical Hollywood of the forties and the star system reign supreme in the Macmahon.

The American cinema is certainly well served in Paris. Revivals are frequent and continuous in the many *cinémas d'essai* (the Paris equivalent of the 'art cinema' or 'classic') which have been mush-rooming with increasing frequency in and around the Latin Quarter and which offer Humphrey Bogart 'cycles', Howard Hawks 'weeks', 'novelties' by McCarey and various other treasures hitherto undiscovered or rediscovered with the help of some veteran film addict/expert. There is always something to see and always something to suit every taste. The quality of the projection may not always be high (although it is certainly better in the *cinémas d'essai* than in the bigger first-run houses on the Champs-Elysées or big boulevards with their often uncertain projectionists, squawking and evil-mannered attendants or *placeuses* who seem to delight in leading you to the worst seat in the place, over-warm seats, eccentric sound system, not to speak of the astronomical prices of the seats) but you will always be able to see films, both old and new, with the original sound-track. A true film addict will always refuse to see a dubbed film. Dubbing is bad enough in itself but in Paris it is worse than anywhere else.

A first exploratory survey of the Latin Quarter cinema scene should include visits to the tiny little *Dragon* (almost no bigger than a corridor) near the church of Saint-Germain-des-Prés (24 rue du Dragon; seats at 6 and 8 francs and don't forget that in every cinema you are expected to tip as much as 50 centimes when the *placeuse* shows you to your seat. You can take another seat if you like but you can't get out of tipping). Next, you should go off the boulevard Saint-Michel to the two pretty little cinemas in the rue Saint-Séverin (*Saint-Séverin* and *Studio de la Harpe*; seats 8 francs) and then to the half dozen or so rather varied cinemas on the rue des Ecoles and along the dark and narrow little rue Champollion running into the Place de la Sorbonne and crowded in the evenings with long queues of students (*Actua-Champo*, from 2 francs; *Champollion*, 4.25 francs; *Studio Medicis*, 8 francs; *Studio Logos*, from 5 francs; *Noctambules*, 4.25 francs; *Quartier Latin*, 7.20 francs).

A little higher up the boulevard and near the gardens and station of the same name, the recently opened *Luxembourg* (67 rue Monsieur-le-Prince; 7 francs) has the added advantage of being a kind of Holy Trinity of cinemas, a three-in-one house with pretty girls dressed in futuristic metallic-looking mini-skirts to guide you to any of three quiet and comfortable auditoriums on different levels where the selection is always interesting and you can see anything from the latest Hungarian masterpiece to the classics of yesteryear. Another good cinema in the same neighbourhood, the *Racine*

(6 rue de l'Ecole de Médecine; 7.30 francs) specialises in midnight shows of horror films for devotees of Dracula and Barbara Steele or else films by young directors unable to get normal distribution.

Far away on the Right Bank, the *Studio Action* (9 rue Buffault, Métro station, Le Peletier, 5 francs) specialises in films which are usually American and which have been unjustly neglected by the critics and public at the time of their first showing (Boetticher, Corman, Kazan, Laughton's one and only marvellous *Night of the Hunter*, Fuller, Ray, and recently a wild series of melodramas by Douglas Sirk). The *Cahiers* crowd have another more luxurious and very snobbish hang-out at the *Napoléon* (4 avenue de la Grande Armée; 7 and 8 francs) near the Arc de Triomphe, another house specialising in midnight horror films. In the same area, apart from the *Macmahon*, you may wish to go to the rather run-down *Studio de l'Etoile* (14 rue Troyon; 7.20 francs) or the venerable *Cinéma des Champs-Elysées* (118 avenue des Champs-Elysées; 3 francs) which opens in the morning at 10 am. Now mainly haunted by old ladies and pensioners, it was for a long time the only *cinéma d'essai* of the early fifties. It is full of memories, rather like the veteran *Biograph* near Victoria Station in London, and a haven for the nostalgic, with films starring Harry Baur, Raimu and Jouvet, etc.

Connoisseurs of unusual cinema architecture should on no account miss the astonishing *Ranelagh* in the Passy district (5 rue des Vignes; 6 francs) with its Renaissance-style auditorium, red plush seats, sculpted wooden boxes, coffered ceiling and huge foyer complete with carpets and stag-heads that might have come straight out of an English country manor, and a permanent display of Surrealist drawings and paintings. On the boulevard Bonne-Nouvelle, the tiny *Bikini* only projects on 16 mm and might have been designed for an audience of dwarfs. (31 boulevard Bonne-Nouvelle; 2.50 francs). Back on the Left Bank, the splendid *Pagode* (57 bis rue de Babylone; from 4.20 francs) has the added appeal of being a real Chinese pagoda full of stuccoes and mirrors. The selection of film classics is well-planned and eclectic, ranging from the Marx Brothers to *Scorpio Rising*. In the heart of Montparnasse, one of the few houses showing a double-feature programme is the *Studio Parnasse* in the picturesque and disreputable rue Jules Chaplain (number 11; 6.30 francs). It is particularly popular with students and artists living near by and the manager, Monsieur Cherey, holds weekly film quizzes and debates with half-price tickets as prizes for those who wish to stay after the last show. Votes are taken on films and addicts are provided with more or less reliable filmographies posted up in the foyer. Beware if the manager is in a bad humour for you are likely to get a broadside if your tastes don't coincide with his. Not far from the boulevard Montparnasse, the delightfully named rue de la Gaîté still has two surviving 'flea pits' (there were three last year but one has now become metamorphosed into the *Translux Pullman Gaîté*, a first-run house), the *Gaîté Palace* and the *Splendide-Gaîté* where for about 2 francs you can follow the adventures of Maciste, the Ringo Kid and Wyatt Earp. The *Splendide-Gaîté* is also popular with *clochards* who give it a rather 'Threepenny Opera' atmosphere. On the boulevard again, facing the hallowed Dôme café, and next to the hideously modernised Rotonde café, the *Rotonde* (7 francs) allows you to smoke and listen to the original sound track, if a foreign film, through rather H. G. Wellsian and highly uncomfortable earphones springing from the back of the seats. Films here are nearly always of the sub-James Bond type, with such typical titles as *Showdown at Singapore* or *Banco at Bangkok for OSS 117*.

The Right Bank has few art houses but many highly characteristic cinemas. The *Jean Renoir* (43 boulevard de Clichy; 5 francs) often has seasons devoted to the work of its namesake, one of France's greatest-ever directors. Near-by, in Montmartre, the *Studio 28* (10 rue Tholozé; 6 francs) is worth seeking out. Even if you can't find it you can always end up in a Pigalle nightspot or just observe the local fauna. In the Thirties, it was Paris' first art house and, with the *Marbeuf* off the Champs-Elysées, it is the most comfortable cinema in Paris with enormous leather arm-chairs in which you can stretch out and go to sleep if you feel like it. Also in Pigalle, the *Scarlett* (34 boulevard de Clichy; from 3.50 francs) offers 'sexy' films (always disappointing) and homages to some unknown genius of the 'B' cinema. On the boulevard Rochechouart (number 80; only 1.35 francs) the enormous, decaying and rather dirty *Trianon* is almost exclusively frequented by Arabs and Africans living in the district. It is certainly worth a visit for the sociologically-minded and has a very noisy and enthusiastic audience who believe to the full in audience participation. In the Belleville-Ménilmontant area, now fast becoming an Arab quarter, there are a few cinemas showing films in Arabic from the Middle East. One such is the open air *Alcazar*, a former circus with beaten earth floor, and the astonishing *Cocorico* (128 boulevard Belleville; from 2 francs) with thirty years of graffiti on its decaying old music-hall walls.

The huge *Wepler-Pathé* (Place Clichy; from 7.30 francs) will take you into another world with its science-fiction glass and metal décor and if you want something even more modern and automatised you should go to the *Publicis-Orly* at Orly airport, with jets screaming overhead and its automatic seats which light up as you make your way towards them. Largest and ugliest of the mammoth palaces are the *Empire* (41 avenue de Wagram; 12 francs), the enormous *Gaumont-Palace* (3 rue Caulaincourt; from 6 francs) and the *Kinopanorama* (60 avenue de La Motte-Picquet; from 5 francs), an outpost of the Soviet cinema specialising in Russian super-colossal epics such as *War and Peace*. The *Rex* (1 boulevard Poissonnière; from 6.50 francs) has a handsome foyer with fountains, is decorated in a pure 1930 style and is one of the rare Paris cinemas which allows smoking. The *Paris-Ciné* (17 boulevard de Strasbourg; from 2 francs though only 1.50 before 2 pm) and the *Strasbourg* (8 boulevard Bonne-Nouvelle; from 1.55 francs) are probably the two dirtiest cinemas in Paris although probably highly popular with performing flea impresarios. The *Studio Universal* (31 avenue de l'Opéra; from 3.50 francs) and the *Obligado A* and *B* (two cinemas in one) cater for children with adventure films and cartoons galore. The *Calypso* (27 avenue des Ternes; 7 francs) and the two *Publicis* cinemas (131 avenue des Champs-Elysées and Place Saint-Germain-des-Prés; both at 10.30 francs) have the prettiest attendants in Paris. The over-rated *Midi-Minuit* (14–16 boulevard Poissonnière; from 2.75 francs) was where horror-film addicts used to come in pilgrimage before it began showing 'daring' nude films. It is still haunted by dirty old men and potential Jack-the-Rippers in search of a new thrill and the graffiti in the Gents is enough to justify a visit anyway. The *Brady* on the boulevard de Strasbourg continues to delight the bloodthirsty and is worth inspecting for its horrific outside decorations. One of its more distinguished visitors is the Spanish playwright Arrabal, a leading exponent of the 'theatre of cruelty'.

The film addict will find all the information on times of showing, etc., in the excellent weekly *Pariscope* (every Thursday; 50 centimes) or the *Semaine de Paris* (every Thursday; 80 centimes). The chances are that he will first look at the programmes of Paris' two cinémathèques which offer the rather indigestible feast of seven films every day between them (*Cinémathèque Chaillot*, Palais de Chaillot; near the Métro station Trocadéro; entrance through the gardens; seats at 3 francs; students 2 francs; *Cinémathèque Ulm*, 29 rue d'Ulm, nearest Métro station, Monge; seats 2 francs; students 1 franc). If you so wish you may see three or four different films at one go, at 6.30, 8.30 and 10.30 pm at the *Ulm* and at 3.30, 6.30, 8.30, 10.30 pm at the Chaillot, but beware: if you stay any time in Paris and make a habit of going you may well become surfeited. After a while the films will always seem to be the same, the 'seasons' rarely of any great importance, new films a rarity and the so-called discoveries often disappointing. There is a great difference between the two *cinémathèques*. In the Chaillot *cinémathèque* you will see films undubbed in a modern and comfortable auditorium with a highly competent projectionist and a silent public; in the second, second-choice films by indifferent directors are shown badly in a dim hall to a noisy student public (you can always tell the Latin Americans by their inability to refrain from making loud comments all the way through the film). All in all, a pretty uninspired, second-rate choice in the rue d'Ulm, unlike Chaillot where you get such attractions as 300 Japanese films shown in one season, special seasons in honour of Hawks, Cukor, Resnais, Truffaut, Godard, Jeanne Moreau, etc., often in the presence of the director or star concerned before a super-elite *cinéphile* audience.

The Cinémathèque has been run and often attended by the now legendary figures of Mary Meerson, the mother-goddess of the Cinémathèque Française, Henri Langlois and Lotte Eisner. The Cinémathèque has become almost a myth ever since the early heroic days when it was situated on the avenue de Messine where most contemporary French film makers began their careers, picking their way through a motley collection of old magic lanterns, optical devices and toys, early cameras and Meliès film props to reach the projection room. The big seasons at Chaillot are now its apotheosis.

The film addict will also find various book-shops specialising in film books and magazines for the French seem to publish more about the cinema than anyone else in the world. Much of it is also more florid and pretentious than anywhere else as well. The *Minotaure* (2 rue des Beaux-Arts) is one of the best with two highly informed and friendly booksellers in attendance. The *Terrain Vague* (14 rue de Verneuil), also near Saint-Germain-des-Prés, is rather more erratically run by a temperamental high priest of the Surrealist movement. Both book-shops abound in studies of unjustly neglected directors, so-called 'minor masters', lengthy exegeses, theses and texts by pompous and sonorous establishment critics or angry young rebels, and a number of intelligent, acute studies of periods and style in film history. But even though the majority of what is written about the cinema in France is chaotic, over-prejudiced, pretentious, foolish or downright unnecessary, it does prove that Paris is the paradise of the *cinéphile* and that, despite all affectations, love for the cinema is genuine, deep-rooted and even mature at times. Many writers have called the cinema the 'seventh art'. In Paris, more than any other city in the world, you can feel that it is the first art.

The Halles District

Perhaps more than a conglomeration of 'villages', Paris is a city of 'quarters', each with its own character, its own population, customs and traditions, and its own brand of charm or beauty. Here are a few of them— the most strongly identifiable, the most famous and, for many people, the most 'Parisian'. . . .

Within the triangle formed by the three churches, Sainte-Eustache, Saint-Merri and the Reformed Oratory church, the central market place of Paris once stood. For over a century the best foods of France and the world ebbed and flowed under the vast steel construction of arched domes to keep the earth's most *gourmand* city well fed.

But nine centuries earlier, in the days of Louis VI, the site already had its *Grand Marché Public*, created along with the *Cimetière des Innocents* to meet the demands of a growing population. Side by side, market and graveyard grew and flourished in what was then an area outside the walls of the *Cité* known as *Champeaux* or 'little fields'. On their way to the market, people would walk through the 'field of rest' where unlimited by walls, children played, *lingerès* hung their washings and *grisettes* conjured up their brief encounters.

Today there is a new market at Rungis near Orly airport. According to sinister rumours, it appears that the old market place and many surrounding houses may be demolished. Time alone will tell what we stand to gain from such a sacrifice to finance *espaces verts* or whatever streamlined dream will flower on the time-honoured site. Such as it is, however, the old *quartier* has its wisdom and pleasures which the builders of the Paris of tomorrow might do well to bear in mind.

Les Halles or *la Halle*, the market place *par excellence*, is familiar to Parisian and foreigner alike, who usually haunted it by night, when most of its activities took place. Hedged in by a maze of some of the oldest streets in Paris, the whole district is still a paradise for the pedestrian. Perhaps the best way to approach the area is from the Left Bank, crossing the Seine by the Pont des Arts and walking through the great courtyard of the Louvre, the Cour Carrée, before crossing the rue de Rivoli past the Temple de l'Oratoire where the statue of Admiral Coligny, in courtly 16th-century attire, keeps watch by his Protestant bible only a few yards away from where the Massacre of the Huguenots began in 1572.

Behind the church, the rue Saint-Honoré narrows into the medieval hamlet road it once was, leading towards the market site where preparations were once made for the biggest feast you never ate and where the foods of the world were still spilling out onto the pavements not so very long ago.

The Halles were the lifeblood of the surrounding tributary *rues* and *ruelles*. Iron-curtained storehouses still remain, small shops still sell their speciality foodstuffs and the smell of meat, fruit and vegetables still clings to the walls of the festering houses that have seen so much of Paris' long and turbulent history.

Opposite the oratory church, at no. 144, a small shop bears the proud sign *Produits Exotiques*, and is still crammed with barrels and bags, sacks heavy with lemon semolina and saffron pollenta, dark brown and coral lentils, and all the beans of France: the broad and the dwarfish, the black and the white, the tender green variety and the deep red bean which the French call the 'cock kidney' ('*foie de coq*'). Rices and coconut midlings and pure flour are still displayed in smaller transparent bags showing every shade of whiteness, and olives are seen swimming in their oil in huge hooped barrels.

This was part of the fascination of Les Halles. Nothing was put away, showcased, sliced, bottled or bound. This was the realm of the wholesale where everything was indeed sold whole and where academicians, poets and lovers would stroll at night intoxicated or fascinated by the abundance of the earth in the very living heart of Paris.

The butchers and *charcuteries* that have survived, often next to an elegant restaurant, display vivid panels and triptychs showing edible animals in the various stages of their beastly after-life. Here, the king of the animals was the pig who lent himself to such impressive variety of succulent forms from the suckling pig placed whole on restaurant tables to the ham-hocks, feet and sausages. In the Halles quarter alone, the pig has given his name to at least three well-known restaurants, the *Pied du Cochon*, *Le Cochon de Lait* and *Le Cochon d'Or*.

Before the market was moved to its present site, such a visible abundance of fresh meat brought out the hunter and fisher in the visitor. The sight of a *pied de cochon* (pig's trotter) being carted off, still hairy and bloody, of a red-faced peasant woman holding a chicken by the feet, or of a black and white lobster fighting it out in a fish tank near a restaurant table, was enough to remind the late-night diner that man was meant to be lord and husbandman of the animal kingdom. Eating at a Les Halles restaurant took on a new meaning, a new dimension. Time was reserved for doing little else. The provincial farmer would come to Les Halles at night to see his lifework in the meal set before him and, subconsciously at least, the boisterous tourists and belly-worshippers who came at night were all craving the sacrificial thrill. Now all this is gone. The restaurants have remained but their vast setting has been dismantled.

Even so, the rue Saint-Honoré has kept its French regional shops. Old allegiances between this part of Paris and the provinces are still strong. At number 99, you may still go to *La Maison du Saumon* with its brightly coloured jars of pickled vegetables, for salmon, sturgeon's eggs, dried cod and ell. At number 102, the *Produits d'Auvergne* is still filled with full-formed cheeses and loaves of rye, mountain honeycombs and twisted sausages, square slabs of bacon and luth-shaped hams smoked during idle winter hours on family hearths tucked away in the hills of Auvergne. At number 73, you may still go to the *Aux Vrais Produits Bretons* for its fat, smooth cylinders of salami and dried cod hanging low over barrels of neatly coiled black pudding and stacks of 'quatre-quarts' cakes the size of Breton round hats.

As in the butchers and the *charcuteries* of the Halles district, most of these regional products are hanging from the walls and ceilings. Odd to think that at the crossing of the rue Sauval and the rue de l'Arbre Sec—once the site of the heaviest concentration of meat in the whole city—there used to be a square and in that square a gibbet. *Arbre sec* or 'dry tree' was just another word for the gallows where bodies were left hanging as a warning to others. On the corner of the rue de l'Arbre Sec and rue Saint-Honoré once stood a cross, the Croix du Trahoir, set there to comfort those on their way to execution. An unusual house, the *Maison d'Andorre*, now stands on the site with a fountain spouting from one wall.

Running roughly parallel with the market place, the rue Saint-Honoré links up with the northern end of the Halles through a series of short, narrow streets opening under the dark, arched galleries of the market place and onto the brightness opposite. Now unencumbered by food products, you may see from the rue Vauvilliers between the Bourse de Commerce and the North Pavilion to the funny little houses in the rue du Jour beside the magnificent church of Saint-Eustache.

Flower market days were held four times a week in the rue des Prouvaires (*Prouvaires* used to be a word for priests) and you could see country folk arranging flower pots on green trestles or spreading them out to make little fields at the dark foot of the church. It is a strange little street that might have come out of some Breton port. The cafés there are squat with low ceilings and shabbily dressed customers. Go to the *As de Trèfle*, *Chez le Basque* or *La Poule au Pot* for a glass of wine but remember that the mere fact of walking through a door in a Les Halles *bistrot* does not automatically make you welcome. Cyrano de Bergerac was born in this street and Henri IV, that great soldier and king who made the phrase 'Poule au pot' so popular by expressing the wish that every peasant home in France might have its 'chicken in the pot' was assassinated only a hundred yards east on the rue de la Ferronnerie next to the inn, *Au Cœur percé d'une Flèche*.

Nearby, the obesity of the Bourse de Commerce—once used for storing wheat—is redeemed by one of the most curious relics in the whole district: a single fluted column built into the building which was traditionally supposed to have been used as an observation tower by Catherine de Medicis, her astronomers and the famous Nostradamus.

The north side of the square where the great pavilions stand is mainly distinguished by its restaurants (Alsace aux Halles, etc.) with their phony chalet-type décors, overpublicised charms and promise of Lucullan banquets to lure the innocent, and Sainte-Eustache with its great towers and flying buttresses. Here, one of the most beautiful hours in the life of the Halles was when the flower vendors used to put their pots away in their big water-willow baskets and women plucked up their flowers and greenery that seemed to be growing out of the pavement. The wholesale flower market lasted from two to six in the afternoon in the rue Baltard and under the galleries of the Halles Centrales, with quick bargains being offered for a further two hours.

The little side streets between the rue Baltard and the rue Saint-Denis specialised in leaves, mosses, branches and nursery trees—in a word everything from the forests around Paris. The atmosphere of the country still lingers and in the rue Berger, even the café names celebrate the country in Paris: *L'Etoile du Midi*, *Au Coq du Beaujolais*, *A la Vallée*, *à l'Ecureil* and *Au Singe* (where you can see a live monkey swinging from the ceiling).

Rue Berger leads into the Place des Innocents, its garden enclosed by iron railings with a sign forbidding access to the very young. For eight centuries, this was Paris' biggest 'field of rest' where the earth swallowed up over two million Parisians. So good was the soil that it was said to be able to 'eat a corpse in nine days'. The name of Innocents was given to the cemetery in memory of the thousand babies slain by Herod.

There is something refreshing and restful about this little square and its surrounding houses, something unfolklorish—like the whole Halles quartier for that matter. A simple square in the heart of the city, a place of romance, as long as they don't turn the aesthetic floodlights on it as they have of late in the Place Furstenberg, or crowd the sidewalk with motor-cars as in defenceless Place Dauphine or Place de la Contrescarpe, or hire phony tramps to stretch out under the trees, pass the bottle and unabashedly make a spectacle of their slapstick dialogues.

Standing in the centre of the square is the Fontaine des Innocents where eight willowy sylphs can be seen pouring water from hips, shoulders, knees and other places. Renoir once came here to gaze at them for hours, hoping to unlock the secret of femininity. And if he did, he confessed it was thanks to these Graces. Forgotten beauties they are, and few Parisians today consider them as forming the capital's loveliest fountain.

In strange contrast with these statues of innocence, are the temptresses striking poses nearby in the rue Saint-Denis. Here, as in the neighbouring rue de la Reynie, rue des Lombards, rue Berger, rue de la Consonnerie, rue de la Verrerie, rue Quincampoix, rue Berger, rue Nicolas Flamel, and rue Saint-Bon, hotel doors are open and entrance ways welcoming with high-coloured women who cluster around the staircases in bright bouquets beckoning to the passer-by.

Prostitutes are one of the more permanent aspects of the quarter. For over ten centuries, they have been standing in these doorways or in those of the houses before them. Charlemagne and later Saint Louis tried unsuccessfully to drive them out of the quarter and both had to compromise by banning them from the streets. They have been standing in the doorways ever since. If the authorities go through with their drastic plan of razing the market and surrounding houses—over 80 acres—these women will have to go and not even a street name will remain to commemorate their ten centuries' standing and the Halles will have lost another of its many faces.

What makes a *quartier* are the people who live and work there. A certain stability and permanence in time and place are necessary to mould a *quartier's* character. The deadly 16th arrondissement has none because it is over-residential and not enough people work there. The Champs-Elysées and Concorde districts are only half-alive because not enough people actually live there—far too many office buildings in proportion to the number of inhabitants. People will tell you that life is 'impossible' in Paris but what made one of the greatest charms of the Halles district was that here, at least, life was 'possible'. The real inhabitants of Les Halles built one of the greatest villages in Paris. Life was self-contained. Wine, women, food, a certain spaciousness—all was to be found here in these few acres. Life was within arms' reach. You could sleep and poach on your own preserves and the rest of Paris was foreign territory. It is a district which inspires an enormous amount of affection.

Montmartre

A large number of visitors to Paris prefer to take their night life in glamorous doses at the Lido, or in the more sophisticated though colourless clubs round the Etoile.

Montmartre is different. It is gritty and always has been. Its night clubs offer the kind of entertainment respectability likes to read about but dares not talk about, in public at least.

Yet even Montmartre has been dusted pretty sharply recently. Before the Second World War police operating in the quarter spent their time tracking down drug peddlars gathered in the Royal Cabaret or the Rat Mort on Place Pigalle. Both are memories today.

There was no time then to worry about opening and closing hours, Montmartre lived almost 24 hours a day. Instead the main concern of the law was the gangs, mostly Corsican—the Bastiani brothers for example—whose business was running women, buying and selling them like cattle and executing them if they did not obey.

A favourite trick for example was rubbing their made-up faces, when they misbehaved, with coarse sugar. Their faces festered after this poisonous treatment and disfigured them. Another pleasant trick was slicing off the tip of a recalcitrant nose with a razor.

Today there are still plenty of pimps and many of them continue

Porte Sainte-Denis

to gather round the Montmartre mountain but they are more discreet.

Most bars now close at 2 am though they may reopen at 5 am if they wish, and some do.

Cabarets stay open until the last drunk has lurched his way out, but the show winds up between 2 and 3 am.

There are, of course, two Montmartres . . . the romantic and the sordid.

Most people, very rightly, prefer the latter because sheer vice as an occupation and a way of earning a living is gradually losing out. What was considered vice years ago is just spice today.

On the other hand the view from Sacré-Coeur, at night, over-looking the misleading fairy lights of a very earthy city, is fascinating. Most people can pick out the Opéra and the Gare du Nord and, of course, the Eiffel Tower. But they get mixed up with the other buildings and are never able to trace the quarter of the city where their hotels are situated.

At one time the Place du Tertre oozed treacle and romance; the sugar being helped down with generous libations of pastis and other delightful if noxious drinks.

Today the famous Place—which is also the commercial heart of the 'Free Commune of Montmartre' has developed into a hard-core haggling market for a couple of hundred more or less talented artists and their 'leg men' who tout for customers.

Yet it would be unfair to criticise this modern Montmartre indiscriminately.

The rue Drevet with its steep and narrow steps leading to the mountain is fascinating if tiring. The rue Durantin with its quaint courtyards—take a look at number 40 where a brilliant film called *Peau de Pêche* was made, is very Montmartroise. The rue de l'Abreuvoir with its ivy-festooned houses, and the rue des Saules and its memorial vineyard owned and exploited by the City of Paris is worth a glance since it is the only vineyard in Europe which flourishes, blooms and ripens in the heart of a vast capital.

Rise like a bird in the cable-car, which starts from the place Suzanne Valten and settles before the Sacré-Cœur. Remember to take field glasses in order to follow Paris lying at your feet.

The Touring Club has set up a useful indicator which should help pick out one or two spots.

A glimpse inside the Byzantine Sacré-Cœur should be enough. Then seek out—about 200 yards away—the *Place du Tertre* which, despite its metamorphosis over the past thirty years, is still worth a visit.

Montmartre has never enjoyed a great reputation for its restaurants or food. *La Mère Catherine* and the *Cadet de Gascogne* both on the Place du Tertre enjoy some notoriety, probably because of their location although *La Mère Catherine* serves a very attractive *Poulet Grand-Mère*.

But it is the coloured parasols planted over white linen table-cloths and the red serviettes which are the great draw.

The Place is intimate. Its trees are powerful and the joy of being served in such surroundings is unforgettable.

Thirty years ago Montmartre's artists were discreet and more concerned with brushes and palettes than with tourists. Now and again a picturesque figure in broad brimmed black hat and, may be, a flowing cloak would approach the tables.

'Madame la Princesse et Monsieur le Prince', he would whisper 'allow me to sketch the nobility of your characters as revealed by your handsome beauty'.

Flattery indeed but preferable to the glinty, granity approach of the modern 'masters' who over-charge for their daubs and hide the sun with their easels planted like artichokes round the Place. However, it is all well worth seeing and, up to a point, paying for.

In one corner is the rue du Calvaire. It possesses a restaurant called the *Auberge du Coucou*. At one time tables were laid out on its terrace. Opposite is an unforgettable scene; the balcony over-looking the city from which Louise sings her famous aria in Charpentier's opera which bears her name.

Unfortunately the Auberge is now a club called *Chez Plumeau* and if the balcony and the scene remain, the terrace alas is bare of tables.

The rue Norvin is narrow. So is the rue St-Rustique where Monet, Renoir, Van Gogh, Emile Zola and Toulouse-Lautrec met to eat in the leafy garden of the *Bonne Franquette*. You can do the same reasonably well for round 50 shillings.

And finally while it is still light walk down the *Allée des Brouillards* which gives onto a charming garden where you still see a handful of Poulbots (the name given to the ragamuffins of Montmartre immortalised in a thousand paintings by Poulbot) playing in the sand. You will also notice St. Denis himself carved for posterity in stone, his head in his hands. Within the shadow of the Saint a half-dozen ageing pensioners will be playing bowls.

The brimming romance of 'la belle époque' which will never be separated from Montmartre may still be absorbed in sickly doses in a museum just off the Place du Tertre in which wax figures and tableaux tell the story. There is another more serious and instructive museum containing many fine paintings by masters who worked in Montmartre.

This is *La Butte* by which name the 'mount' of Montmartre is known. Until the Revolution it was a mass of vineyards, and a Benedictine sanctuary which was destroyed during the Revolution.

It is rumoured that a fabulous treasure, hidden at that time by the Benedictines in one of the galeries with which the *Butte* is riddled, has still to be found.

May be it is buried beneath the foundations of the timbered *Moulin de la Galette* on the rue Lepic immortalised by Guy de Maupassant.

In those days the Moulin was a 'bal' frequented by the riff-raff as well as gentlemen of leisure; ladies of easy virtue and the sleazy apaches so dear to short-story writers; and to Hollywood also in its early days.

Today the Moulin has lost both its lustre and charm. Saturday night dances are still held but most of the building has been turned into television studios.

Nevertheless, its gardens still perfume the quarter with the romantic essence of the past.

Walk down the hill to the market in the rue Lepic, taking at the same time a fleeting glance at the rue Véron (Véron was director of the Paris Opera at one time) and at one or two of the other thread narrow and winding streets. John Huston made his famous film *Moulin Rouge*, based on the tragic life of Toulouse Lautrec, in the streets which the artist knew so well.

But romance does not go down with the sun in Montmartre for the quarter's night life is as turbulent as its days are smooth.

Montmartre nightlife is divided into two water-tight sections. The fountain in the Place Pigalle is the hub of a turbulent roundabout embroidered with 'come hither' women and doused with champagne and whisky.

La Butte however still provides the kind of entertainment which made Montmartre famous ... the chansonniers where one may still hear such typical old songs as *Ma Femme est Morte*, *Le Fiacre* and *La Jolie Vigne* not forgetting the last chorus which goes 'piss, piss, piss'.

The *Chat Noir* and *Aristide Bruant* have long disappeared but La Butte still provides similar artistic fare.

In the rue des Saules the *Lapin Agile* will charm and, if the night is hot, stifle for it is very small, always crowded and practically airless.

The drink is cherries in alcohol, the price of which climbs steadily as the years pass. Small glasses are sipped while sitting at long heavy oak tables surrounded by cobweb-festooned figures including a life-size and rather ominous crucifix. Dusty pictures showing Montmartre in all seasons decorate the peeling walls. An upright piano stands in one corner and next to it a harp, both of which provide the musical accompaniment to the singing. Some knowledge of French is a help for the words are often more amusing than the music and if the romantic poems are to be appreciated, French is absolutely necessary.

Remember, hats should be removed when climbing the three steps leading to the cabaret. If they are not a chorus of 'chapeaux!' will greet the newcomer and will continue until it is.

In the old days chansonniers not only improvised poems on any burning subject of the hour—political and mondaine—they also rocked out sarcastic but uproariously funny little ditties about the audience, particularly as patrons walked in. The French adored this and never took umbrage though foreigners who had no idea why, suddenly, they should be the targets of derisive laughter—not understanding the language—were often annoyed.

Those days are passed but with an ace of luck, it is still possible for gentlemen to get their ties clipped off *Chez Patachou* in the *rue du Mont Cenis* just behind Sacré-Cœur.

Patachou, a delightful blonde who sings happy, fruity songs, once served St-Honoré pastry in her pâtisserie next door. She was persuaded by friends to open a cabaret and leave the pastry shop to her family. This she did and it was an immediate success.

Patachou was certainly not the first to sing songs with doubtful choruses and she won't be the last, but she is probably the only one who snips off patrons' ties in order to suspend them in decorative rows from the ceiling. Whatever the indignation, at first, most visitors are delighted at the thought that part of their vestments would now be an integral part of Montmartre.

Patachou is not always on the bill as she travels a great deal but the songs are always fruity.

Chez Ma Cousine, on the rue Norvin, provides dinner, dancing and attractions, all impregnated with the atmosphere of *La Butte*. Songs and stories laughter and champagne rip through the night till dawn breaks. Some French is advisable. A meal costs round £4 10s. 0d., a large scotch a couple of pounds and Coca Cola 17s.

Le Poulailler also on the rue Norvin offers similar entertainment at a similar price.

Such then is the Montmartre of silk, lace and pretty rêveries. Down the hill in the hub of Pigalle romance, different if delightful and certainly very expensive, is something of a change.

The boulevard Rochechouart and the boulevard de Clichy, from the corner of the rue des Martyrs to the Place Blanche and the surrounding streets, include enough cabarets, strip-tease joints, bars and clandestine brothels enough to satisfy several woman-hungry battalions back from a desert war.

After the liberation of Paris and the invasion of Montmartre by hordes of American troops on heat, the famous place Pigalle was fondly referred to as 'Pig Alley'.

Pigalle should be visited alone or definitely all stag. How the head of the family manages to persuade his wife to retire early with a good book and some aspirins is his business, not mine.

One evening, emerging from the bowels of the Métro at Place Pigalle, I was asked in atrocious French if I could recommend a cabaret.

The South Africans who asked the questions made their meaning perfectly clear after I had replied in English to their question. They were looking for some scalding *niterie* where they could watch, at a safe distance, Paris in the raw.

Because there were two ladies in the party I could give no satisfactory advice. Montmartre *is* raw. It has always been raw. Years ago it was possible to take the whole family to the Bal Tabarin. The show was good and if, as I once saw, a fond mother cover the innocent eyes of her young son with her hand when the bosom-nude mannequins floated elegantly across the floor, there were enough talented star turns the young man could enjoy without risk of his being debauched. The Tabarin has gone. The *Moulin Rouge* on the Place Blanche remains, of course, but it no longer resembles the narrow galleried establishment where Toulouse-Lautrec sketched La Goulue and a hundred others.

Today it is semi-circular, over-decorated, and caters for tourists;

offering first-class variety attractions and the only authentic, long legged *Can-Can* girls in existence. Champagne can be obtained at the reasonable price of £2 a half bottle, or £3 with dinner.

The Moulin Rouge is eminently respectable and probably the one Montmartre spot the family can visit together without a *scène de famille* ensuing later.

I suppose the same may be written about the *Nouvelle Eve* on the rue Fontaine. This cabaret has a history. Between the two wars it was, at one time, run by Briton's own night-club queen, Mrs. Merrick, after she had been forced by British puritanism to leave London. It was then called The Gaity. Later it became a cinema and is now a cabaret once again but it opens and closes with some irregularity.

It offers lavish costumes and plenty of talent, but the settings are poor because the stage is small. Entrance costs round a pound and drinks average at £2 for half a bottle of champagne. A few attractive 'pieces' sit round the bar for the benefit of the unaccompanied.

There is also the *Théâtre de Dix Heures* and the *Deux Anes*, both on the boulevard de Clichy but they are *chansonniers* and demand a fluent understanding of the French language.

The *Cabaret du Néant* on the rue Puget founded in 1892 is the last cabaret of its kind in France, or in Europe for all I know, and lives exclusively on tourist parties. It provides sombre entertainment such as sitting at tables shaped like coffins and includes a fair offering of skeletons. It should be seen just once, before, eventually, it follows the late and lamented 'Heaven' and 'Hell' cabarets of the same order which have given way to a vast supermarket.

On the corner of the rue des Martyrs and the boulevard Rochechouart is a café known as the *Atlantique*. Between ten and eleven pm it might well be filled with a bevy of tall, heavy and somewhat ungraceful ladies drinking coffee. They will have dined before starting work at *Madame Arthur* round the corner at *75 rue des Martyrs*. The reason they are ungraceful is that they are not ladies at all, they are gentlemen.

Madame Arthur was started in 1947 by a personality who must be nameless. He was a washer-up *Chez Isis* a cabaret at the other end of the boulevard, famed for its travesty or impersonation of females by males.

In that year he took over the *Divan Japonais* on the rue des Martyrs, redecorated it and opened *Madame Arthur* where homosexuals might find a little comfort. There were others at the time,

Ton Ton on the La Butte was one for example. This was to die eventually but *Madame Arthur* lived on despite the authorities who, after the murder of a famous Paris homosexual couturier by the man he loved, decided to trim homosexual establishments.

Madame Arthur's ladylike gentlemen who served the drinks and were becomingly dressed, had to peel off their petticoats. Today they resemble doubtful Highlanders in kilts.

The acts are amusing but seem to have been toned down since the days when Floridor said the 'unsayable' without a blush. Maslova, a rather unlovely gentleman who changes his ornate pyjamas at least thirty times during the show animates everything and everybody.

Those who wish to know more about the 'ladies' whose artistic talents are not to be derided, need offer a few banknotes and a kind word sent via one of the Highlanders. Whisky costs 35 shillings and champagne round £6 or more a bottle, according to the colour of the label.

Most of the smaller cabarets have either disappeared or been transformed into striptease 'joints'. And in any case Cabarets such as the *Eden*, on the rue Fontaine, *Eve* and *Pigalls* on the Place Pigalle are little more than glorified striptease shows.

The striptease establishments such as *Narcisse* on the Place Pigalle, *Show Boat* (ex-Le Royal cabaret) on the rue Pigalle or the *Roulette*, also on the rue Pigalle offer raw entertainment at high prices— whisky runs round £2 a glass—but the girls or hostesses who look after solitary patrons at the bar will suggest champagne at £6, £7 or even £8 a bottle because they earn an attractive 25% or more on each drink.

Striptease talent is of no importance. The cabarets could discover a little, no doubt, but it is not so much what to see as what to do.

Narcisse and *Pigalls* along with a number of cabarets dotted all over Paris are owned by Helen Martini, an attractive young woman who is never seen without a hat.

She inherited the cabarets from her husband Nachat who, before he died from a heart attack, ran Montmartre—more or less. Helen was one of his dancers.

One of her great aims and objectives has been, since his death, to restore to Montmartre the name it once enjoyed. That is when it was still possible to have a roaring time at a reasonable price. Today the roars follow the sight of the bill.

Madame Martini tries to keep her prices as reasonable as possible and at one time issued tickets, obtainable in tourist agencies, which gave a discount to visitors to her establishments and struck an average of thirty shillings a head. The tickets have gone but the cabarets are certainly not clip joints.

She took over the old Athens Café on the Place Pigalle and turned it into *Narcisse* a cabaret intended for homosexuals. Because her clientèle might have objected to the peripeticians outside, she installed green lighting which made the customers' faces turn green and ugly. The whores of Montmartre avoided the lights of *Narcisse* like the plague but even this effort did not help the cabaret to compete with *Madame Arthur* and so Madame Martini turned it into just another strip joint.

Most of the bars and joints on the rue Pigalle have histories even if their present glories are tarnished.

Méphisto was once Madeleine Barry, a worthy cabaret with pretty girls and funny songs. There was no show. Today it is a bar, not too expensive, and festooned with young ladies with a ready eye for what the French call a 'pigeon' or male of the species out for a good time with his life savings in his pocket to pay for it.

Next door, *La Roulotte* one time a cabaret, was owned by a lady of considerable dimensions. She was known as Lulu de Montmartre who preferred the affection of her sisters to those of her brothers.

This led Lulu into trouble for—and this goes back to before the war—she turned very nasty when the fair-haired, blue-eyed cashier she had befriended and sent to Switzerland to be cured of tuberculosis showed a preference for a young man.

It all led to a violent scene in which menaces and a revolver were brandished. The police intervened and poor Lulu was out of circulation for six months.

Her's was an amusing cabaret. She loved politics and was something of a minor power in the Resistance during the occupation so it is a pity that her one-time *boîte de nuit* should now have declined to the level of a rather abysmal strip joint.

Montmartre bars and strip establishments are innumerable, monotonously similar but always exciting if the choicest of the Seven Mortal Sins are the objectives.

The young ladies who show their pretty legs and display intoxicating cleavage, live as much by their wits as by their charms.

Montmartre 'post-midnight' forms a devoted brotherhood and sisterhood. Baal is its god. Pan and Venus trail unhappily behind the glittering glory of gold or what has replaced it.

Its network includes hostesses, barmen, 'racoleurs', taxi drivers, waiters, restaurant owners and pimps.

A 'racoleur' by the way is that eminently persuasive gentleman who invites tourists with smiles and oily looks, to spend an evening in any of the establishments for whom he operates.

He receives his percentage on the drinks served and sold to all clients who follow his advice. Needless to say, the girls, the taxi-drivers and anyone else involved receives a rake-off, so it is not surprising that a bottle of champagne wholesaled at £2 can easily cost £10.

Superb is the comedy played in a couple of dozen bars and strip joints as the day breaks.

It is time to go. The question is ... where? Juliette, Mado or whatever her name may be will place her soft persuasive hand on the all-too-willing thigh of her escort and at the same time whisper 'Shall we have a *gratinée*?'.

Gratinée is a good old French word for any dish including grated cheese cooked under a grill.

The normal 3 am *gratinée* is generally onion soup enjoyed with a loving spouse in a Les Halles restaurant after a visit to the Folies-Bergère.

But to the ladies of Montmartre it is a lavish meal with good money behind it.

Invited to buy a *gratinée* the slightly dazed but immensely happy escort generally agrees and is led to one of the half-dozen all-night restaurants found in and round the rue Fontaine.

The lights are low, the waiter obsequious and the menu rich in inviting morsels such as Persian caviar, foie gras stuffed with truffles, gentle and inviting layers of smoked salmon, lobsters, lamb from the Orient prepared with herbs from the same direction, and, among a couple of hundred other delights, strawberries out of season.

Prices, considering the ambience, the pile on the carpet, the discretion of the lights, the time of day and all the rest, are reasonable.

The lady will probably start with caviar, followed by lobster and then spitted lamb, all washed down with a Bordeaux of great character.

During the meal a gentle old soul with a soft, appealing smile and white hair will come up to the table and propose a death-white gardenia at an impossible price which will be bought and duly presented with becoming gallantry.

Juliette or whoever she is will place it gently on the table, at the

O

same time caressing the libidinous and hopeful thigh of her escort. Her gesture will be followed by a wish to receive a little gift, just a small piece of paper guaranteed by the Banque de France, for favours desired and hoped for but not yet enjoyed.

The hazy-eyed escort now throws to the winds what few of his wits remain. But he will return to earth when presented with the bill. If he is in a condition to count he will call for the waiter and ask to consult the menu in order to check the prices. His request will be met instantly and the price will add up correctly because the menu receiving his attention will not be the one from which he ordered. The prices on this one will be double.

By this time he will have dived into his pocket, extracted his last francs, paid his bill and persuaded himself that it was all worth while because having paid in advance the rest of the night will be bliss.

Alas! When he looks round for his Diana she will have vanished. The gardenia will have been returned to the sweet old lady with the gentle smile and the cashier will have handed 50 per cent of the cost of the meal to the girl of his fleeting dreams. An expensive night, an unlearned lesson for sure, but a lovely story to recount over the bar at the local at home with, of course, a few slight amendments for obvious reasons.

A genuine *gratinée* by the way can always be obtained in any one of the numerous all-night brasseries.

Nor do all the nocturnal restaurants round the rue Fontaine lend themselves to the nefarious practices described above. The *Cloche d'Or* on the rue Mansard for example. Favoured by show people after the show, it is open all night, has an excellent menu with an inviting *plat du jour*, and its prices are reasonable.

Women: The French police start every criminal investigation with one sole objective: *Cherchez la femme.*

Behind most crimes there is always a woman. She may play no direct part in the crime but she may well provide the reason for it.

When a lady called Marthe Richard marshalled her troops and closed the *maisons de tolérance* and the *bordellos*, the Police were unamused. For the elucidation of most crimes rests on informers and bordellos are beehives of information.

This is just one of the many reasons why after Madame Richard's resounding victory, certain 'maisons clandestines' were left in peace. There were other reasons, of course. Montmartre without a couple of whorehouses would be like cheese without wine, or should it be the other way round?

On the rue de Douai there are several. They are easily recognisable since they are bars installed in hotels. The girls are becoming, beautifully dressed and manicured, generally stupid but always inviting.

Once settled at the bar the devotee will be approached by one and then by another if the first or second or third receive a brush-off.

The approach will be for a drink, a glass of champagne generally. The soft white hand on the thorny thigh, the obvious question and the inevitable reply . . . how much?

There is no tariff but a bottle of champagne is 'de rigueur'. The rooms are well furnished and clean, the *femme de chambre* expects to be lavishly tipped and the lady who produces the main course will not take what may be offered, if it is not enough. The 'dream the breath the froth of fleeting joy' can cost between £20 and £25. If it is worth that amount of money is a matter of personal opinion.

One house, to be recommended if recommendation is necessary, is at the top of the rue de Douai. It is discreet and may well be missed. There are no lights, just *Bar-Hôtel* marked up outside. The lady who runs it speaks very good English.

Montmartre starts with the faubourg Montmartre which gives onto the boulevard Montmartre. This is the centre of a business section of the city far removed from the romance of the *Butte* or the 'stews' of Pigalle. Nevertheless there is still the *Folies-Bergère*, probably the world's best known music-hall—in a district surrounded by clothing manufacturers and furriers. It is not necessary to introduce either the *Folies* or the *Casino de Paris* on the other side of Montmartre in the rue de Clichy. Both are famous, offer similar entertainment lavish settings, beautiful girls, international talent, etc. Both have suffered, slightly, from the scintillating eminence of Jean Louis Guérin's *Lido* on the Champs-Elysées, but both are well worth visiting.

The Folies has an interesting history. Today it is run by Madame Paul Derval whose husband died at the age of 86 in 1966.

Paul Derval, a giant of a man, announced his retirement every year but never retired. Every day he received offers to buy his music-hall from show-biz tycoons, mostly Americans. Only once did he accept an offer. This is what Madame Derval said about it: 'The lawyers got to work, the deeds were drawn up. The sale was complete but for the signatures.

'The buyers signed the documents and then pushed them across the table to my husband. He looked at them for a minute or two, tears welled into his eyes. He picked up his pen. For a second or two he held it in a trembling hand and then, throwing it down sobbed, "I am sorry I simply cannot sign away the Folies" '.

That indeed is Montmartre. Whatever its faults, however phoney its glamour, it just gets under the skin. Maybe it is a little tarnished and fading here and there, but it will never die.

Guide

RESTAURANTS
La Mère Catherine, Place du Tertre.
Cadet de Gascogne, Place du Tertre.
La Bonne Franquette, 18 rue St-Rustique.
La Cloche d'Or, 3 rue Mansart.

MUSIC-HALLS AND CABARETS
Moulin Rouge, Place Blanche.
Nouvelle Eve, 25 rue Fontaine.
Eve, 7 Place Pigalle.
Pigalle's, 9 Place Pigalle.
Eden, 40 rue Fontaine.

CLUBS AND CHANSONNIERS
Chez Plumeau, 7 Place du Calvaire.
Lapin Agile, 4 rue des Saules.
Patachou, 13 rue du Mont Cenis.
Chez Ma Cousine, 12 rue Norvins.
Le Poulailler, 14 rue Norvins.
Théâtre de Dix Heures, 36 boulevard de Clichy.
Théâtre des Deux Anes, 100 boulevard de Clichy.
Cabaret du Néant, 2 rue Coustou.

TRAVESTI (HOMOSEXUAL)
Madame Arthur, 75 bis rue des Martyrs.

STRIPTEASE AND BARS
Narcisse, Place Pigalle.

La Roulotte, 62 rue Pigalle.
Mephisto, 64 rue Pigalle.

BORDELLOS
Rue Victor Massé.
Rue de Dousi.
Rue Pigalle, etc.

The Marais

It's only a ten-minute bus ride from wherever your centre may be, Montparnasse, Place de la Concorde or Saint-Germain-des-Prés, to the remotest region in Paris. It is set apart by its slow-changing life, its ancient stones. Disparate peoples live there, many with foreign tongues and ways, in a *quartier* both old and profoundly French. The Marais has preserved what Léon Daudet described, when he lived on rue Pavée with his father Alphonse, as 'that indestructible something that cannot age or wear'.

At one time, the quarter of the hundred and one palatial mansions grouped around a royal square was just a marsh, a *marais*. Whoever dreamed the six uncultivated letters would be hung with the city's most polished legend and the common noun made proper? They were. This is the *Salon* of Paris, where Madame de Sévigné, Ninon de Lenclos, Mademoiselle de Scudéry, Queen of the Précieuses, held court, silhouetted against the splendid creations of Mansard and Lebrun.

Obviously the *Grand Siècle* moulded the Marais and impressed its residential stamp upon it. But to say that was all is uncatholic. Centuries are spanned in the monumental presence of its past, and people from more walks of life live in the district extending along the Seine between the Bastille and Les Halles than in any other part of Paris. A walker through the narrow misleading streets finds contrasts at every step, as well as the finest in French names and stones.

On the most secure knolls of the original marshland, churches arose, Saint-Merri, Saint-Gervais, and, by degrees, monasteries, Notre-Dame-des-Blancs-Manteaux, and les Carmes Billettes (with the only remaining Medieval cloister in Paris). Charles the Wise, who became king of France in 1364, had his rustic pleasure dome along the river, where a street still bears his name. On rue des Lions was the royal ménagerie, on rue Fauconnier the falconers, while orchards and trellised gardens grew in rue Beautreillis, rue du Figuier, rue des Jardins-Saint-Paul. The street names are still signposts to a lost world.

In the Middle Ages, artisans and shopkeepers huddled around their bishops and king. Monks helped peasants drain ground on the overflowing Seine, heaping up earth for their crops or *coutures* as they called them. But the old river, younger then, would slip out of bed overnight and Parisians wake up to a new world of little islands everywhere.

On a sunny morning, after a rainfall, strike inland through the Medieval *ruelles* behind the Hôtel de Ville, to the hillside where a garden climbs against the flying buttresses of Saint-Gervais. A bright little scene where you picture the place revisited by clear waters. Skin divers would have enjoyed exploring the deep for pumpkins and pre-washed salads at the *coutures* Saint-Gervais. At rue des Barres, the last dike always gave out, and only the granary remained above water at rue du Grenier-sur-l'eau. Somewhere between flood and sky, in the stained glass of Saint-Gervais, shepherds tend their white flocks against the blue, and rue de l'Ave Maria echoes with the ancient prayer as people call out the name. The Medieval Marais rested on faith.

In the *Grand Siècle*, after a final hesitation between land and water, an island of stone emerged. The Marais crystallised. A masterpiece mellowed in the light of the Sun King.

The best introduction to the quarter is along rue Saint-Antoine, the royal way into the city through what used to be the Porte de la Bastille. This broad axis is the genesis of the Marais, where styles are superimposed like the layers of geological ages. The Renaissance comes to a close at Hôtel de Mayenne and Hôtel de Sully, and classicism appears in the cupola of Temple Sainte-Marie, which was later to serve as a model for the famous dome of the Invalides. The 17th century cohabits with the Middle Ages, as columns coupled and classic rise to the heights of the Gothic vaults of Saint-Gervais. At Saint-Paul an elaborate façade yields to Baroque temptation, and until quite recently, in a more modern fashion, Hôtel de Sully wore the eyepatch of a shoemaker's black frontage, shining with the golden letters L'INCROYABLE.

Today rue Saint-Antoine is a busy market street. Opposite the church, Métro Saint-Paul provides a steady flow of customers and a good underground approach for those who like to come upon a quarter by surprise.

Walk into the dark streets which branch out on either side of rue Saint-Antoine, to find or lose yourself in the Labyrinth of Paris. Taxis and buses have been scared away by the maze of *ruelles*, one-ways and dead-ends. An occasional tri-car runs small errands. Pedestrians take their time, and slow motion is made slower by the contrasting bustle of the quarters which enclose the Marais, by the Bastille, the Halles, and the Grand Boulevards.

The Marais is the capital's quiet valley where flowers of the mind may grow. Madame de Sévigné snubbed court life to cultivate her mind and *belles-lettres* in her quiet Marais abodes, all ten of which she chose for their tranquillity. In little rue des Oiseaux, surrounded by her kinglet and garden warbler, her chameleon and parrot, the bluest stocking of them all, Mlle de Scudéry, compiled her dictionaries of precious love. We laugh with Molière at the expense of the 'Queen of the Précieuses' and her entourage, but are they so ridiculous? The great Leibniz, after all, deigned to sing of her parrot, in a poem addressed to the Maid of the Marais. And today, her maps of gallant geography seem an appropriate guide, when buffeted by the waves of modern traffic, you sail from the *Sea of Imprudence* onto a *River of Douceur*.

Nothing has changed less than some of these sweet-flowing streets, rue des Guillemites, rue des Blancs-Manteaux, rue Payenne, rue du Parc Royal. After the Revolution, the quarter was taken over by shopkeepers and artisans who haven't budged since. Many of the grand 'hôtels' are occupied by goldsmiths or toymakers who disfigure façades with signs, clutter up courtyards with their wares, put sheds in the place of gardens. Some of them stand half-ruined and unoccupied, as though waiting for a wealthy resident. But the body of the quarter is still strong, sometimes intact. The Paris of the *Grand Siècle* is alive in the midst of ours, unimpressed by change and the world without.

Its life is within. The rulers of Europe flocked to Versailles to see a king on parade. When they came to the Marais, they saw a model of domestic life, the ideal house in the city. The most stately Marais dwellings shun display, spouting fountains, and perspectives. They hide between courtyard and garden, behind sober walls and façades.

The centre and birthplace of the Marais is the Place Royale, now the Place des Vosges, which was designed by Henri IV. Up to King Henry's time, the general layout of Paris followed what urbanists term the 'road city' pattern, houses had grown spontaneously, that is, along streets and roads. When the king came to Paris in 1594, he intended 'to spend his life in this city, and stay there like a real patriot; to make it beautiful and peaceful, and as full of comforts and ornaments as possible; to make of this city a whole world and a miracle of the world'. He designed the adjoining manors of the Place Royale with identical façades, pink brick and white cornerstones, mounted on arcades and grouped into a perfect square. A city within a building, the Place Royale prefigured a world he did not live to see. At some cost to their pride, peers agreed to live together behind a standard façade, and the peacable atmosphere ushered in an age of elegance.

The deep-gardened mansions attracted the nobility. The arcades were a market gallery for the sale of luxury articles and an agreeable promenade for the cramped *populus*. Today the roomy arcades still harbour ancient arms and antique shops, Japanese prints, and a bookstore whose owner treats residents of the Place to a puppet show in the evening. A café with tables in the sun and shade serves choice wines *au comptoir* and you can dine lavishly at the expensive Coconas. Here, at last, according to the menu and to the good king's wish, is a 'chicken in every pot'.

The King intended the central area of the Place as a kind of playfield for Parisians, where tournaments, cavalcades and all manner of sport, including some famous duels, could and did take place while the ladies looked on from their balconies. Today it is a playground for children. Fewer people hang over the balconies; the one at No. 6 where Victor Hugo lived is gone, but the windows of his second floor apartment, now a museum, offer the best free view of the square. In the gay 1820's, if you happened by the Place at dawn, you could see two early birds—the other was Théophile Gauthier who lived at number 8—exchanging greetings while they lathered and shaved as the sun rose.

These romantics and others, like Gérard de Nerval, who liked the 'grave harmony' of the Place, were no doubt attracted by the feeling of dormant life which pervades the enclosed area, perhaps too by the quiet contrasts which inspired *Les Rayons et les Ombres*. Théodore de Banville described the *soirées* at the Poet's house as 'true and good hospitality, the kind offered by kings and also by lumberjacks'.

Great places, like great men, lead double lives. Behind the elegant façades of the Place, beckon opportunities for quick getaways—back alleys like Impasse Guémenée which led from Victor Hugo's house, secret gardens and stairways designed for the heroes of Hugolian drama, streets of love and intrigue like rue des Tournelles where Ninon de Lenclos lent her 'yellow room' to the amorous frolics of Scarron, while in her salon Molière gave his first reading of *l'Avare* to the select audience of La Fontaine and Racine.

At number 1 bis—Hôtel de Coulange—Madame de Sévigné was born, but the finest of her Marais dwellings was the Hôtel Carnavalet, now the Historical Museum of Paris, where she spent her last years. Tourists rarely venture off the beaten path which leads them from the Musée Victor Hugo on the Place des Vosges to the Musée Carnavalet, just around the corner and back to Métro Saint-Paul. Until recently, the 'Châteaux of the Seine' were not even listed by the tourist agencies specialising in visits of Paris Historique.

The ways of the famous dead are respected, however, and touching care is taken to keep things as they liked or left them. At the Hôtel Carnavalet, the fastidious Grand Lady of the Marais would find her writing desk in perfect order, should she be tempted to pen one last famous letter. The atmosphere is even graver at the Musée Victor Hugo, where groups of workers have been seen to visit his reconstituted death-room with respectfully doffed hats. Yet the poet who knows that 'You' is really 'Me', would no doubt be quite unperturbed to find so many strangers at the window where he listened in the evenings to the *Voix Intérieures* of the Place des Vosges.

Only a few steps off the tourist circuit, right behind Hôtel Carnavalet, rue Payenne forms a T with rue du Parc Royal. In this unnoticed street, you step back a few centuries into a garden city, as it appears in Turgot's bird's eye view of 1739. Trees bow in, partly hiding Hôtel de Croisille at the far end. The mansions here, Hôtel de Marle, de Vigny, de Châtillon, are like neglected beauties, aloof with gardens. Discreetly, they flash fine points, mascarons, sun dials, basket handle arches or gable windows, a reclining goddess leaning away from her oval mirror—things you remember and miss in other *quartiers* of Paris. A dwelling more welcoming than Hôtel de Châtillon is hard to imagine, facing the many-levelled gardens, separated by a wing of the Hôtel le Peltier. Once the whole Marais was like this leafy haven.

'The French who have so many architectural treasures are the most neglectful when it comes to preserving them', deplored Rousseau. A few years ago, Hôtel de Vigny, after many others, was marked for demolition and the family of artisans, who had been making automat dolls there since the 19th century, was heart-broken. But a young man who loved the Marais persuaded them that the plastered ceiling of their workshop concealed a treasure which could save their dwelling from destruction and themselves from eviction. Thanks to friends who helped with the scraping, Louis XIII beams painted with flying cherubs were uncovered, and the doll-makers' house was classified and saved.

The Marais has many lovers. From distant corners of the capital, young votaries of ancient beauty come together here to seek out its secret stones and colours. Marais residents call them the *bénévolents*. They work in blue overalls, the girls with scarves tucked in at the neck and heads wig-white with dust, and you see them emerging from cellars and attics to charter a hidden treasure, or to pass around petitions to save a noble mansion's life.

Such generous efforts to save old dwellings are not in vain. The city has given the young restorers a place of their own for an annual token rent of one pound: a simple 16th-century house with a vaulted Medieval cellar and a roof with old-fashioned hook-tiles. Even more important, the recent Malraux Law codified the principle of preserving not merely an isolated monument but an historic 'ensemble' like the rue du Parc Royal. It protects 'all or part of a group of buildings which by their æsthetic or historic character, justify conservation, restoration, and development'.

It was the *bénévolents* who started the Marais Festival with make-shift props and amateur actors, and who had the brilliant idea of using gardens and courtyards as settings for plays, thus enabling uninhabited mansions like Hôtel de Sully, d'Aumont and Lamoignon to resume a seasonal role in the art of living.

'It is the charm of aristocratic quarters', according to Marcel Proust, 'to be at the same time *popular*.' For the Marais, one might add exotic. The occupation of the quarter by artisans in the 19th century was coincident with immigrations from mid-European countries. It is since known as the *Platzel*, where you come to ask settlers of longer standing about the chances of work and housing. Some are directed to other quarters. Those who stay become rooted.

Much that is foreign is welcome in this classic French quarter: the shop for Hungarian Specialties in rue Sévigné, the Produits Exotiques, the Polish restaurants with sausages and vodkas displayed

Hôtel Fieubet, Marais

in the window on rue Saint-Paul, or the homely Franco-Yugoslav restaurant where neatly dressed old Slavs gather volubly.

The most universal is Rosenburg's on the corner of rue des Rosiers and rue Fernand Duval, formerly rue des Juifs, whose awning boasts of World Specialties. Built into what is left of the Hôtel d'Herbouville, Goldenburg's restaurant and delicatessen is a place of taste and freedom. You can sit down at the counter to a plate of chopped chicken livers and egg salad, and Goldenburg may come and eat at the counter too. You can say this was just an appetizer and move to a yellow tablecloth where Goldenburg will serve you a square meal. Who is Goldenburg? He is any one of a dozen brothers belonging to the once rival restaurant families on this street who decided to merge. Thanks to their phenomenal presence, Goldenburg is permanently open, at all times.

Other shops on rue des Rosiers, the heart of the Jewish quarter, look reserved beside this summit of sophistication. They close Saturdays and the Hebrew letters on the windows have the remoteness of an ancient tongue. The kosher meats, the castle-building cakes and buns, the bread like spikes of corn, all breathe unspeakable wisdom. And bearded, darkly-dressed-and-hatted-men stop to chat softly in the middle of the street on their way to a synagogue of a few chairs and tables in a former café.

The Marais took a long time. And when you walk away into other quarters, other towns, a spicy smell clings to you of accumulated ages and exotic lands, the essence of its atmosphere. It brings back the memory of the rue des Rosiers with its unleavened bread shops and you remember other worlds you came near to knowing, where mint and verbena grew in the fields of Saint-Gervais and orange groves in the rue du Parc Royal.

Montparnasse

What Montmartre was to the Right Bank, Montparnasse has been to the Left Bank with the one important difference: Montmartre has been submerged by its foreign tourists and sold its soul whereas Montparnasse has always been the cosmopolitan quartier *par excellence*. Montparnasse is still the heart of 'artistic' Paris.

Lying to the south of Saint-Germain with its new-found flashiness, its drugstores, its boutiques, its *yé-yé* population, snobs and intellectual mandarins, Montparnasse has retained its slightly parochial, conservative air. It has a life of its own, its traditions and its *style*. If Saint-Germain is a city village, Montparnasse has remained something of a village outside the centre. It is situated higher than Saint-Germain and the Seine. Its inhabitants will tell you proudly that the air is cleaner and the light purer than 'down there' at the other end of the long—and oh so monotonous—boulevard Raspail and rue de Rennes. The boulevard Montparnasse is one of the widest and most pleasant in Paris, its great cafés have become legendary and the little streets near it have seen the explosion of some of the greatest talent in the history of modern art.

Picasso, Braque, Douanier Rousseau, Van Dongen, Blaise Cendrars, Derain, and Modigliani all lived and worked there. So did Giacometti, one of the last of the great 'giants', and so do Jean Paul Sartre and Simon de Beauvoir, the sculptor César and the great singer-poet George Brassens. After Henry Miller and Hemingway, thousands of young Americans have come and still come to Montparnasse in search of the Great Paris Dream, and so do thousands of young Italians, Germans, Latin-Americans, Spaniards, Dutch, and Japanese.

To all these, Montparnasse has been welcoming and it has absorbed them into its population with ease and grace, offering those who stay the chance to become real *Montparnos*.

It is significant that few other parts of Paris have a name for their inhabitants. The native of Saint-Germain-des-Prés does not call himself a *Saint-Germano-Pratin*, a *Montmartrois* is simply someone who lives in Montmartre, and as for the Latin Quarter, people there are either 'students' or—well, just Parisians. The term *Montparno* is fairly recent: it was coined in 1924 by the writer Michel Georges-Michel who used it as the title of his novel *Les Montparnos* in which he related the tragic love story of Modigliani and Jeanne Hébuterne. The book was not particularly distinguished but nonetheless it helped to contribute to the prestige of Montparnasse in Paris and in the world. *Montparno* became the proud title of all who came to the *quartier* in those wonderful years between the two wars when the whole of artistic Paris seemed to be migrating southwards across the Seine.

The process started in the last years before World War I when the café *Rotonde* became the great temple of the arts and letters. Apollinaire, Max Jacob, Vlaminck, Reverdy, Othon Friesz, Giorgio de Chirico, Foujita and Marie Laurencin—they were all to be found at the *Rotonde*. The *soirées de Montparnasse* were immortalised by Guillaume Apollinaire and it is revealing that Apollinaire was not a Frenchman. Artistic Montparnasse was cosmopolitan from the very beginning and it is still the home of the most cosmopolitan assembly of artists in the capital. After the dark years of the First World War, Montparnasse entered into its great Golden Age and new legends were born almost every day. The café *Rotonde* had become world famous. Everyone who was eccentric, everyone who wanted to gain his laurels as an artist, every adventurer and pleasure seeker seemed to be coming to Montparnasse. Such was the invasion of foreigners that the French artist Guy Arnoux hung up a sign outside his studio in the rue Huyghens announcing a 'Consulat de France'. Night clubs opened everywhere, the most spectacular and frenetic being the *Jockey*. The roaring twenties roared at Montparnasse as nowhere else in Paris. 'Never go to Montparnasse' Max Jacob said jokingly, 'the orgies are in the south of the city. The orgies are at Montparnasse.' Most long-enduring of these orgies was that of the arts. Every self-respecting café seemed to be holding its own exhibition. You went to see works by Russian artists at the *Café de l'Observatoire*, the *Rotonde* once displayed a great canvas by Gauguin surrounded by the works of young and unknown artists and at the *Closerie des Lilas*, the 'Company of professional painters and sculptors' used to hold their Lucullan meetings. Every nationality seemed to have its own café: the Russians at the *Observatoire*, the Scandinavians at the restaurant *Stryx* in the rue Huyghens, the Americans at the *Dingo* bar and everybody at the *Dôme* and the *Select*. For the *Montparno* the years 1919–1930 were a never-ending party and it was in Montparnasse that everything was 'happening'. With the depression of the Thirties and the Occupation the party was over. After the Liberation, Saint-Germain took its revenge on Montparnasse and still another legend was created in the capital. The gaiety and madness of Montparnasse had gone for ever and yet, even today, something still remains of the old magic. And, what is perhaps most important, it is still the most tolerant and cosmopolitan of all 'artistic quarters' where to be poor is not so much a crime as elsewhere in the city. It is used to a large colony of foreigners and it it is there that the love affair between the Americans and Paris lingers on although the fires of the earlier passion have died down, giving place to a homely and affectionate domesticity.

For the visitor who wants to enjoy his 'idea' of the Left Bank, he could do no better than to escape from Saint-Germain and make straight for one of the great boulevard cafés of Montparnasse. If you don't speak French, if you don't know anybody in Paris, don't waste time or money at Saint-Germain-des-Prés. At Saint-Germain you will never escape the feeling of being a tourist. If you go to the café *Lipp*, the *Deux Magots* or the *Flore* you will be surrounded by the smart and intellectual life of Paris and by sight-seeing 'provincial' Parisians who have come to gape at the *yé-yé* and miniskirts from their fastnesses in Passy and Neuilly, all supremely indifferent to your existence. At Montparnasse you may only be a drop in the ocean, but at least it is *your* ocean, and by the mere fact of being there—no matter for how long—you are a part of its life and the chances are that you will feel 'at home'. The truth is that Montparnasse is 'cosy'.

By some miracle, the quarter has escaped being vulgarised. There has been talk of a *Drugstore* on the Boulevard but so far—thank God —it has not happened. In fact, very little seems to have happened at Montparnasse in the last thirty years. There is still an indefinable 1920's air about the place. The *Rotonde* has suffered most and been overwhelmed with chrome, plastic and formica. It has become stiflingly bourgeois and not even the ghosts of the great personalities who made it famous can be bothered to haunt it. All that remains of the formidable personalities who gave it lustre are their names, recorded by two giant plaques inside the *Rotonde* cinema next door which specialises in bad gangster films and Italian westerns (its most unusual feature is that you are allowed to smoke in it). On the same side of the Boulevard, the *Select* has kept much of its 1920's graciousness. Founded in 1923, it has kept its original beige décor and its wicker seats and is a favourite with many young intellectuals, aged Spanish politicians and young Catalans in exile. It endures as one of the most authentic, living vestiges of the feverish Montparnasse the *années folles* as the French call *their* twenties.

A little further down the boulevard, past a truly hideous church, another institution—the *Foyer des Artistes et des Intellectuels*. It was founded in the early fifties by Monsieur Vaux, a passionate lover of the arts who decided to cater for needy artists and students by giving them a restaurant-cum-coffee-bar and art gallery. To belong to the *foyer* a membership card is needed (10 francs a year) but *if* you are young, or at any rate look like an 'artist' or 'intellectual' don't be afraid to go in. Service is rough and ready and the food is rather 'self-service' in quality but sufficient (steak and chips, chicken and salad 2.90 francs; a meal for about 4 or 5 francs) but who can complain? Towards the Place du 18 juin, facing the former site of the old Gare de Montparnasse, all is vulgarity and banality. The only redeeming feature is the tiny *Théâtre de Poche-Montparnasse*, tucked away at the end of a little alley. It has only sixty seats but the productions there are excellent. One of its greatest successes was François Billetdoux's *Chin Chin*. The continuation of the boulevard is mainly distinguished by its horrid cafés and truly execrable restaurants. *Rougeot* is cheap and has a pretty 1900 style décor but is certainly no place for a gourmet and *Roger la Frite*, as its name implies, is a rather dingy 'chips with everything' establishment. On the other side of the boulevard: a bit and brassy *brasserie Dupont* and two great cafés, the *Coupole* and *Dôme*.

The *Coupole* is by far and away the most exciting café in Montparnasse. It is also the only one that is fashionable with snobs and the *tout-Paris* who come to see and be seen. It is both the biggest and the grandest of all Montparnasse cafés and also has a restaurant service (excellent steaks, good Bordeaux and Muscadet wines and oysters galore though expensive). Many artists and eccentrics of the district come there every night and half a bottle of white wine brought to you in an ice bucket costs only 3.50 francs. Although it was founded in 1927 (and has kept its décor) its true glory began comparatively late, in the 1950's. To see it at its most lively, go at about 11 o'clock at night and sit inside if you can find a seat. The noise is deafening. If you are really thirsty ask for a *formidable* of beer. The glass holds a litre.

The *Dôme*, where you buy your cigarettes, may once have been frequented by Modigliani, Stravinsky, Trotsky and Picasso, but now verges on the sordid. The clientèle that gathers nightly around the horse-shoe zinc bar inside is 'mixed', to put it mildly. Nonetheless, there is no denying that it has an atmosphere—rather raffish. It is a great favourite with young Cubans for some reason. Across the boulevard Raspail, the *Rond Point* serves Watney's Red Barrel bitter (aerated and almost indistinguishable from French beer) and stays open all night. The juke box is deafening.

At the far end of the boulevard, where the Latin Quarter begins, the *Closerie des Lilas* that Hemingway loved so much (read his *Moveable Feast*) is now an extremely expensive restaurant with a small café section. But the old *Closerie* had a long and distinguished history. Murger, the author of the *Vie de Bohême*, Verlaine, Sartre, Beckett, Giacometti, Ionesco and Sagan have all been frequent visitors there. It began as a dance hall in the early 19th century, the famous *Bal Bullier* where students and *midinettes* came to dance the quadrille and its shady trees and rustic gardens attracted poets and painters, Baudelaire and Ingres. By the end of the 19th century, it was the headquarters of the 'moderns' and the Symbolist poets and writers: Paul Fort, Mallarmé, Moréas and Valéry. Charles-Louis Philippe, the author of that classic of 19th-century Paris low-life, *Bubu of Montparnasse*, came there and so did Gide and, later, Cocteau, Braque, Marie Laurencin, Modigliani. Lenin and Trotsky used to play chess there (ask to see their chess board) and after they had prepared their revolutions, the Dadaists and Surrealists came to prepare *theirs*. Today all that remains are their names written on the tables near the bar where Jean now serves the affluent but uncreative *tout-Paris*. It's all very luxurious, rather quiet and somewhat depressing.

Montparnasse is, of course, more than its boulevard. It has its night clubs, its 'bars', its prostitutes and its clip-joints. In the rue Delambre, famous to generations of expatriates, the *Rosebud* is fashionable at present. The *Falstaff bar* (42 rue du Montparnasse) is open day and night and is decorated in atrocious mock-Tudor style. It is a favourite with Anglo-Saxon journalists and Sartre and Beckett have been seen there. The *Norland*, in the rue Bréa, is pleasant but the customers often tend to have a conspiratorial air. It has a large and rather snooty chow dog who likes to lie across the threshold. The rue Jules Chaplain, near by, has an excellent art cinema, a few fading prostitutes, and a pseudo-American night club, *Jacky's Bar*.

If the boulevard sector is the heart of the 'artistic Montparnasse', the boulevard Edgar Quine tand rue de la Gaîté are very definitely 'popular Montparnasse'. Henry Miller used to like to read in the café on the corner of the rue de la Gaîté and the boulevard (*Café de la Liberté*) and the décor is pure 1930-Constructivist. The short street is famous above all for its theatres (the *Bobino, Gaîté Montparnasse*) and is a strange medley of cut-price refrigerator and radio shops, cheap tailors and 'fleapit cinemas'. The *Restaurant des Milles Colonnes* is cheap and—well it's cheap. The boulevard Edgar Quinet has even more of a provincial air than the boulevard Montparnasse, although it has now been disfigured by a hideous block of modern flats and a huge self-service supermarket (very useful for expatriate residents). There used to be a famous brothel opposite, before the last war. Try and guess where it was. The façade has remained.

The other side of the avenue de Maine is a curious extension of the old Montparnasse. It is a genuinely working-class quarter with low houses, narrow streets and an abundance of horse-meat butchers' shops and workers' *bistrots*. Unfortunately vast areas are being rebuilt and the whole is overwhelmed by the towering blocks of Paris's most ambitious, most brutal building project and by the new Montparnasse station. Douanier Rousseau used to live in the rue Vercingétorix but now most artists have fled and an atmosphere of doom hangs over the whole district.

This is the 'other Montparnasse' and there is nothing gay about it. Far better to go back once more to the heart of Montparnasse, where the boulevard intersects with the boulevard Raspail at the

P

carrefour Vavin and sit outside the *Dôme* or even the *Rotonde* on a fine evening and watch the night fall. As the neon sign of the *Coupole* lights up and the nightly procession of *Montparnos* and sightseers starts, you may still catch something of the atmosphere of the *années folles*. You find an empty seat, you order your drink, you watch the passing show, someone asks you for a light in halting French spoken in a Spanish accent, and like the young painter from Chile or the would-be writer from Denver City, you too are a *Montparno*. . . .

Saint-Germain-des-Prés

Saint-Germain-des-Prés and Montparnasse have a kind of see-saw relationship, and when one is fashionable or exciting the other tends to go through a quieter phase. Before the last war, for instance, Montparnasse was the centre of Surrealist groups of painters and intellectuals who haunted cafés like *La Coupole, La Rotonde* and *Le Dôme* while Saint-Germain was a silent onlooker. But after the war things began to change. Existentialism and its adjuncts came to Saint-Germain: Jean-Paul Sartre wrote at the *Café de Flore,* Juliette Greco sang her earliest successes—words by Prévert, music by Cosma—at *La Tabou,* one of the best known cellars or *caves*. It was the time, too, of Boris Vian and of the top Dixieland jazz players. Régine opened her famous night club, *Chez Régine*. During the fifties and early sixties Saint-Germain was at its best, it was the fashion. This state of affairs did not altogether last—Régine emigrated to Montparnasse and opened *New Jimmy's*; once again it was rather important to be seen at *La Coupole*. But does this mean that Saint-Germain has faded? Not at all, for the atmosphere is unchanged and the good places are still there, except for the famous *Royal Saint-Germain*, the traditional café where you could have a dozen Belon oysters and champagne sent up to your room at any time of day or night, has disappeared. In its place—the inevitable drugstore. But *Chez Lipp* remains, one of the most famous Brasseries in Paris, where you can have marvellous choucroute, oysters and Alsace wines. At *Chez Lipp*, though, your neighbours are perhaps of greater interest even than your food. You may well find yourself at the next table to Georges Pompidou himself, or to his rival Valéry Giscard d'Estaing (or both, which could be amusing).

Even better, you may be eating your oysters while Françoise Sagan and Alain Robbe-Grillet eat theirs.

Opposite *Lipp*, on the other side of Boulevard Saint-Germain, are two very well known cafés. *Les Deux Magots* is on the corner of rue Bonaparte and faces, on that side, the beautiful church of Saint-Germain-des-Prés. This café still claims to be 'Le rendez-vous de l'élite intellectuelle'. But in a city where the notion of the 'élite' has changed quite radically, such a rendez-vous is perhaps more likely to be the excellent bookshop next door. *La Hune* has the widest possible selection of books on any subject from philosophy to gardening, an excellent library of French literature, novels, poetry, magazines and art books—and much foreign literature. In addition to all this, it is a very good art gallery where you can certainly find an etching or a print by Zao-Woo-Ki, or Poliakoff, or an engraver like Piza whose talent is already well established. Across the Boulevard from *La Hune* another, more recent, combined bookshop and gallery called *La Pochade* plays its part in maintaining the intellectual tradition of Saint-Germain. The other well known café here is, of course, the *Café de Flore* where you will see people of every conceivable kind, fashionable and artistic; upstairs it tends to be homosexual in ambience.

All these places are, naturally, the shop windows for the deeper intellectual life of this district. For instance Gallimard, the publishers, have a bookshop in their name on the place Saint-Germain but their heart is in the rue du Bac, an area which houses about half a dozen publishers, among them Editions de Minuit (rue Bernard Palissy), du Seuil (rue Jacob), and Julliard (rue de l'Université).

One of the interesting features of this lively part of Paris is its proximity to the traditional university, La Sorbonne, and to the famous 'grandes écoles'. There is the Polytechnique (rue Descartes) for mathematics and higher technology, and for business and civil management; École Normale Supérieure (rue d'Ulm) for sciences, arts and philosophy. From there, you would probably go in for research and an academic life, while the Ecole Nationale d'Administration (ENA) in rue des Saint-Pères trains you for a career in diplomacy, finance or the civil service. L'Institut National des Sciences Politiques or, briefly, Sciences Po, is the nursery for the future 'ENArques'. The gardens of the two colleges adjoin, and a student moving up to ENA from Sciences Po need only cross the lawn.

The smarter students frequent the Café de Flore, mixing with the painters, writers and film people, and with the teenage 'minets' (kittens), those versatile young boys who also haunt the drugstore. If you are a minet, one of the most important things is to be well dressed and there are a variety of places to get your gear. There is the tailor, Jack Romoly, at the corner of Saint-Guillaume and Saint-Germain, or, for something more English in style, Berteil at the corner of Saint-Germain and rue de l'Ancienne Comédie, Arnys at Sèvres Babylone, and a host of others selling clothes and shoes along the Boulevard. There is also, a little to the west of *Les Deux Magots*, a boutique called *Fleurmay* where you can buy modern jewellery of all sorts, particularly in baroque and oriental styles.

But setting frivolities like this on one side for a moment, it is important to remember that Saint-Germain is a melting pot of cultural elements, an arena into which ideas and influences are bound to emerge from the shadow of the universities, where they are bred, and the publishers. Such a concentration of intellect sometimes explodes—as in May 1968. A constant reminder of Saint-Germain's part in those troubles can be seen on the streets of the district, where a heavy layer of asphalt has replaced the paving stones which provided such effective missiles for the rioters. But the value of the thoughtful atmosphere of this district now would be appreciated by Egon and Maximilien de Furstenberg who had their own problems with students in the middle ages when they founded the Abbey from which the beautiful church of Saint-Germain-des-Prés has grown. The church is the oldest in Paris, and the steeple, dating from 1014, one of the oldest in France. There are many things of interest to be found inside, including sensitive frescoes by Flandrin, and headstones of the tombs of Descartes and Boileau, while outside in the churchyard there a head by Picasso has been placed as a memorial to Apollinaire. The name of the founders of the Abbey is also given to the charming and peaceful place Furstenberg with its old globe lamp-posts. This is a part of Saint-Germain which is generally not so well known. The shadowy rue Jacob with its antique shops, rue Bonaparte with art galleries where you can find some really good modern prints, rue de Seine, Quai de Conti with all the hotels along the banks of the river, rue Mazarine, rue de Buci, rue Dauphine and rue de l'Ancienne Comédie. In this area people hunt for food in the big open markets and satisfy their cultural needs in the galleries and bookshops. In the early summer cars are banned at night and a Festival is held—rather like a mini Festival de Marais.

In the rue de l'Ancienne Comédie is the oldest café in Paris, the

Procope, where Diderot played chess and Voltaire talked. It is now a restaurant, but it hasn't lost its character and you can get a very good meal at a reasonable price—not always easy—and you can get excellent couscous at *La Fourchette d'Or* in rue Mazarine.

If you want to find the heart of Saint-Germain-des-Prés by night, you must go straight to rue Saint-Benoît, a narrow street between the *Café de Flore* and *Les Deux Magots*. There you will find a number of restaurants, from the fairly traditional *Pizzeria* to the Swedish *Akwavit*, and the *Bilboquet*, which is a restaurant-night club similar to *Annabel's* in London. If you prefer a good old Parisian atmosphere, you will certainly enjoy the tiny snack bar called *l'Epicerie*. It is not that comfortable, but it is very congenial indeed and for less than ten francs you can get a perfectly good steak and fried potatoes. Across the street at the *Petit Saint-Benoît* you will find the atmosphere of a typical Parisian *bistrot* with a combined art nouveau and provincial décor. If you pursue this quasi-Mediterranean street further you will reach *Les Assassins* at the bottom where you can eat a meal to the accompaniment of pop music and limericks.

Not far from there, near *La Pochade* and opposite the famous pissotière reputed to be the rendez-vous of a number of fashionable writers and film makers, is rue du Dragon. The only dragon in the street, however, is a fine cinema, where the best new films are shown continuously with a performance starting even at midnight. The other attraction of rue du Dragon is a series of Auvergnat restaurants where the food is cooked on charcoal. These Grillades au Charbon du Bois are delicious—especially the beef, and it is a perfect place to go at the end of an evening.

On the Place Saint-Germain one of the most interesting moments of the day comes at five o'clock—tea-time in France. Then the outdoor cafés fill up, and sitting at a table with a *citron pressé* or a cup of coffee you can watch the world go by. Here and there a contract may be signed, and the plans for a new book or film discussed (especially in a little restaurant—which doesn't look particularly interesting—at the corner of rue des Saint-Pères and boulevard Saint-Germain called *Restaurant des Saints-Pères*).

It is not easy to define Saint-Germain-des-Prés. It is not just geographical, not simply an administrative area or a postal district. Its characteristics are living ones; it is a great scene, but not a façade, for the backstage activity is equally vital. If good and interesting things ever cease to come out of Saint-Germain, the legend and the ghosts will always be worth a second glance.

The 'East End' of Paris

The East End of Paris extends between two green oases: the Buttes-Chaumont to the north and the Père Lachaise cemetery to the south. Because of the changes being made in the city recently, these two landmarks will soon be the only pleasant refuges in the midst of a forest of new blocks of flats and skyscrapers. Not long ago, the districts of Belleville and Ménilmontant brought a breath of the country to Paris with their streets lined by little country villas surrounded with gardens. Today, thank heavens, they have not been completely destroyed and what remains is still an invitation to the solitary pedestrian in search of an older Paris to lose himself in a rapidly vanishing and yet recent past.

If you are an inveterate explorer of cities and you start from the centre of Paris, you should make two halts on your itinerary towards the eastern city of the 19th and 20th arrondissements. First at a hospital—and what a hospital! The hospital of Saint-Louis (71 Place du Docteur Fournier) is the oldest in Paris and for many years was the home for plague victims in the city. It was founded by Henry IV in 1607 while the plague was raging throughout the region, and was completed in 1612. After being shut down in the 18th century, it was used as a grain warehouse before becoming a hospital again during the Revolution.

Architecturally it is a joy, and with its noble stone and brick buildings set in a square, their one-storey pierced with tall narrow windows and tiled roof decorated with charming dormer windows, and pediments, the whole place resembles the beautiful architectural composition of the Place des Vosges, and is an example of the Louis XIII style at its finest.

South of the hospital, at number 39 in the rue du Château d'Eau you can see the smallest house in Paris: it only measures three feet in width by five yards in height.

Your second halt should be in the Place de la Bastille itself, where the massive fortress once stood as a symbol of royal power until the Revolutionaries pulled it down and gave France its national holiday. Today, you can still see its size by the outlines traced on the ground. Apart from having been held and besieged on innumerable occasions during the wars between the Burgundians and the Parisians, the Parisians and the Armagnacs, the French and the English, etc., it was the most famous prison in France. The Man in the Iron Mask spent some time there and so did the Marquise de Brinvilliers, that famous lady poisoner, Voltaire and a host of other notabilities. After it was pulled down some of its stones were used in the completion of the Concorde bridge. In 1899, when Paris' first métro (the Vincennes-Neuilly line) was being built, workmen uncovered the foundations of one of the eight towers of the fortress. They put them up again, stone by stone, in the Square Henri Galli by the Quai des Célestins, and you can see from them how thick the old walls were.

The huge column in the middle of the Place de la Bastille had its first stone laid by King Louis-Philippe on July 28th, 1831 and it was inaugurated exactly nine years later. The door at the base of the column opens into cellars in which the victims of the 1830 and 1848 Paris revolutions are buried and the names of 615 of the buried dead are on the column itself. The somewhat charmingly frivolous statue at the top of the column represents the 'genius of Liberty', holding the fragments of a broken chain in one hand and the torch of civilisation in the other.

History galore in the Place de la Bastille, pleasure and gaiety in the nearby rue de Lappe. The little street is the capital of Paris popular dancing and the Champs-Elysées of the traditional *bal-musette* where young workers came to dance with their girls on Saturday and Sunday nights and where hopeful tourists would come to catch a glimpse of the mythical *apaches*.

The rue de Lappe has been devoted to dancing since the beginning of the century. After being almost entirely colonised by Auvergnats from the mountain region of central France, almost every shop had its own *bal musette* where the immigrants would meet again and dance to the sound of the *cabrette* or *musette* that gave its name to the dance: a kind of provincial French version of the Scottish bagpipes. The dance halls were simple enough: no admission fee was charged although you paid about ten centimes for each dance and the main drink served was a bowl of wine, and the orchestra was just the one player who beat time with his foot. Later, for some mysterious reason, the bagpipes gave way to the accordion and the local *apaches* and *filles de joie* practically took over the rue de Lappe. Quarrels were quickly settled with a knife in the best *apache* tradition, and guide books of the time warned tourists not to go there unless accompanied by policemen, which was hardly an appealing idea and not likely to make you popular with the locals. The *apaches* went in their turn and the tourist agencies moved in. Out-of-work actors would be dressed up for the occasion and hired by the different dance halls to give visitors the agreeable feeling that they were really participating in the high jinks of the Paris underworld. But even since then, many of the old bals have disappeared although a few—the *Boule Rouge*, the *Balajo*, the *Guinguette*, and the *Petit Balcon* in the passage Thierée—are still places where you may dance at night only a stone's throw away from the Bastille.

Today, the rue de Lappe is still an Auvergnat colony and the centre of this colony is number 41 in that street, the *Galoche d'Aurillac*. The *Galoche* is not a *bistrot* like the others. Its owners, M. and Madame Bonnet, both of them solid Auvergnats, have succeeded in giving it a character and an atmosphere not to be found in any other of the city's 19,000 odd cafés and *bistrots*. As you might expect, it has, of course, got its bar where you can join the locals and drink a glass of 'the wine of the house', but it also has its extraordinary décor provided by a vast selection of smoked hams, sausages and clogs hanging from the ceiling and, perhaps even more important, a concert of *cabrettes* (Auvergnat bagpipes) every Friday evening from 8 o'clock onwards.

The concerts take place in the back room under the direction of Maître Georges Soule, a winner of the Grand Prix de Rome for music, a skilled organist and teacher of the *cabrette*, mostly played here by young Auvergnats who keep their old village traditions alive in Paris despite juke-boxes and television sets in bars. It's a rare sight and one you shouldn't miss if you have the chance. And don't forget to try Mme Bonnet's real country *charcuterie* while you're there.

If you're in Paris in the week before Easter, another reason for heading eastwards in Paris is the annual *Foire de la Ferraille*, on the boulevard Richard Lenoir, just off the Place de la Bastille where, besides a large selection of old junk and ironware (whence the name 'Ferraille') you can buy gastronomic specialities (cold meats, pâtés, sausages) from all over France, sold to you by vendors in regional costume. It's quite as entertaining as the Flea Market and even if the selection of 'antiques' leaves a lot to be desired, it has its gastronomic compensations.

Beyond the Bastille, the district of the faubourg Saint-Antoine has been a home of artisans and craftsmen for centuries, and especially for cabinet makers, and is still full of shops selling every kind of furniture, fitting, carpeting and mirror, with workshops

at the end of almost every yard or alley way. Until the 17th
century, the village of Saint-Antoine had been outside the walls of
Paris and had grown up around an ancient convent whose abbesses
protected the craftsmen who came to escape the rules laid down by
the city guilds. The abbey has gone but the tradition of fine crafts-
manship remains and the population is one of the oldest established
and most stable in all of Paris.

Few buildings of any importance have survived in the whole of
this area, but it is still rich in historical memories. Today, the best
known, and most sinister monument of Paris' past is the prison of
the Petite Roquette—poetically named after a wild flower that
used to grow in the wastelands of the district. The grim, six-sided
prison was first used for convicts awaiting transportation to the
bagne or convict-yards at Toulon or elsewhere. Since 1932 it has
been a women's prison but it's main claim to fame has been that it
was in front of the main entrance, in the rue de Roquette itself,
that public executions were held for many years. Five black,
rectangular stones set in the roadway still show where the guillotine
used to be set up.

If you follow the rue de la Roquette it will lead you—appropriately enough—to Paris' most famous cemetery: the Père
Lachaise. It was once a country house with magnificent gardens
which had been given by King Louis XIV to his confessor, the
Jesuit priest Lachaise, but after the expulsion of the order in 1763,
the property was sold to pay debts. In 1790, the Revolutionary
Assembly prohibited the burying of the dead within churches and
a few years later Napoleon continued to apply the prohibition by
ordering that four new cemetries should be built outside the walls
of Paris. The Père Lachaise was one of them. The architect
Brougniard was set to work, he kept two rows of lime-trees and
an avenue of chestnut trees that had belonged to the Jesuits' magnificent gardens, built the cemetery chapel, did some landscape gardening and, even more important, built the neo-Gothic shrine for the
remains of those famous lovers of the Middle Ages, Héloïse and
Abelard. The shrine was built with stones from the cloister of
Paraclet where the lovers had been originally buried and the two
13th-century effigies had new heads added which had been modelled
after the skulls of the corpses. Even today, the tomb is still a place
of pilgrimage for romantics drawn by the pathos of one of the
world's great love stories.

Quite a different pilgrimage to the cemetery is that to the *Mur des Fédérés* every May 26th—the anniversary of that tragic day in 1871 when the last defenders of the Paris Commune were hunted down amidst the gravestones and funeral monuments by the victorious government troops and shot in batches against the wall at the farthest end from the main entrance.

This enormous cemetery is the largest in Paris and has some fifty-thousand tombs. It is also one of the most picturesque and a feast for the connoisseur of funeral architecture and sculpture. Famous people buried there include Napoleonic marshals, Chopin (next to Sarah Bernhardt), the actress Rachel, the poet Musset, the painters Delacroix, Ingres, Corot, Daumier; Oscar Wilde, the most famous exile to be buried in Paris, and a galaxy of writers and scientists including Apollinaire, Molière, La Fontaine, Colette, Balzac, Beaumarchais, Michelet, Champollion, Cuvier and Claude Bernard. The Père Lachaise also has its ghosts. Young women on their own are said to be attacked at nightfall by a giant cat, three yards long, according to some of the older inhabitants of nearby Ménilmontant, a ghost plays the piano on moonless nights at the highest tomb in the cemetery, that of one Félix Beaujour, and if you lay your hand on the head of the statue of Alain Kardec, founder of 'spiritual philosophy', your erring wife will at once mend her ways. And speaking of curious happenings at the cemetery, the index and little finger of the right hand of the sculpted muse playing the lyre over Chopin's grave have just been cut off again for the twentieth time by some determined fetishist. . . .

The rue de Charonne outside the cemetery is the main artery in another hive of craftsmen like the faubourg Saint-Antoine and it is worth exploring it if only for the little church of Saint-Germain-de-Charonne in the Place Saint-Blaise which has kept the prettiest and most rustic churchyard of any in Paris.

But the heart of 'popular' and 'East end' Paris is Belleville-Ménilmontant: two districts that have always been linked together in the folklore of the city. This is the territory of Edith Piaf and Maurice Chevalier, the singer Aristide Bruant and other Paris immortals who have sung of the simple life and loves of working-class Paris. Until not so very long ago, Belleville and Ménilmontant were both villages with farms and country houses, until the city swallowed them up after having first brought them within the city limits in 1830. But despite wars and revolutions, the two districts managed to keep their provincial, country charm for more than a century. Now, alas, the city-planners have decided to build Paris

2000 AD on the windy heights of Belleville and a whole way of life is dying out as the bulldozers move in.

By the time these lines are printed, it is probable that little will be left of the old village life of the district. The twice-weekly market in the rue du Télégraphe will probably have moved and the barrow women with their black dresses and wooden high-heeled clogs will have disappeared from the narrow, low streets. At least, let's hope that the streets won't lose their names. Each one has a story of its own.

In the 18th and 19th centuries, Belleville-Ménilmontant was one of the centres of Paris pleasure—a kind of earlier Montmartre. The centre of this pleasure was the 'Courtille', a wooded valley with a running stream on the flanks of the hill of Belleville, covered with cabarets, estaminets, rustic restaurants, open air dance halls and *rôtisseries*. So famous was the area that the 18th-century visitor to Paris would be told that 'to see Paris without seeing the *Courtille* is like seeing Rome without the Pope' and until 1840 it was renowned for its annual carnival when merry-makers would come streaming down from the heights in a noisy, bucolic procession to the boulevards below.

But Belleville did not only have its pleasure-seekers; it had its cranks, eccentrics and even its own cults. One of the most curious to have left its traces was that founded by a curious 19th-century personage, Prosper Enfantin. Having decided to create a new and somewhat bizarre religion he founded a 'phalanstery' for its maintenance and greater glory in a property inherited from his mother between the present rue Pixérécourt and the rue de la Duvée and took the name of Father, regulating every detail of the life of his brethren to the smallest detail, insisting on such hygienic (or mystic) rituals as daily washing of feet and the wearing of a rather bizarre tunic consisting of a blue blouse, white trousers and a red-bordered, white waistcoat bearing the letters 'Le Père' in red and buttoned up from behind, with the wearer thus requiring the assistance of one of his fellow *Saint-Simoniens*, as the members were called. Precisely what the locals thought of this brotherhood is not recorded, but after a number of scandalous rumours had circulated it was closed down by the authorities.

The Belleville cemetery in the rue du Télégraphe is the highest point in Paris (128 metres) and *not* Montmartre as most people think, which is a metre lower at its summit. It was here that an 'optical telegraph' device was first tried out by its proud inventor, Claude

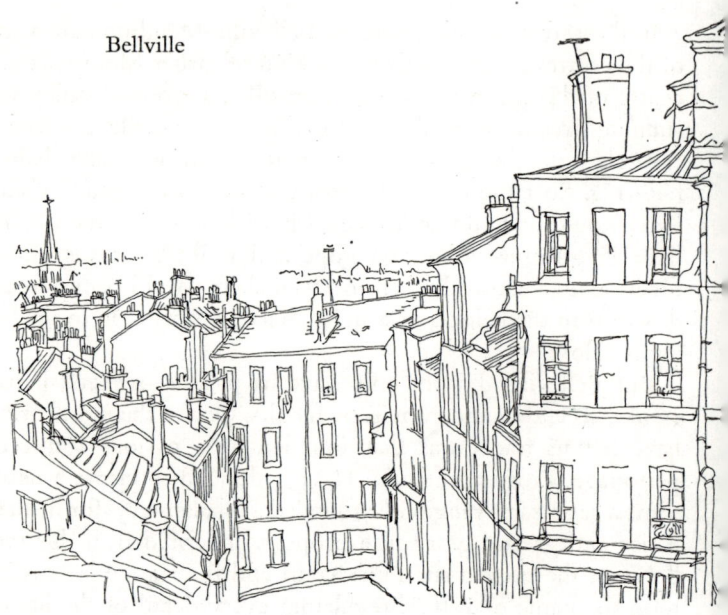

Bellville

Chappé, in 1794, and that the living heart of the old village used to beat. Many of the old streets, mysterious passage-ways and alleys are now disappearing for ever, but the rue Julien Lacroix and the 220 metres long Passage Notre-Dame-de-la-Croix, only six feet wide and intersected by other passages even narrower still will give you an idea of the old, maze-like network of alleyways. If you go up the rue Piat to the Villa Fauchère, you will be rewarded with one of the most breath-taking views of Paris to be had anywhere in the city, and if you include archery among your hobbies, then you might care to visit the *Café de l'Arc* at 63 rue des Rigoles, which is the official headquarters of Paris' only company of bowmen, founded in 1847.

The Buttes-Chaumont is the pride of the 19th arrondissement and

its park is one of the most unusual in a city not particularly noted for its green spaces. Once the site was a quarry, near the sinister medieval gibbet of Montfaucon where criminals would be strung up in tiers, and it was only a hundred years ago that Napoleon III decided to show his admiration for things English by transforming it into an 'English' garden. His faithful prefect Haussmann and his municipal engineer Alphand accordingly set to work, and the picturesque result is the 'Grecian' temple, rocky promontory, chalets, artificial lake, hanging bridge, grotto and waterfall and ponds where—if you've got a permit—you can enjoy that most traditional of French open air pleasures—angling. But whether you catch anything is another matter. . . .

Salon Paris

Paris high-society tends to group around certain salons. To make your entry into them, the question of 'contacts' is all-important.

A short and light-hearted look at Paris at its most hermetic. . . .

So you're young, presentable, fairly well-off and you'd like to break into Paris society via the salon? You've read your Balzac and Proust and you have a touching belief that you need only be invited into one or two of the great houses of Paris for all doors to be opened to you? The chances are you will be disappointed if you believe that the salon still lays down the law in Paris society life. True, there are still a few old-fashioned salon gatherings where you may rub shoulders with Academicians, go-betweens, countesses, lady poets, bankers and boutique owners, but though they may all be very amusing, they are quite unimportant—especially to the true snob. You should also beware of the so-called Tout-Paris, whose names you may find in the papers when describing the attendances at first nights. They are mentioned mainly to impress provincials.

The fortunate few who still have the necessary leisure, houses and money to have salons now prefer to invest in Swiss banks, to buy antiques or even to work. Work is the new blessing of the privileged classes and the luncheon party and business 'cocktail' have taken precedence over the old-fashioned salon and are often far more amusing. The fact is that top people are no longer in fashion in Paris. Youth is now the rage and it has eclipsed all the ageing lions of the political and literary drawing-room parties.

The new heroes in Paris society life are young people like Comte Jean de Rohan Chabot and his pretty wife Joy and the count's sister, Marthe de la Rochefoucauld who injected new life into the Paris social scene when she brought together a group of pretty girl cousins and relatives to form a group of hostesses who would liven up even the stiffest gathering. Should you be fortunate enough to be introduced to her, you will be looked after, you won't have a moment to yourself, you'll go from one ball and week-end party to another and you may even flit through a few genuine salons in the noble Faubourg Saint-Germain where your Proustian heart will beat a shade faster.

The youthful spirit of these gatherings saves them from formality and even though the days of the salon are numbered, you may be sure that wit and good conversation will survive. But, the determined salon hunter can still find a few salons although how he will gain entrance to them is another matter. Ambassadors and men of letters still meet at the Duchesse de Rochefoucauld's, politicians still congregate at the houses of Madame Thome-Patenôtre, the Princesse de Robech and the Comtesse de Fels, and music lovers and scholars still go to Madame Dujarric de la Rivière's. But if you are a beginner, the best place for you to make your social début is at Madame Faure Dujarric's.

After you have made your way in by some means, no one will be in the least surprised if you know no one there, and you will soon find that you know everyone present. You will be introduced to Jouhandeau, Ionesco and other celebrities and the conversation will mainly revolve around literary prizes, music and gastronomy. You might bear in mind that fresh praise from anyone young and unknown is always welcomed there by writers bored with swopping compliments with each other in their impeccable French.

You may never succeed in getting an invitation to the famous Bal des Débutantes, but you may have the good luck to find yourself at one of the Viscomtesse de Noailles' lively luncheon parties which are a perfect combination of the Bohemian and the courtly. Be careful not to say anything silly or pedantic, be on your best behaviour, be prepared to dance with ancient upper-crust hostesses and give a more unassuming address if asked, if you should happen to live in the stuffy 16th arrondissement. It helps if you like painting and are good looking. The odds are that you'll be invited again.

Circumspection is recommended when moving in these exalted circles. Repeat nothing you have heard there—not even nice things, for then you may be taken for a patronising foreigner. Look as if you are always learning something when important people speak to you and remember that important people are Academicians, associates of the Comédie Française, inspecteurs des finances, worldly musicians, duchesses and newspaper owners and, naturally, all the people known to share their beds.

Don't make anti-Semitic remarks, *don't* make wisecracks about Sodom and Gommorah, *don't* run down drug addicts, Pétain supporters, big time gangsters and people with acquired titles, for you never know whom you may be speaking to and try not to waste time with all the various fossils of the Fourth Republic who

227

can always be seen clustering around the buffets at embassy parties given by the under-developed countries.

If you are a social climber, no interior decorator is worth mentioning but quote Jean or Thierry Feray. *Don't* suggest amusing outings to the Flea Market to any young ladies you may meet but *do* take them to Valentine Andy's charming shop or to Jensen's where the assistants are extremely pretty and the Princess Gaetani occasionally holds salons. Above all, *don't* compare Paris to London in spite of any resemblances you may detect. Never forget that the French are more conventional than the English and that seating arrangements at lunch and dinner parties are more important except among the very young who all sit on the floor anyway.

With the right combination of luck, persistence and a few introductions, you should be able to get to know a lot of people; you will never have an evening to yourself and will try to write a novel. You will be entertained at vast expense by people who have convinced themselves they have finally made it in Paris society and you will probably end up by becoming a pundit on society life and lamenting the passing of that splendid old-fashioned institution—the Paris salon.

Expatriates' Paris

And then, there is the Paris of the expatriate ... Paris has a tradition of attracting self-made exiles and you too, perhaps, may become one of them. But before the beauty and fascination of Paris, and your own illusions get the better of you start looking for that Left Bank attic or studio in which to compose your masterpiece, or just 'live', a warning:

The foreigner who expatriates himself and comes to settle in Paris will find himself changed by the city. If he leaves Paris for a time and tries to renew the love affair he once had, he may find the city changed out of all recognition. The familiar old landmarks of the heart and senses are no longer the same.

We asked an expatriate ex-Parisian to define the 'expatriate experience' for us. The story of a love affair and its end.

The number of private Parises of the heart being carried around in people's memories must be enormous. Paris, more than any other city, is the traditional locale of the Expatriate Experience and, physically, its complex beauty and wholly urban pseudo-simplicity lends itself to the expatriate's intense but artificial vision.

Anglo-Saxon writers as disparate as Cyril Connolly, Henry Miller, Hemingway, Scott Fitzgerald and George Orwell have all reconstructed the city in their own images. For some, like Connolly, it has become a map of their own spiritual and emotional experiences, a Paris which is 'another country' both actually and emotionally, where activities are conceived of as happening in a different element and almost a different dimension of time from those in the native land. For Hemingway the city tended to become a kind of backdrop for his own life and both he and Scott Fitzgerald provided a perfect illustration of how to live in a European city with the minimum of appreciation for it and the maximum of emotional and spiritual isolation, with the Ritz bar as the place where the heart really beats. Henry Miller, the most direct expatriate inheritor of Hemingway's bull-dozing attitude, would also have sat in the Ritz bar if he could have afforded it, but because he couldn't he ended up by converting his dead-beat view into a more genuine way of life than Hemingway's. Orwell's attitude was equally genuine though more circumscribed, matured through force of circumstances in the greasy sculleries of restaurants where he washed the dishes. But Orwell saw Paris through a lens of social awareness and an Anglo-Saxon sense of fairness, an approach as idiosyncratic in its way as that of a writer like Connolly.

What all these famous expatriates did was to pass on their individual Parises to their readers and imitators who, in turn, grafted them on to their own experience thereby creating a million more variegated Parises and self-perpetuating cities of the mind. The Beats who came in the early fifties to look for the Paris they had learned about from the previous generation, have in turn superimposed their own public fantasies on what they were looking for. The result is that what are now being passed on to newcomers are personal interpretations of the city that were second- (or even third- or fourth-) hand to start with—reflections of reflections of reflections....

Although it may be argued that reflections are, like dreams, often more poignant and sometimes more meaningful than a prosaic single representation, the trap is that the reflections are taken for reality and the dangers of expatriation frequently ignored. The basic pitfalls were stated by Orwell thirty years ago: '... leaving your native land ... means transferring your roots into a shallower soil. Exile is probably more damaging to a novelist than to a painter or even a poet, it's effect is to take him out of contact with working life and narrow down his range to the street, the café, the church, the brothel, the studio'.

Notice that Orwell specifically confined his remarks to novelists, thus partially exempting other types of expatriate. Artists, in fact, seem to thrive in Paris, but this is for practical reasons connected more with the light and the European art market than with the type of life they lead there. But writers are not 'different' from other people who come to live in Paris. They are exactly like everyone else only more so, since they live their expatriate lives more consciously. In fact, the same creative ability that makes them vulnerable, in Orwell's opinion, to a false environment also provides them with a defence against that environment.

It is the non-creative expatriate who is more vulnerable—especially if he has little real immediacy of view or originality and comes to Paris hoping that the experience lived by Miller or Hemingway will be easily accessible to him too.

You may argue, when it comes to the point, that the 'working life' and all that goes with it in the way of home-founding and

child-rearing, is not *necessarily* a deeper or more personally significant experience than those to be found in a foreign café or studio.
But what is factually true is that a large proportion of people, both
the genuinely innocent and those who ought to know better, *think*
that café and studio experiences, not to mention brothel and street
ones, are not only more striking but also in some way more profound and more personal, even, than those to be met with at home.
Admittedly the outsider's café-terrace view is a heightened one,
but what is 'experienced' in an alien setting is liable to remain alien
in every sense: because it is largely unrelated to previous living it
does not get evaluated or assimilated; it does not, in short, become
part of the personality. Time, you note, does not exist in 'the Paris
where all good Americans go when they die'—a cliché more telling
than it first appears. Typically, expatriate experience is 'found'
rather than created, and it is apt to be both unindividual and
phantasmagoric—a hyper-reality in which concrete details of daily
life assume an exaggerated importance while the real nature of the
situation is passed over or possibly misinterpreted.

How familiar is the congenital expatriate, with his almost mystical
preoccupation with foreign food and drink, his conviction about
the 'narrowness' of the life available in his native land and, in
contrast, the 'freedom' of that he finds in his elected new environment where he feels 'so much more at home'! It is fairly obvious
that such an escape is usually one not from the motherland but from
the self, and from self-knowledge and commitment. By joining a
heterogeneous, polyglot society the expatriate has rid himself
neatly, he thinks, of the identity tags of nationality, class and
education. Actually, what he is likely to have shed is half his wits;
there is nothing like parroting a foreign language and play-acting
foreign customs for believing yourself cleverer than you were at
home while in fact you are being rather more stupid. The 'new
identity' is really a partial loss of identity. Also, since the lack of
close involvement with the environment is not merely a side-issue
of expatriation but is, secretly, the main attraction for many
expatriates, the experience inevitably brings diminishing returns.
The varied yet homogeneous 'foreign-ness' of even so adequate an
expatriate terrain as Paris is changed by familiarity, and in the wake
of familiarity come the inconveniences of increased thought,
cooler perceptions, resultant areas of criticism and contempt, and
a gently accruing burden of habit and commitment. Time, in fact,
makes its presence felt.

At this juncture the refugee or involuntary exile (who has little alternative but to stay) has, perforce, to make the transition from outsider to assimilated foreigner. Paris, in fact, has many such—Levantine, White Russian, Spanish (Red)—and has been enriched by them. To be truly 'Parisian' is not necessarily to be French. But the genuine, boat-burning adoption of another country is not easy, and most voluntary expatriates are by nature disinclined for any such effort. The very traits that have made them expatriate themselves are the same that prevent any real metamorphosis of the personality in that situation. When reality begins to impinge, and the inescapable, awkward self threatens to make its true nature felt once more—help! The expatriate ex-patriates himself once more, sets off for Rome or San Francisco, Athens, Majorca or Tahiti. Is there another Paris to find?

The fact that the Expatriate Experience in any one place is inevitably transitory accounts for the static quality of an expatriate atmosphere. The décor barely changes, nor do the walk-ons. But, as in a University, the faces only *seem* the same; their sameness lies in the fact that they are actually new people having the same old experience, not, as in a society less parasitic and with more continuity, the one set of people developing and growing older at individual rates. The names are different, the faces and clothes less so; the preoccupations with art, sex, pot, food, knowing other people and the current poetry-and-jazz Happening organised by the Something-group have hardly changed at all.

To be repelled by a return trip to expatriates' Paris is the direct reverse of nostalgia: a disgust at the tide-marks of out-of-date emotion. For nostalgia, one realises on reflection, is the result of an attachment to a place which is merely sentimental. But if you have ever attempted to invest a more serious emotional capital thus turning the Paris Experience into something more than a diverting and instructive interlude, innocent nostalgia is out. If, in fact, you have tried to effect the transformation and convert an expatriate world into a Parisian one and have subsequently, for whatever reason, drawn back from the undertaking, it is difficult ever again to revisit Paris as a happy outsider without experiencing two conflicting distresses—the distress of feeling that you have wandered back into a past life which you no longer much want to inhabit (will you, awful thought, be able to get back again to the present?) and, at the same time, distress at being unable to find again whatever it was that you originally possessed there. Once the affaire, whether with an individual or a way of life, is over, the 'holy places' of the exile's Mecca become not simply devoid of meaning in the literal, harmless sense, but threateningly and depressingly so. The happy dream assumes an almost nightmarish quality; your beloved little Paris, gives way on the spiritual street-plan to a wide, anonymous boulevard up which you walk and walk, wearily uncertain whether you are going in the right direction at all. A standard, anonymous *Pharmacie* sign winks green in endless rhythm by day and night, and at a vast, unknown meeting point of five ways a huge, character-less café serves standard, overpriced dishes at any and every hour to strangers in dark clothes among a wilderness of plastic chairs. . . .

I have been writing as if the nature of expatriate existence and of life in Paris were one and the same thing. Obviously this is not entirely true—not, at any rate, for five million Parisians—yet it is true to a surprising degree. Paris, the French agree, is a place to drink and eat in, and to walk and talk. It is the setting for a life of consumption, not of accumulation. Unlike London it is not, by and large, a place in which to have babies, or drop in on your neighbours—*impensable!*—or to save up for a new carpet, and there are no gardens in which to grow things. There is one café for every seventy inhabitants, men, home-bound women and pinafored tots, yet even the well-off, professional families frequently live round echoing courtyards in apartments so cramped that anything re-sembling what educated Anglo-Saxons regard as family-life is impossible in them.

The apparent paradox of contrast in the space devoted to external areas—café terraces, wide boulevards, vast *rond-points*—and that devoted to interior living, is actually causal: the existence of terraces and broad-walks has made it possible for the Parisian to keep his home a secluded eyrie if he so wishes, while the cramped, internal, secret quality of the traditional Parisian *ménage* has, in turn, made the external spaciousness essential. Paris more than any other city thus looks like a theatrical set, almost a *trompe-l'œil*. Superficially, since the Haussmann plan of the last century was arbitrarily imposed upon the existing street-pattern, Paris has given an impression of magnificence and slightly chilly beauty—now, admittedly, somewhat distorted by the loud, continuous sound of fast traffic on cobbles and the ever-thickening vapour of diesel. The avenues retreat between a series of wings which seem to have been placed to *suggest* acute perspective; a sky-cloth with its painted domes is motionless behind an artistic arrangement of grey roof-tops; the huge apartment blocks of the late nineteenth century with their wedding-cake decorations could surely only be occupied by lofty, plaster people wearing 'Parisian fashions'—whatever they are, or were. But there is another Paris, on quite another scale, built in another age, populated by a darker, more emphatic, race. The original Paris of small streets, small shops, crowded *carrefours*, passages and cul-de-sacs and courtyards within courtyards smelling of food and butane gas and wet stone, is still preserved, behind the façade of the Second Empire city.

Moreover this secret Paris exists even within the large blocks, for behind the grandiloquent façades and the airy rooms fronting the boulevards, lie cramped, dark corridors, windowless bathrooms, cliff-steep servants' stairways, and always, at the top, a warren of small, brick-floored rooms initially without water or heat in which the most Parisian of Parisians live like resourceful mice in the crannies of a dwelling built for a mythical race of giants. To 'arrange' and contrive—*aménager, bricoler, se débrouiller*—is the language of Parisian habitation. It is as if the Parisians were camping in their own city, and for them, too, the thunder of cars on the boulevard is crushing, the jerking lift that carries them to the top of their high building a source of secret fear, the commercialism of this fabulous world's theatre a relentless pressure. The more articulate classes talk much of the pressure of life, and of the sense that their attachment to Paris (which means to them Parisian conversation) may be costing them something both in health and happiness. By Anglo-Saxon standards, social life tends to be competitive, ruthless and heartless—though a true Parisian will usually only admit this to himself.

And yet Paris invites you to wander through it as a rich yet chaotic countryside invites marauding gipsies and all manner of other congenital wanderers to batten of it. You can have a physical relationship with the stones of Paris comparable with that a primitive man or a child has with his rural territory, making its landmarks into totems, till the city itself becomes a substitute for home and family. But it is just *because* Paris is uniquely well constructed for expatriate living that it is in some ways a hard city to live in.

Superficially, it is easy. Here is this marvellous setting, with layers behind layers to be peeled off, here is conversation, culture, art, style, all the famous Parisian *douceur de vivre* . . . in practice, it is all rather too much. Settling in an archetypal city one tends, in fact, to be swamped by one of a limited range of stereotypes. There is a little scope for genuine, original eccentricity in Paris, for the city's overpowering 'character' tends to crush the individual response. For the marvellous sense of 'belonging' to those stones and to the life with which they beat, you pay a price: do not make a mistake about who is doing the belonging. 'Paris Nous Appartient' more often means 'Paris has consumed us', as the film of that name made clear. With a reputation for cynical tolerance Paris actually invites, even forces, conformity—to one recognised mode of life or another. '*Bourgeois*' or 'emancipated', *de bon standing* or a licensed jester—defined by the places he frequents, the social group to which he 'belongs'—the Parisian must stand up and be counted. The Parisian is conscious of playing a social rôle, in many cases almost a character part, in a way alien to most Anglo-Saxons. *Le style, c'est l'homme* is not a phrase that commends itself to the Anglo-Saxon viewpoint and that preoccupation with style which so charms the casual visitor to Paris is the very thing which may, on closer acquaintance, alarm and even repel him. The expatriate is in danger of suffering a crisis of identity. Who is he? He is a Parisian, isn't that enough? Yes, but what has he built up in himself, what new system of values arising out of his Parisian experience? The answer is nothing. Paris is already built—she doesn't need the expatriate.

Once you find yourself engaging in such reflections, then know that this is your life giving you the signal for departure. The Parisian Experience has given you all it can and if you quit it at that point you may do so with gratitude. But for the committed Parisian it is a different matter. For him, the problem can have no such simple solution.

Revolutionary Paris

Every now and again, Paris has its 'revolution' or, at least its riots. People 'come down into the street' as they say. It's not always very pleasant. French police are about the worst in the world when they get rough. Our expert knows: he was there in May 1968. Read him carefully: it could happen again. . . .

If all you wanted was a quiet time in Paris and you happened to arrive during a revolution, it is worth remembering that the French observe official holidays religiously, so that there are at least ten days every year free from revolutionary activity. Even if you can't plan your stay so precisely, the extent or lack of your involvement with the revolution will depend largely on which *quartier* you go to. Outsiders always get the impression that the entire city is aflame during an outbreak of violence, yet New York during the Harlem riots of 1964 or London during the Notting Hill riots of 1958 remained supremely unaffected—indeed their inhabitants knew less about what was going on than foreigners. So if you read about 'violent outbursts' in Paris, don't be put off. You can stay clear of them if you know where not to go.

The Latin Quarter should be avoided, and indeed the Left Bank between Notre-Dame and the Pont de la Concorde, extending as far back as Montparnasse. If anything is happening you can bet your life the Sorbonne will be at the heart of it, so postpone visiting your friend's children who are taking the Cours de la Civilisation Française. You won't be missing much by being denied the boulevard cafés of St-Germain: the resident intellectuals will either be fighting, lecturing, in gaol, in exile, or occupying a nearby civic building. If you want to drink overpriced cups of chocolate while watching Paris pass you by, stay on the Right Bank and go to the Café de la Paix. Apart from public buildings, the Right Bank as a whole is quite safe, especially the smart 16th arrondissement. If you normally inhabit Mayfair or Sutton Place and you are simply seeking a change of air, the 16th will be just like home.

Avoid, also, the slum areas, the ghettos, the new university campuses such as Nanterre, the industrial suburbs (if the workers occupy their factories there might be police reprisals), the headquarters of the political parties, the large railway stations, the ORTF building, the Eiffel Tower (as a radio mast it might be seized), the Opéra, Madeleine, Elysée, Palais Bourbon, US and UK Embassies, and Les Invalides (usually safe as it is surrounded by chic wide boulevards, but it remains a favoured rallying-point for old soldiers). This, admittedly, doesn't leave you much—especially as during the troubles of May 1968 even the Louvre was closed because of occupation by the staff—but you could always go to a cinema, as long as it's on the Champs-Elysées. You won't do too well on theatres, alas, because if you try during an official holiday they will be closed and if you try during a revolution they will mostly be occupied. The Zoo usually remains open, however. Major public buildings do not—those not occupied are surrounded by police against seizure by the revolutionaries.

Life in revolutionary Paris outside the areas of uprising is tolerably normal. Of course if there is a general strike, there will be few shops open, no banks, no trains, buses, taxis, or aeroplanes, no gasoline, and quite likely no tobacco. Some of the great restaurants will probably be closed, but there is no need to fear that you will starve. The French have long ago passed the stage where their revolutions subsisted entirely on cake, and short of a cataclysm you will find that the supplies of food and wine remain uninterrupted. Be warned, however, that the Parisians are terrible hoarders: at the first sign of trouble they begin laying in stocks against a siege, perhaps a memory of the 1870 Commune when things got so bad they ate the elephant in the Zoo. Do not panic if you see long lines outside all the food shops; there will be enough. A last warning for Right-Bankers: the staff of the most luxurious hotels may also decide to strike, in which case you can either hire a car and bribe enough gasoline out of someone to get you to the border (easy if you know any journalists, who are usually to be found in the bar of the Hôtel Crillon)—or you can throw in your lot with the revolutionaries.

For those who missed the Spanish Civil War and who are getting fed up with Aldermaston-style marches, revolutionary Paris may fulfil that oft-sought 'bliss was it in that dawn to be alive' feeling. As a foreigner you can at least work off all your hate against the Establishment on someone else's forces of law and order, and the worst they can do, apart from beating you up until you can no longer stand (assuming you do not have the misfortune to get shot dead), is to deport you. You will not be able to claim a refund on your fare money, however; there is no appeal; and it is unlikely

237

that you will ever be allowed in the country again. But revolutionaries must take risks.

At the outset it will be useful to identify for those who might get involved the three types of police used to crush revolutions. Everyone, it is assumed, can recognise the Army, who usually travel in tanks. If you see them in the suburbs, they will be 'on manœuvres'. If you see them in Les Invalides, be wary. If you see them on the bridges of the Seine, leave the city while you still can.

The ordinary cop wears blue and is familiar from countless Maigret serials on TV. They salute when you ask them a question (in daylight), travel in blue vans, carry truncheons, guns, and heavy capes weighted with lead which can knock you over in a riot, and are most sinister when loitering behind what look like individual *pissoirs* but are, in fact, gun-shields, a relic of the days of the Algerian troubles when it was customary to whizz by police stations firing machine-guns and throwing grenades.

The only people who still indulge this habit are the CRS, a sort of special riot police founded after the war to cope with what looked like a Communist threat of insurrection. It is these gentlemen whom you are likely to see most of. They never salute, and their faces are obscured by grey crash helmets plus, if things are quite hot, a sort of chicken netting to protect them against flying missiles. They are all in grey, with long trench coats and heavy boots, a combination which makes them sound like outraged swans when running, and they carry assorted guns and two sorts of truncheon, one rubber filled with lead, the other plain old wood. They travel in grey vans and have an unnerving habit of brooding in them, so that it is not uncommon to see a whole posse of stationary vans filled with these evil sadists presumably working themselves up into the appropriate frenzy. They sweat a lot too.

The CRS are recruited from the provincial towns of France so that when called into the metropolis they will not feel tempted to settle any old scores. They are extremely racist and profoundly ignorant; also well-paid, and often drawn from those on Assistance Publique—orphans, bastards, and the like. They are doubtless godfearing family men when off-duty, but do not smile at them or in any way attempt to make them your friend. It isn't worth it.

The third type of police is the Garde Mobile who are slightly mysterious and whom few people are able to describe. Their reputation is that of well-built men with a surprising turn of speed, whose speciality is a body blow with the butt of a rifle swung with great force from the barrel. To receive such a blow could seriously impede the normal functioning of the kidneys, and it is wise to run in what you conceive to be the opposite direction at the mere rumour of the Garde Mobile's presence.

Unless you are an industrial worker, who will therefore consider your place to be in an occupied factory, it is safe to assume that the storm-centre of revolutionary Paris will be the Latin Quarter. This is because of the volatility of the students and the inviolability, until recently, of the Sorbonne. The events of May 1968 were indeed sparked off by the Rector calling in the police, the first time the holy precincts had been invaded for 700 years (not counting the Nazis). It is to the Sorbonne you must go for all the information on what is happening, assuming it is occupied by its students. Nothing much happens before 10.30, because the students will be exhausted either by interminable meetings or police charges. From slogans, discussions (which you are at liberty to join), wall-posters, leaflets, loudspeaker announcements, and, best of all, from the incredibly pretty, clean, and dedicated girls who wander purpose-fully around, you will learn what is afoot.

A word about these girls: contrary to all notions about the French romantic temperament, and the promiscuity of revolutionary movements, you will not find that the 'freedom' of revolutionary Paris also includes free love. There were no orgies either in the Sorbonne or in the Odéon in May, contrary to many foreign press reports: if there had been there would have been no need for the forlorn notice which appeared inside the Sorbonne bewailing the lack of sexual freedom and announcing the creation of a 'Comité d'Action Pédérastique Révolutionnaire'. Girls play an enormous role in the revolution, marshalling, victualling, passing paving stones for barricades, and shouting insults at police. But I never believed the stories I heard of foreign revolutionaries nipping off for a quick one with whomever they found themselves next to between police charges. It is inadvisable to make this the main reason for your support for the revolution.

Not all Parisian demonstrations will be violent: many are English-style marches with vague purposes, vaguer destinations, and the vaguest organisation. But let us assume that you have heard the Prime Minister banning all demonstrations, that you have wandered down to the river (assuming you are on the Left Bank; if you're not you've had it, since you will remain cut off from what is happening) and seen the grey vans and the CRS guarding the bridges, that you have noticed that there is a certain tension in the air and that the Sorbonne is filled with heated and militant argument, and that you are still foolish or dedicated enough to want to see what happens. The first thing is to know what to wear.

Avoid anything red: the CRS equate the colour with Communism and tend when excited to pick you up on any excuse. By the same token trim your hair and/or beard. If you have red hair, it's safer to dye it. Dress respectably but not in your best, though you ought to know at once that, if they get you, not even a City suit will preserve you inviolate. Take two handkerchiefs, a little money (to prove you're not a vagrant), empty your pockets of political reading matter—the CRS are not notable for their literacy and are decidedly suspicious of newsprint without pictures—and take your passport. This last is essential and if you are brave enough to insist you are an innocent foreigner when picked up, it might go more easily with you, though there is no guarantee: a Japanese tourist was grabbed, beaten and accused of being a Maoist. When he insisted that he was Japanese he was beaten some more and informed that 'everyone knows Japan is the capital of China'. Only after the greatest perseverance did he persuade the sergeant to look up the Japanese Embassy in the telephone directory, and even then suspicions were not allayed until the sergeant had dialled the number and heard for himself that they did indeed represent an independent country.

The two handkerchiefs are for use against tear gas, one to wear over the mouth and nose (remove it before being picked up, as it is considered incriminating evidence), the other to dab the eyes and blow the nose gently. If you are going to make a night of it, a small shatter-proof container with bicarbonate of soda or lemon juice is good for soothing the skin; for the eyes, water, or the special preparation which the student medical service administers.

For those who are going to play a passive role, the only rule is to avoid contact with the police at all costs. They are in no mood to answer questions about the way to the riot, and they tend to beat you up as soon as look at you, especially if you are young, infirm, or bandaged. They have no taste or chivalry, so neither looks nor sex count. If it is early in the evening their beating will take the form of a severe blow on the head with whatever truncheon is handy; if it is late and they are a bit fed up it will include anything from severe and sustained truncheoning and kicking of your most private parts, to rape. If you are female and not totally repellent it is extremely unwise to wander alone in any area, however remote and far from the storm-centre, where the CRS are likely to pass. Cases of rape are legion, and unless you like that sort of thing—and they tend to leave you bleeding on the street, having stripped and beaten you for good measure—don't risk it. It ought to be firmly emphasised that whoever you are, however innocent you look, wherever you wander, if the police are on the prowl and feel like it they will clobber you. There is nothing you can do about it except run, and though you are likely to run into the arms of their comrades (an intimate knowledge of the geography of the area is invaluable; the CRS are certainly ignorant of such things), don't be a hero. If caught cover your head, or in the case of the Garde Mobile, your kidneys and neighbouring areas, and try not to show pain too obviously because it only excites them. If you wear spectacles remove them quickly, as they love the sound of broken glass. When they are tired of kicking and beating they will ask for your papers. Now is the time to speak English, but don't act enraged since they won't understand and if they do will redouble the treatment. If you happen to have a Press armband it might save you from arrest but not from insult and beating. Whatever you say, do not state that you are a student: the CRS have scant respect for higher education.

Should it be your bad luck to be carted off for interrogation there is no appeal, no possibility of contacting the Embassy, and nothing whatever you can do about it. I will not shock you with the details of what happens once they get you inside, but it is very nasty and can last a long time—days, even. If you are staying with someone whose friendship you value do not give their address to the kindly sergeant and ask him to call to say you're all right: the next thing you know your friend will have joined you and there will be all sorts of unpleasant things marked on his record. Try saying that you are staying at one of the better-known hotels though if you are wearing shabby jeans they will not believe you if you babble of the Crillon, Ritz, or Georges v. *That* stupid they are not.

If it is early and you would bloody their van because of the superficial scalp-wound you have just received, if you were miles away from an actual riot and you manage to convince them, in an abject sort of way, that you are totally innocent, you might just avoid being dragged to gaol. But don't count on it.

Those who wish to play an active role will arrive in what was christened *l'équipe anti-flic*. A crash helmet is essential, as well as goggles to allow you to penetrate the gas. You should be lightly yet warmly clad, so that you can both run and survive the cold mists of dawn. It is not essential but very useful to have a transistor radio because the commercial stations, especially Europe numéro 1, give minute-by-minute coverage of what is happening so that you will know where the police are. This is always assuming that the Government does not impose total censorship, in which case the light music you will hear might while away an hour, though this can also be filled by perfecting your knowledge of the words and music of the Internationale or the latest anti-police obscenity. Or you could make Molotov cocktails.

You will be able to pick up a dustbin lid to use as shield, and a stave for the attack, if any, so that all you have to be certain of is your ability to survive in a fight with toughs indifferent to the Queensberry rules.

For the barricades being American is a great advantage, and if you are not one, stay near one. Baseball training is invaluable, since the Parisians have no idea how to hurl a *pavé* effectively (*pavés* being the main constituent of French streets, about the size of half a brick, though twice the weight. They are laid in a bed of tar, and you should also carry with you a small container of alcohol or surgical spirit—not for internal use but for the rapid cleaning of the hands if you have been throwing *pavés*, since the police redouble their beatings on those with black palms). Barricades are erected, usually on no sort of plan, from anything that comes to hand. Before helping to build one it is wise to verify that there is an escape route: the police will undoubtedly crush the thing, if necessary with a bulldozer, and it does not help morale to know that they have you from both ends. Tactics are not the students' strong point, so you may have to take a lead. Again let me impress on you the importance of knowing the geography. If the area is foreign to you attach yourself to someone who knows it. Usually these are girls, who on these occasions wear dark corduroy trousers. If they are, in addition, sporting red armbands that does not denote their political sympathies but the fact that they are marshals. They will probably be too busy to direct you anywhere, so find another.

The first things to drag into a barricade are the iron grilles that surround the bases of most Parisian trees, but this is only a start. Melting the tar comes next, so that the *pavés* can be uprooted and properly piled to make a strong barrier. Trees, railings, garbage, and anything that will help can be used, but if things get really tough you will have to overturn a few cars. To English and American tourists, certainly, there is something horrific about taking the car of someone you don't know and setting fire to it in the middle of the road. This was also horrifying to some Parisian students at first, but it is surprising how quickly you will overcome your scruples if cars are the only thing between you and a charging squad of howling police armed with guns, grenades, percussion bombs, and truncheons. Besides, legal-minded tourists should take heart: some of those whose cars were burnt in May 1968 were reported to be clubbing together to sue the City of Paris for negligence.

It must be remembered that barricades are rarely in such advantageous positions that they can be used for last-ditch stands. Indeed the only way in which a victory, however temporary, can be achieved, is if a few of you find yourselves behind something fairly solid facing only a few police. Then skill in *pavé* throwing is really essential, which is why American expertise is needed to make this strategy work. Throwing a *pavé* requires strong shoulders and wrists, and the courage to wait until you can see the wax on their moustaches. Aim for the head, because the chances are your target will duck and the *pavé* hit someone behind him. If there are a lot of police you will have to run, so your casting the stone can only be an act of defiance. If there are only a few of them you might be able to drive them away, but they will be back.

A word on fleeing. Most private houses in Paris have street doors opening, at the touch of a button situated where bell-pushes are in England and America, onto courtyards. It is possible to seek shelter here, but it is not safe. The police penetrate even private apartments if they are worked up, and they have been known to drag out innocent people along with wounded ones. Also many concierges, amongst the most conservative forces in the nation, took to locking the street doors during the May troubles, whether on their own initiative or on orders from the police is uncertain. So do not rely on private hallways. Shop fronts are little better, and you are in danger of being showered with broken glass. The best thing is to comfort yourself with the thought that the police cannot really be *everywhere* and run as fast and as far as you can. Only you really do have to know where you are going, though in these situations solidarity usually holds up long enough for you to keep up with an expert if you are lost.

There are no victories on the barricades, and the only success is to survive. That in itself is a considerable achievement. Even if the police do not catch you—and if they do it is a painful experience—you will get bloodshot and extremely sore eyes from the tear-gas, plus the danger of lung damage from the other gases they use. Do not, by the way, touch or keep as souvenirs any unexploded canisters you may find: they are extremely dangerous.

If you are opposed or indifferent to revolution do not visit Paris during an outbreak. It really is boring to be confined to the 16th arrondissement, unless that is the life you normally lead. If, however, you arrive and find yourself caught up in events, if you yearn for radical political activity and the complete freedom of ideas, if you are seeking the genuine revolutionary spirit in all its romantic realism, Paris brings to the event that peculiar sense of excitement, dignity, and garlic which is her hallmark on all things. You might get deported, you will probably be clobbered, but if you want to be present at, and totally participate in, the making of history, you will have to be in the city during a revolution.

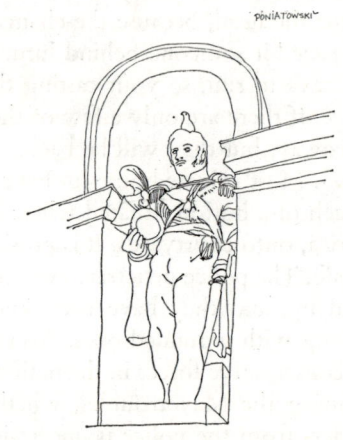

The 'Clochards' of Paris

*The real, traditional Paris tramp or clochard belongs to the class of Paris'
voluntarily under-privileged citizenry.*

*You can see clochards by the banks of the Seine, in certain streets and bars,
sleeping on the pavements or staggering along the boulevards, bottle in
hand. They form their own society, speak their own language, and have
their own rules for survival. Above all, they remain passionately attached
to their independence—the right to be a clochard.*

They're as much a part of the city as the Métro.

First the word itself: *clochard* is derived from the slang *cloche*. A
clochard is consequently someone who lives and sleeps out of doors
with only the sky for his roof. The *clochard* has no fixed abode, no
job, no resources and no income. First and foremost he is an indi-
vidualist and, perhaps, one of the last few surviving *bona-fide*
anarchists, living on the fringes of society and at its expense. If he
does exact an income from society it is through begging. He is
completely *déclassé* and free from all social shackles for he has
chosen to live life as he pleases and is so attached to his independence
that nothing in the world would ever induce him to resume his
position in so-called 'organised' society.

An old negro told me once that it is easy to become a *clochard*.
He had been one himself for a number of years and as he explained:
'One day, you put on a jacket and you say that's my shirt, and then
you put on another jacket and you say that's my jacket. Come
winter-time you put on a third and you say that's my overcoat and
then you go and sit on the quaysides where you'll find other bums.
You drink red wine and smoke fag-ends with them and that's it. . . .'

Reality isn't quite as poetic. Anyone can become a *clochard* overnight. No need to believe in predetermination to find yourself in
the *zone*, as they say, one fine day. Many of the *clochards* were
something quite different before joining the army of their ragged,
hairy, tattered brethren. I myself know a priest, a teacher, a lawyer,
an accountant and a notary who all became *clochards* and are now
indistinguishable from their fellows in the kind of ragged Foreign
Legion they elected to join.

Although you can become a *clochard* by the force of circumstances, because of drink, gambling or trouble with the wife, most
clochards are simply misfits, often from birth as a result of their
social origin. National assistance, the army, and their own hard-
pressed family, have all been unable to prepare them to take their
normal place in society. Even more important, they are often
defeated from the start by the other members of the human jungle
in which they have had to fight for their daily subsistence. Shedding
their past as easily as leaving a coat in the cloakroom, they join the
ranks of the *clochards*, drop their surname out of a kind of shame
and lead their new lives known only by their Christian name or a
nick-name.

Considering that there are several thousand *clochards* in Paris and
that you hardly ever see them working you may well wonder how
on earth they keep alive and even get money. The truth is that the
clochard doesn't do any work as such: he simply does the odd chore.
Every *clochard* has his own system, his *combine* or *défense* as he calls
it and he will jealously keep the secret of his system to himself. At
night he uses it to 'defend himself' and in the daytime he will
usually go to sleep whenever and wherever he may feel like it,
whether it be on a bench, on a grating with warm air coming up
through it, on the pavement or the banks of the Seine. If he sleeps
in a hostel he can't earn his living since the flop-houses open their
doors at about five in the afternoon and only free their inmates at
six-thirty next morning. He has to make his choice and he usually
prefers to do his chore to sleeping with a roof over his head.
Another disadvantage of the hostels is that they are always closed
down between Easter and All Saints Day.

Apart from a wide variety of little trades, most *clochards* still have
one main resource: dustbins at three in the morning. The *clochard*
who earns his pittance from dustbins is called a *biffin* or, if he has no
permit to exercise his trade from the Prefecture of Police, a *coureur*.
The work is simple: leaving his *berline*, a kind of child's pram in
which he wheels his belongings, by the door, he brings out the
dustbins from a house and lines them up on the pavement ready for
the vans. The *concierge* of each house will pay him so much every
month. After bringing out the bins, he will scavenge through the
rubbish and keep anything he can sell to the scrap merchant: paper,
cardboard boxes, rags, cloth, metal, bread and bones. Once gathered
in sufficient quantities, they can all be used again in trade or industry.
Bottles are sold to wine and spirit manufacturers, rags to paper

makers, metal to scrap merchants, bones to button makers, coarse hair to brushmakers and bread to the pig breeders living near Paris. Any time he thinks he can get a better price for some bit of salvaged junk, he keeps it to sell the following Saturday and Sunday at one of the flea markets on the outskirts of Paris.

As a rule, every Paris *clochard* is a potential beggar. Even if he isn't one to begin with, the odds are that he will eventually become one. In this evolutionary process, a large part is played by example. The only place in which the *clochard* can go for a drink is one catering for his kind and where he will meet other *clochards* who are all beggars and thereby never quite out of funds. . . .

It's not certain whether you need a certain kind of face before you can get satisfactory results as a beggar although you might well think so, looking at some of the pariahs of the Paris streets and boulevards. But physical appearance is not enough: other qualities are necessary before you can hope to be a successful beggar. Otherwise, it would be only too easy to simply display your gargoyle-like features under some porch or at some street crossing and wait until you had made your pile. There are some who do this, of course, and you can see them desperately clinging on to their chosen church or monument for years on end until they end up by becoming a permanent feature.

Like all professions, that of the beggar has its system of titles, ranks, castes and categories. It's more than a profession: it's an art. It's no good just holding out your hand and expecting money to drop into it. You must first condition your client by a series of psychological stimuli before his hand will go to his pocket. The beggar knows this and will favour one variety or another of begging according to his own appearance, his clothes and his infirmities.

The Paris Métro is a good hunting ground for beggars and much favoured by *clochards* despite the risks of prosecution. One type of beggar will stand at the entrance, endlessly begging for tickets. He hasn't the money to get home. . . . As soon as he is given a ticket he offers it for sale to the next comer. It's all he's got and twenty centimes would buy him a piece of bread. . . . So you give him his twenty centimes and of course you let him keep his ticket and so it goes on. . . .

Another kind of beggar will stand in the corridors of the Métro under that well-known notice 'Toute quête est formellement interdite dans l'enceinte du Métropolitain' (all begging formally forbidden in the precincts of the metropolitan railway), exhibiting a stump, a wooden leg or a frightful sore. 'Yes, good lady, just look what I'm risking.' After pointing at the warning notice and explaining that he hasn't had a bite for two days, coins will begin to fall into his cap. Another more unusual type of beggar is the man who fakes a faint while his accomplice passes around the hat on the pretext of needing enough to buy medicine.

But the street is the beggar's real 'beat'. It is here that the beggar can leap upon each passer-by, always offering him the same old postcard, the same old pencil or packet of lighter flints, or showing him the same much thumbed and almost illegible certificate of release with the accompanying explanation: 'just out of prison . . .' 'just out of hospital . . .', etc.

Any pretext is valid on the various pitches such as the fronts of railway stations, bus-stops or almost any well-frequented public place.

In the summer, many open-air cafés also have their own accredited cripple or deaf-mute. The deaf-mute's 'gimmick' is simple enough. A man quickly goes around the tables leaving envelopes on which you may read something like 'Ladies and gentlemen, I'm a deaf-mute. Please buy my good-luck tokens. It's up to you, Thank you'. In the envelope you'll find a sprig of lily-of-the-valley or a piece of coloured paper cut into shape of the four-leaf clover and that's all. The deaf-mute will then go around the tables again, pick up the money left on them and disappear to repeat the operation elsewhere.

Motor cars also provide opportunities for the Paris beggar. He can work as a 'door-man'. The system is simple: he watches each coming or departing car. As soon as he sees a car door about to open or shut he rushes forward to help the driver or the passenger and then takes off his cap to reap the fruit of his courteous gesture: a coin which is rarely refused.

Beggars are very keen on getting themselves photographed by the army of kind-hearted tourists that invades the city every year. After all, a snap you've taken yourself is a much nicer souvenir than one of a million identical postcards and it seems that a photo of a *clochard* is one of the most typical Paris souvenirs there is. As soon as you've pressed the button, your subject will come forward cap in hand and you'll do the expected, not without an uneasy inner twinge of guilt.

When caught in the act of begging, the vagrant will be quickly judged by a court and sentenced to a term of prison varying according to his past record. The sentence will always be complemented by a compulsory stay of thirty or forty-five days in the departmental *hospice* at Nanterre.

He will serve this second term in the First Section, known as the 'forty-five' or 'legion' as the inmates say. There, the detainee will have his hair cut short, be given a uniform and a number.

'A normal de-intoxication cure' I was told by an old beggar who had just been back to Nanterre for the seventeenth time. 'Mahomet invented *Ramadan* so that Arabs who ate too much could fast. Not that it's very religious, mind you. *Ramadan* only has one purpose which is to put you back on form. The government of the Republic puts us into quarantine where there's no chance of drinking. It is a good thing, but what a booze-up when we come out!'

As a general rule, the Paris *clochard* hangs out in certain relatively restricted areas. You'll meet the odd *clochard* almost everywhere, of course, and every district will have a *clochard* of its own but he'll usually move in a regular pattern according to his three greatest needs: drink, food and sleep.

The capital of *clochard*-dom in Paris is undoubtedly the Maubert district, in the Latin Quarter. It has been so for centuries for the simple reason that it was near Les Halles, that now-vanished vast food store in the centre of the city, and the banks of the Seine where you can take your rest after performing your chores for the day or the night, as the case may be. Maubert also has the advantage of having a very large number of wholesale rag-dealers and *bistrots* reserved for *clochards*.

Clochards also assemble in the rue Mouffetard, in the Gobelins district, along the Quai de la Gare, in the Amandiers district in the 20th arrondissement, by the banks of the Seine, at the '*portes*' of Paris as at Clignancourt, for example, or in the *zones* around the former Paris fortifications, at Saint-Ouen, Lilas, Vanves and Montreuil.

Clochards don't like going to hostels if they can help it but they do meet around them. Apart from the Nanterre *hospice*, there are at least thirty refuges for down-and-outs in the Paris region including a dozen run by the Armée de Salut (the French Salvation Army). The main ones are: *l'Etoile du Matin*, 33 rue des Cevennes; *l'Armée de Salut*, 12 rue Cantagrel; *Le Palais du Peuple*, 29 rue des Cordelières; *Le Refuge Nicolas Flamel*, 69 rue du Château des Rentiers and the *Mie de Pain*, 16 rue Charles Fourier.

The *clochard* hates hostels for he is essentially a free man jealously guarding his independence. He knows only too well that once he has gone through the doors of a hostel he will have to submit to various hygienic measures, administrative formalities and be slave to a time-table. *And* he will be deprived of drink—a prospect as daunting as going to hospital to which he will only consent when at the point of death.

Arab Paris

Arabs may be seen everywhere in Paris—refugees from France's North African colonies. They're often desperately poor, shamefully underpaid, the worst of the reverse side to France's prosperity. They're France's biggest social problem. They have their ghettoes and their shanty towns. They live like a race apart: their miseries are all too often ignored. But they are an essential part of that other Paris—the Paris of the under-privileged foreigner.

Go down to the quayside at Marseilles if you happen to be there and you will see the daily exodus of an army of unemployed workers from the former French colonies of North Africa. You will see them coming in rags, dark-skinned, eyes feverish, each holding a shabby suitcase in one hand and a brand new passport in the other. All the measures taken to dam this human flood have proved ineffective, for all these exiles from hunger have been able to avoid the traps set for them by the French authorities, with the open or tacit complicity of their governments. They come in a flood, tirelessly, every day helping to swell the human magma forming the lowest and most subterranean layer of the French population. There are more than three hundred thousand of them in Paris alone and they have come from every corner of North Africa. Berbers, Kabyles, Algerians, Tunisians, and Moroccans from the North and the South—soon they will merge into one vast pariah-class to be despised, ignored or merely tolerated by the average Frenchman. They will be reduced to the level of an anonymous crowd with interchangeable faces. They have their own streets, their own cafés, their own cinemas and their own brothels. There are so many of them that Paris has been called the 'fourth city' of North Africa. Their presence has made an essential contribution to the present face of Paris. With their *casbah*, their restaurants and Moorish cafés, certain Paris streets seem to be living according to the throbbing rhythm of the East. But this Moslem Paris bears little resemblance to the romantic Orient as suggested by the sumptuous *cous-cous* at *Aissa fils,* the charming *trompe-l'œil* mirage of the Bey's Palace at the Parc Montsouris or the marvellous little patio in the Paris Mosque with its shaded divans, its fountain, and its cage-birds singing in the trees in an anachronistic evocation of André Gide's Blidah.

It is a world well worth exploring if only because you cannot say you know Paris if you have never seen it and because it is here more than anywhere else perhaps, where you begin to realise the immensity of the problem now facing France since it left its North African colonies. The sad-faced Moors tramping the Paris streets are distorting mirrors in which we can all see ourselves and see what we have made them—disturbing, indecipherable and nourished, we wonder, by what secret hatreds? Now, since they are no longer to be feared, they are simply ignored. They are regarded as not being entirely human and how can you convince the police overnight that an Algerian citizen is no longer a *bicot*, something you can shove off the pavement with impunity, whom you can search, strike and *tutoyer* without the slightest risk? Not long ago, every Arab sitting in a bus became a terrorist, a *fellagha* ready to cut the throat of the Frenchman sitting opposite. Not so long ago, the district between the boulevard Barbès, the boulevard de la Chapelle, the rue Ordener and rue Max Dormoy in the 18th arrondissement was like a fortress in a permanent state of siege, surrounded by armed *harkis* day and night, a forbidden city into which no European would dare venture.

The Paris *medina* is no longer impenetrable but few Parisians take the risk of entering it. Once you plunge into the maze of narrow streets lined by sordid little hotels where each room sleeps five or six boarders and vaguely Moorish-looking cafés with tiled walls and pseudo-Moorish windows where the Arabs listen for hours on end to their monotonous chanting music, in all these little streets with the Goutte d'Or as the main artery, you are liable to an immediate fear—a fear underlined by the discreet but constant presence of *paniers à salade* with their cargoes of *flics*.

Not all Parisians refuse contact with the North Africans for some even search them out under cover of night. But, sexual curiosity apart, they seek them for the same reason which makes most of their fellows avoid them. They are attracted to the Arabs since they seem to symbolize danger, the unexpected and the irrational in a world where the mysterious is diminishing every day. The former pariahs become princes of darkness while their masters imitate their downfall and disgrace in a game which sometimes ends with a few terse lines in the daily papers.

Like most Parisians, you may never have ventured into the district around the rue de la Goutte d'Or but you will have seen Arabs everywhere for this district is only the nucleus of the vaster colony scattered throughout the four corners of Paris. You will see Arabs in Les Halles, in the *Marais*—in the little narrow streets between the rue Saint-Denis, the boulevard Sébastopol and the rue du Temple; you will see them at the Bastille, at the Nation, at the Gobelins, in the rue de la Huchette, the rue Xavier Privas, the rue de Bièvre, around the Place Maubert, in the 15th arrondissement, at La Motte Picquet, near the Métro station Commerce and the Citroën factory. You have to be blind not to see them for they form a city within a city like some malignant tumour continually spawning new diseased cells, eating away at every district, gnawing away at every piece of wasteland, proliferating with a dumb persistence and monstrous patience that defy every remedy. But their insidious progress is free from any secret design or attempt at subversion. On the contrary, it is a sign of a purely sociological phenomenon.

Paris is an old city, heavy with its centuries, weighed down by its thousands of old houses, its old blocks and streets threatening to collapse into ruin as they await the pickaxes of the demolition gangs. This North African infiltration follows the lines of decay and squalor with an unfailing precision. Let a building become empty, let it be evacuated, let it risk collapsing in ruins and there you will find the Arabs installing themselves like human termites, ready to fight with every rat for the holes they have dug themselves there.

Don't be too impressed by all the indignant protests of those who cry out against this 'invasion'. The only result of their outcry is that it tends to allay the conscience of the average Frenchman. France needs this unskilled labour force. The French proletariat may be affected by unemployment and specialised workers and trainees may have difficulty in finding jobs, but there is a constant, growing demand for this army of unskilled hand labour. Arabs will perform tasks that the more 'evolved' Frenchman will no longer accept since they are the most tiring and the worst paid. Hence the embarassment of the authorities and public opinion every time that the question is raised. Two attitudes are then possible: the Frenchman can feign distress and declare that he would like to put an end to this invasion if only he had the means or he can accuse the Arab of every conceivable vice and crime, insinuating that he has nobody but himself to blame for his state. The two attitudes are in no way incompatible and are often to be found combined. The extreme right-wing weekly *Minute* shifts from one to the other with rare dexterity and incontestable success. It is *they* who bring every disease with them, *they* crowd all our hospitals, *they* are dirty, *they* are the low and the thieving, *they* rape our women and *they* are responsible for most of the crimes committed in the capital and its suburbs. . . . Still, as there is no point in frightening industry by appearing to demand the deportation of this sub-proletariat which is the raw material of French industry, the racist Frenchman will hasten to add that he is not a racist, that many Arabs are good and honest workmen and that he is only against the idle and the criminal. . . .

The Arabs are not the only sub-proletarians to be kept at a distance by the French. Negroes, Italians, Poles, Portuguese, Yugoslavs and Greeks often share the same way of life, the same occupations, the same difficulties and lodgings, but there is something which separates the Arabs from the others. The European workers share a deep-rooted social instinct which encourages them to group themselves together by nationalities and to re-create an atmosphere of human warmth and solidarity which helps them to salve their wounded susceptibilities and forget the many subtle snubs they have endured. As for the Negroes, they are held to be *braves gens* who have become more or less assimilated into French society. But the Arabs, as ferocious individualists unconsciously obsessed by the memory of their former grandeur and predisposed to despise those who ignore them, and adepts of a religion which many obscurely feel to be the rival and hereditary enemy of Christianity, stagnate in a mortal ghetto which isolates them even more than their poverty. They are more than just foreigners: they are the 'others'. The Spaniards, and the Portuguese especially, tend to form cells, to regroup into their clans and villages and often send for their wives and children and hold family reunions every Sunday. But hunger has exiled the Arab from his land and his family and he knows no other social framework than the rigid one imposed upon him by Islam. He can never bring himself to expose his wife to the eyes of the French or his own compatriots. He sends half, or even more, of his wretched wages home, only keeping enough to ensure his painful subsistence. If he mingles with his co-religionaries it is not so much by volition as the pressure of exterior circumstances. He will remain in the centre of his artificial ghetto, a man always, absolutely, desperately, alone. He is a man without roots. If you go to find him you will be undertaking a voyage to the end of the night of human misery.

There are many ways of making such a voyage but perhaps the most direct way would be to visit that part of Paris which for almost thirty years has been the preserve of the Arabs: the district of 'La Goutte d'Or'. Take the Métro to Barbès-Rochechouart and there, once you have stepped out onto the boulevard de la Chapelle, all you need do is mingle with the flow of people going towards the *Jaurès* station. You will soon find yourself jostled and hemmed in by men all equally dirty and badly clothed, all with the same weary, blighted expression, all with the same hard, yet resigned eyes, filled with secret greeds and rancours. You will pass one café after another and little 'hôtels' with crowds around the door. Poverty confines many men to the role of *voyeur*; the women here work around the clock and to see them is often reward enough for those without the means to buy more physical pleasures.

Arabs in their hundreds roam in the streets to the left of the boulevard. You must venture into them to see what is hidden by such 'picturesque' streets as La Charbonnière, la Goutte d'Or, Polonceau, Oran and, ironically, de Suez: a swarming, despairing universe of poverty. A vague smell of washing hangs in the air between the blackened facades of leprous houses which, you may be sure, will escape the general cleaning-up ordered for Paris. You will choke on foetid, stale smells from courtyards opening like wells at the end of dark and narrow corridors and see restaurants where the men—for you will never see women there—are eating *cous-cous* reduced to its simplest form. You are now in the very centre of this immense tumour whose other abscesses, such as that at Belleville, are also disfiguring the capital.

Only recently, Belleville was still a kind of 'Whitechapel' of Paris, a district with a certain provincial air where farmyards and rustic houses remained to remind you of the country origins of the town. You could find little inns there, *bals-musettes* and *guingettes*. It was a district of artisans, shopkeepers and workmen, where you rubbed shoulders with the local 'bad boys' who might have come straight out of a song by Aristide Bruant, and *midinettes* wearing their hearts on their sleeve. It was the parish of 'Titi', Maurice Chevalier and the birthplace of Edith Piaf in the rue de Belleville. Now both lower Belleville and the heights of Ménilmontant are being abandoned, street by street, house by house, with windows either glassless or walled-up with only an occasional poor piece of linen hanging to remind you that these ghost streets are still inhabited. Here, the Arabs have made their homes against the background of the new and unattainable blocks of flats rising on the heights above the ruins of demolished houses. The rue Vilin, the rue du Sénégal, rue des Envierges, rue du Pressoir, between the Métro stations Belleville and Couronnes, where a much older Jewish quarter begins—it is here in this labyrinth of sloping streets, amid the culs-de-sac and dark passages, that an army of silent men seem to have found asylum. You will see them standing idle on the pavements, lost in groups or walking alone like all the wretched of the earth, aimlessly, listlessly, eyes lowered. And at the corner of the street and the little Place Vilin you will find a café bearing the name *Floréal*.

Visit the *Cité Floréal* if you want to have a clear idea of the way in which our society is behaving towards those isolated communities it exploits without having the courage to acknowledge or hide the fact.

Go to the Porte de la Villette in the north of Paris and take the bus number 150 to Stains via Aubervilliers, a grey suburb where many North Africans live in an industrial setting that you will find repeated in any capital city in the world. After going under the viaduct of the boulevard Périphérique, that superb *auto-route* being built around Paris, you will suddenly emerge into a futuristic landscape with a certain grandeur and beauty of its own. Get off the bus at the stop named 'Cité Floréal' and you will find yourself in the midst of an immense, open no-man's-land stretching between the city and Stains. To the north, you will see groups of new housing estates, with flower-filled balconies, grey-and-white striped window blinds, surrounded by lawns; to the west, a sports ground bordered by beautifully kept parterres and trees; to the south, the beginnings of Paris with its high blocks and the flyover of the boulevard Périphérique on its thick concrete columns; and lastly, to the east, surrounded by all these new estates, autoroutes and gardens, a conglomeration of huts standing in the midst of a muddy, bumpy, rain-furrowed wasteland covered with garbage and the occasional patch of wild, coarse grass, a huddle of old cars picked off the scrap heap and ramshackle caravans forming a kind of wretched *lager* in which men, women and children live surrounded by the magic sight of a civilisation from which they forever remain excluded. The 'village' is protected by a barbed wire fence and access to it is by a bumpy path. Only three hundred yards separate this shanty town from the highway. Here you will find the reverse side of the Paris of Notre-Dame, of the Eiffel Tower, of the Ritz and the *Café de Flore*. It is here, in this *bidonville* of La Courneuve, facing the Cité Floréal where posters offer flats to be bought over a twenty-year period, with a down-payment of 8,249 francs plus monthly payments of 650 francs.

The village has its different quarters: those of the Portuguese and the Spanish, of the Yugoslavs and the Poles, and lastly, that of the North Africans. In the first two you will see swarms of children and women going to fetch water from the only tap in the *bidonville*; in the last you will see only the occasional woman and hardly any children. It is a strangely silent place, the silence made even more disturbing by the distant ceaseless rumbling of the traffic along the highways. There is a smell of rotting meat and old potato peel, a stale fetid odour of rancid oil oozes out of huts built onto each other with sheets of corrugated iron, old doors and mouldering planks awkwardly assembled, with worn out tyres on the roofs to prevent the wind from carrying them away. You walk past rotting hulks of thirty-year-old lorries on which you may read 'for sale' scribbled in Arabic and French. You walk among old tins and stagnant puddles, thinking of the long Parisian winter in this windswept corner of France. You pass shelters barely three yards wide, gaping open with huddled families cooking, eating and sleeping in a frightening promiscuity and you think of the rats swarming to fight over the various scraps thrown by the doors. But most surprising of all, in the midst of this limitless squalor, you will suddenly come across a tricolour flag streaming in the wind at the top of an improvised mast. It is not there to mark the site of any school, dispensary, or police station: it is a kind of symbol that the inhabitants of the Zone Floréal have set up, perhaps to proclaim their attachment to France, or else to keep bad luck away. For they all know that one day they will be condemned to move away in search of another, equally precarious, refuge. Certainly, the *bidonville* will be razed to the ground as soon as public opinion demands it. You may be sure of that but you may be equally sure that it will disappear only to form itself again, perhaps at Pantin, perhaps at St-Ouen or at Gennevilliers, or along the Canal St-Denis which has just been drained, and where you may already see the first hovels beginning to cluster along the embankment. . . .

Veteran Parisians will insist on telling you that Paris night life 'isn't what it used to be'. Don't be too impressed by their nostalgia—it's the privilege of the ageing.

Of course the commercially 'gay Paree' of the Sixties isn't the same as that of the Twenties, Thirties or Fifties—why should it be? The scene may have moved down from the heights of Montmartre and Pigalle, the cabaret of yesteryear has given way to the night club of today. Some of the old institutions, the 'Folies', the 'Moulin Rouge' and the 'Lido' have survived while others have become transformed, but Parisian wit, humour and spectacle continue to flourish until the early hours in many of the establishments we have pleasure in recommending to you.

Here is our selection, ranging from the super-spectacular girly show to the intimate cabaret for the discerning few. And a few places to avoid. . . . A slice of Paris' night life as it is now. . . .

'PRIVATE' NIGHT CLUBS

As almost any veteran of Paris' nightlife in the twenties and thirties will tell you, the age of the old-style *boîtes de nuit* is over. Nowadays, old-timers, young Paris and tourists rub shoulders together from midnight onwards in a variety of establishments exactly similar to their predecessors except in name. The old *boîtes* have gone and the term *night-club* has come to stay in Parisian mœurs and language. Like the *boîtes*, they offer you a refuge until the morning hours, various drinks at prices ranging from the expensive to the exorbitant and even the outrageous, the occasional 'spectacle' or singer, food of generally indifferent quality if they have a restaurant, glimpses of Parisian celebrities in the better type of club, various pretty girls, the often illusory hope of finding some kindly, kindred soul if you go on your own, and, in a few of the more fashionable clubs, the pleasant feeling of mingling with the fabled Tout-Paris who, if they are there, will be sublimely and obviously unconscious of your existence.

Outside many such clubs you will see the sign *privé* and if you are a stranger inside one of these clubs you may well feel that the whole place is simply a highly exclusive and very private meeting place for those happy few initiates who hold the keys to the secret of Paris's night life. Nothing could be further from the truth, with one or two exceptions: French law upholds your right to be admitted into any such places of entertainment and refreshment, no matter what the sign or the motto of the place, and refuses to recognise the category 'private night club'. All the sign *privé* does, in reality, is to reassure clients who like to feel that their favourite club has the right to refuse admittance to anyone unknown or considered as persona non grata. Precisely how a person is considered as such no one knows. However, it is a matter of history that the Shah of Iran was once refused admission by one of Paris' best-known hostesses and a member of France's solemn Institut de France was once only allowed entrance after his name and age had been confirmed over the telephone by a Minister of the Interior.

You may therefore, insist that they let you into the club of your choice, as long as it is of a patently commercial nature, i.e., one making a profit by serving drinks, food, providing entertainment, dancing, etc., and be secure in the knowledge that the French administration will back you up in your efforts to buy a whisky at a vast price in any club reluctant to let you enjoy this privilege. You can even summon a policeman if they get too difficult at the door, or sue, with the prospect of being awarded a nominal one franc's damages. But once safely inside, nothing and no one can help you integrate into the different groups who regard these clubs as their private territory. The so-called Tout-Paris that French newspapers like to talk about are organised into stratified cells held together much less by any common tastes, criteria or convictions than by their common inclination to show an aggressive non-awareness of the existence of anyone so uninteresting as to ignore *them* and not to have anything to ask of them. No one has ever quite defined this society and the fact remains that many celebrities who go to the clubs in favour with this semi-mythical class would be highly indignant if you suggested that they were among its more august members. They go to the night clubs for the same reasons as anyone else: to meet friends, to drink, see the show (if there is one), to dance, talk politics and scandal and, for the most favoured, to while away the night with the *patron* whose friendship bestows the highest social accolade of all in Paris' night society.

The most 'in' clubs of all at the time of writing are indisputably the 'New Jimmy's' which is known as 'Chez Régine' to all its clients who fear to be thought 'provincial' (a fate worse than any death) and 'Castel' named after its owner. It is by these two clubs, both enjoying tremendous snob-appeal, that we shall begin our selection of Paris' night spots. They are the most famous clubs in Paris, they are the most fashionable by far, they have the prettiest girls and of all the night-clubs they are by far the most 'private'. We can't possibly omit them but neither can we guarantee that they'll let you in if you go there alone in all innocence. Anyway, you can also try for that one franc's damages. . . .

CLUB PRINCESSE, 15 rue Princesse. Tel: 90-22. About 20 francs for a drink.
The real name is 'Chez Castel'. There is a restaurant on the first floor where you can eat reasonably well. Apart from that, there's nothing to attract the attention of the hurried visitor. On the ground floor, a small bar and banquette is almost always occupied by the staff. The only place to go is to the *cave* downstairs where almost anything goes. Its many nooks and crannies have been carefully draped in shadow and the waiters wouldn't dream of disturbing you in your profound meditations on Parisian *mores* should you happen to be alone. A record player plays hit tunes of the moment full blast and after a while you can hardly breathe which doesn't seem to matter to the more blasé Parisians who soon give up any attempt to hide the exquisite torpor induced by so much noise and movement and the comforting sense of just *being there*.

One of the secrets of Castel's success is that he makes you feel perfectly at home without doing anything to make his presence known to you. He is perfectly content to leave the young girls to their dancing while he drinks with all his intimate friends to the healths of other friends and fleeting friends of friends whom he has never seen and hopes never to have to meet. If you do happen to be a friend of a friend of his it's no good your proclaiming the fact to him since the mental effort of having to remember someone not present will distract him from his essential duty as host which is to preserve his exquisite air of idleness.

As far as décor goes, it's pretty awful. An assortment of old bits of stuff picked up here and there make a pathetic attempt to mask the banality of the wall decorations in what is simply a large cellar badly lit by Art Nouveau style lamps. The miracle is that such a lugubrious place should succeed so well in setting off some of the loveliest women's silhouettes and faces in Paris. Many connoisseurs even maintain that the most beautiful of all the city's beauties are only to be seen here, and by 'beauties' we do not mean film stars, actresses and fleeting feminine celebrities for whom to be seen at Castel's is a sign of professional success. Nor do we mean the various very young girls in miniskirts who add to the décor by simply dancing and who ask for nothing else than to be allowed to go on dancing. The real attraction is the sight of those extraordinarily beautiful girls of the so-called 'high society' who know that a fairly strict vetting at the door will always shield them from being seen at Castel's by any of their father's employees or even by the pretty little seamstress who comes once a week to work for their grandmothers. Castel's cellar gives them the opportunity to be initiated into libidinous delights in the nicest possible way and to take a regular evening course in elegant dissipation.

The 'Club Princesse' is a drawing room or *salon* in which people talk less than they dance and in which they dance less than they pretend. What counts is to be seen there, to try to find out by whom despite the surrounding gloom, and thereafter reach the proper conclusions, prompted by the lateness of the hour and the imperious demands of charming if fleeting emotions.

NEW JIMMY'S, 124 boulevard du Montparnasse, Paris 14. Tel: DAN 74-14. Closed on Sundays. Prices: from 20 francs a drink.
The first thing to be said about this famous club is that it is known as 'Chez Régine' and that without Régine, its celebrated hostess, it is completely devoid of interest for the connoisseur of Paris' night clubs. Nothing could be less inspiring than the décor: four black, shiny walls decorated in an unconvincing pastiche of the thirties style, a bar that an indifferent carpenter with ambitions to qualify as a coffin maker might have knocked up in a spare moment, a few gilt decorations and a murky lighting system are far from explaining the success of this almost mythical night spot which brings together a brilliant public almost invariably aged between thirty and fifty night after night. No matter what has been said and written about the place, the 'New Jimmy's' is almost exclusively reserved for the elder generation of Parisians in the public eye. Neither the lackadaisical welcome nor the absent-minded service add in any way to the graceless décor which has become the

traditional late night surrounding for Paris' 'society' as it enjoys its last fling. Ageing Academicians go there to live it up, fashion designers to be smart, the aristocracy to laugh a little too enthusiastically at the witticims of some famous dancer too long absent from the stage, and Françoise Sagan to indulge her nostalgia and sulk at not being considered 'quite serious' as a writer.

If Régine herself is not there, there's really no point in going. She alone can bring a breath of life and inspiration into this funereal establishment which she is now unfortunately abandoning with increasing frequency since she has become a singing star. She is a great 'personality' first and foremost and her appeal is not due so much to her undoubted abilities as a hostess, to her skill in reconciling literary or political rivals nor the spontaneity in which she will join in the celebration of some fleeting celebrity who has been dying to meet her. What has made her into one of the most justly admired personalities on the Paris scene is the fact that Parisians recognise themselves in her with her wit and spirit, her almost childish pleasure in luxury and merrymaking and her determination never to show surprise at anything—in first place, her own astonishing success—whereas everything quite obviously fascinates and amazes her. She has managed to symbolise and resume all the virtues long attributed to the typical *parisienne* and her own wit and personality do the rest. That these virtues and attractions now appear out of date and that the 'real Parisienne' is a fast disappearing animal is of no account: Régine has rehabilitated them and triumphantly projected the image to a clientèle she rules completely and who come to adore her. *That* is the real and only reason for going to 'Chez Régine'.

LE NOUVEAU SAINT-HILAIRE, 24 rue Vavin, Paris 6. Tel: ODE 90-95.

The third of the 'smart' and 'private' clubs after Régine and Castel. Unlike the other two its décor is completely modern: metallic and gleaming. A favourite place for young actors hoping to meet some ageing film director and rising starlets. While they talk business and exchange propositions, the *patron*, François Patrice, makes a point of gathering some of the wittiest people in Paris around his table. No need to warn you that nothing could be more difficult for a stranger (especially a foreigner) to join his group. But as the canned music is always so loud that you have to yell at each other to make yourself understood, the judicious eavesdropper can pick up some of the raciest gossip of the moment from Patrice's friends who are generally well-informed on the latest goings-on. A good place then, to improve your understanding of idiomatic French. Whether you find anyone to practise it with at 'Patrice's' is another matter.

GIRLY SHOWS—MUSIC REVIEWS—CHAMPAGNE

You want to see a typically 'Parisian' show: girls galore, cabaret acts, dazzling costumes, lavish seats, dancing and music. Each of the three following establishments is famous and each is manifestly patronised by tourists, businessmen and provincial Frenchmen. Don't let that put you off: there are plenty of dismal and expensive 'cabarets de spectacles' throughout Paris which will avidly take your money without giving you even a quarter of its worth. The Folies-Bergère, the Lido and the Moulin Rouge are the best and as such they need no other excuse. Go and enjoy yourself: they are the best value to be had and that's why they have lasted so well.

FOLIES-BERGERE, 32 rue Richier, Paris 9. Tel: PRO 98-49. From 10 francs in the 'promenade' to 40 francs.
An institution with a long and glorious history. Once the symbol of gay and naughty Paris—now a place for a family outing. The once-famous 'promenade' which had a reputation like that of the Alhambra in London of the nineties, is now entirely respectable. Times have changed in the first hundred years of its life (it opened in 1869). The historian Michelet and the fiery Second Empire journalist Henri Rochefort used to hold patriotic meetings here in the early seventies and the first modern 'revue' was presented here in 1886. Yvette Guilbert, Mistinguett and Josephine Baker were all consecrated here but memories of such former glories are the last thing that bring the crowds here today. On the average we would say that only about one in a thousand among the public is a native of Paris. The rest come from just about every province in the world to gape at lavishly staged numbers featuring pretty girls in the nude accompanied by cohorts of male dancers and a variety of 'boulevard' numbers that have gone rather stale in an atmosphere of ostrich feathers and glitter. If you find the whole thing a bit too trite you can console yourself by observing the reactions of those around you. The very banality of it all is enough in itself to send them into transports and make elderly and obese spectators positively roll in their seats and go purple in the face with joy. The formula

of the 'Folies' has become a cliché but it is one that still has the power to bind a butcher from the States, a businessman from Toulouse, a Westphalian politician and a Welsh paper salesman in a spell as indestructible as it is banal of a kind of triumphant vulgarity on an international scale, put on the stage with enormous skill and no expense spared.

LE LIDO, 78 avenue des Champs-Elysées, Paris 8. Tel: ELY 11-61. Dinners from 8.30 pm. Dinner-dance and stage show at 11.15 pm. and 1.15 am. Dinner from about 80 francs. ½ bottle of champagne (compulsory), 50 francs.

Parisians have proudly claimed that the 'Lido' is the 'most famous cabaret in the world' which is only half exaggeration since it is undoubtedly the most splendid show of its kind in Paris. It is dazzlingly professional and the most fantastic numbers and scenes follow in breathless succession without the slightest break: conjuring, acrobatics, breath-takingly beautiful nudes in profusion, dances, glittering costumes and Cecil B. De Mille-type special effects (cascades of feathers, water effects, storms, fountains and waterfalls, etc.). Whether you actually like this kind of thing is a different matter, but you will find it impossible not to admire the way it is done here, i.e., with supreme expertise and assurance. A piece of advice: do try to book a table near the stage.

MOULIN ROUGE, Place Blanche, Paris 18. Tel: MON 00-19. Dinners at 9 pm. Prices much the same as at the *Lido*.

Under the same management as the *Lido* and, of course, famous ever since Toulouse-Lautrec's stumpy form first appeared there in the great days of the 'Can-Can'. The Can-Can is still performed there, of course (and rather better than a few years ago) otherwise the attractions are much the same as at the *Lido*, although the sets are often more ambitious and the submarine ballet in a giant aquarium is always positively hypnotic. Even the most sophisticated visitors have been known to forget their sophistication and to have enjoyed themselves at the Moulin Rouge together with honest bumpkins from the world over.

CASINO DE PARIS, 16 rue de Clichy, Paris 9. Tel: TRI 26-22. Every night from 8.30 pm. Seats from about 12 francs.

The owner of the *Lido*, Henry Varna was once known as the 'Diaghilev of the Big Show'. He's aged a lot since then but not as much as his show which mainly consists of performers who are as *passé* as they are uninspired. But unlike the *Folies-Bergère*, the *Lido* is an excellent place in which to study the real French little bourgeoisie at its most uninhibited. Monday is the best day to see them.

STRIP TEASE

Pigalle is still the traditional home of old-fashioned Parisian strip-tease and what passed for 'naughtiness'. Between the average 'strip club' in Paris and that in Soho, there is little difference. You see the same lugubrious public, the same weary girls going through their sad ritual of disrobing, appearing in chains or tickling each other with whips without much conviction, and sit in the same type of drab cellar in an atmosphere conducive to suicide, with the uneasy feeling that 'it's your money they're after'. Some strip clubs are distinctly 'tough', most are sordid. If you must see 'strip' and if you want to see it as an art rather than a pseudo-titillation, then jump in a taxi and flee from Pigalle and Clichy to the avenue Georges V, to the one good 'strip-tease' show in the whole of Paris. It's really extraordinary.

CRAZY HORSE SALOON, 12 avenue Georges V, Paris 8. Tel: BAL 69-69. Minimum charge: 30 francs at the bar. Show at 11.15 pm. and 1.10 am.

'A temple of the flesh' a rather puritan journalist once called the Crazy Horse Saloon. He was quite right: it is. For all its mock Wild-West decoration, it is the one place where you can see strip-tease in Paris raised to the level of a fine art in elaborately staged and rehearsed shows which practically banish all vulgar stirrings of sensuality and in which the girls can only be called 'superb'. The vulgar-minded in search of a cheap thrill will only be disappointed here. The others won't. There is a small dance floor and the ventilating system is still rudimentary but the shows are so intelligently and humorously staged that you can almost forget it. Of all Paris's cabarets it is by far the most 'artistic' and by 'artistic' we really mean *art*.

AU CLAIR DE LUNE, 28 boulevard de Clichy, Paris 18. Tel: MON 39-37.
The entrance fee is cheap enough (2.50 francs at time of writing), but of course you won't be exactly popular if you don't have a drink and the prices of the drinks, it should be noted, are almost as high as in the very best Paris clubs.

Not to hide anything from you, let it be said at once that the successive strip-tease numbers presented by the *Clair de lune* every evening are about as bad as could be. The only reason we mention this club rather than another, such as the nearby *Boule Noire*, *Moulin à poivre* or the *Tabaris* is that the seats are the most comfortable to be found in this part of 'Pigalle by night': about the only thing to be said in its favour.

As for the actual 'numbers', they're much the same as in the other clubs. The famous 'Coucher de la Mariée' ('the bride goes to bed') that used to send our grandfathers into ecstasies is now sadly out of favour, mourned only by elderly Pigallians. At the moment, the star turns have such names as 'summer months in the Tropics', 'the awakening of sensuality in a cosmonaut' or 'flagellation in a mini-slip'. The girls performing these melancholy exercises seem to have been recruited from among maids and shopgirls who seem to be labouring under the delusion that a foreign pseudonym, be it Spanish, Scandinavian or Scots, is enough to make up for their lack of professional expertise. In such exotic numbers as 'tortures of Bali' it is all too noticeable. From the way they perform, one can only gather that 'the mysteries of sensuality' they advertise are still a mystery as far as they are concerned and likely to remain so.

Deplorable as it all is, the place undoubtedly enjoys great popularity with a public largely made up of Germanic travelling salesmen who undoubtedly believe they're seeing Paris at its most madly diverting.

CABARET-RESTAURANTS

TETE DE L'ART, 5 avenue de l'Opéra, Paris 1. Tel: OPE 64-45. Dinner and show for about 150 francs. From 9 pm. Closed on Sundays.

A pocket-sized music hall where you can eat well. Both the shows and the food are among the best presented in Paris and the stars who appear here are all of the first rank: Raymond Devos, Charles Trenet, Barbara, Fernand Raynaud, etc. To appreciate the songs and variety turns a sound command of French is advisable, other-otherwise you'll feel rather lost among a public often largely composed of solid bourgeois who tend to wax sentimental and swop memories of their Paris sprees in times past in between bottles of champagne.

SHEHERAZADE, 3 rue de Liège, Paris 8. Tel: TRI 41-68. Dinner for about 100 francs. With caviar and champagne: 180 francs.

Russian-Byzantine type décor, reminiscent of the Ballets Russes, with lashings of red everywhere. Discreet lovers whose minds are on anything but the show can dine in semi-seclusion behind gold-embroidered curtains in luxuriously administered recesses. The food is equally Russian style, with an emphasis on caviar, salmon, blinis, beef Stroganoff and vodka. Entertainment is provided by various singers and players with a repertory ranging from old Ukranian folk tunes to American musical comedy hits and the latest pop songs. In between the violins weep and so do some of the more nostalgic Slav clientèle who might have strayed in here for a little bit of 'Old Mother Russia'.

LE PORT DU SALUT, 163 bis rue Saint-Jacques, Paris 5. Tel: ODE 32-03. Dinner for about 70 francs. Drinks at 20 francs. Show at 11 pm.

The entertainment is provided by actors and singers who either became famous or who are about to become famous at the *Galerie 55* (see page 268) to take one example. You can hear them here while you dine. It is a tradition of the house that you have a plaster-cast taken of your face on the spot by an expert attached to the house. The atmosphere is charming and the *patron* is genuinely pleased to see you and shows it unreservedly.

LA MAXEVILLE, 14 boulevard Montmartre, Paris 9. Tel: PRO 72-85. Dinner and show until midnight. From 15 to 30 francs.

Few Parisians seem to know about the *Maxé*, a huge, surviving vestige of the old days of the Parisian café-concerts so beloved by Toulouse-Lautrec. The décor has been 'modernised' which is a pity; otherwise the place remains faithful to the old traditions with Italianising tenors and raucous Montmartre songsters bellowing away vigorously. You may not care for this kind of music but the uninhibited atmosphere, and public, and the friendly familiarity of the waiters are those of an older and more charming Paris before neon lighting and American type drugstores came to the city.

'LEFT BANK STYLE' CLUBS

Here are three of our favourites. But first, a word of warning: you may find the atmosphere enchanting and drink yourself silly but if you don't know French well enough you'll miss all the humour of the songs and gags—which is to say the main attraction of the cabaret. 'Left Bank' cabarets are an old institution and the humour is typically non-conformist and Parisian. If you can't appreciate it, then don't go.

GALERIE 55, 55 rue de Seine, Paris 6. Tel: DAN 63-51. Show at 11 pm. Drinks at about 25 francs.
   A kind of Comédie Francaise of variety, with a galaxy of performers who once made their name here and who continue to make an appearance on the tiny stage. A public of habitués and one of the best places for savouring the most Parisian of French humour. The *patron* never announces his programme in advance.

LE CHEVAL D'OR, 33 rue Descartes, Paris 5. Tel: MED 50-11. Show at about 11 pm. Drinks at about 15 francs.
Tiny stage and excellent young and not-so-young singers and comedians who keep alive the spirit and traditions of Saint-Germain-des-Prés in the great period of the early post-war years. The *patron*, M. Léon, discovered such stars as Anne Sylvestre and Raymond Devos.

LA CONTRESCARPE, Place de la Contrescarpe, Paris 5. Tel: MED 44-63. Drinks at about 10 francs. From 7 until 3 am. Show at 10 pm. Drinks at about 10 francs. Closed on Sundays.
Very popular with students. Rather heavy emphasis on guitars, folk songs and political songs of protest (or lament). But there are

nearly always some good numbers during the show, which owe nothing to the political situation or the miseries of 'under-developed' countries.

L'ALCAZAR, 57 rue de Seine, Paris 6. Tel: DAN 53-35.
The Alcazar is an attempt to recreate the atmosphere and entertainment of a typical 'café-concert' of the Parisian Nineties. Whether the proprietor, a Parisian from Toulouse, Jean-Marie Rivière, has been successful it is still too early to say. At the time of writing, the clientèle of this large cabaret-restaurant with its uninspired décor is difficult to classify. So is the show which ranges from various old popular songs sung by elderly gentlemen with little voice left to strip-tease turns by over-nervous girls. The whole thing needs to be tightened up and given cohesion. In any case, the Alcazar is likely to be besieged for a time by Paris's smart society who so far have remained blissfully unaware that Paris still has an authentic surviving representative of the real café-concert of the time of Toulouse-Lautrec: the Maxéville (see page 267).

'SPECIALISED' NIGHT CLUBS

Known as 'cabarets particuliers' in French. 'Particular' is certainly the word for some of them. Each has its speciality: some have 'drag shows', others make their fortune out of their Lesbian reputation while one or two are still genuine representatives of a very special form of Parisian wit at its cruellest and most deliberately obscene. They are all hugely popular: with tourists seeking Paris at its 'naughtiest' and, in a few cases, with genuine connoisseurs of a type of Paris night life that, alas, became rarer in the stifling climate of Gaullist France.

First, the 'drag shows': the best place is:
MADAME ARTHUR, 75 bis rue des Martyrs, Paris 18. Tel: ORN 48-27. Every night at 11 pm. Drinks at about 25 francs.
'Madame Arthur is a woman' was one of the great popular songs of the 1900 period but history matters little in this Montmartre temple of drag and double-meanings where the historical references which occasionally serve as pretexts for 'strip-tease' turns are vague in the extreme.

'*Madame Arthur*' is certainly not a place you visit in order to recapture the atmosphere of the good old days in Montmartre and the habitués of this club, which we esteem the liveliest and most original of its kind in Paris are here for quite different reasons. Everything that is said, sung and performed on the stage is of the utmost, the most uninhibited, aggressive, explosive vulgarity imaginable. The young transvestites who prance and waggle their hips and bosoms for the delight of the audience are no different from those you see in any other comparable type of show anywhere. The difference is that here they accompany their friskings with an endless stream of repartee and running commentaries in a language so deliberately crude and apparently, so unselfconsciously obscene that even a hardened trooper might well blush. An old man who successively appears as a concierge, a society lady or a *midinette* acts as compère. His name is Maslova and he binds the whole show together with a deliriously insane patter which now and again attains pure genius. His pathetic clowning, his deliberate bad taste (to put it mildly) and his striving after the utmost excess of the obscene by means of gesture and facial expression rather than by his wild ravings are the high-spot of a show which may not be the best of its type but which, with him, is the most unique, the most unforgettable in the whole of Paris' night life. Even if you don't like 'drag' it's more than worth your while to see Maslova.

CARROUSEL, 29 rue Vavin, Paris 6. Tel: DAN 66-33. Show from about midnight. Drinks at about 25 francs.
For a long time a haven of the 'third sex' in a rather old-fashioned sort of way with a variety of slender transvestites whose impersonations are all to often limited to rather *passé* idols such as Marilyn Monroe, Maria Callas and Brigitte Bardot whom they mimic with varying degrees of conviction and success. Now and again they also do Marlene Dietrich. The general lack of originality in the entertainment seems to reassure the habitués who go there knowing very well what the evening's bill of fare may be. Remarkably few queers in the audience which is made up for the most part by solid, respectable bourgeois and tourists, and even family parties. Relaxed, even soothing atmosphere; well staged revue numbers but no surprises.

BRASSERIE 'AUX CASCADES', 60 boulevard Rochechouart, Paris 18. Tel: MON 63-75. Closed on Thursdays. Drinks from 4 to 10 francs.
The *Cascades* is an Alsatian type of brasserie like so many others in Paris with a clientèle largely made up of truck and taxi-drivers.

In the evenings it comes to life with various musical numbers and, above all, a drag act performed by an elderly mechanic who will appear in a flowered miniskirt and sing a repertoire of old patriotic songs and less respectable numbers for the delight of his audience. Some people find it rather sad—others, like several well-known Parisians—find him fascinating. Armando is the name of the 'star' and if you dare to ask him why he should have taken up his unusual profession he will tell you in no uncertain terms that he is an entirely normal, ordinary family man.

'FEMININE CABARETS'

Gaping tourists naïvely imagine that a visit to a 'feminine cabaret' is a voyage of discovery in the depths of Paris's lesbian world. Why disillusion them? They're good for business and business is what these clubs are there for. Lesbians, in Paris as in other cities, conduct their lives discreetly and those you see flaunting their proclivities in clubs do so for the best of commercial reasons. The clubs are not for pick-ups (of course, they do happen) but essentially for entertainment. Sometimes they are hilarious, at other times provocative and even aggressive. If you're a male visitor, you may find the girls taking the mickey in no uncertain fashion. Some nights are quiet. It all depends on the clientèle and the humour of the girls.

LA MONTAGNE, 46 rue de la Montagne-Sainte-Geneviève, Paris 5. Tel: ODE 15-59. Show from about 11 pm. Open until dawn. Closed on Mondays. Prices at about 15 francs.
The 'Montagne' was originally a rather dingy little popular dance hall, a *bal musette*, before an enterprising and very butch lady made it into one of Paris's most famous meeting places for ladies in search of a sister soul. Times have changed since and although the place is no less dingy, no one will stop you setting foot in there if you are a male—although you will not be made particularly welcome or invited to stay with any enthusiasm. Young couples come to gape and your girl friend may sometimes be raucously invited to dance and that's about all. The show is generally abysmally bad but of course, it's the habituées of long standing who are the main attraction. The music is deafening.

ELLE ET LUI, 31 rue Vavin, Paris 6. Tel: MED 29-52. Show at about midnight. Drinks at about 25 francs, (less at the bar).

271

Elle et Lui is the pendant of the *Carrousel*. Not only is there a communicating door between the two clubs but the management is said to be the same. The atmosphere is completely different: there is none of the humour the good humour and even the wit that makes for the naïve charm of the *Carrousel*. The ladies who perform their strip-tease numbers or who solemnly pretend to whip each other on the stage take themselves very seriously since they know that other women are watching them and make a valiant effort to arouse their desires. The general lack of humour that characterises these proceedings is underlined by the solemn gravity with which the waitresses in male uniforms serve drinks. For the voyeur rather than the tourist, the female audience is more interesting than the show but it's worth taking in the *Elle et Lui* with the *Carrousel* if only to cover the old-fashioned 'homosexual Montparnasse' scene in both its aspects.

CHEZ MOUNE, 54 rue Pigalle, Paris 9. Tel: PIG 64-64. Show at 11.30 pm. Open every evening from 10 pm. until dawn. Drinks at about 25 francs (or 15 at the bar).
Middle-aged Lesbians in three-piece suits. Unexceptional 'show' with a few 'strip-tease' numbers. Openly Lesbian atmosphere with habituées only too ready to show their interest in any young female visitors who may have been attracted by curiosity.

FRED CARROL'S, 12 rue Saint-Anne, Paris 1. Tel: RIC 97-86. Every night from about 10.30 pm. until dawn. Drinks at about 20 francs. 'Fredé' (always dressed in a dark suit) was the high priestess of Sapphic love in the good old Paris of the 4th Republic. Since then, her feminine friends have remained commercially faithful to her in a cabaret which is distinctly passé.

Finally, for connoisseurs of 'unusual' cabarets, the most unusual of all: there is no show, no music, only . . .

RENE COUSINIER, Impasse Marie-Blanche, Paris 18. From 10 pm. Closed on Mondays. Drinks from 10 francs.
Parisian journalists have been asked by the owner not to reveal the exact address of this practically 'clandestine' cabaret which the police apparently only tolerate on condition that it never advertises —not even to the extent of putting up a neon-sign. But every night it's packed to overflowing. It's strictly a one-man show and the most amusing, if disconcerting, in the city.

From about ten o'clock until the early hours of the morning, René Cousinier provides the sole and entire entertainment with perhaps an hour's break around midnight. His act consists of a non-stop commentary on subjects theological, scientific, political, literary and topical with endless gags and double meanings of more than Rabelaisian obscenity, with a wealth of meaningful gestures and untiring enthusiasm for everything salacious. He's an artist in the obscene—in fact he's an artist full stop. But to appreciate him and understand why he's such a sensation you *must* have a great knowledge of spoken French and be able to hold your own in *argot*.

Gambling

Gambling is rather a sober, even depressing activity in Paris. It's very strictly controlled by the law, rather secretive and anything but light-hearted. With the exception of Enghien (where roulette is forbidden) there are no casinos nearer Paris than Le Touquet. The smart set prefer to go to Cannes and Monte Carlo for their gaming—so do most foreigners. Paris gambling is mainly for Parisians who have to gamble, no matter where they are.

Horse racing is a different matter. Some of the courses are among the most famous in the world—Longchamp, Auteuil.... That's where high-society and the aristocracy of the Paris turf go. The man in the street, the ordinary punter, plays the tiercé, a kind of state-run sweepstake. To the French it's the equivalent in popularity of British football pools.

In France all gambling is controlled by the law and is under the 'high patronage' of the State which means the tax authorities. A special police force has been established to control it and a special tax department to reap the fruits. France's lawgivers may pretend that gambling isn't 'moral' but it still doesn't stop them from taking their cut of the winnings.

In Paris, there are three ways in which you can lose (or even win) your money. You can play Baccarat, Chemin de Fer and Trente et Quarante in establishments called Cercles de jeux if you get in; you can buy a lottery ticket for the National Lottery (winning numbers published in the press every Thursday. The draw is held the night before); and you can go to the horse races. Greyhound racing, for some reason, never caught on in France. The last attempt to introduce it ended in a resounding bankruptcy in 1938 (it was an English enterprise).

We can't guarantee that you'll win any money but chances are high as everywhere else. If you do win at the races don't forget the cut taken by the tax-man, which ranges from 16% at the least to 40% at the most. Never gamble except for fun.

THE LOTTERY

Tickets for the National Lottery are on sale in kiosks and at cigarette counters in cafés. Tickets generally cost 3 francs for a *dixième* (literally a tenth) which simply means that if you win, you only get a tenth of the winning sum for that number. Other special draws are more expensive and the amounts to be won are correspondingly higher. Tickets are sold on behalf of recognised charitable organisations such as the *Anciens combattants* (ex-servicemen), blind people, widows, orphans, etc.

The draw is held every Wednesday night and the winning numbers published in all the French daily papers the following morning.

GAMING CLUBS

Gambling has been legalised in France for foreigners and it is due to an amendment to the law (passed in 1907) that French nationals may now frequent gambling clubs or casinos, that of Monte Carlo being the original model.

In the beginning only a spa or a seaside resort could open an establishment of this nature 'During the Season of Foreigners'. Later, this ruling was applied to all holiday resorts which, before the First World War, had been frequented either by rich foreigners such as English lords (sic), Russian princes (sic), Latin Americans, or by rich French bourgeois and the titled nobility who derived their income from their enormous industrial, financial or mining holdings or else their civil lists paid by the State.

The money (then in gold) that they might lose only represented a tiny fraction of their global income. Everyone played for very high stakes in casinos in a kind of family atmosphere, for all those in the 'Europe of the Aristocracy' knew each other and there was never an unknown face to be seen at the casino.

It was in order to make the stay of these 'foreigners of the family' as agreeable as possible that the laws were passed. After all they had to spend their time somehow.

At the present time, certain professions are excluded from gambling. Employees of the Treasury, administrative officers and bank cashiers are prohibited in France (and in Monte Carlo) from entering any private gambling premises, even to risk a mere 20 francs. Gambling fanatics may, at their own request, be barred from gambling rooms!

Furthermore, gambling debts are not recognised by the State and consequently you cannot bring a lawsuit for recovery of such debts.

It is easier to say what gambling is *not* in Paris than what it *is*.

There are no roulette, fruit machines, grand-style gambling and no display. A gambling club rarely draws attention to itself and the inhabitants of a block of flats only a few yards away from the most famous gambling room in Paris would never know of its existence. The wealthy buildings sheltering it have nothing of the baroque flamboyance of the Monte Carlo Casino. Everything which constitutes the faded charm of the classic casino is absent. Only the necessary tools of the trade are present.

Paris gambling hides itself as though it were ashamed. No glittering façades, no neon signs, no publicity, only the occasional visiting card of some important club left casually on the reception desk of some great Parisian hotel or skilfully slipped into the right room by the bell boy.

Official gambling is as discreet as possible for it is better not to provoke the 'working man'. This dissimulation is even greater when clandestine gambling houses are looking for their clientèle.

The best clubs in Paris insist on certain formalities before accepting new members. You have to be introduced by two sponsors and prove your identity before a member's card is given to you, after both the club and the police have made investigations. The card, known as a *gris-gris* gives you the right to lose your money and to win at Baccarat, Chemin de Fer and Trente et Quarante. This first advantage is enhanced by the addition of such pleasant little items of comfort as excellent free meals—nearly always on the house. For less than five francs you may dine before going back to the gambling table of your choice. After all, a well-fed gambler will more readily sacrifice himself to his demon.

All the adepts are fanatics, the curious and the 'worldly' being excluded from the start. People go to clubs and meet there for one reason only: to gamble.

A 'newcomer' is someone who has already begun to play in casinos 'just to see', and whose taste for gambling has grown into a passion. It is perhaps for this reason that more people are inscribed as members of gambling clubs immediately after the holidays than in the other ten or eleven months of the year.

Whether they are fanatical or not, such members have an income of at least £10,000 a year.

There are of course hundreds, if not thousands, of small fry in the gambling world—often the most fanatical. Crooks and penniless old men alike are life members who meet every afternoon at 3 o'clock in the clubs on the boulevards, where you may also meet

'incognitos', members of some luxurious gambling club, all consumed by a common mania. Many habitués come every day to
play (*faire leur matérielle*) even before doing their shopping. They
belong to the second category. But both ordinary and luxurious
clubs—those that don't cheat—are often frequented by a very mixed
clientèle.

Gambling clubs in the west of Paris are chic and luxurious, those
in the east markedly more popular, but even when the trimmings
are different the substance remains the same.

Foreign gamblers also frequent one or another of the two main
categories of clubs according to their origins but they are generally
recruited in the most banal and barefaced manner, especially when
they are slightly tight.

Americans are the most popular, being the most credulous; but
nationality is of little account as long as you have the look of an
idle tourist not knowing what to do next and with all those Marks,
Dollars or Pounds in your wallet. . . .

The potential gambler will be scientifically picked up, conditioned
and led at the right moment to some clandestine gambling-den in a
deserted street. A fairly spacious casino-apartment will await him
in a house which will appear to be empty and in which all the
shutters are closed. There will be a roulette with 37 sections but no
double zero as in London, for the legal rule applies here although
the wheel may behave a little too docilely.

The croupier will be in evening dress and rather a comic. Nonetheless he is both genuine and expert and will pronounce the ritual
phrases ('Faites vos jeux, les jeux sont faits' and 'rien ne va plus' with
the same arithmetic toneless precision that you find in any casino
in the world whether at London, Las Vegas, Genoa, Monte Carlo or
Deauville.

The newcomer will enter a smoky room with heavy curtains
looking rather like some *fin de siècle* lovers' boudoir. Accredited
players known as 'jockeys' will make room for the new arrival.
Gaming is quick. Champagne (Veuve Cliquot) or Cognac is
handed around with everyone quenching their thirst in an atmosphere
of smoke and excitement.

The *étranger* (the initiate whether he be French or not) can win
sometimes—it is known to happen—but if he gives signs of leaving
too early, other 'players' standing around will stare at him with an
insistence bordering on moral constraint. Not that he will suffer any
physical harm. He plays again and loses. Isn't that what he's there for?

This kind of establishment does not offer the same guarantees as the official clubs. The tax man certainly doesn't know of it and the police pretend to ignore its existence although it may have its 'narks' there.

Things are different if you happen to be presented by Big Joe: you are a *friend* and they know you'll come back. The Negro by the door will bow to you which will cost you 10 francs (compulsory). Your favourite brand of Havana cigar will be offered to you and it won't take you long to realise that you are expected to pay for it. The croupier will be as amusing as ever and spin the wheel with his usual dexterity. You will lose in the normal way and the end of the night it will always be the owner who wins.

Between two games, you will be offered another drink (a quadruple cognac) and a few subtle hints that all kinds of supplementary pleasures are to be found on the upper floors where trained and skilful staff will satisfy every desire, and still more notes will change hands.

Few tourists can resist the attraction of these forbidden fruits and some will come back with their friends a few days later.

Faro is a little known card game with 32 cards. A 'friend' takes the bank. The 'punters' bet on squares numbered from 7 to the ace, lengthwise. On the right the banker picks up, on the left the bets are laid.

If the first card is a seven you win the stakes, if the second is a queen the sums bet on the queen are paid out and so on. This children's game is highly profitable to the banker but is always played straight.

Standard playing cards replace cards 'of legal format' in the clandestine clubs. Generally, if the cheating is organised it is by the management so there is no need to use the official cards.

Authorised clubs of the first or second category use the large size cards since too many quick-fingered players were found to have the right cards ready for the big wins. The playing cards that you will see will be slightly larger than usual so that you can't palm them.

Three kinds of police will be keeping watch over the play. First, the police of the management with inspectors wearing special glasses, who will at once denounce any irregular cards, second and third, inspectors of the Gambling Brigade, both known and unknown. They may also keep an eye on their colleagues and always on the establishment, its staff and its clients. If a player wins too many high stakes at a time, or loses more money than his social condition would appear to allow, they will soon check up on his resources. Thanks to this system, professional cheats are sometimes discovered.

Clubs with a house of their own are the most adviseable for players but if you want an extra thrill with all the trimmings then go and get picked up without too much money on you, which you should consider as already lost. The game's worth the candle.

SOME CERCLES DE JEUX

Le Grand cercle, 12 rue de Presbourg, Paris 8. Tel: 553 30-60.
Very comfortable, very good and cheap restaurant.

Cercle Haussmann, 22 rue de la Michodière, Paris 2. Tel: 742 67-82.

Nouveau cercle des Capucines, 6 boulevard des Capucines, Paris 9. Tel: 073 62-80.
Very classy. Two sponsors needed.

Cercle Bonne-Nouvelle, 206 boulevard Raspail, Paris 14. Tel: 033 96-11.
Very democratic indeed.

And remember, women are *never* admitted in the gambling rooms —only in the restaurant.

HORSE RACING

In France as in England, you need to spend at least thirty years on the courses to know about horses and how to bet on them, let alone knowing how to win. *Turfistes* are the same breed everywhere.

Whether it is because of the money, the risk or the horses themselves, racing is very popular in France and the racecourses are crowded every day of the season. Punters, owners, jockeys and trainers all speak the same language with words like *canasson* for the horse and *bifton* for a betting slip. Horse racing is 'big business' in France with an annual turnover of six thousand million francs (over £50 million) and represents a livelihood for thousands of people including crooks, tipsters, turnstile attendants, taxi-drivers and journalists.

There are nine important courses in the Paris region: LONGCHAMP (flat racing), AUTEUIL (steeplechasing), SAINT-CLOUD (flat racing),

T*   279

MAISON LAFITTE (flat racing), ENGHIEN (steeplechasing and trotting), VINCENNES (both day and night racing: flat racing and trotting), CHANTILLY (flat racing), DEAUVILLE (flat racing), COMPIEGNE (all categories). The former course at Tremblay was closed in May 1967 to be turned into a children's sports- and play-ground. Access is easy to all race courses: you may go by underground, train, bus or taxi and even by private car since car parks (paying of course) have been provided, which is rather rare for Paris.

When two different meetings are held on the same day (this happens quite often in winter) the afternoon public is to be found again at Vincennes in the evening thanks to a special private or public bus service between one course and another (3 francs). Before the evening racing begins, you can nibble a stale sandwich or treat yourself to a gastronomic dinner (expensive for what it is) while watching the first race.

The temptation to go to the races is greatly encouraged by posters (although now less than in the past), television, the racing section in all the main papers such as the *Figaro*, *Le Monde*, *Combat* and *l'Humanité*, and the two racing papers *Paris Turf* and *Sport Complet* (50 centimes each) which also cover racing events abroad throughout the world, including Russia. If you buy one of these two racing papers at a kiosk don't be surprised if it is handed to you inside a *France Soir*: it's a way of hiding the fact that you bet. Although you need no longer be ashamed of betting the tradition goes back to last century when the rich bourgeois forbade their servants to bet.

Organised horse racing in France started in 1776. The first racing society, the *Société Sportive d'Encouragement* was founded in the 18th century under Louis XV. The king (Louis XVI) lost his head during the Revolution but, naturally enough, horse racing survived. The same society, now headed by Marcel Boussac, land-owner and industrialist, controls three race courses: Longchamp (the smartest), Chantilly and Deauville. Being one of the richest societies (some are relatively poor) the *Société Sportive d'Encouragement* has invested thirty-five million francs at Longchamp, providing the course with new stands, complete with escalators. Set in the middle of the Bois de Boulogne, this is the most 'automatised' course of them all. Tickets are distributed by electrical machines, and you can watch the races on closed circuit colour (SECAM) television inside the buildings.

Longchamp has the world's longest racing track and with its three thousand metres and uneven surface it is one of the most difficult for riders. To win at Longchamp you need an exceptional aptitude for the course which is why foreign horses used to absolutely flat tracks (with the exception of Epsom) are often at a disadvantage.

About a hundred meetings are held a year, each consisting of seven races. They are attended by the greatest international champions and the best racing stock in France and abroad.

The most interesting steeplechases are organised by the *Société des Steeplechase de France*. Casualties are high among the runners, especially during the big races which are held at Auteuil (the three most important being the *Prix Draggs*, *Prix du Grand steeple* and *Prix du Président de la République*).

The *Société du cheval Français* organises trotting races which are run at Vincennes during the colder months. Meetings are held both in daytime and at night, after or during dinner (*Prix d'Amérique*).

The other racing societies (*A la race chevaline*) which own race tracks complete the number of meetings organised by the three preceding societies, as in the case of the *Société Sportive d'Encouragement* with its meetings at Saint-Cloud, Enghien and Maison-Lafitte.

Many of these meetings should not be missed if at all possible, for it is there that you will see the ritual and splendour of the French racing world at its most impressive. The greatest of all the *grand prix* races are held at Longchamp. They are the *Prix de l'Arc de Triomphe* (prize of 1 million francs) and the *Grand Prix de Paris* (700,000 francs), held on the last Sunday in June. Ever since Napoleon III, it has been the custom for the President of the French Republic to watch the race from his own box in the grandstand, but during De Gaulle's term of office his absence was regular and conspicuous, to the great regret of Marcel Boussac, since the ceremony in which the two Presidents shook hands is now a thing of the past. . . .

This meeting is attended by the greatest names in society, the French and European racing world, and, traditionally by ambassadors (except the Papal Nuncio) and unless you want to be accused of being naked, afternoon dress is necessary, although only *de rigueur* at the weighing-in.

The last Friday (a smart day) before the closing of the season is when the *Draggs* is run at Auteuil. It is the elegant meeting *par excellence* being that chosen by Paris *Haute Couture* for a display of the latest fashions. The models from all the great fashion houses ride to the races in mail-coaches with teams of six. After a hunting horn has been sounded, they set off in procession from the Place de la Concorde, up the Champs-Elysées and to Auteuil by way of the avenue Foch and the Bois de Boulogne. The band of the Republican guard plays between each race.

Once inside you have three choices: you may go to the Weighing-in (8 francs, very smart and covered), the Pavilion (4 francs, covered) or the *Pelouse* (1.50 francs, open air) inside the tracks. The odds then go up automatically to the nearest centime. When the races are announced everyone surges towards the paddock where you may see various celebrities such as the leading jockeys (Poincelet, Saint-Martin), owners (Madame Volterra, Aly Khan, Rothschild) and the trainers (Mathet, Alec Head) appraising the horses while the over-worked betting officials take bets at their windows, at 5, 10, 50, 100, 500 and 1,000 francs. A bell rings, the current is switched off, late-comers can no longer place their bets, and they're off!

If you want to come back often, hire your own box for the year like the Begum: it'll only cost you 4,000 francs.

You can of course go to the races without betting, and enjoy the natural beauty of the site and the races and the clean air (not to be overlooked, if you live in Paris). But the real punters simply come to see, to observe and to place their bets accordingly.

An even larger number never leave their quarter of Paris when betting. They use the PMU. (*Pari mutuel urbain*), an institution even more solidly entrenched than the Constitution since bookmakers were outlawed in 1899. There are of course clandestine bookies but you need to be known by them and they never give any receipts.

Bets are taken in *bistrots* and cafés where tobacco and cigarettes are sold (*bureaux de tabac*) everywhere in France. For a café to have a PMU licence is a rare privilege for they are harder to obtain than a licence to practise as a notary.

You will generally see long queues at these establishments every Sunday morning, with little middle-aged women sitting at their desks, a Ricard beside them, taking down bets and handing back little betting slips. You have a choice of various betting permutations: *pari simple* (straight bet), *gagnant* (to win) and/or *place* (place) for the very prudent, the *couple* and the *jumelé* (first and second) and lastly, the *tiercé*. The *tiercé* is a bet on the first three horses in a race, either in winning order or not and is only held once a week on Sundays. Winnings of course are far less if your horses (all numbered) come in 2nd, 3rd, 1st or in any other combination than 1st, 2nd and 3rd.

To prevent the French spending all their rent money on horses, the maximum stake allowed for the *tiercé* is 60 francs and the amount you can win for one franc, say, varies from week to week. The biggest ever win was in 1956 when 360,000 new francs were paid for a two franc bet on the right order of winners.

To bet on the *tiercé* is almost as easy as buying a lottery ticket. Just buy a paper, look for the race marked *Tiercé*, and ask the girl at the betting counter of the nearest PMU to give you a slip for the three numbers of the horses you pick in any order you like. You pay your money and take your chance. The winning *tiercé* combination is displayed in little score-cards (usually under the name of some apéritif) in every café all over France.

Prostitution

It's certainly no exaggeration to say that prostitution in Paris is nothing like it used to be. The Liberation put an end to the traditional French brothel, state-supervised and immortalised by Toulouse-Lautrec and Guy de Maupassant. You can still be solicited in the street but with the removal of Paris' central market from Les Halles to Rungis, nearly Orly airport, the picturesque, 'tough' prostitution of central Paris has practically suffered a death-blow.

But prostituion remains—it's always been there, as in every other capital city. But now it's largely a matter of call-girls, and motorised amazones. It's losing what one of our Parisian colleagues called its 'democratic aspect'. . . .

Gaullism or no Gaullism, despite official puritanism, the Loi Marthe Richard of 1948 and police zeal, prostitution in Paris is still a flourishing industry with some several thousand workers. There is no reason to doubt that the industry is still important even though it has had to contend with a number of repressive measures, although prostitution as such is not prohibited by the legal code.

The authorities aren't interested in suppressing prostitution, you will be told. Not at all—if the police close a *hôtel de passe* it's only to discourage the practice of pimping (known in French by the formidable term *proxénétisme*). As for forbidding the girls to parade up and down the pavements, it's only to prevent soliciting in the open or 'recruiting'—a practice very much frowned upon by the inspectors of the Paris vice squad, the *brigade mondaine*. But the law is still vague—all that happened *officially* is that the brothels were shut after the last war and the *official* conclusion is that prostitution no longer exists in France—*officially* that is. . . . Everything depends on the mood of the government which is periodically assailed by a fit of puritanical zeal, with the result that the street walkers (*péripatéticiennes*) take refuge in the corridors of their little hotels until the wave of morality subsides, when they are free to resume their usual pavement 'beat'. But come what may, the girls are unfailingly resourceful and nothing can really stop them from plying their trade.

As for their clients, they have nothing to fear from the law: the worst that can happen to them is to be picked up in a police raid and taken to the local station where they must provide proof of their identity. One very important warning for would-be street Casanovas: don't follow obviously very young girls. French law is ferocious about picking up 'minors' and anyone caught will end up before an assize court.

The geography of prostitution in Paris has remained relatively stable. Admittedly, the arcades of the Palais-Royal are now totally deserted after being the rendez-vous *par excellence* of the town ladies in the 19th century, but this did not happen overnight. When the areas of intensive prostitution shift, it is mainly because of real estate transactions and developments which transform working class or entertainment districts into residential or business districts, but the process is slow. The greatest and most rapid change of all is due to the shifting of the Halles market from the heart of Paris to Rungis, nearly Orly Airport.

Most Parisian prostitutes defy any kind of general definition. They are usually rather stupid girls who have either 'had a misfortune' obliging them to live this way, or they are victims of a pimp. Others are franker and will say that they have taken up prostitution simply because they find it the least tiring profession and the most remunerative. Hypocrisy is rare among Paris prostitutes and there's no mistaking them. But although we certainly do not recommend anyone to treat the girls as out and out whores, there's no need to beat about the bush with them. As a general rule, a broad Gallic frankness characterises all such venal dealings.

The favourite haunt of the Paris prostitute is the street.

In Paris, the 'street' goes beyond the mere pavement. It extends to the ground floor of little hotels where the girls will stand behind a glass door, smiling and making inviting gestures at the passers-by and hesitant, would-be customers.

The 'street' of course, may also be the roadway where the most expensive and 'up-to-date' ladies will ply their trade from the safety of a fast and usually rather American-looking car.

Unlike Hamburg and certain other big cities, Paris has no 'special quarter' although certain streets are traditionally reserved for the oldest profession in the world. But although it may seem to be in the normal course of things that Pigalle and Montparnasse have their street-walkers, given the number of night-clubs and bars in these neighbourhoods (not to speak of the tourists), what seems less explicable is that some of the more sedate, middle-class residential roads should see a nocturnal flourishing of venal *l'amour*. The true reasons for such unexpected apparitions are lost in the mists of time. We have to go far back in the history of the Paris underworld to find why such and such a street has always had its nightly contingents of prostitutes. Tradition is strong among the underworld and the prostitutes. Without knowing it, the *péripatéticiennes* of the rue de Provence are the last direct descendants of the '*lorettes*'—the women of easy virtue who were the (secret) delight of the good honest bourgeois of the Restoration period after Waterloo.

Upper-class Paris—the 'beaux quartiers'—is to the west of the city. The prostitutes there are correspondingly better-class. They are younger, prettier, better dressed, more expensive (of course) but also far more conscientious. Given the high price of a *passe* (a 'short time') they are not obliged to aim at a maximum 'quota' each night and can therefore give more of their time to each client.

The eastern limits of Paris prostitution are to be found in the neighbourhood of the Bastille, in the little streets on each side of the boulevard Beaumarchais, particularly the rue des Tournelles and the rue de la Roquette. Here the *professionnelles* are of what is generally considered to be a 'respectable age' and somewhat in their cups (to use the charming French expression: *entre deux vins*). Their clients are as a rule desperate and poor but given the scarcity of custom the poor dears will generally lower their prices if anyone has the courage to accost them: 10 francs and pleasure in proportion to the low price. Anyone really feeling himself to be in need of a little feminine consolation would be well advised to go further west in the city—to Les Halles for example.

The heart of the prostitute area (the *quartier chaud*) in Les Halles is that limited by the rue Saint-Denis, the rue des Lombards, the rue Beaubourg and the rue Rambuteau. It is here that the prostitute population is the densest. You may see the girls gathering by dozens in some ten narrow, badly paved alley ways and little streets, either standing on the pavements or at the counters of little bars which communicate directly with the corridors of the *hôtels de passe*. Unfortunately for them, the new town planning projects for Paris have made most of them emigrate. But despite everything, a certain number still remains, clutching on desperately to their last stronghold in the rue Quincampoix or the rue des Lombards. This hard core represents a fairly accurate cross-section of Paris' prostitute population: old women nearing the end of their working life but still not sufficiently decayed to be relegated to the Bastille district or to Barbès (Barbès-Rochechouart—this quarter has an almost exclusively North African population), young but already expert débutantes who might be ugly or pretty, soberly or seductively dressed.

This is also the only Paris district in which the girls will unhesitatingly publicise their 'speciality'. You may see several *fouetteuses* wearing black leather high boots and holding a whip in one hand. They are the *fortes femmes* who administer 'correction' to those in need of it, and who are also ready to restore order should things prove unruly. Indeed, it has been by no means rare to see one of them rush out of a bar when a street fight has broken out and separate the combatants with blows of her whip.

One 'speciality' that was peculiar to Les Halles was the girl who would shut her client in a kind of cage as a prelude to undressing and indulging in various auto-erotic pastimes. Upon being paid a modest 'extra', the girl would give the client a few strokes of the whip but she would always avoid any direct physical contact. If the client were still unable to derive full satisfaction from beholding her antics, he had to call upon the services of the girl's lover—and pimp—who would offer him oral or manual gratification. Unfortunately, the police intervened but when the pimp came up in court he pleaded not guilty on the grounds that he could hardly be accused of pimping since his mistress had never had any true sexual contact with the client and therefore could not be considered as a prostitute. The French, remember, pride themselves on their logic. . . .

But such cases *are* the exception. Sexual perversions, especially of a sado-masochistic nature, are so little practised by street prostitutes that some ten or twelve 'specialists' on the streets are enough to cater for their restricted clientèle. But, as we shall see, the situation is different with regard to the clandestine brothels and the call-girl networks.

The prices charged by the girls of Les Halles are in the region of 25 francs for the *simple passe*. For the girl to undress completely, another 10 francs are needed. But even after being paid this 'extra', the prostitute will only have one thing in mind: to bring her client to the desired orgasm as quickly as possible and then to be rid of him. In order to have, let us say, more friendly service, the client will have to resign himself to spending 50 francs.

The same prices are charged by the girls of the rue de Provence and the rue Taitbout, where the choice is rather restricted, and those of the streets around the Place Pigalle and the Place Blanche. Near the Madeleine, the rue Godot-de-Mauroy, the rue Caumartin and the corner of the boulevard des Capucines and the rue Daunou, the prices increase by between 20 and 30 per cent. But there, the *professionnelles*—generally in their thirties—are better dressed and less vulgar. Although they are not averse to being given a tip in addition to their *petit cadeau*, at least they don't aggressively demand it as their right. Even when they meet with a refusal they are still likely to display professional conscientiousness in their work.

Still further westwards towards the Champs-Elysées, to the rue du Ponthieu, the rue du Colisée or the rue de Berri, you will find the élite of the Paris pavements. Dressed with sober elegance, often wearing a fur coat, and made up like some *Vogue* model, these ladies have reached the peak of the profession. To become a member of this élite clan is far from easy: the girl must have made her mark in the *métier* and have been accepted by her colleagues. The lowest tariff is 100 francs the *simple passe* but the service is excellent. Anyone wishing to spend the whole night with a girl must be able to afford between 300 and 500 francs. For such a price the girl will do everything to give satisfaction to her client and to make him want to come back. Once a customer has made up his mind to pay there is little likelihood of his being disappointed.

Prostitutes are also to be found near the Etoile and in the little streets running perpendicularly to the avenue de Wagram. They are less classy than their sisters in the Champs-Elysées—in fact they're rather like the girls in Les Halles—but they take advantage of the situation by demanding high prices. There should be no hesitation in haggling with them and you may be sure that the girl of your choice will lower her fee once she has been convinced that you're not a *pigeon* (mug).

The Left Bank of the Seine has far fewer prostitutes than the Right Bank. The few girls to be found there cluster around the *carrefour* Vavin at Montparnasse, and are rather indifferent-looking but relatively cheap: about 30 francs. As they are few in number and the demand is considerable, the choice is limited and anyway, the client will usually end up with a lady of uncertain age nearing the end of her professional road. Conclusion: if you're looking for venal love don't bother to cross the Seine from the Right Bank. It just isn't worth it.

With very few exceptions, the girls you see on the streets work in hotels. The price of the room is in addition to that of the *passe* and varies between 8 and 15 francs. Like the girls, the rooms vary in quality. They tend to be sordid at Les Halles or Pigalle and well appointed around the Madeleine.

Although the pavement is the traditional domain of the Paris prostitute, her livelihood is being threatened increasingly by the clandestine brothels, call-girl networks, certain *entraîneuses* in bars, and the motorised *amazones*.

Brothels were closed down in France by the *loi Marthe Richard*. The law was voted by the Parliament shortly after the Liberation, as the result of a successful campaign waged by the moral-minded Madame Richard whose astonishing virtue compensated for her somewhat murky past. After a confused period in which the fierce resistance put up by the brothel owners would seem to have deserved a better reward, morality won the day. But ever since, the old institution has been making its slow but steady comeback—this time in the form of the *clandé*.

The *clandé* is, of course, simply a clandestine establishment employing a small number of carefully selected prostitutes whose clientèle is hand-picked to protect the owners from the curiosity of the authorities. Naturally, such establishments are far beyond the means of the Paris working man. Prices being what they are, you are not likely to spend much less than 500 francs for an hour with a girl and a bottle of champagne besides. On the other hand, the girls are always beautiful and well educated. The question of payment is settled with discretion and tact, guests are welcomed like princes and you may enjoy a drink with your friends before you go upstairs.

The difficulty is getting inside a *clandé*. Knowing an address isn't enough: you must have an introduction. Don't rely on hotel porters for most of them will send you to a Pigalle night-club or bar full of *entraîneuses*. If you do want to go, then you must ask your friends in the diplomatic service, parliamentary deputies or influential businessmen who will either give you the necessary introduction or even regard it as a pleasure to go with you.

A word of warning lest you fall into a trap—quite likely if you have been foolish enough to ask a taxi driver for the address of a *clandé*—nearly all the *clandés* are in either the 16th or 17th arrondissements and have discreet plaques by the doors announcing that you are at the 'Villa —' or 'Résidence —'. Some may be straightforward *maisons de rendez-vous* where erring wives come to spend an afternoon with their lover.

It is equally difficult to contact a call-girl network. Once again, to get the telephone number of a top-class courtesan you must have contacts in a certain Parisian society. Also, there is no question of discussing prices: they are extremely high but the girls are the aristocrats of their profession. They aren't *really* professional prostitutes strictly speaking. They have just enough clients to enable them to live in luxury and they are not interested in soliciting. There is, in fact, nothing to distinguish them from their more virtuous sisters. Before spending the night with them, there is nothing to stop you from taking one of them out to dinner at a three star restaurant. No one will suspect the true vocation of your charming partner—unless one of her former clients should happen to be dining in the same restaurant but he is hardly likely to reveal the secret. . . . As for afterwards—nothing as vulgar as a *hôtel de passe*! You will either go to your own home or to some pleasantly furnished studio flat.

Another advantage: in their determination to be considered a class apart from the ordinary prostitute, a call-girl will willingly practise perversions that would horrify a street girl. It is the call-girl who caters for the masochist, the would-be necrophile, the copro-phagist, scopophilist, etc., and it is the call-girl alone who will satisfy the more bizarre tastes of certain clients whose unusual demands would scandalise the ordinary prostitute.

As for the *entraîneuses* in the bars, their *mœurs* are those of their pavement but their prices those of the call-girl. Like their sisters in every big city, the *entraîneuse* you will find smiling at you in the dim light of a Pigalle or Montparnasse bar is simply 'leading you on'. If, after buying a number of drinks at exorbitant prices you do eventually manage to get as far as the girl's room the chances are you won't be in a fit state to do anything anyway. Your unsatis-factory night out will cost you about 500 or 600 francs and it serves you right.

The last class of Paris prostitutes is that of the *amazones*. Like the street girl, a motorised prostitute can be approached by anybody who cares to do so. In the daytime they charge between 150 and 200 francs, at night (when they prefer to work for obvious reasons) anything from 300 to 500 francs. One slight saving: no hotel room to pay for they will take you home. Like the call-girls, they are quite willing to cater for the oddest tastes.

Their favourite itineraries are along the Champs-Elysées and the wide avenues radiating from the Arc de Triomphe, particularly in

Prostitutes in a doorway

the avenue de la Grande Armée and the very classy avenue Foch. They are generally to be recognised by their powerful sports cars, the quality of which is proportionate to their price.

All the above categories constitute what we might call 'official' Paris prostitution. The one last remaining class of prostitute is that of the 'amateurs'—housewives desperate to make ends meet, poverty stricken students or simply nymphomaniacs who like to combine pleasure with profit. They are rarely to be found on the streets for even if they weren't picked up by the police they would certainly be sent packing by their irate professional sisters. You will usually find them in certain cafés along the Champs-Elysées, or at Montparnasse and Saint-Germain-des-Prés. Their usual method of approach is by asking you the time or for a light. You can recognise them at once by their awkwardness and embarassment which immediately distinguish them from the type of lady simply out to 'have fun'. They will agree to be taken to the first hotel in sight and their uncertain position and fear of eventual scandal makes them agree to almost any sum you propose. On the other hand they are far more likely to be contaminated by VD than the professional prostitute. Their exact number is uncertain although some authorities estimate that as many as 500 are working each day throughout Paris. What is certain is that they have contributed appreciably to the alarming rise in venereal infections, which certainly cannot be said of the professionals who usually take every precaution.

Most Paris prostitutes are honest. You have nothing to fear from call-girls or the inmates of a *clandé* for the slightest attempt at cheating would be fatal to the reputation of the 'house' or network. Similarly, the street girls are rarely dangerous and the progressive disappearance of the pimp (which leaves them free to enjoy the totality of their earnings) discourages them from risking anything dishonest. Still, this doesn't mean that you should be careless with your wallet. Nor should you hand the girl a 100 franc note and expect change for a *passe* at 30 francs. Such behaviour is regarded as highly provocative.

There is nothing attractive about street prostitution in Paris— nothing picturesque and only minimal pleasure to be bought. To choose a girl in the street, to suffer the ironic comments of the lookers-on (especially if you are a tourist), to climb up several rickety flights of stairs to a sordid little room and to have to submit to the humiliation of the *toilette intime* at the hands of your partner means that you really are in desperate need. . . .

As if all this wasn't bad enough, some prostitutes have even worse surprises in store for their clients. Some are pregnant and succeed in hiding their state until the last moment when the customer will fling down his money and flee. One girl, lately seen around Pigalle, even had a wooden leg but this is exceptional.

As far as masculine prostitution is concerned, there is very little organisation. The homosexual clubs in the rue du Cherche-Midi or the boulevard Montparnasse on the Left Bank or on the rue des Martyrs near Pigalle are straightforward rendez-vous. The type of Turkish bath patronised by Marcel Proust is a thing of the past. Only the pavement remains for men, and even there, things are far from easy for them. If they're not picked up by the police they are victimised by the passers-by and with the disappearance of so many pavement *pissotières* or *vespasiennes*, their favourite haunts are rapidly vanishing with the notable exception of that in the Place Saint-Sulpice, only a few yards away from the police station of the 6th arrondissement!

Even so, you can still see a few brave souls, with eyes made up, hair permed and dressed in tight fitting suits strolling up and down

the rue du Colisée, the avenue de la Grande Armée, and around
Saint-Germain-des-Prés where their favourite beat is between the
rue Mabillon and the rue des Saints-Pères. Most male prostitutes
are young amateurs who only know one law—that of the jungle.
They are often dangerous. Although their prices are usually as
low as 20–50 francs they will do everything they can to rob the
client. One should *never* follow them to any place of their own
choosing. To take them home is just as imprudent for, as recent
criminal cases have shown, one of their favourite tricks is to have
an accomplice to follow them and, at the crucial moment, burst
into the room and blackmail the victim at gun or knife point.
More than one murder has resulted and there have been tragic
cases in which Parisian families have preferred to drop proceedings
rather than let it be known that their son was a homosexual. Far,
far better for anyone in search of his own kind to go to a well
known club or bar. After all, friendships can be struck up quite
easily in Paris. . . .

Homosexual Paris

---

*Homosexuality in France is not considered as an offence by the law.
'Corruption of minors' is.*

*Paris has its homosexual society, its cabals and its traditions, its bars and
its cafés, but by and large Paris' homosexuals don't feel the need to have
their own, special clubs. They're more 'integrated' than in London or
New York and have less social complexes. Many foreign homosexuals
find Paris a haven for them: it's less depressing, more tolerant, less
neurotic. In Paris you can be a* person *first, a homosexual secondly.*

So that he might continue to take an interest in young boys without
fear of being disturbed, one of Napoleon's ministers succeeded in
restricting the applications of the French penal code. Thanks to his
efforts, homosexuality in itself does not constitute an offence in the
eyes of the French law. But in reality the position is not quite so
simple and in France, as in all Latin countries, people have an
extremely ambiguous attitude towards the homophile. . . .

Whereas in Holland, for example, you can't help feeling that
anything's possible and that certain rather unusual kinds of marriage
may even take place one day without public opinion being unduly
shocked, the French have a far more hesitant attitude. Among the
working-class, in particular, although homosexuality is a frequently
mentioned subject, boys who 'aren't like the others' are often very
cruelly mocked. A 'normal' man, i.e., someone attracted by women,
is allowed to have his weaknesses (as long as his behaviour remains
'virile') but young men who devote themselves exclusively to the
same sex have strayed too far from the path of the *petite bourgeoisie*
for them to be forgiven. They must either hide their inclinations
by marrying (and thus increasing the episodic homosexuality that
occurs in the new housing estates where they are likely to live) or
leave the provinces to take refuge in the cities, which is to say Paris,
since it's the only really big city in the eyes of the French. They will
come to find work and often try to enter into a milieu in which
they can 'be themselves' without any risk, generally taking up the
professions of antique-dealer, couturier, hairdresser or actor.

They will of course try to be 'discreet', even more than their
follow homosexuals in London who are not afraid of being ex-

tremely obvious. On ballet nights or important first nights, the Paris Opera or the Théâtre des Champs-Elysées resemble a meeting of '*créatures*' but they often prefer to dissimulate themselves to some extent by going accompanied by more elderly lady-friends covered with furs and jewels, which gives them the feeling of passing unnoticed. As for the ladies, they have the pleasure of being escorted by well-dressed and attentive young men even though they have passed the age of being able to command the favours of young men.

But, of course, this reserve doesn't deceive anyone and even in Paris, any over-effeminate young man walking in the streets is liable to arouse the smiles and jibes of passers-by. As for the police—one of their favourite pastimes is persecuting over-adventurous homosexuals. Woe betide anyone imprudent enough to venture in the public gardens and to behave too freely and woe betide anyone letting himself be tempted by the promiscuity of a *vespasienne* (pavement urinal), making passes in the darkness of a cinema, or seeking to rid himself of his frustrations in a Turkish bath! ... The policeman will patiently wait for his advances to become sufficiently obvious, will even pretend to join in (and, it appears, he may even go quite far) before abruptly transforming himself back into a representative of the law ready to cart the guilty party off to the police station.

Once there, treatment at the hands of the police will vary according to the social position of the offender. If he appears to be anyone of consequence, he will be released to give him a chance to call upon his friends for help and to obtain the necessary interventions likely to prevent a trial. But if he is someone of no social status, or even worse, a foreigner, he will have to suffer the vindictiveness of the police or even preventive imprisonment. In any case, he will be accused of having committed an offence or an outrage against modesty in a public place (cinemas and Turkish baths are considered as public places for this purpose) even if it was the over-zealous policeman who initially encouraged the offence. Such curious contradictions show that, like French novels in earlier days, the French are at the same time more daring than their neighbours and yet more puritanical.

Admittedly, most police are recruited from among the *petits bourgeois* and even if they do count numerous homosexuals in their ranks (as in all essentially masculine and virile professions), they are far from tender to those who stray too outwardly from the norm. If you want to be quiet and undisturbed, you should keep away from any place frequented by the police and limit yourself to sure friends and to the elegant but corrupt society known as 'Nescafé society' since it is international, cosmopolitan and even rather shady. The real high society—at least, what remains of it—is more demanding in its family traditions and greater circumspection is called for. But a few years ago, the *à la mode* 'creatures' had found a banner to follow: a couple of rather elegant young men who were considered to be the twin arbiters of Parisian elegance. The finest parties, and most successful dinner parties were given in a mansion on the Ile Saint-Louis and for many people; to have been present at them was a kind of consecration in itself. The world of *haute couture*, the most important antique dealers and even a few worldly ladies all flocked around this couple which included a legitimate wife since she alone could wear the jewels which were accounted among the finest in Paris and which she displayed for admiration on fashionable evenings.

In this world, homosexual *ménages* practise adultery with both discretion and parsimony and certain decencies are always observed. Conversation has its own code-language and *Saint-Trop, Hermès, l'Opéra* and *Cartier*, the ballet and mad nights spent at *Castel's* are all so many conversation pieces which you must have ready if you are to be known and deemed worthy of gracing the right cocktail parties. You must go out in the same *milieu*, and have the same idols. Many pretty boys believe that they have finally 'arrived' because they have succeeded in making their way into these circles. To maintain yourself in them, you must either get yourself 'married off' in one way or another (marriage with a genuine heiress who has strayed into this world is the most decried but also the most certain way) or distinguish yourself in some particularly striking fashion. Scientific treatises or academic attainments don't count for anything at present. Ideally, you should write a successful *roman à scandale* (or a puzzling *roman à clef* as a talking point) or else manage to get a part in a fashionable film; television has also made its way into the *mores* of this small world and has quite as much snob appeal as painting or antiques—charming pastimes which allow pretty boys to grow old gracefully.

If you already belong to this little world at Geneva (in which case you'll have less advantages), London (a great advantage), or New York (you will be respected; Parisians still have a certain idea regarding American wealth) all you will have to do is obtain an introduction and choose the right hotel or district. But of course, best of all, you should contrive to get yourself invited at once by a 'locomotive' i.e., one of the clan leaders who lay down the law as they like. . . .

If you aren't already known, but only very beautiful and very prudent, with a certain silent, romantic charm, you can still always manage to get yourself introduced into this world by tagging behind someone else: you alone will be the judge of the means and the price involved. Otherwise, you can always wait in front of the door of *Castel* in the rue Princesse, or the *New Jimmy's* on the boulevard Montparnasse to watch the passing round of fashionable snobs who may have been worn out by their late nights but who are still bursting with energy to continue their merry rounds.

The most effective way to draw attention to yourself would be to go down to the terrace of the Sénéquier at Saint-Tropez at about midday or seven o'clock and to aim only at those Parisians likely to be going back to the capital, but you have still another opportunity open to you: in the rue Sainte-Anne (in which the 'dikes' also have a very well known night-club) there is a 'club' which is crammed to capacity on certain evenings when the 'boys' crowd in it, all holding a glass in their hand. It is still the best club for mingling with people who are *à la mode* although not for long, perhaps, since the geography of Parisian life is highly unstable. The other fashionable night-club is in rue Guisarde, near the church of Saint-Sulpice and very close to *Castel*. There, 'good class' people who are not afraid of admitting their inclinations, gigolos on the make and habitués all mingle together. Of course, it is the charm and youthfulness of the gigolos who give the place its atmosphere and it is their very discretion which is a sign of the quality of the establishment; if there are enough well-behaved beauties, even those who do not come alone and who leave without having caused any disturbances can take pleasure in contemplating the evolutions of these youths through the smoke and a clammy heat which is sometimes like that of the Métro.

There are, of course, all kinds of other Paris *boîtes*. Dancing is permitted in some of them although a police regulation formally forbids men to dance together. We won't give their addresses to spare them any trouble with the law but simply tell you that they are to be found between Saint-Germain-des-Prés and the boulevard Saint-Michel, near the Bibliothèque Nationale or at Montmartre, in basements, back-rooms or on the first floor which makes it possible to 'check' newcomers. In these places, 'sentiment' triumphs and men dance cheek to cheek with the same tenderness as anywhere else. But appearances remain decent once you have agreed that there is nothing shocking about a boy holding another in his arms in public.

Such *boîtes* provide places for encounters which can lead to 'marriage', facile adventures and every possible sort of combination. They are more numerous than in London and, to take one example, on certain summer evenings the rue du Cherche-Midi is crowded by a numerous public on both sides of the street as if to confirm that the pavements can be just as rich a hunting ground as certain bars and night-clubs.

In the streets, of course, there is every hazard but also every possibility. There you may meet young male models from the Faubourg Saint-Honoré, workmen in the Métro (for enthusiasts, the best times are during the rush hours, i.e., eight in the morning and six in the evening), students near the Sorbonne, sailors around the Gare Montparnasse (even though the new station is much less inviting than the old), North Africans in the Barbès-Rochechouart district, Negroes almost everywhere, and everybody at Saint-Germain-des-Prés. You must have a keen eye, know how to stroll, or as the French say, 'flâner', you must not be afraid of walking and should know where to go if successful. Above all, you mustn't forget that the police are very severe in dealing with 'outrages to modesty' as we have already said. You can be charged with this offence if you:

1. Linger too long in a *vespasienne*. There are now fewer of them in Paris since a recent wave of puritanism, imputed to the Gaullist régime, has removed most of them from the boulevards and cross-roads. In the Place d'Iéna, we have even seen a wreath laid on the pavement in honour of happy memories on the site of a former *vespasienne*. Those that survive have their days numbered and as they are very well-frequented they are closely watched by the police. Beware of the one on the corner of the avenue de Maine and a street running along the cemetery to rejoin Denfert-Rochereau, that very near the police station in the rue de la Pompe, and that in the gardens of the Rond-Point des Champs-Elysées, romantic as it is, in the middle of the bushes with its beacon light which gilds the heads of contemplative visitors at night. There are others but they all have the same dangers and, apparently, the same attraction. On the boulevard Sébastopol, men even queue up on certain evenings.

2. Stray a little too much in specialised cinemas like those at the

Porte Maillot, the Gare Saint-Lazare or near the main Right Bank boulevards. The mediocrity of the programmes or their commercially erotic character doubtless explains why the audience come for something else than mere cinematic pleasure. Hands have a way of straying, heads draw together . . . but anyone who's let himself be taken in is only too likely to be led out in the direction of the nearest police station by the man who led him on the better to catch him out.

3. Like gardens and wandering in them at night. Naturally, people are far more discreet in the daytime as in certain pathways in the Bois de Boulogne where workers from the Renault works pass by, or on the terrace overlooking the water by the edge of the Tuileries gardens. There, you can see 'creatures' you'll see nowhere else without any risk and engage in conversation with them while looking at one of the finest views in the world or between visits to the Jeu de Paume or the Orangerie. But at night everything is different. Only a very small part of the Tuileries Gardens remains open to the public which is often far from respectable with satyrs and police abounding, the latter chasing the former. The Bois de Boulogne is swarming with police cars, prostitutes of both sexes and cars seeking each other out, caressing each other with their lights as a prelude to going somewhere else to get acquainted. The gardens of the Eiffel Tower, those of the Quai Branly and the Ile au Cygne between the Pont Bir Hakeim and the Pont de Grenelle are very well-frequented at night since they have welcoming bushes and a darkness favourable to every kind of human activity.

4. Have contracted the habit of taking Turkish or sauna baths. You might go to one of the establishments patronised by 'creatures' and married men gone astray, tourists and policemen in their birthday suits, near the Bastille, the church of Saint-Roch, the Place des Ternes or the Gare Montparnasse. You are certainly likely to meet someone interesting but beware of that indifferent and dignified young man standing there so motionless and tempting: he may sometimes be accompanied by police inspectors in similar state of undress who may tarry a little to watch the fun and games before brutally carting off all that *joli monde* which had imagined itself safely disporting itself at Amsterdam or elsewhere.

As if all this wasn't enough, we must tell you that there has been a terrible recrudescence of venereal diseases, as much at Saint-Tropez as in the gardens of the Quai Branly, at *Castel's* as at Barbès-Rochechouart. Once again, it's all a question of chance.

And don't think you are running less risks with elegant rather than professional pick-ups for they have all come into contact at one time or another. . . .

But if you haven't got the time to go for a drink in some fashionable bar or club and wait to be introduced or make yourself known, if you aren't afraid of running the risks of the Ile au Cygne or the gardens of the Eiffel Tower, which is to say if you've got well-exercised enough muscles to be able to resist any eventual attempt at arrest, and if you aren't looking for someone with whom you can swap views on Marcuse or the Quattrocento, then you might find what you are looking for:

1. Near Pigalle where a little hotel frequented by writers or famous actors offers shelter to likeable young who've been in prison and who are comforted by a saintly woman who helps them in a spirit of genuine philanthropy. But to be presented to one of her protégés you must be warmly recommended to her and also inspire her sympathy.

2. Around the rue du Colisée where there is no saintly woman to introduce you, where there is no proximity of intellectual activity to sanctify what is nothing but prostitution pure and simple, without trimmings and without joy.

3. And still at Saint-Germain-des-Prés since it is a world centre for all such activities. Amateurs abound there but so do the professionals waiting for customers on the 'beach' ('sur la plage') which is to say between the *Café de Flore* and the rue des Saints-Pères or under the arcades of the Drugstore—a new place although these arcades are simply a modern equivalent of the old arcades of Paris like the Passage Véro Dodat or the arcades of the Palais-Royal. The young people haunting them—no doubt because the lighting is favourable to their night-bird complexion—are also perpetuating an old tradition. The fun of the game is in trying to win the favours of one of these venal beauties for nothing—something not everyone can do and which, if successfully accomplished, is an exploit that can illuminate a stay in Paris.

The Paris Underworld

The Paris 'underworld', the milieu, *has become decentralised in the last few years. The apaches of old have become the delinquent youth of today. Foermerly, gangs used to stay in their own districts and even their slang changed from one part of Paris to another. Now, the 'folk-lore' side of the Paris underworld has practically died out. The new breed of gangsters, robbers and racketeers dress and look like executives and bourgeois. Their meeting places change: it's getting harder and harder to say exactly which bar or restaurant is their favourite haunt. Customary meeting places are usually only for the small fry.*

But shootings and vendettas still occur—sometimes in broad daylight. And the police are armed. But the ultimate deterrent, the guillotine, is now rarely used. But it still exists. . . .

Nowadays, it is difficult to describe the exact geography of the Paris underworld since the *milieu,* as it is known, has discovered the virtues of discretion and the advantages of having a respectable 'front'. The gangsters have abandoned the neon-lit streets of Pigalle and the Hôtel des Trois Canards, now just another little undistinguished Paris hotel after having been the headquarters of one of the biggest and best-organised rackets of recent years.

Originally, the whole affair had started with a few Marseillais of whom one was picked up in New York for drug smuggling—a scandal which also involved Jacques Angelvin who now presents *Paris-Club* on the French television.

The whole gang had flourished at first in the south of France where they had ransomed victims after first kidnapping them. A very well-known bookmaker on all the best racecourses of the Côte d'Azur was 'detained' for a couple of days at Carry-le-Rouet near Marseille and was only released after paying up three *briques* (three million old francs) and handing over his car. A VIP from London met the same fate. But it was at Paris, under the sign of the 'Trois Canards' that the enterprise flourished on a truly alarming scale.

The exact number of victims was never known, although they were said to be as many as 300 or 400. They were mostly hotel-keepers who had dabbled in prostitution, shopkeepers who were more or less on good terms with the tax inspector and owners of bars and clandestine brothels. When the gang could not find any good grounds for blackmailing these worthy gentlemen they simply invented them. A woman would serve as bait and when the victim fell into the trap, a member of the gang would play the part of the jealous, vengeful husband. The expression 'on va te descendre à la cave' (we're taking you down to the cellar) became so well-known that you only had to mention it to make your victim tremble with panic. Millions were made under this reign of terror and as no complaints were ever brought to the police, the 'Trois Canards' gang could operate with impunity. One of the gang who made his pile is since said to be busying himself with improving the breed of his racehorses, having left one kind of *turf* (the pavement, i.e., prostitution) for the other.

All the police could do in this racket was to observe. For lack of evidence, they had to collect files that became bulkier and bulkier with monotonous regularity until one day when the unexpected happened. Christian David, known as *le Beau Serge*, gunned down police inspector Galibert one night in a bar in the rue d'Armaille, in the middle of the Ternes district. David was almost unknown to the police although he was known to have been sentenced for a hold-up and to have escaped. Since then he had been lost from sight although he was living under the nick-name of the 'American' at Cassis where he seemed to have a strange fascination for pretty girls with whom he launched into amorous careers.

It was only after the murder of Inspector Galibert that the police learned that the *Beau Serge* was also a right-hand man of the brothers Guérini, famous hotel- and cabaret-owners at Marseille where the eldest was mysteriously shot down on June 23rd, 1967. But, exceptionally in the history of crime detection, his traces have since never been found.

The shooting took place in the *Saint-Clair* but the club has since changed hands. Now apparently respectable, the little bar has even been recommended by the Touring Club of France. In the old days, it was a discreet enough establishment in a street full of children and landed proprietors but at night . . . Saint-Clair was the name of the woman owner who had worked as Sylviane Saint-Clair, a strip-teaser. But now Montmartre is no longer the exclusive nocturnal domain of the *truands* who used to gamble away their ill earned gains, or settle their accounts in the narrow dark streets.

Gambling is one of the favourite amusements of the Paris under-world. With the exceptions of only a few districts, notably the

7th, 8th and 6th arrondissements, illicit gambling clubs are to be found all over Paris still. They are variously known as *tripots*, *clandés*, *flambés*, *sirops* or *tapis* and not only attract a large proportion of gangsters but an equally important clientèle made up of foreigners: Chinese from the 12th arrondissement, Vietnamese from the 5th, North Africans from the 18th, and Portuguese from Ivry, Armenians from Alforville or Issy-les-Moulineaux.

The police raid these establishments almost every night—somewhere in Paris. Uusually, gambling parties take place in a backroom or cellar. The habitués of poker, faro, *passe anglaise*, baccarat, *ronda* or *cochinchinette* to only mention a few of the most popular games, include a good sprinkling of professional players well versed in the various forms of cheating, the most frequent being the altering of the chequered backs of cards. One recently prosecuted card-sharp used cards with criss-cross patterns on the backs: the ace had a slightly thicker line on the top row, a king, a thicker line on the second row down and so forth. They were as easy to read as a book.

Such minute alterations are very difficult for the victim to notice. One victim, who had lost more than £400 at poker in a single evening, simply refused to believe that her loss had been due to anything other than her bad play until the statements of the 'sharps' had been read to her.

In 1967, 687 organisers of occasional clandestine gaming clubs, 20 *clandé* owners and 27 card-sharps were arrested. The stakes confiscated amounted to nearly 20,000 old francs. But besides the clandestine *tripots*—that in the rue Capron near the avenue de Clichy is exclusively frequented by the *milieu*—10 *cercles de jeux* and 10 *maisons de jeux* are officially controlled by the authorities. Seven of them are devoted to the *Multicolore*, a game somewhat like roulette: the wheel has 25 compartments in five different colours. According to the number and colour that comes up, players can win three, four, five or 25 times their stake.

For some time now two rival groups have been fighting for control of the *cercles*. The well-known Grand Cercle near the Etoile has nearly been burnt-out twice and its owner, the former *patron* of the 'Grand Monde' at Cholon, in the suburbs of Saigon, received a dose of buckshot in the stomach. A bomb was also set off at Bougival, near Paris, in the doorway of the house belonging to the boss of the Cercle Haussmann (a former *cercle* owner in Beirut) but the only casualties were the men who set the bomb.

Unlike the good or bad old days, the Milieu can no longer be identified with certain areas of Paris at night. The old, pre-war *pègre* (underworld) did not conceal itself. It had what we might call its 'uniform' and its traditions were handed down from father to son, and the destiny of an outlaw often seemed to have been established at birth. Not all who became thieves had sisters in Saint-Lazare (the old women's prison, now demolished), their mothers in the hospital and their *dab* (old *argot* for father) in the condemned cell at Pantin, but by and large they were all born in a world of poverty and vice. There were, of course, occasional criminals and those who only murdered in a fit of amorous passion but there were no amateur criminals. You became a thief or a pimp by instinct since you were born in a milieu of thieves or pimps. You became a specialist burglar or you lived off women not as an amateur but as a fully qualified professional. No one wore masks or false noses. At that time, the men of the *milieu* lived dangerously but without cheating. You knew the penalties and you took your risks, knowing that one day you might have to pay the bill.

Now, the Milieu (especially at Paris) has become fluid and faceless. Without being restricted, as it once was, to the world of duels *à la loyale* (to the death) and *gigolettes* (molls) in flowing skirts in the Paris slums, the milieu has now broken out of its traditional confines.

Between the two wars, in the thirties, if you went to the Place Blanche at about midnight, you could go to a café with three façades dominating the square and see a basement room reserved to the milieu. Only men were there and they were all well-dressed with the exception of their somewhat garishly coloured tailor-made suits. Similarly, as though in a synagogue, no one who met in this peaceful spot ever took his hat off. They all wore very expensive felt hats in the best tradition of the fictional gangster of the period and looked their parts. They would gamble without money: all you would ever see on the cloth were straightforward chips and bits of folded paper. The players simply relied on each others' word as they took their chances. They had all 'done' the two Americas, and had come back with their pile to keep prosperous brothels in Paris or the provinces.

It was a world which has now disappeared and lost its privileges. You can still find bars reputed for their disrespectable clientèle but you will find it hard to distinguish the *truands* from the honest bourgeois.

The Lizeux, with a beamed façade at the corner of the rue Fontaine and the rue Duperre, is still the rendez-vous for the Corsicans of Montmartre but now its atmosphere is simply that of a morose provincial café. Even so, if you go in there, unknown to the habitués, everyone will suddenly stop talking. The waiters will gaze up at the ceiling dreamily while the drinkers at the bar will pick up their glasses and go and sit at the back of the room. Don't trust to appearances there: it was there that a little small-time pimp from the South who had hoped to make his fortune in Paris was found with a belly full of lead. He had simply refused to pay his dues to the kings of the Paris pavement.

Even though the *truands* have given up their flashy suits and their crocodile-skin shoes, they still have to live among people who speak, think and act like them, whence the need for certain places where they know they'll be at home, among 'men'.

They will even eat at the same places but instead of Montmartre, the restaurant preferred by the cream of the Paris underworld is in the 16th arrondissement, in the rue Lauriston where a block of flats was the headquarters of the 'French' Gestapo during the dark years of the Occupation. Another rendez-vous of the Milieu is in the rue de Provence which was famous from the time that the 'one two two' drew lovers of erotic pleasure there.

The Corsican *truands* still meet in the rue Berthe on the hill of Montmartre, at Pappi and one of the cafés in the Place des Vosges has become a spot where ex-prisoners go to seek aid and assistance. But apart from these few spots, only known to initiates, do not believe that the Paris gangs automatically meet in their accredited bars and that their headquarters are fixed. A gang will be formed to prepare a robbery. After the *coup*, and the division of the spoils, the gang will disperse unless there was any quarrel over the division of the booty when summary executions cut short any discussions that threaten to be too lengthy.

1962 was the peak year for hold-ups in the Paris region. Almost a hundred were recorded. In 1966 there were only six, but in 1967, the total had gone up to twenty, the reason being, according to the police, that new, unidentified gangs had been formed.

Robbery with violence in the streets of Paris has increased recently but less taxi-drivers have been attacked. On the other hand, more women on their own have been attacked. Pocket-picking has remained fairly stationary in Paris and is mostly practised in the Métro.

The constant increase in the number of parked cars is a permanent

Monumeut, La Bastille

temptation for *roulottiers* (car thieves). More than fifty are stolen every day now. If you lose your car you still have about four chances in five of getting it back in the end. 25 per cent of car thieves arrested are under eighteen years of age. Juvenile delinquency is on the increase and, interestingly enough, the number of girls arrested had increased more than that of the boys. But none of them has anything to do with the classic *milieu*. There is a *nouvelle vague* milieu admittedly, but it is one made up of young criminals who shoot out of fear and are consequently more dangerous than the old style *truands* who only made use of the *calibre* (gun) in really exceptional circumstances.

In the old days, shootings only took place in certain very restricted areas of Paris at night. In succession, these areas were the Halles, the Butte Montmartre, the Faubourg Saint-Martin, the Bastille and La Chapelle, where accounts would be settled after midnight. In the Thirties, the rue Fontaine in Pigalle became a kind of preserve for fusillades between rival gangs and a new milieu made its appearance in Montmartre: the milieu of the Corsicans.

At the top of the rue de Douai, the bar *Chez Dante* was the headquarters of the newcomers. At the other end of the street a dance hall, the *Ange Rouge*, was opened. It soon became a favourite hunting ground for *truands* in search of fortune. They killed each other for indelicate behaviour and for breaking their words with a casualness that left the few late passers-by breathless with astonishment.

Today, the old *Ange Rouge* has been replaced by the Bus Palladium and the only violence there is that of the neo-rock'n' roll played there. Apprentice gangsters hoping to *lever une cavette* (to pick up a girl—never a prostitute) still go to the dance hall of *Le Petit Jardin* in the avenue de Clichy or the *Boule Noire* on the boulevard Rochechouart. But the little *bals musettes* in the rue de la Lappe near the Bastille have lost their more hoodlum clientèle. The atmosphere is now a family one and you can go there quite safely as an honest tourist.

The sad truth is that the *milieu* is now just as likely to meet in a night-club on the Champs-Elysées or in a snack-bar in Montparnasse. It's what they call a question of 'standing'. As for the crackle of small arms fire, you are now just as likely to hear it, if at all, in the respectable and wealthy *beaux quartiers* as in the more ill-famed districts.

But are guns used that often? You might think so, from seeing French thrillers on the screen but really spectacular shooting matches are rarer than ever, and the *truands* generally prefer not to shoot it out with the police, as witness the following case that occurred not long ago:

The driver of a blue Aronde car that the police had been watching from their car, was behaving in an increasingly suspicious manner. The second time the Aronde passed the police, they were surprised to see that its number had been changed. Four new plastic numbers had been pasted over the old registration plate. It was late at night and the streets were deserted. The Aronde went towards the Place de la Concorde and then accelerated abruptly in the rue Royale. The police gave chase and followed the car to the boulevard des Capucines, at the corner with the Passage Edouard VII. The Aronde was about to be overtaken by the police car and tore onto the pavement, knocking over a shelter of a parking attendant. The police saw two windows in the side of the car being smashed and two automatic guns pointing in their direction, There was a brief volley with the police shooting back at point blank range. One of the men in the Aronde was wounded in the arm and took shelter under the car. Another, hit in the leg, managed to get away while a third was overcome after a brief struggle.

After finding an impressive arsenal in the car and discovering the identity of the *truand* in their hands the police saw that they had been only too justified in following the car.

The arrested man was Petit René, a bosom friend of one Pierre Colombani who had been gunned down recently in front of his home in Ajaccio. In the car, a Tommy gun—which had happily jammed after the first burst—a Colt 11, a 43 and a sawn-off Italian shotgun were found.

It was clear enough that with such hardware the passengers of the Aronde meant business—somewhere, somehow. The whole thing smacked of a vendetta. Petit René had accompanied his Corsican friend to his last resting place in Ajaccio. There had been no need for any melodramatic oath. He had come to Paris and was combing it carefully in the hope of a showdown which would have made a spectacular mark in the annals of Parisian vendettas. You may imagine the firework display there would have been on the boulevard des Capucines if the Tommy gun hadn't jammed. Petit René apologised profusely to the police for having opened fire on them:

'We wouldn't have fired if we hadn't taken you for killers of the *milieu*' he said abjectly.

And he meant it!

Speciality Services and Useful Paris

What you should know, what you might like to know and what you almost certainly don't know. From the trivial to the essential. Where to buy the best honey, where to ring a taxi, where to hire a bed or a bicycle, where to lose weight and where to hire a magician should you wish to throw a children's party in Paris. You might, one day.

ANIMALS (FOR HIRE)
Mostly horses and donkeys. From GASCARD, 36 avenue de la Motte-Picquet, Paris 7. Tel: INV 32-81.

ANIMALS (FOR SALE)
For pythons, alligators, white mice, koala bears and canaries go to the SAMARITAINE department store, 75 rue de Rivoli, Paris 8. Tel: 508 33-33.

The livestock is guaranteed young and in good health. The attendants somewhat elderly and the smell abominable.

AUCTIONS
Practically everything is sold at the auctions held in the HOTEL DROUOT, 9 rue Drouot, Paris 9. If you can't afford to make a bid for a Cézanne in one of the grander sales, you might acquire something for a few francs at the more humble sales held on the ground floor every afternoon from Monday to Friday inclusive. Most of the stuff is on view the afternoon and the following morning previous to the sale.

BABY-SITTERS
Some Parisian baby-sitting agencies are more concerned with the father's pleasure than with the child's welfare. The following three, alas, simply look after the baby:
Institut Catholique, 21 rue d'Assas, Paris 6. Tel: LIT 31-70.
Copar, 39 avenue de l'Observatoire, Paris 14. Tel: CAN 07-49.
Etudiants en médecine, 26 faubourg Saint-Jacques, Paris 14. Tel: ODE 25-44.

Give 48 hours notice. Maximum length of time for baby sitting: morning until following night. Price: generally 4 francs an hour.

And, in case you were wondering: the French for baby-sitter is usually 'baby-sitter'.

BALLOONING

If you feel like ballooning, then Charles Dollfuss is the man for you in Paris. A charming young man of seventy-odd years, he's a great admirer of Jules Verne, and avid balloonist and the creator of the wonderful Museum of the Air (*Musée dé l'Air*) at Meudon, near Paris. M. Dollfuss has so far made well over five hundred balloon ascents, with more than four hundred in 'free balloon', over the seas, in the States and in Russia and to an altitude of 20,000 feet, and has broken several records as well as establishing new ones. Although he's suffered a few bruises and broken bones in his time, he tells us that he's ready for at least another ten years of ballooning.

You only have to ring him up and for about 250 francs you can make an ascent with him. The only drawback is that you can never be quite sure in advance exactly when the balloon will go up. Persistence is everything and if you can stay in France long enough to make eight solo ascensions and to pass a short test, you will get a licence as a balloon pilot. You will then be able to hire one of M. Dollfuss's balloons for about 750 francs an hour or have one built to your own specifications for about 15,000 francs.

And the best of luck and favourable wind!

Charles Dollfuss, 82 rue du Ranelagh, Paris 16. Tel: 288 91-89.

BEDS (FOR HIRE)

You've rented a two-room flat in Paris and your friends joyfully descend on you and they certainly don't intend to stay in a hotel if they can help it. Happily you've all got a friend in Monsieur Paul Desprets: he'll lend you as many beds, mattresses, sheets and blankets as you like—although only for a minimum period of two weeks, and you can't have sheets or blankets without the beds. Anyway, ring him up, he'll deliver in less than 48 hours and everything will be impeccably clean and in the best of condition.

La literie familiale, 14 boulevard Ornano, Paris 18. Tel: MON 59-85.

BICYCLES (FOR HIRE)

Very useful for getting about if you're not afraid of the traffic. You can hire them for a minimum duration of three days from GUEBET, 58 rue La Fayette, Paris 9. Tel: TAI 47-59. About 40 francs a week.

BRONZE FITTINGS

Aubier et Cuny, 74 faubourg Saint-Antoine, Paris 12. Tel: DID 36-36.

Fittings in every style. Also mirrors. Very useful if you buy a 'period' flat.

BUSES

Paris still has many splendidly old-fashioned buses with rear open platform where you may smoke and watch all Paris go by. Others are more modern and a few are double-deckers. All are hideously expensive as a result of endless successive fare increases. You pay according to the number or parts of fare stages you travel. Many stops have a numbered queue ticket dispenser: the person with the lowest number gets on first and so on. ... It's one way of settling disputes during rush hours. Most bus lines stop running before 10 pm.

It's always better (and cheaper) to take the Métro if you don't suffer from claustrophobia.

If you still like buses, then buy a *carnet*, a book of 20 tickets from the conductor: this will save you about a third of the normal fare.

CAR HIRE

Hertz is the best. They are open every day until midnight at 27 rue Saint-Ferdinand, Paris 17 and their telephone number is GAL 99-69.

CARS (STOLEN)

If your car is stolen, don't just report it to the police. The O.R.T.F., France's state broadcasting system, has a special 'stolen cars service' on its 'France Inter' programme, and will try to trace it with the help of enthusiastic listeners.

Ring BAL 33-33 and ask for *'Service voitures volées'*. If you can't speak French get someone to do it for you.

CHOCOLATES

The best in Paris are at:

La Marquise de Sévigné, 11 boulevard de la Madeleine, Paris 8. Tel: 073 72-77. And in all branches of the same name.

Other excellent hand-made chocolates can be bought at:

Boissière, 7 rue des Capucines, Paris 2. Tel: 073 69-06.

Foucher, 17 avenue Victor Hugo, Paris 16. Tel: 727 50-21.

Le Lotus d'Or, 5 rue de Suresnes, Paris 8.

Le Marquise de Pompadour, 49 faubourg Saint-Honoré, Paris 8. Tel: 265 89-45.

CLOTHES (HAUTE COUTURE: TO BE HIRED, BOUGHT SECOND HAND AND SOLD)

Saint-Frusquin, 1 villa Juge (1st floor), Paris 15. Tel: 273 13-56.

A rather secretive establishment, haunted by starlets and young girl friends of businessmen, ministers, etc.

CLOTHES (OLD)

Antique women's lingerie, corsets, pantaloons, etc., in 1900 or 1920's style:

Catherine, 52 rue Vavin, Paris 6. Tel: 376 72-24. Specialises in shirts and slacks imported from America and twenties' dresses.

Newman, 14 rue de l'Ancienne Comédie, Paris 6.

Philomène, 15 rue Vavin, Paris 6. Tel: 633 62-01.

Second-hand clothes:

1. Knitted wear: *Sèvres 33*, 33 rue de Sèvres, Paris 6. Tel: 548 66-73.

2. Tailored suits and de luxe leather goods: *La Boîte à Soldes*, 113 rue de Rome, Paris 8. Tel: 924 38-14.

Bargains from couturiers:

Violette Benistan, 4 rue Chambiges, Paris 8. Tel: 359 91-44.

COMFORT (MORAL)

Many would-be suicides and people in despair and anguish have found comfort and relief by ringing VAL 70-50, the number of *S.O.S. amitié*, Paris's version of the Good Samaritans organisation. They don't like to offer advice except in really exceptional cases, but you can pour out your woes to a sincerely sympathetic listener. It often helps.

COOKING AND KITCHEN WARE

Dehillerin, 18 rue Coquillière, Paris 1. Tel: CEN 53-13.

The largest shop of its kind in Paris with the greatest range of casseroles and every imaginable kind of copper utensil. Caters for all the great European restaurants.

CUTLERY

Peter, 191 faubourg Saint-Honore, Paris 8. Tel: CAR 88-00.

A very great craftsman.

DEMOLITIONS

Not so much for pulling down any building you may happen to hate but for the extraordinary selection of garden and household objects and odd furnishings 'salvaged' you should go to:

Fauvet et Bernard, 1 boulevard de la Chapelle, Paris 10. Tel: NOR 23-04.

Old staircases, marble fireplaces, balconies, doors, windows, and ancient sanitary appliances all in satisfactory state may be bought at remarkably low prices.

DINNER JACKETS AND DRESS SUITS (FOR HIRE)

May be hired in Paris for about 70 francs for 48 hours.

The *Cor de Chasse* at 40 rue de Buci, Paris 6, is one of the best known establishments for hiring suits and dinner jackets. But even better, go to *Jean-Jacques* at 36 rue de Buci (Tel: ODE 25-56). The shop was founded in 1867 and is now run by Monsieur Boc-Ho, a native of Britanny who will hire you clothes of a cut you will find in no other similar establishment in Paris. Your size or physical peculiarities are of no importance: alterations can be made in a maximum time of four days and no supplement will be charged. Should you wish to keep your dinner-suit (which will only have been worn four or five times before you) you can buy it for just under 300 francs. Reasonable enough, don't you think?

ENGLISH THINGS

The French are mad about English things, from pubs to Union Jack decorated ash-trays and marmalade. *A London*, 1 rue Goethe, Paris 16, sells useful and useless English odds and ends to a smart clientèle.

ENTERTAINERS (AT HOME)

For musicians and singers in your home, call:

Les Baladins du Crépuscule at GRA 88-11 (day and night).

A young singer who is assuredly not a professional but not quite an amateur will come and entertain you during or after your dinner party for 60 francs for 45 minutes. You can have a jazz quartet or a chamber music quartet for 200 francs for the same time. They will stay as long as you (or the neighbours) like.

Magic and conjuring:

Mystag, also known as 'the creator of the impossible' or 'the human Radar' will perform for about two-and-a-half-hours for 300 francs.

Variety artists:

Janine Marchand (58 boulevard de Strasbourg, Paris 10; Tel: COM 94-40) can supply an excellent ventriloquist (1,800 francs the hour), a pair of conjurers (350 francs for 20 minutes) and a flea trainer (450 francs for 20 minutes).

Monsieur Priolet (8 rue d'Enghien, Paris 10; Tel: PRO 07-97) will provide you with clowns (400 to 500 francs for 40 minutes), burlesque musicians (same price) and marionettists (400 to 450 francs for 30 minutes).

EVERYTHING (OR ALMOST)

Ladislas de Diesbach will find you everything—or nearly everything. As the French television was saying not so long ago, 'Impossible isn't French'. He and his team will find everything from your missing cat to a white rhinoceros and negotiate various business deals for you in the more troubled parts of the world. So far, he's already found Pacific isles for sale, an 1880 tram in good working order (for Jean Castel of *Castel's* night club) and various other 'unfindable' objects.

So don't despair if you can't get your heart's desire. Ladislas and his world-wide team will find it somewhere, somehow. Ring him at:

Impossible, 17 rue de Beaune, Paris 7. Tel: BAB 91-10.

FANCY DRESS (FOR HIRE)

Vachet, 17 rue Rodier, Paris 9. Tel: TRU 70-85.

The most popular fancy dresses and carnival costumes at the time of writing are: Napoleonic hussars, early 19th-century dandys, Japanese, Cleopatras, and Empire ladies not to speak of 1900 femmes fatales and Twenties flappers.

Some costumes, like those of a papal guard, are genuine. Others are carefully made after period designs. They are all rather expensive: 60 to 250 francs for a day, according to style and period, and at least twice that amount for a deposit.

FORTUNE TELLING

Paris is full of fortune tellers and people who will cast your horoscope. A magazine called *Horoscope* and the more popular papers (*Ici-Paris, France-Dimanche*) will give you all the addresses you need. More amusing we think is the ASTRO-FLASH electronic horoscope at 138 avenue des Champs-Elysées which will deliver a written character analysis or forecast for the next 6 months for 10 francs each after you've told it your date and time of birth and place of birth.

FURNITURE HIRE
Lanzani, 19 rue Bafroi, Paris 11. Tel: ROQ 78-56.
  Senac, 36 bis rue Ballu, Paris 9. Tel: PIG 35-82.
They will lend you every imaginable kind of furniture, both genuine and imitation.

GADGETS
Very fashionable in Paris. Every sort of gadget from automatic cigarette lighters and dispensers for motorists to handy kitchen things can be had at *La Gadgetière*, 1 rue Georges Bizet, Paris 16. Tel: POI 61-31.

HAUTE COUTURE (FOR DOGS)
If you want to turn your dog (assuming it's a 'she') into a perfect four-legged *Parisienne*, then the only *couturière* for you is Anne Suzler. After being treated like a dog, she says, for more than thirty years by the great Paris *couturiers* she used to supply with leather goods, she now devotes all her time to treating dogs like *parisiennes*.
  She sells everything for the dog: collars, leashes, coats, raincoats and even pyjamas—yes, pyjamas! You can even bring your own materials and she'll tailor them for you (or rather, your dog), and make a delightful little spring or autumn coat in the best Balenciaga style, complete with a pocket holding a handkerchief for wiping dear little doggie's paws after his walk.
  Prices vary according to degree of luxury and size of course, but you may be sure of getting something splendid for about 100 francs (150 for lamé or lambskin). All her collars are hand-made and can be decorated with just about everything, including precious gems. Collar and leash on their own cost between 40 and 50 francs.
  Anne Suzler, 13 cité du Retiro, Paris 8. Tel: ANJ 50-59. Every day from 2 to 7 pm and Saturdays by appointment.

HONEY
You'll find Francis Francq's honey shop by the smell of beeswax in the rue de Clickh from early morning onwards. He mainly sells honey from his own bees (at 7.20 francs the kilo) but also stocks other more unusual kinds such as pine-tree honey, forest, orange, rosemary, acacia and linden tree honey. Some of his most faithful customers are ageing actors afraid of losing their voices and such famous figures as Sacha Guitry and the tragedians of the Comédie Française have made his shop famous in the Paris theatre world.

315

M. Francq also sells flower pollen (from 4 francs the jar) and 'gelée royale' which was once reputed to have such miraculous therapeutic properties but which is now rather demythified by the medical profession. Still, if you believe in it, this is the place to buy it.

ICE CREAM

Aux Délices, 39 avenue de Villiers, Paris 17. Tel: 924 71-36.
Berthillon, 31 rue Saint-Louis-en-l'Ile, Paris 4. Tel: 033 31-61.
The oldest and the newest ice-cream shops in Paris.

JAM

Tandrade, 18 rue Vignon, Paris 8. Tel: 073 26-99.
Cavex, 68 rue Legendre, Paris 17. Tel: 627 84-49.
Excellent French jams. Very expensive.

KEEPING FIT (FOR MEN)

For 80 francs a month you can keep fit and exercise yourself to your heart's content at one of the three *'Le Président'* health-clubs. Addresses are as follow:
11 rue Chanez, Paris 16. Tel: BAG 95-90.
6 rue Déodat de Séverac, Paris 17. Tel: MAC 51-37.
5 rue de Lagny, Paris 20. Tel: 344 74-14.
They are all open from 9 am to 9 pm, have saunas, swimming baths and solarium, masseurs and P.T. instructors with a fully equipped gymnasium.

Or you can go to the *Carita-Messieurs* at 11 rue du Faubourg Saint-Honoré, Paris 8. Tel: ANJ 10-70. Closed on Mondays. There you can have a Japanese 'Shiatsu' massage which will both stimulate and relax you (but not slim) for 60 francs the hour.

Most luxurious of all, if you can afford it, is the Japanese-style *Tekki,* 125 rue de Sèvres, Paris 6. Tel: SEG 13-57. Closed Thursdays. Open from 9 am until midnight. You can be bathed, frictioned and massaged by a charming young lady, with a cup of jasmine tea at the end of it all, for 50 francs, practise gymnastics, judo, karate, French boxing and cane-fencing, and yoga for an annual subscription of 350 francs entrance fee *and* 150 francs quarterly charge.

KOSHER SHOPS

Five of the best Kosher food shops are:
Goldenberg, 7 rue des Rosiers, Paris 4. Especially for pastries.

Schwarz, 47 rue Richer, Paris 9. For cakes, cold meats, wines.

Charcuterie Alsacienne, 5 rue Cadet, Paris 9. Preserves, smoked tongue, smoked herrings, cold meats, wines, flour, etc.

David Koubbi, 7 rue de la Présentation, Paris 11. Excellent Kosher butcher's shop.

Boutboul, 16, rue du Pont Louis-Philippe, Paris 4. Another good butcher.

Kosher Shop

LANGUAGE LABORATORIES

For learning French as quickly and efficiently as possible. The following have all the latest equipment: tape-recorders, individual cubicles with speakers, closed circuit television, etc.

Lanco, 6 avenue de Messine, Paris 8. Tel: 522 33-72. They have a crash course lasting two and a half months of 25 hours per week in classes not exceeding fifteen pupils. Price: 660 francs a month. Also a four-month course with 3 hours' tuition a day at 400 francs a month.

Cetav (Centre d'Etude des techniques audio-visuelles). 64 bis rue Dulong, Paris 17. Tel: 267 39-22. Prices on demand. Ask for their prospectus.

317

LAVATORIES

Most public conveniences are still pretty vile. Some of the better cafés have now reached quite a reasonable standard of hygiene and comfort (the Brasserie Lipp and the Drugstore, both at Saint-Germain-des-Prés are among the best). The best authority on the subject is *The Loos of Paris* by Jonathan Routh, published at 3*s*. 6*d*. by Wolfe Publishing Ltd.

LIGHTING UP THE CITY (LITERALLY)

If you want one or several Paris monuments or buildings lit up at night, then make your request in writing to:

La Direction Technique de la Voirie Parisienne, 9 Place de l'Hôtel de Ville, Paris 4.

The fees are as follow:

All public buildings and monuments in Paris with lighting facilities: 2,000 francs an hour.

The Eiffel Tower: 275 francs an hour.

The Arc de Triomphe: 132 francs an hour.

The Sacré-Cœur: 42 francs an hour.

The best bargain: any local war memorial: only 4.40 francs the hour.

LOST PROPERTY

Lost objects found in the streets, public places of entertainment, buses and the Métro may end up at the Préfecture de Police offices at 36 rue des Morillons, Paris 15 (Métro station Convention). They're open every day from 9 to 5.30 except Saturdays (mornings only, till 12) and Sundays.

MARRONS GLACES

Tanrade, 18 rue Vignon, Paris 8. Tel: 073 26-99.

From Balzac to André Gide, French writers have been praising the excellence of the *marrons glacés* sold in this two-centuries old shop.

METRO

Much better than the bus for getting around Paris quickly (if not comfortably). You can travel any distance first or second class for a fixed fare (1.50 francs or 1 franc) and buy a *carnet* of 10 tickets at a third reduction. The Paris underground system has been praised for its layout and efficiency but many people still need to be told that each line is named after its terminal station and that *correspondance* simply means a connection with other lines.

The most beautiful and modernised Métro station in Paris is now the 'Louvre'. You'll see why if you get out there.

MORNINGS AFTER (WHAT TO TAKE)
Try a Fernet-Branca. Available in almost every café or bar. Some people even drink the stuff for pleasure. You won't.

ODD JOBS
If you have any that need doing you can call upon the willing services of a needy student by ringing the Bureau de Placement des Etudiants at DAN 20-26 or by calling in at 18 rue du Four, Paris 6.

OLD PARIS
The Librairie G. Simone Barbier, 14 rue de l'Université, Paris 7, has a wonderful selection of books and journals on old Paris. Madame Barbier is herself an expert and gives lecture tours sometimes (in French). She will gladly give you a list of forthcoming walking tours and visits to various historical parts of the city.

OLDEST HOUSE IN PARIS, THE
Number 3 in the rue Volta. It dates from the 12th century. You can go up the medieval stone, spiral stairs to the top if you wish. It's still inhabited and looks appropriately dingy.

'PASSAGES'
Paris has a number of covered arcades known as *passages*. Some are picturesque and curious, with shops, cafés and restaurants, others are depressing and sadly neglected. Most were built early in the 19th century and are to be found on the Right Bank of the Seine, especially in the 2nd arrondissement. Connoisseurs, antiquarians of Paris and the historically minded in search of the picturesque all have their favourite passages. Here are a few of ours:

Passage du Caire, Paris 2. Between the Place du Caire and the rue Saint-Denis.

Passage de Choiseul, Paris 2. Between rue des Petits-Champs and rue Saint-Augustin.

Passage Jouffroy, Paris 9. Between the boulevard Montmartre and the rue de Grange-Batelière.

Passage des Panoramas, Paris 2. Between rue Saint-Marc and the boulevard Montmartre.

Galerie Vivienne, Paris 2. Between rue Vivienne and rue de la Banque.

PASTRIES (FOREIGN)

Danish: *Pâtisserie Danoise,* 4 avenue de l'Opéra, Paris 1. Tel: 073 08-28.

Viennese: *Pâtisserie Viennoise,* 8 rue de l'Ecole de Médecine, Paris 6. Tel: 326 60-48.

North-African and Near Eastern: *Pâtisserie Franco-Orientale,* 38 rue Monsieur-le-Prince, Paris 6. Tel: 326 78-95.

American and English: Fauchon (on order only), 26 Place de la Madeleine, Paris 8. Tel: 073 11-90.

PASTRIES (FRENCH REGIONAL)

Alsatian: *Pâtisserie Alsacienne,* 15 rue de Strasbourg, Paris 10. Tel: 208 74-16.

Pâtisserie Alsacienne, 58 rue de Passy, Paris 16. Tel: 288 33-61.

Breton: *Pâtisserie de Bretagne,* 28 avenue Pierre Ier de Serbie, Paris 8. Tel: 727 66-40.

Au gourmet breton, 4 rue de Babylone, Paris 7. Tel: 548 52-15.

Le Berre, 179 bis rue de la Pompe, Paris 16. Tel: 727 43-55.

Gueguen, 49 rue de Rennes, Paris 6. Tel: 548 06-98.

PAWNING

There are several state-run municipal pawnshops in Paris, called 'Monts de piété' unofficially and 'crédits municipaux' officially. They look more like labour exchanges than pawn-shops and are even more depressing. Foreigners wishing to pledge anything must produce proof of identity and signed, documentary proof of their domicile in Paris. If you're still interested, the addresses of the two most central *crédits municipaux* on the Left and Right Banks respectively are:

112 rue de Rennes, Paris 6.

98 bis rue de la Victoire, Paris 9.

Others are listed in the phone book under 'Crédit municipal'.

PERFUMES

Unfortunately perfume shops no longer give tourists 20 per cent discount if you pay by travellers' cheque, as they used to. Chemists and beauty shops sell just about every perfume and beauty product everywhere, except *Guerlain.* They only sell in their own shops.

They are at:
  68 avenue des Champs-Elysées, Paris 8.
  2 Place Vendôme, Paris 1.
  93 rue de Passy, Paris 16.
  29 rue de Sèvres, Paris 6.

'PNEUS' (OR 'PNEUMATIQUES')

A real Paris speciality this: you can send a letter almost anywhere in Paris by pneumatic tube from post offices, and it will be delivered in under two hours. You can post one until 7.30 pm. Special letter-boxes outside post offices are marked 'pneumatiques'. They're cheaper than telegrams.

POSTAGE STAMPS (FOR COLLECTORS)

A 'Stamp Fair' is held every Thursday, Sunday and public holiday from 8 am until 7 pm in the open at the corner of the avenues Gabriel and Marigny near the Champs-Elysées Métro station. Mostly collectors, although a few elderly men have been known to come here not so much for the stamps as for the younger philatelists.

RECORDS

The best record shops in Paris are:
  For classical music: *Pan*, 11 rue Jacob, Paris 6. Tel: 326 18-25.
  Passacaille, 146 rue de Courcelles, Paris 17. Tel: 924 47-85.
  Ploix, 48 rue Saint-Placide, Paris 6. Tel: 548 82-85.
  Variety and jazz: *Sinfonia*, 68 Champs-Elysées, Paris 8. Tel: 359 53-60.
  F.N.A.C., 6 boulevard de Sébastopol, Paris 2. Tel: 887 29-49.
  Raoul Vidal, 41 rue de Rennes, Paris 6. Tel: 548 33-13.
  Lido-Musique, 78 Champs-Elysées, Paris 8. Tel: 225 30-86.
  And if you wish to collect old and rare 78 r.p.m. records, particularly of some of the most fabulous variety stars between the two wars, then go to:
  René Brunel, 87 rue de Seine, Paris 6. Tel: 633 28-09.
  Edouard Pécourt, 58 bis rue du Louvre, Paris 1.
specialises in old records of Latin American music, Tangos of the vintage years of Rudolph Valentino and French *bal musette* accordion music of the Twenties and Thirties.

SHOE REPAIRS

René Clarasso, 34 rue Godot de Mauroy, Paris 8. Tel: RIC 49-79.

The master-cobbler René Clarasso and his forty workmen have been repairing an average of 150,000 pairs of shoes a year since 1939. You can send them to him from anywhere in the world and you'll get them back after a week as good as new. Expensive, but postal charges are included.

'SHOPPINGSERVICE'

Going to the market in Paris can be a delightful experience but if you're tired, in a hurry or simply lazy, you can buy your coffee, tinned peas, olive oil, shoe polish or wine by simply marking off each item on the 28 page catalogue that Shoppingservice, 5–7 rue Garibaldi, 93 La Courneuve, will be happy to send you. They can deliver any of 800 different items in any quantity you like. Some prices are slightly higher than those in the average Paris supermarket but think of the time saved!

In certain conditions, you can order by telephone. Ring up FLA 62-65 and find out.

SKELETONS (HUMAN AND ANIMAL)

Make an unusual present for newly-weds wondering what to put in their new flat. You can get most types of skeleton at:

N. Boubée et Cie, 3 Place Saint-André-des-Arts, Paris 6. Tel: 633 00-30.

You can get a nicely mounted long-legged bird skeleton for only 99 francs, or even a toucan for between 180 and 220 francs. The maison Boubée can also offer you a choice of some two million samples of stones and coloured minerals from 20 francs upwards. They're very fashionable in interior decoration in Paris just now.

Similar novelties are to be found at:

Deyrolle, 46 rue du Bac, Paris 7. Tel: 548 81-93.

SLIMMING (FOR WOMEN)

You can go to *Silhouette*. They have five Paris branches and are all in the telephone book. *Silhouette* promise they will slim you by the natural method, rapidly, removing excess fat wherever you desire. They even say you can lose up to a total of 30 centimetres all over your body in one 30-minute session. Results guaranteed or your money back. They also have swimming pools, saunas, solariums, mechanical and individual massage.

SPYING EQUIPMENT

Comptoir commercial d'outillage, 31 passage Thiers, Paris 11. Tel: ROQ 05-54.

Although at least 80 per cent of the customers of this fascinating shop belong to one branch or another of the State secret services, and another 18 per cent work for industrial concerns and private detective agencies, the 'Comptoir commercial d'outillage' manufactures and sells what are charmingly called 'domestic spies' for the more than merely curious amateur.

You might like to acquire an 'N.A. 101' and an 'N.A. 103': two gadgets stuffed with microphones, transmitters, receivers and tape-recorders. Excellent for recording conversations in your presence (from 7,500 to more than 10,000 francs). Another similar toy can be hidden in a book. Even better, how about the 'N. 251' transmitter which is no bigger than a halfcrown? Transmitting range is 100 yards. You slip it in your pocket before going to that secret interview and your accomplice in a car outside can pick up everything being said on his receiver. It only costs 1,500 francs. A slightly bulker toy tells you the time as well since you wear it as a wristwatch. A telescopic aerial will increase the range (gilt metal model: 3,895 francs, silver-plate: 3,750 francs).

Various mikes include a fountain-pen mike for 299 francs and a suit-button mike for 299.50 francs. And even better than all the anti-bugging devices you might be tempted to buy (since there are always anti-anti-bugging devices on the market as well) is the 'N. 266'—a box no bigger than a cigarette packet. You can attach it to a telephone wire, in your Paris flat for example, where you have to leave your pretty wife while going on a business trip to London, for example. All you have to do is to dial the number of the flat and you'll hear everything being said. Don't worry: the telephone won't even ring. It only costs 2,500 francs. The next model may even have video as well if you wait. . . .

SWEETS (ALL KINDS)

Sweets and chocolates from every part of France are to be bought at *Spécialité de France*, 44 avenue Montaigne, Paris 8. Tel: 359 58-77.

The other best sweet shops are:

Meurisse, 49 bis avenue Franklin Roosevelt, Paris 8. Tel: 225 06-04.

Fauchon, 26 Place de la Madeleine, Paris 8. Tel: 073 11-90.

Hédiard (particularly for *glacé* fruits), 21 Place de la Madeleine, Paris 8. Tel: 265 77-36.

Berthonneau: '*A la mère de famille*', 35 rue du Faubourg Mont-martre, Paris 9. Tel: 770 83-69.

TAXIS

Day or night you can ring for a taxi at the following numbers: 205 77-77; 253 94-00; 587 67-89; 707 89-89; 735 22-22; 742 32-00; 797 36-50.

To book a taxi 24 hours in advance, ring 742 28-30.

TELEPHONE NUMBERS (USEFUL)

Answering service: dial 13 for the official post office answering service. Better but slightly dearer is the privately run service at 288 11-27.

Alarm calls: '*service réveil*': dial 13.

Speaking clock: 033 84-00.

Ambulance: 887 27-50.

Firemen: 18.

Police: 17.

Weather forecast: 705 97-39.

Night doctor (for urgent cases): 707 51-99 (from 8 pm to 8 am. You pay 50 francs for the visit).

TELEPHONING

The inland telephone service in France is notorious (try ringing Nice from Boulogne or Nancy from Biarritz if you're in a hurry!) but it's not too bad in Paris itself. Most post offices and Métro stations have call boxes for which you need a *jeton*, costing 40 centimes. Cafés and restaurants generally have a call box known as a 'Taxiphone' and sell you a *jeton* for 50 or 55 centimes. In older cafés and *bistrots* you either make your call from an antiquated telephone on the bar or get the barman to dial for you before making your way to the telephone somewhere next to the loo. If you don't get through, the price of your *jeton* will be refunded by the cashier but don't try to use it in another café later: they won't like it if they find out it's not one of theirs.

If you're using someone's private phone, you can dial direct to England (London is 19—pause and wait for the so-called musical tone) 44-1 and then the number. The dial arrangement is the same as in England).

If you're using an operator or having a call put through for you, it's worth remembering that a reversed-charge call is a 'P.C.V.'

(pronounce pay-say-vay) and a personal call is 'avec préavis' (aveck pray-avee) followed by the name of the person you want to speak to.

TIPPING

Quite dreadful in Paris: you tip in the cinema when shown to a seat (about 50 centimes is considered usual), you tip when you use the lavatory in a café or restaurant, you leave a tip at the bar of any café where you may happen to have a quick drink and of course you are expected to tip about 10 per cent to your taxi driver.

CAFES: if you sit down, you pay more for your drink than if you stood at the counter. Even so, you are expected (and strongly advised) to tip. Most bills have 'service not included' printed on them, and lately a lot of them have gone so far as to advise you that 'service 12½% pas compris'. What 'service'? Ah, you may well ask.

In some cafés, like *Les Deux Magots*, the waiter calculates the amount of 'service' himself and adds it to the price marked on the bill. Then, you really needn't leave anything over. Honestly, you needn't.

RESTAURANTS: not so bad. Most restaurants tell you on the menu how much the service charge will be: from 10% to 15%, and they automatically add it to your bill. You only need leave a little something if you feel like it, but naturally, if you've had a long, pleasant lunch somewhere and the waiter was suitably helpful, you should leave a franc or two—especially if you're coming back again.

TELEPHONES AND LAVATORIES (in large cafés): most of the larger cafés have a fierce lady of advanced years guarding the telephone-toilet installations. Sometimes it is from her you buy your *jeton* for the telephone. Depending on the degree of luxury offered by the establishment, you are expected to leave anything from 20 to 50 centimes on her plate.

VETS

If your pet needs urgent treatment, ring the veterinary service at 288 67-99. (*Centre d'urgence vétérinaire*); if it needs burying *Animaux-Service*, 40 rue Laugier, Paris 17 will do the job very nicely for you. Ring them at WAG 71-50.

WHAT'S ON IN PARIS?

Two French weeklies, *Une Semaine de Paris-Pariscope* (every Wednesday, 80 centimes) and *l'Officiel des Spectacles* (every Wednesday, 60 centimes) and one quaintly written 'English-language' weekly, *Paris Weekly Information* (Wednesdays, 60 centimes) will tell you what's on in the cinemas, theatres, night-clubs, music halls and provide you with a long visit of restaurants. Cinemas, incidentally, generally change their programmes on Wednesdays.

All these weeklies are sold at every newspaper kiosk.

The *New York Herald Tribune* (daily) covers films, exhibitions, plays, etc., in Paris. The *Figaro*, *Le Monde*, *France-Soir* and *Paris-Presse* also give details of shows, films and concerts.